TRUTH AND LAMENTATION

TRUTH AND LAMENTATION

Stories and Poems on the Holocaust

Edited by

Milton Teichman and Sharon Leder

UNIVERSITY OF ILLINOIS PRESS

Urbana and Chicago

Publication of this work was supported in part by a grant from
the National Endowment for the Arts.

This book is printed on acid-free paper.

Library of Congress Cataloging-in-Publication Data

Truth and lamentation : stories and poems on the Holocaust / edited by
Milton Teichman and Sharon Leder.
    p.   cm.
  Includes bibliographical references (p.   ).
  ISBN 0-252-02028-6 (cl : acid-free paper). — ISBN 0-252-06335-X
(pb)
    1. Holocaust, Jewish (1939–1945)—Literary collections.
I. Teichman, Milton, 1936– . II. Leder, Sharon.
PN6071.H713T78   1994
808.8'0358—dc20   92-40178
                                                                CIP

To the memory of our friend and teacher,
ERWIN ZIMET, 1912–89

And if, for even one of the days of my life, I should forget how I saw you then, my people, desperate and confused, delivered over to extinction, may all knowledge of me be forgotten and my name be cursed like that of those traitors who are unworthy to share your pain.

—Rachel Auerbach

Contents

I. Transmitting Truths

STORIES

POEMS

II. Lamentation

STORIES

POEMS

Acknowledgments

It is a pleasure to express our thanks to many colleagues who offered their support and advice: to Betty Jean Lifton, Gerald Sorin, and Matia Hendelman, who encouraged us in the early stages of our work; to Alvin Rosenfeld, Richard Fein, Irving Buchen, Adam Gillon, Joseph Belanger, Meta Plotnik, and Larry Badendyck, who read preliminary drafts of our manuscript and offered valuable suggestions. We offer our special thanks to colleagues who read the final manuscript and suggested refinements that could come only from the most careful reading: Leslie Brisman, Sivia Kaye, Arline Kuznetz, and Robert Karmon. We owe a special debt to David Roskies, whose scholarship helped us recognize how extraordinary are the creative works written in ghettos and camps. We will always be grateful for the advice and friendship of Jerome Regunberg.

We wish to acknowledge the assistance of Dina Abramowicz of the Yivo Institute for Jewish Research for locating biographical data not readily available. The exceptional skills and limitless generosity of Cheryl Pollard, research librarian at Marist College, Poughkeepsie, New York, benefited us in every phase of our work.

We extend our appreciation to the members of the University of Illinois Press—in particular to Richard L. Wentworth, director; his assistant Lisa Warne-Magro; and Mary Giles, our editor—for their encouragement and patience.

Work on this project was supported by a summer research grant and a sabbatical leave from Marist College. Finally, this project would not have reached fruition without generous grants from William and Sadie Effron, the Nassau Foundation of Nassau Community College, and the Max and Clara Fortunoff Foundation.

Copyright acknowledgments appear at the end of the book.

Introduction

This volume is a selection of stories and poems drawn from one of the most arresting and valuable literatures of our time—the literature of the Holocaust. Responding to the systematic destruction of European Jewry by the Nazis during the years between 1933 and 1945, this literature of moral power and stylistic inventiveness calls up perplexing questions about the human propensity for good and evil, the nature of God, the meaning of culture, civilization, and scientific advancement; questions about the nature of the world in the aftermath of the Holocaust; questions about how a decent human being is to live in the post-Holocaust era. It is a literature that leads inevitably to mind-numbing questions, How could such a catastrophe have taken place? How could the world have allowed it to take place?

There are some who believe that all artistic responses to the Holocaust are inadequate, in spite of the noblest sentiments, the noblest words. The most appropriate response, from this perspective, is silence. The Yiddish poet Aaron Zeitlin, who fortunately was saved from the fate that befell his wife and family in Warsaw, declared, "Were Jeremiah to sit by the ashes of Israel today, he would not cry out an *ekhah,* a Lamentation. . . . The Almighty himself would be powerless to open his well of tears. . . . With the lost millions of his people, He, too, would maintain a deep silence. For even an outcry is now a lie, even tears are mere literature, even prayers are now false" (Niger 14).

Zeitlin is not alone in believing that silence is better than any utterance. "The world of Auschwitz lies outside speech as it lies outside reason," wrote the influential critic George Steiner. "In the presence of certain realities [ghettos, death camps] art is trivial or impertinent" (123).

Although we ourselves have, at times, wondered whether there can be, or should be, such a thing as Holocaust literature, fundamentally we share the more widely held view advanced by such penetrating critics as Lawrence Langer, Sidra Ezrahi, Alvin Rosenfeld, and David Roskies, to name a few, that a literature of the Holocaust does indeed exist, that it is a literature of great moral and literary value, and that it is "among the most compelling literatures of our day" (Rosenfeld 4). This literature exists because, despite great difficulties, writers felt compelled to speak. And in so doing, they found imaginative and subtle ways of entering into and rendering the Holocaust experience.

Although readers have had access in recent years to many diaries, memoirs, novels, and plays on the subject of the Holocaust, they have not had as convenient access to outstanding short stories and poems dealing with the subject. This is regrettable, considering that some of the most creative and profound responses to the Holocaust appear in the genres of the short story and poetry. Indeed, a number of writers who have made the Holocaust a central theme of their work—Nelly Sachs, Paul Celan, Uri Zvi Greenberg, Tadeusz Borowski, Aharon Appelfeld, Elie Wiesel—have written in these forms. Unfortunately, much of this excellent short fiction and poetry is scattered in volumes that do not focus specifically on the Holocaust. When we consider, also, that many excellent pieces appear in volumes that are out of print (we think, for example, of the poems of Nobel Prize–winner Nelly Sachs and of stories by Pierre Gascar and Giorgio Bassani), the need for an anthology like this one becomes evident. A number of fine anthologies have appeared presenting various forms of creative or expository writing from or on the Holocaust.[1] However, none has focused, like ours, on an international collection of poetry and short fiction of high literary merit.

We have included works by victims who perished, by those who survived, and by those who never experienced the terrors directly—works by writers Jewish and non-Jewish, male and female. Represented are writers who have written a few pieces on the Holocaust and writers, as mentioned earlier, who have made the Holocaust a major theme of their work. Our selection is international in scope, including works translated from Polish, German, Dutch, French, Italian, Russian, Yiddish, and Hebrew, as well as works originally written in English. Some of the most outstanding writers of our time are represented, as well as writers who deserve to be more fully known. Although we can present only a selection from the great number of stories and poems treating the Holocaust, that selection can nevertheless demonstrate how impressive is the work accomplished in these genres.

Each piece in this collection is tied directly to the historical event we call the Holocaust. Because we view the literature of the Holocaust as a literature based upon historical fact, we have omitted poems that use the Holocaust as a metaphor for other things. Such well-known poems as "Daddy" and "Lady

---

1. We think of such volumes as *Anthology of Holocaust Literature*, edited by Jacob Glatstein, Israel Knox, and Samuel Margoshes (1969); *Out of the Whirlwind: A Reader of Holocaust Literature*, edited by Albert H. Friedlander (1968); and, more recently, *To Live with Honor and Die with Honor*, edited by Joseph Kermish (1986); *The Literature of Destruction*, edited by David G. Roskies (1988); *Lodz Ghetto: Inside a Community under Siege*, edited by Alan Adelson and Robert Lapides (1989); and *Blood to Remember: American Poets on the Holocaust*, edited by Charles Fishman (1991).

Lazarus" by Sylvia Plath are notable examples. We do not include these pieces because they do not treat the Holocaust as their central subject. Rather, they employ Holocaust imagery as metaphors for internal horror and female victimization. We do not deny the right of poets to draw their imagery from all areas of human experience, but we have chosen not to include works that subordinate the historic event to other problems or afflictions.

We also exclude traditional forms of fiction that use historical fact to make their fictions more believable. Such popular treatments as William Styron's *Sophie's Choice* and John Hersey's *The Wall* serve as examples. Such works use history, or even alter it, to serve their imaginative ends. The fiction writers included in our volume have a different purpose in mind—to make imagination serve fact, rather than the reverse. When, during the Holocaust, history became stranger than fiction, ghetto writers, as well as writers who wrote after the war, made use, paradoxically, of fictional techniques—characterization, dialogue, dramatic conflict, and narrative point of view—to help make outrageous history more credible. What seemed so thoroughly unreal had to be made real.

While there have been attempts at genocide directed at groups other than Jews, we use the term *Holocaust* in this volume to refer specifically to the Nazi application of science, technology, and bureaucratic efficiency to the mass destruction of European Jewry, including the debasement and dehumanization of victims before destroying them. The term *Holocaust,* although we use it, gives the catastrophe a theological meaning we cannot accept. The word derives from *Holokaustos,* from the Greek translation of the Torah, third century B.C., and means the burnt sacrifice dedicated to God and to God alone. We reluctantly use this intrinsically theological name for a secular atrocity because the term has by now become thoroughly common and almost thoroughly accepted, even in the most scholarly discussions.

Although this anthology consists mostly of post-Holocaust writings, we have included representative works written during the catastrophe itself. Despite hunger, exhaustion, and fear of reprisals, writers in ghettos set up by the Nazis produced a remarkable amount of literature: diaries, expository prose, plays, songs, poems, and stories. They wrote mainly in Hebrew, Yiddish, and Polish in an effort to chronicle the destruction, to make sense of it, or to inspire or instill hope. We have included poetry and fiction by such outstanding writers as Simcha Bunim Shayevitsh and Jozef Zelkowicz of the Lodz Ghetto; Yitzhak Katzenelson, Leyb Goldin, and Wladyslaw Szlengel of the Warsaw Ghetto; and Abraham Sutzkever of the Vilna Ghetto. Also written during the Holocaust and included in our volume are poems by Miklos Radnoti, who wrote in Hungarian in the labor camp of Bor in Yugoslavia, and poems by Czeslaw Milosz and Mieczyslaw Jastrun, who wrote in Polish on the aryan side of occupied Warsaw. Of these writers, only Sutzkever, Milosz, and Jastrun survived the war.

Although much was written in the ghettos, much was also lost—confiscated, burnt in ghetto buildings, or never unearthed. But thanks to the efforts of editors Alan Adelson and Robert Lapides (*Lodz Ghetto*), Joseph Kermish (*To Live with Honor and Die with Honor!*), David Roskies (*The Literature of Destruction*), and other scholars, readers now have access in English to some of the writings that have survived. That Nazi brutality and terror could not blunt the creative spirit of ghetto victims is one of the extraordinary facts of the Holocaust.

Transmitting Truths

> I do not know whether we shall survive, but I like to think that one day we shall have the courage to tell the world the whole truth and call it by its proper name.
>
> —From Tadeusz Borowski, "Auschwitz,
> Our Home (a Letter)"

In reading dozens of stories and hundreds of poems in preparation for this volume, we have observed two broad categories of literary response to the fearsome historic events. One is the transmission of various truths about the Holocaust; the other is the expression of grief, the response of lamentation. Presented in styles ranging from realism to surrealism in fiction, and from the plain and direct in poetry to the fragmented and oblique, these two multifaceted responses are characterized by a deep sense of moral urgency. We shall discuss truth-telling first and describe it under three aspects: historical, psychological, and philosophic.

Historical Truth-telling

Works in this anthology that present the historic reality are apt to focus on the unspeakable brutalities of camp and ghetto life and the extraordinary efforts of victims, women as well as men, to resist their tormentors. During the Holocaust itself, creative writers in ghettos and in camps were unequivocal in their determination to chronicle the persecution and the suffering so that after the war the historical record could be set before the world. Like ghetto historians, they wanted their writing to be a form of testimony. The great ghetto poems of Katzenelson and Shayevitsh are full of specific factual reference to the destruction, even though their dominant tone is that of lamentation. The narratives of Leyb Goldin and Jozef Zelkowicz included in this volume were actually part of the Warsaw Ghetto and Lodz Ghetto secret underground archives, respectively, the purpose of which was to reveal to the world one day what the Nazis were bent on concealing. Indeed, one of the most compelling reasons for writing during the Holocaust was to bear testimony to what would otherwise not be believed.

Zelkowicz anticipated disbelief when, in September 1942, he spoke to future generations from the Lodz Ghetto: "Listen and believe this, even though it happened here, even though it seems so old, so distant and so strange" (Adelson and Lapides v). In these words Zelkowicz foresaw the aura of remoteness that surrounds the Holocaust for many individuals today, for whom it is almost outside the realm of reality.

Of course, witnessing and giving testimony regarding the historical truth were also powerful motives of writers who survived the Holocaust—Jews and non-Jews alike—although it took time, as we shall note later, for many survivors to overcome an impulse toward silence. "I had a torrent of urgent things to tell the civilized world," Primo Levi recalled in his memoir *The Reawakening,* which first appeared in Italian in 1963 (40). And Peter, the narrator of Pierre Gascar's story "The Season of the Dead," who probably stands for the author, asserts: "There were still many things to which I should have to bear witness later, many sufferings to be shared." Sometimes survivor writers felt compelled to be the voices for those who could no longer speak the truth. Eugene Heimler, author of the memoir *Night of the Mist,* declared after his liberation from a concentration camp: "There were messages I had to deliver from the dead. . . . Of their dead, burnt bodies I would be the voice" (191).

And even writers who did not experience the terrors directly, Jews and non-Jews, have felt compelled to remind us of what took place in our civilized time. Sometimes they have made use of German documentary footage, as in William Heyen's poem "Simple Truths":

> when we see the films of the bulldozed dead
> or the film of one boy struck on the head
> with a club in the hands
> of a German doctor. . . .
> when we read these things or see them,
> then it is clear to us that this
> happened, and within the lord's allowance.

Or else, they have based their treatments on victims' diaries or memoirs (Ruth Whitman's *The Testing of Hanna Senesh*), or visited European sites of atrocities or acts of resistance (Marge Piercy's "The housing project of Drancy" and "Black Mountain"). Survivor writers as well as those without direct experience of the Holocaust have a further motive in asserting the historic truth—

the growing tendency on the part of extreme rightist groups to deny the magnitude of the Holocaust or, indeed, its very existence.

Writers who bear witness to the ordeals of camp and ghetto life often attempt to draw us as fully as possible into this brutal world. Especially for victims and survivors, the world of camp and ghetto was so overpowering that it often eradicated the sense that reality was ever any different, ever rational or just. These writers seek to reproduce some equivalent of that world within a world that they experienced. Hence, they search for strategies that can place the reader within the inferno. In Leyb Goldin's penetrating piece of psychological fiction "Chronicle of a Single Day," the use of present tense, first person, stream of consciousness enables the reader to experience the narrator's condition of being totally consumed, from moment to moment, by his hunger. By allowing us to identify fully with one starving human being, Goldin communicates the reality of mass starvation in the ghetto.

Overwhelmed by an actual massacre of Jews in the Lodz Ghetto in 1940, and fearing that the incident will be erased from history, Jozef Zelkowicz tells a story with the unexpected title "25 Live Hens and One Dead Document." Zelkowicz draws us into a world of atrocity by employing a sardonic, third-person narrator who hopes for future readers to whom he can explain the meaning of a seemingly innocent ghetto document: "This piece of paper you found by chance in the ghetto archives says nothing about 24 dead Jews." The narrator presents himself as one who has the true facts about the senseless slaughter and will reveal what is behind "such an unimportant, trivial document." In this manner, the narrator seduces us into involvement.

Tadeusz Borowski's "This Way for the Gas, Ladies and Gentlemen" is an even more rigorous attempt to draw the reader into the cruel reality—this time the reality of Auschwitz which, as Borowski presents it, is a world without courage, compassion, or heroism, where the line between murderer and victim has been erased. Borowski eliminates all references to past or future, so there is no possibility for consoling distractions away from the present. Unlike the narratives by Goldin or Zelkowicz, Borowski's story offers no character to represent the pre-Holocaust world of moral values. He thus confines readers to the brutal and brutalizing nature of the camp experience.

The terrible conditions under which victims lived exposed them to a range of moral dilemmas. Does one expend energy caring for family members who are sick and aged, or does one focus exclusively on one's own survival? Does one give primacy to the good of the oppressed group, or does one make one's own way easier by cooperating with the Nazis or by exploiting other victims? In short, does one resist or submit to the corrupting and dehumanizing effects of Nazi oppression? At times, the line between resistance and submission becomes blurred. Is a woman who aborts the birth of her child because the life of that infant is at great risk resisting or submitting to the Nazi system? A significant aspect of truth-telling is the dramatization of these moral problems. Often, writers during and after the Holocaust took a critical view of those who, in one way or another, were complicit with the enemy.

Such a critical view appears in Zelkowicz's story. A Jew and a Pole in the Lodz Ghetto degenerate morally under the Nazi occupation. Both enrich themselves by smuggling hens into the ghetto and selling them for exorbitant prices. The Pole, allying himself with the occupying force, becomes a murderer of Jews no less cold-blooded than the Nazis. Neither the Pole nor the Jew is spared the author's cool and derisive contempt.

As Alan Adelson points out, "ghetto dwellers' selfishness . . . family members stealing food from their loved ones . . . official corruption . . . the brutality of the Jewish police" were considered appropriate subjects for ghetto writing (xxi). We should note, however, that with the mass deportations from European ghettos beginning in 1942, some ghetto writers withheld or muted their criticism of other Jews, viewing all Jewish victims as holy martyrs (Roskies, *Against the Apocalypse* 222–24).

In survivor-writer Sara Nomberg-Przytyk's fictionalized memoir of Auschwitz "The Block of Death," the character Cyla is judged for her complicity with the Nazis. A fifteen-year-old Jewish girl from a respected, religious middle-class family, Cyla exchanges sex with a S.S. man in return for handsome clothes and hefty portions of food. More amazing to Sara, the Jewish narrator, is Cyla's willingness to collaborate in the gassing of female victims no longer capable of work. When—with trepidation—Sara asks Cyla how she can participate in the destruction of her own people, Cyla replies, "I put my own mother in the car that took her to the gas. You should understand that there remains nothing so terrible that I could not do it. The world is a terrible place. This is how I take my revenge on it." Rationalizing her brutal conduct, Cyla directs her rage not at the evildoers but at the victims. Sara, on the other hand, struggles to preserve her humanity, reflecting Nomberg-Przytyk's view that individuals can still exercise some degree of moral choice, even in a death camp.

Borowski's "This Way for the Gas, Ladies and Gentlemen," mentioned earlier, provides one of the most dramatic instances of an individual complicit with the Nazis. Like Cyla, Borowski's narrator has identified so completely with the executioner that he vents his rage not at the Nazis, but at the victims he unloads from the trains arriving at Auschwitz. He submits to the Nazi system in order that he can eat abundantly and live. What is most surprising is that Borowski withholds criticism of his dehumanized narrator. Borowski, himself a survivor of Auschwitz, suggests that the Nazi system is the enemy, and no individual has the power to resist it.

We speculate that when survivor writers portray characters who submit to the Nazi system, they may be seeking ways of dealing with their own guilt for having survived. Perhaps they are reminding themselves that their own survival was not bought at the price of complicity, or else that some degree of complicity was inevitable, given the Nazi terror.

Yet writers who treat the world of ghetto and camp also show great interest in characters who struggle successfully against dehumanization. The sensitive narrator of Leyb Goldin's "Chronicle of a Single Day" has a double source of anguish: his hunger and his fear that he is sinking morally, that hunger will turn him into a beast. Has he not taken an extra soup in the communal soup kitchen, one to which he was not entitled? Has he not had thoughts of stealing bread? Throughout the story he struggles to maintain integrity in the face of starvation. An unusual sight through the window of the ghetto hospital strengthens his resolve to hold fast to his humanity: Hunger ravages us, he thinks, gives us "the mourning look of foxes, dingoes, kangaroos. . . . But we are not animals."

In Arnost Lustig's story "The Lemon," also about starvation and disease in the ghetto, the young Ervin could, if he chose, take the path of his friend Chicky and focus only on his own survival. He could reason that his mother and sick sister are soon likely to die. Instead, he is willing to undergo the emotionally devastating experience of removing gold teeth from his father's corpse to buy a lemon to ease the distress of his dying sister. As the critic Alvarez rightly observes, Lustig's stories "have something of Borowski's directness" but lack the sense of "decadence and corruption" found in the Polish writer's fiction (29).

Fiction, with its representational function, lends itself to the recreation of the concentrationary world, incomplete as that rendering may be. It is also well suited to dramatize conflicts and dilemmas like those described previously. But poetry also contributes to the form of truth-telling that illuminates the realities of Nazi oppression. Focusing as it often does on states of feeling, poetry can be highly effective in externalizing subtle states of suffering and anguish. Joseph Kirman's prose poem "Doves on Wires," written in the Warsaw Ghetto, expresses the unusual sadness of having to hate even the sight of birds because they are being fed by the murderous hands of the oppressor while humans are starving. With sorrow and compassion, Gertrud Kolmar contemplates the disintegration of human beings in "In the Camp," written as early as 1933 before her poetry took its more conventionally literary direction. In "The Seventh Eclogue," Miklos Radnoti evokes the complex feelings of a prisoner in a labor camp—the terrible longing for home, the fear that home will be obliterated, the deprivation of being separated from loved ones, the endless waiting, and the failure of even sleep and dream to provide relief.

Paul Celan's "Death Fugue," one of the most celebrated poems on the Holocaust in Western Europe, presents the voice of a death camp victim ground down by relentless oppression:

> Black milk of dawn we drink you at night
> we drink you at noon and at daybreak we drink you at dusk
> we drink and we drink.

These lines, repeated throughout with subtle variations, constitute the poem's ominous refrain and evoke what Primo Levi, in another context, called the Nazi "demolition of man." The absence of logical sequence and punctuation in the poem and the blurring of syntax help underscore the unrelieved anguish and disintegration of the speaker.

The poetry of truth-telling takes special note of the particular vulnerabilities of women in the ghettos and camps. Because of their biological role, Jewish women were primary targets of the Nazis. The Nazi plan of genocide required the annihilation of mothers. From memoirs we learn that deported women with children under the age of fifteen were marked for death along with their children, and that women were subject to various forms of sexual abuse—from verbal humiliation and forced sterilization, to physical violence and rape (Heinemann 14, 18). It is not surprising that Robert Mezey in "Theresienstadt Poem" imagines the possibility of sexual abuse as part of the terrors of life in the camp for thirteen-year-old Nely Silvinova, or that Primo Levi alludes in "Shema" to the physical humiliation and loss of fertility that women experienced in the camps:

> Consider whether this is a woman,
> Without hair or name
> With no more strength to remember
> Eyes empty and womb cold
> As a frog in winter.

A number of poems in this volume portray with great poignancy the particular anguish of mothers and their vulnerability through their children. Shmerke Kaczerginski's moving song "Still, Still," written in the Vilna Ghetto, presents the pain of a mother whose husband is in hiding and who is left to care for her child alone in a perilous time. Her child's cries, she fears, may endanger them both and bring their own lives to a close at Ponar, a killing site outisde of Vilna:

> Still, still, let us be still.
> Graves grow here.

> Planted by the enemy,
> they blossom to the sky. . . .
>
> Somewhere a mother is orphaned.
> Her child goes to Ponar.

In Kaczerginski's song, memorable for its effective use of nature imagery, only the frozen Viliye River shares the mother's grief.

Simcha Bunim Shayevitsh, the leading poet of the Lodz Ghetto, provides a glimpse of what deportation from the ghetto meant for mothers and their children in the ironically entitled "Lekh-lekho" which is Hebrew for God's words to Abraham, "Go forth" (Genesis 12:1). On this fatal journey, mothers carry frozen children thinking they are still alive; pregnant women "kneel in weariness. . . . their wombs aborting in the snow, / Fertilizing the field with blood and tears."

Nelly Sachs, in "Already embraced by the arm of heavenly solace," undertakes the immensely difficult task of rendering the mind of a mother who knows that her child has gone skyward in smoke from the crematorium:

> The insane mother stands
> With the tatters of her torn mind
> With the charred tinders of her burnt mind.
> Burying her dead child,
> Burying her lost light,
> Twisting her hands into urns.

That countless mothers witnessed their children desperately struggling to survive or ruthlessly being murdered explains the lines in Miklos Radnoti's "Fragment":

> I lived on this earth in an age
> when a curse was the mother of a child,
> when women were happy if they miscarried.

The suffering of women during the Holocaust is a subject that has only begun to receive scholarly treatment (Ringelheim 742; Heinemann 6). It is likely that scholars will turn to the creative literature written during and after the Holocaust for insights into the nature of women's experiences.

Finally, historical truth-telling goes beyond Nazi evils and horrendous suffering to record the resistance of men and women caught in the maelstrom. Selections in this anthology present the remarkably varied forms of resistance of the victims themselves. We think, for example, of such ghetto and post-Holocaust works as Hirsh Glik's songs, Wladyslaw Szlengel's "Counterattack," Abraham Sutzkever's "On the Anniversary of the Ghetto Theater," Marge Piercy's "Black Mountain," and Irena Klepfisz's "Poland, 1944."

Some scholars, notably Bruno Bettelheim and Raul Hilberg, have alluded to the passivity of victims who faced Nazi persecution. Recent scholarship (Krakowski; Mark; Trunk), however, has shown that resistance—both physical and spiritual—was greater than has been assumed. Scholars such as Vera Laska and Margaret Rossiter have also pointed to the important role that women played in various forms of resistance. In addition to revolts in many places less known than Warsaw, Jewish victims found countless ways of resisting their oppressors, from smuggling food to survive, to publishing underground newspapers, to educating their young, to holding religious services. The creative literature reflects the multifaceted nature of resistance during the Holocaust.

Selections in this volume show that resistance on the part of women constitutes a moving aspect of the literature of truth-telling. Resistance efforts specific to women are clearest in the camps, where women were separated from men. In Nomberg-Przytyk's story "Esther's First Born," the narrator, Sara, and the female inmate physicians in Auschwitz resist the brutal Nazi policy of destroying mothers together with their newborn infants. Risking their own lives, they secretly kill the newborns in order to save the lives of the mothers. Like Ervin in Lustig's story, they steel themselves to commit a morally repulsive act in order to preserve lives that the Nazis are bent on destroying. In two stories not included in our volume, "Salvation" and "Morituri te Salutant," Nomberg-Przytyk relates how her own life was saved by women who formed an underground political resistance movement in Auschwitz and were actually instrumental in blowing up a crematorium.

The American author Cynthia Ozick did not experience the death camps herself, but probably based her compressed and metaphoric story "The Shawl" on actual records of female resistance in the camps. Rosa, the protagonist, resists the Nazis by attempting to preserve both the life of her infant, Magda, whom she is hiding in the camp, as well as her own. When her infant is murdered—a scene she witnesses—she resists the voices of traditional motherhood that "hammer" through her "nipple," commanding her to "fetch, get, bring!" Had she listened to those voices, she would have been shot and would have given the Nazis yet another victory. In one of the most memorable passages of post-Holocaust literature, she stuffs Magda's shawl into her mouth to stifle the screech of anguish that would have meant her death. We sense Ozick's admiration of Rosa's courage, despite unspeakable pain, to think rationally and resist impulse in a milieu that would rob her of rationality and choice. Given the Nazi plan of genocide, to keep oneself alive was itself an act of resistance.

Women resisted the Nazis in ghettos as well as in camps. In his poem "And There You Were," the Vilna partisan and survivor Abba Kovner pays tribute to courageous Zivia Lubetkin, one of the leaders of the Warsaw Ghetto uprising, who hid in the sewers of Warsaw to remain alive. Similarly, the Polish poet Jerzy Ficowski in "Both Your Mothers" recognizes the heroism of two mothers in Warsaw. One in the ghetto effects the secret transfer of her infant to the aryan side of Warsaw in the hope that it can survive; the other is a Christian woman who risks her life to rear the infant. Anna Swirszczynska, also Polish, introduces a note of honest realism when in "Building the Barricade" she acknowledges the fear and anxiety of those who, like herself, participated in the Warsaw Ghetto uprising:

> We were afraid as we built the barricade
> under fire.
> The tavern-keeper, the jeweler's mistress, the
> barber, all of us,
> cowards.

Two American women poets represented in our volume are inspired by the heroic resistance of Hanna Senesh, who left Palestine in 1943 to join a parachute rescue brigade behind enemy lines in occupied Europe and was captured by the Nazis in Hungary. Senesh is the dramatic speaker of Ruth Whitman's imaginative poem *The Testing of Hanna Senesh*, based upon Senesh's diary. The poet Adrienne Rich, emphasizing the complex nature of Senesh's mission in "Letters in the Family," also recognizes her essential heroism.

Historical truth-telling does not ignore such realities as the world's indifference ("Campo di Fiori" by Czeslaw Milosz, "Here Too as in Jerusalem" by Mieczyslaw Jastrun, and "Say This City Has Ten Million Souls" by W. H. Auden) or the humanity and heroism of Christians who risked their lives to save Jews ("1980" by Abraham Sutzkever and "A Poem for Anton Schmidt" by William Pillin). Its greater focus, however, is upon the crimes of the Nazis, the suffering of the victims, and the valiant efforts of the victims to fight back.

Psychological Truth-telling

Psychological truth-telling, as distinguished from the rendering of camp and ghetto life, focuses upon the exploration of individual psychology. The paradoxical mind of the oppressor, for example, is presented in such poems as Louis Simpson's "The Bird," Denise Levertov's "The Peach Tree," and Charles Reznikoff's "Research." In each, the mind of the oppressor encompasses startling contradictions. In Simpson, love of song and love of comrade coexist with "loathing / For every size of Jew"; in Levertov, routine meal-taking is on a par with giving orders to murder thousands; in Reznikoff, dedication to research and science is combined with enthusiasm for sadistic experimentation on humans. These poems lead us to ask how educated, rational individuals with traditional religious upbringings, living in the center of civilized Europe, were capable of directing and inflicting crimes of such unprecedented enormity. We are not likely to find definitive answers to this question in the literature in this volume or, for that matter, in Holocaust literature in general. The poems do, however, offer vivid pictures of the twisted mind of the oppressor and some fragments of truth about the human capacity for extraordinary evil.

In this collection, the poets who explore the Nazi mentality are Americans. This may not be coincidental, because psychological analysis implies a more detached, less emotionally involved stance than could be expected from European writers with firsthand experience of the Holocaust. The use of various shades of humor and satire in the previously cited works also implies a distance from the actual events. Jewish-American novelists, it so happens, have not as yet attempted to deal directly with the perpetrator (Kremer 19).

Also part of the psychological approach to truth-telling is the examination of the mind of the survivor. Writers in this volume who attempt to render the psychology of the survivor testify to the impossibility of ever putting the terrifying experiences of the past to rest. No longer victims of brute force, survivors are still victims of their memories. In addition, writers illuminate the isolation of the survivor from those not touched directly by the conflagration, the psychic gap between those who experienced the Holocaust and those who did not.

It is interesting that Abraham Sutzkever, writing in the Vilna Ghetto in 1943, actually anticipated the distress he and other survivors would know at the time of liberation. In the poem "How?" he realized that, paradoxically, freedom would bring the memory of death and degradation, the pain of loneliness, as the mind digs through layers of the past:

> memory will resemble
> An ancient buried town.
> And your estranged eyes will burrow down
> Like a mole, a mole. . . .

On one level, Nelly Sachs's poem "Chorus of the Rescued" may be read as an elaboration on the paradox of survival expressed in Sutzkever's "How?" Although Sachs's speakers have been rescued from the camps, "the nooses wound for our necks still dangle / before us in the blue air—." Even the innocent experiences of daily life—the "song of a bird" or a "pail being filled at the well"—can evoke the painful past, can "let our badly sealed pain burst forth again / and carry us away—." The chorus of speakers in this poem knows that their history has permanently separated them from the human community, that all they have in common with the living is death itself: "all that binds us together now is leave-taking, / The leave-taking in the dust." The poem is noteworthy in that it touches on all the important motifs relating to the mind of the survivor.

Like Sachs's poem, Elie Wiesel's autobiographical narrative "An Old Acquaintance" shows how "badly sealed" is the pain of survivors, how easily they can be carried back to the traumatic past. What is unexpected in Wiesel's story—and deeply ironic—is that the sophisticated narrator, many years removed from his camp experience, becomes a victim all over again after encountering the barracks-chief who was his tormentor in Auschwitz. The present vanishes; years that have intervened are as nothing. The narrator is in Auschwitz once more, overcome by impotence, defeat, humiliation: "My hands in my pockets, I turn around and begin to walk, slowly at first, then faster, and faster, until I am running. Is he following me? He let me go. He granted me freedom."

The separateness of survivors, their isolation from the rest of us—one of the motifs in Sachs's "Chorus of the Rescued"—is a central concern in the story "A Plaque on Via Mazzini" by the Italian-Jewish writer Giorgio Bassani. Bassani's use of a well-meaning but insufficiently discerning narrator helps ironically to underscore the theme of separateness. A chasm divides Geo, the survivor who returns to Ferrara from Buchenwald, from the rest of his townsfolk who were not victims of the camps. Geo's bizarre behavior—which includes his talking obsessively to the townspeople only of the death of his relatives—reflects his rage at the town's indifference to what he, his family, and the Jewish citizens of Ferrara have undergone. If only Geo had been a bit more patient, thinks the narrator, time "which adjusts all things in this world . . . would finally have calmed even him, would have helped him to return to the fold, fit in once more." We know better than the narrator, sympathetic to Geo though he may be. We share the author's perspective that Geo cannot "fit in once more" because the suffering of the camp survivor belongs to a new order of experience.

If Bassani focuses upon the separation of the survivor from the rest of us, Aharon Appelfeld's related concern in his story "Bertha" is the arrested life, the great difficulty for the survivor of going forward after past traumas to pursue an ordinary life. Bertha is a young woman whom the protagonist, Max, himself a survivor, saved during the war when she was but a child and whom he still looks after in Jerusalem. She represents an extreme form of life stopped short, for she has retreated into autism and solitude, blocking out the traumatic past completely. Max gives the appearance of normalcy: he has a job; he would like to marry and lead a life like others. What he says to Bertha to encourage their separation applies more realistically to himself: "You must understand, Bertha, you're already grown up; one must marry, set up a household." But when he takes the step to form a serious relationship with a typist at his plant, he undergoes great mental distress. His anxiety and disorientation are mysteries to himself. When at the close of the story he sees his hands not as hands but as "iron rings," it is as if he has a glimpse of his being somehow less than human: Iron rings cannot touch, hold, embrace. By introducing this surreal element, Appelfeld seeks a new way of illuminating the troubled mental state of his survivor.

Philosophical Truth-telling

We call another form of truth-telling reflected in this volume "philosophical" because details of atrocity are presented not to underscore the historic truth that must be transmitted, but to support insights and reflections on a wide range of matters pertaining to the Holocaust—reflections on the essential nature of Holocaust reality, on the nature of the post-Holocaust world, and on the persistent human capacity for violence.

Some writers in the philosophical mode view the Holocaust as a radical departure from the past. In previous eras, civilization and humanism had meaning and value. But the Holocaust unleashed the horrific side of human nature, and for these writers, the Holocaust has a continuing contaminating effect. They tend to focus, among other things, upon the new meaning of death under the Nazis—the hideous process of dying, the unheroic aspects, the lack of ritual—and, directly or indirectly, they compare such gruesome death to the way individuals died in previous historical periods.

The poet Anthony Hecht's presentation in " 'More Light! More Light!' " of the sixteenth-century Christian martyr who is burnt at the stake suggests that brutal death is not a new invention. But Hecht's contrast between that death and the deaths of two Jews and a Pole under the Nazis implies a dimension not seen before. A rupture has taken place between past and present. This same attention to the Nazi transformation of death appears in two poems by Randall Jarrell, who served in the U.S. Air Force during World War II at the time the camps were liberated. "Protocols" may not make explicit the distinction between death before and during the Holocaust, but the dramatic situation presented in the poem—children remembering in contrapuntal voices how they died—can serve readily as an objective correlative for the new world we inhabit. It is Jarrell's second poem, "A Camp in the Prussian Forest," that juxtaposes the barbaric nature of death under the Nazis with more civilized methods: "The needles of the wreath" that the speaker fashions for a grave "are chalked with ash" from the crematoria.

In Pierre Gascar's "Season of the Dead," which Irving Howe has called "one of the very few masterpieces of Holocaust fiction" ("Writing and the Holocaust" 36), death in the inherited, civilized conception appears in the burial ground that the narrator, Peter, helps to create, adorn, and tend for fellow French prisoners who die in the German camp. Death as atrocity—anonymous and markerless—is emblemed in the hastily covered mass grave that the narrator and his fellow gravediggers discover at the edge of their own beautifully cared for cemetery. It is further emblemed in the endless trains of Jewish deportees, "full of stifled cries and shouts," on their way to gas chambers and incineration. Two distinct eras in human history are represented in Gascar's story—an earlier one in which civilized values were still observed and an era in which those values are overturned and abandoned. The new era, suggests Gascar, is the "season of the dead," a season in which death has taken on a meaning hitherto unknown to humankind.

Other writers in the philosophical mode use the Holocaust as a heightened example of the way reality always has been and will inevitably continue to be. They view the Holocaust as an extreme and exaggerated version of the brutality that has always resided in human interaction, although sometimes disguised by a veneer of civilization. This view is reflected in Jacov Lind's surrealistic and grotesquely humorous story "Journey Through the Night." (It also appears in Borowski's "This Way for the Gas, Ladies and Gentleman," a title that juxtaposes brutality and civility.) An Austrian Jew who survived the war, Lind dismisses conventional realism as inadequate to represent the modern world, where reason and civilization are illusions. Lind presents the post-Holocaust world as rational and civilized on the surface only and cannibalistic at its core. Outwardly sophisticated, the cannibal in the story could be taken for a doctor with his black bag, except that this bag contains instruments for neatly severing the body parts of his victims. The urbane cannibal's perversion of reason as he justifies eating a fellow passenger is both amusing and shocking. He is Lind's symbol for what humanity essentially is. The present is thus merely a deceptive continuation of the grotesque past. Although Lind makes no explicit reference to the historic facts of the Holocaust, his use of the train journey and his yoking of urbanity and savagery are allusions to the Nazi era.

Finally, there are those writers in the philosophical mode who resemble Lind in viewing the Holocaust as a magnified version of the past, but who are nevertheless hopeful that individuals yet have the power to improve the world. Included in this group are a number of poets who see in the Holocaust a reminder of the capacity in each one of us for violence or indifference to suffering. Denise Levertov in "When We Look Up" and W. D. Snodgrass in "A Visitation," for example, both use the figure of Adolf Eichmann to offer indirect warnings against self-righteousness and self-deception and to suggest that no person is without the propensity for the fierce and the savage.

There is something of Eichmann in each one of us, suggests Levertov, when we fail to see in another face "a person, . . . an I." Looking at Eichmann standing isolate in a bullet-proof witness stand of glass, we may see our own potential to separate ourselves from others, to forget that we are related, "member / one of another." Snodgrass's stylized dialogue "A Visitation" creates the fiction of Eichmann's ghost still roaming the world, attempting to absolve itself of guilt by pointing to the hypocrisy of others. The ghost of Eichmann says to the poem's speaker, who may represent all of us:

> Once, your own hand
> Held a nightstick, .45 and sheath knife;
> You've chained men to a steel beam on command.

Reluctantly, the poem's speaker faces the half-truth in Eichmann's words—that even decent people can slip into the evil that initially repels them: "How subtle all that chokes us with disgust / Moves in implacably to rule us, unaware." If we approach Eichmann only from the perspective of moral superiority, suggest these poets, we can fail to see our own potential for inhumanity. Both poets also imply our potential for treating others as persons.

The Polish poet and Nobel-laureate Czeslaw Milosz also examines with some hopefulness truths about humanity in "Campo di Fiori," written on the aryan side of Warsaw during the war. When the sixteenth-century philosopher Giordano Bruno was burned at the stake in Rome, the flames were hardly extinguished when "the taverns were full again / and hawkers carried on heads / baskets with olives and lemons." When the Warsaw Ghetto went up in flames, becoming a new Campo di Fiori, and while Jews in the Ghetto perished alone, Poles outside the Ghetto simply continued their recreations and amusements:

> wind from the burning houses
> blew open the girls' skirts,
> and the happy throngs laughed
> on a beautiful Warsaw Sunday.

Nothing has changed, suggests Milosz, a Polish Christian, only the magnitude of human persecution and the magnitude of human indifference. Through passivity in the face of evil, Milosz implies, Christian Poland betrayed its Jews to the worst inquisition the world has known. Milosz believes that inhumanity is likely to erupt on a "new Campo di Fiori," but his cautious hope is that poets of the future will be the new priests to jar us out of moral apathy.

In the multifaceted literature of truth-telling and truth-discerning, we hear victims and survivors, as well as those who did not experience the calamity, indirectly telling us: These are the painful and sometimes inspiring realities we must acknowledge and learn from if the human tragedy of the Holocaust is not to be repeated. Stories and poems that reflect the truth-telling impulse appear in Part 1 of this anthology.

Lamentation

Can I mourn?
I am an elegy.
Lament?
My mind is lamentation.

—From A. L. Strauss, "Lament
for the European Exile"

The second major pattern we have observed in Holocaust literature—lamentation—is a mode of literary response that David Roskies and Sidra Ezrahi have described in some detail (*Against the Apocalypse* 15–52; *By Words Alone* 96–115). In the lamentation response, writers express—sometimes directly, sometimes obliquely with understatement and restraint—their grief and heartbreak over the suffering and destruction of European Jewry. It is important to say at once, however, that this elegiac response is often more than an outpouring of sorrow; it is strongly infused with anger and with theological, ethical, and social concerns.

Most of the writers who lament the tragedy are Jewish, and they strongly identify with other Jews, those destroyed as well as those still living. Their works evoke a sense of kinship and solidarity deepened by the great tragedy. The pronouns *we, our,* and *us* are common in this category of response. A line from Ida Fink's story "A Scrap of Time" is representative: "We, who because of our difference were condemned once again, as we had been before in our history, we were condemned once again."

The Criticism of God

Jewish writers who lament the devastation are part of a literary tradition that goes back to the Book of Lamentations, a work of elegiac poetry occasioned by the destruction of the first Temple in Jerusalem in 586 B.C.E. Later persecutions during the Crusades, the Spanish Inquisition, the period of the Cossack massacres, and beyond produced additional elegiac literature, the Book of Lamentations often serving as prototype. Composed mainly by liturgical poets, these lamenting elegies are called *kinoth* and *seliboth*. Their authors describe contemporary persecutions and express deep sorrow over the sufferings of their people. Only a selection of the vast number of these compositions is now recited in the synagogue. Over the centuries, these liturgical pieces helped to commemorate martyrs and to pay tribute to their courage, heroism, and faith. The underlying beliefs of traditional lamentation literature are that Israel's suffering was caused by her sins, and that repentance and submission to God's just punishment could bring an end to suffering.

Jewish writers lamenting the Holocaust do not share the theological assumptions of earlier writers in this genre who viewed both the destruction of the Temple and succeeding catastrophes as caused by Israel's sins. Rather, most writers responding to the cataclysm of the Holocaust perceive the suffering as grossly unmerited, as God's violation of His covenant with the people of Israel. They see the destruction of their people as a sign of God's impotence rather than His control of events. If the traditional lamentation literature presents God as showing His wrath against Israel, Jewish Holocaust writers often direct their anger at an uncaring God. If humility is the characteristic tone in traditional lamentation literature, a certain spiritual audacity characterizes the response of modern Jewish authors.

Hayyim Nahman Bialik (1873–1934), who in his poem "In the City of Slaughter" responded with shock and rage to the 1903 Kishinev pogrom against Jews in Czarist Russia, was the first major Jewish writer to express anger at the absent God. In his poem "Spring 1942," Simcha Bunim Shayevtish responds in grief and indignation to the mass deportations of Jews from the Lodz Ghetto and calls upon the revered Bialik to wake from their sleep mother Rachel and the Saint of Berdichev. Shayevitsh implores all three—Bialik, Rachel, and the Saint of Berdichev—to go before God to thunder, demand, and plead that God be "the Savior / Of Living Jews" and not "the Savior of Corpses." The questioning of God's justice is implicit throughout the poem as Shayevitsh asks again and again how a beautiful spring can coexist with deportations. Shayevitsh is well aware of Bialik's famous lines: "The sun shines, the acacia blossoms / and the slaughterer slaughters."

More explicit in his criticism of God is the Warsaw Ghetto poet Yitzhak Katzenelson, whose epic *The Song of the Murdered Jewish People* is sometimes regarded as a latter-day Book of Lamentations. Also with Bialik in mind, Katzenelson asks angrily,

O why are you so beautiful, you skies, while we are
being murdered, why are you so blue? . . .

Millions . . . raised high their hands to you before they
died. . . .

You have no God above you. Nought and void—you
skies!

(Canto IX)

The criticism of God, appearing with various degrees of audacity and
springing from sorrow and anguish, is expressed in such postwar poems as
Kadya Molodovsky's "God of Mercy," Jacob Glatstein's "Without Jews," and
Paul Celan's "Psalm." To denote God's absence, Celan refers to Him in the
repeated words "No one," as if God no longer deserves a name after the destruction. The conventional language of piety in the second stanza, and indeed in the title of the poem, suggests a mocking of the absent God. Ezrahi
sees this poem as "a prayer of defiance which is perhaps the most anguished
of the blasphemies to be encountered in the literature" (144).

Sometimes the criticism of God for abandoning His people is expressed
indirectly in the form of an inversion of biblical themes or archetypes, a tendency especially noticeable in Yiddish and Hebrew poetry, with its high degree of allusion. "Lekh-lekho" by Simcha Bunim Shayevitsh, written in
response to the first deportations of Jews from the Lodz Ghetto in January
1942, concludes with a traditional affirmation of faith, but its very title suggests the author's equivocal attitude toward God. The Hebrew words of the
title, meaning "Go forth," allude to God's words in Genesis 12:1 and constitute a mocking of God's promise to Abraham. Now the Nazis are giving the
command, not God, and the promise of greatness is now the reality of destruction. Ezekial 37:1–10 and its consoling vision, at the time of the Babylonian exile, of the dry bones of the Israelites coming back to life is the
passage subversively used in "Draft of a Reparations Agreement" by the Israeli poet Dan Pagis. The same archetype is even more explicitly employed for
critical purposes in Katzenelson's *The Song of the Murdered Jewish People*:

Woe and grief!
Not even a bone remains from my murdered people.

No bone is left for new flesh, new skin,
For a new spirit of life—

(Canto II, stanzas 5–6)

The *akeda,* or the binding of Isaac, is the biblical episode dramatizing Abraham's unquestioning submission to the divine will and God's intervention to spare the life of Isaac. But the Israeli poet Amir Gilboa rewrites the episode in his poem "Isaac" to emphasize the absence of divine intervention during the Holocaust. In Gilboa's poem, it is the child who witnesses the slaughter of his father just as countless child survivors witnessed the extermination of their parents' generation. It is the child—that is, the survivor—who will be haunted and scarred by what he has seen. The inversion of biblical passages is not new in the history of Jewish literature. It is a technique that goes all the way back to Lamentations. But modern Jewish writers frequently employ this technique as a way of questioning God's justice and mercy. (For a Christian writer's critique of God, see William Heyen's "Simple Truths.")

The criticism of God in Holocaust literature is not confined to poetry and the short story. Alan L. Berger has pointed out that the quarrel with God is also a persistent feature of American-Jewish novels that respond to the Holocaust (16). It is important to note, however, that this pattern of criticism and accusation has exceptions. For example, in "Elegy" by the Canadian-Jewish poet A. M. Klein, anger is directed not against God but against the perpetrator. Klein turns to God in prayer and supplication, asking that He avenge the murdered, heal the survivors, and "renew our days . . . as they were of old." In a like manner, the character of Hersh in Chaim Grade's story "My Quarrel with Hersh Rasseyner" holds fast to his faith in God in spite of the catastrophe. Similarly, the Yiddish poet Aaron Zeitlin, whose work strongly reflects the Jewish religious and mystical tradition, asks in "I Believe,"

> Can I then choose not to believe
> in that living God whose purposes
> when he destroys, seeming to forsake me,
> I cannot conceive;
> choose not to believe in Him
> Who having turned my body to fine ash
> begins once more to wake me?

But such uncritical attitudes toward God are hardly representative in modern lamentation literature. More prevalent are questioning and confrontation.

In spite of complaint, accusation, and defiance, however, Jewish writers cannot altogether reject the God of their fathers. "However loudly we call out to heaven and demand an accounting, our outcry conceals a quiet prayer for the Divine Presence" says the narrator, a writer, in "My Quarrel with Hersh

Rasseyner." Similarly, beneath the reproach of God in Glatstein's "Without Jews" is a longing for a God to whom the poet can feel bound. If your people vanish, says Glatstein addressing God,

> Who will dream you? . . .
> Who yearn for you?
> Who, on a lonely bridge,
> Will leave you—in order to return?

In spite of Auschwitz, Jewish writers cannot separate themselves from their God.

Traditional lamentation literature contains little or no reference to the foe or executioner, probably because he is viewed as a mere instrument of God's will. In modern Jewish lamentation literature, however, the destroyer and his accomplices can be a target of anger and rage. This tendency is apparent in the concluding lines of "To Spring" by Shayevitsh and in such postwar poems as "Elegy" by A. M. Klein, "Sometimes I Want to Go Up" by Rachel Korn, and "For Adolf Eichmann" by Primo Levi. Levi's treatment of Eichmann differs markedly from that of the American writers Levertov and Snodgrass. Given Levi's rage at Eichmann's barbarity, it is unlikely that he would humanize Eichmann by comparing him with the rest of humanity. In the work of no modern Jewish writer, however, is criticism of the oppressor—and, indeed, the entire Christian world—so pronounced as in that of the Israeli poet Uri Zvi Greenberg. Many of his poems explode with wrath. In "We Were Not Like Dogs," he exclaims:

> There is no retribution for what they did to us—
> Its circumference is the world:
> The culture of Christian kingdoms to its peak
> Is covered with our blood,
> And all their conscience, with our tears.

The critique of Christianity appears also in the work of a few Christian writers in this collection, for example, in Charlotte Delbo's "Street for Arrivals, Street for Departures" and in Czeslaw Milosz's "Campo di Fiori."

Where the tradition saw an explanation for Israel's suffering in its sin, contemporary writers perceive no explanation for the calamity, hence their demand for an accounting. The sense of sin characteristic of traditional lamentation at least opened the possiblity for consolation, for there was the hope that acceptance of—and submission to—God's will could bring an end to suffering. However, consolation is seldom offered in modern lamentation literature, although the poetry of Nelly Sachs may be considered an exception. Essentially, mod-ern Jewish writers, although often conscious of being part of a tradition, have not been able to share readily in the affirmations of faith found in traditional lamentation literature.

Loss and Disillusionment

In the modern literature of lamentation, the delineation of details of atrocity as well as the attempt to uncover psychological and philosophic truths—features prominent in the truth-telling mode—are subordinated to the expression of sorrow. But that expression of sorrow is suffused with a variety of motifs that go beyond the criticism and accusation of God. Sorrow often leads to the remembering of individual victims as well as the destroyed millions. Writing is thus a way of resurrecting the dead, as in Uri Zvi Greenberg's poem "At the Rim of the Heavens," Boris Slutsky's poem "How They Killed My Grandmother," or Ida Fink's lyrical and elegiac story "A Scrap of Time." Writing is also a way of communing with the dead, as in Abraham Sutzkever's *Green Aquarium,* H. Leivick's "I Hear a Voice," or Jacob Glatstein's "Nightsong." In the literature of lamentation, remembering the dead can be seen as a "matzevah," to use Elie Wiesel's term, "an invisible tombstone, erected to the memory of the dead unburied" (8).

In several of these pieces, as well as in Jerzy Ficowski's poem "5.8.1942" and Isaiah Spiegel's story "The Ghetto Dog," remembering prompts tribute and homage. Elegy and eulogy merge. In the poetry written in the ghettos of Poland such tribute is anticipated in memorable passages praising the average, simple Jew who clings to life or who has already been murdered. Even the great and wrathful Bialik, who mocked and ridiculed Kishinev's passive Jews, asserts Shayevitsh, would bow his head to the ghetto Jew "and murmur with ecstasy, 'Holy, Holy, Holy'" ("Spring 1942," section 9). And Katzenelson, speaking of the "simple, ordinary Jew from Poland," declares in "The Song of the Murdered Jewish People":

> Compared with him, what are the great men of a past
>   bygone?
> A wailing Jeremiah, Job afflicted, Kings despairing,
>   all in one—it's they!
>
> (Canto IX, stanza 8)

In the modern literature of lamentation, remembering can extend to the recollection of the entire East European Jewish culture that perished with the victims. Gone, says Katzenelson, are the characters that the beloved Yiddish author Sholem Aleichem (1859–1916) wrote about in his fiction—Menachem

Mendel, Tevye, and others (Canto XV, stanza 10). Dead and gone, by implication, are most of the shtetl folk of Eastern Europe who inspired Aleichem's fictional creations and were also his enthusiastic readers. Similarly, the American poet Irving Feldman indirectly elegizes a culture lost in "The Pripet Marshes" when he imaginatively places his American friends in the shtetl, "visiting, praying in *shul,* feasting / and dancing." On one level, I. B. Singer's story "Hanka" may be read as a lament for the passing of the Yiddish-speaking culture of Eastern Europe. Hanka is emblematic of that vanished world, and Isaac, the writer-protagonist of the story, still writing in Yiddish, yearns for that which has perished: "I was calling to Hanka, 'Why did you run away? Wherever you are, come back. There can be no world without you. You are an eternal letter in God's scroll.'"

The sense of loss that pervades the lamentation mode of Holocaust literature can give rise also to an indignant criticism of Western cultural values. Did not the lofty ideas about love, equality, freedom, and progress all prove to be a facade hiding the most blatant forms of savagery? This criticism is evident in such poems as Jacob Glatstein's "Good Night, World," more indirectly in Dan Pagis's ironic "Draft of a Reparations Agreement," and in Chaim Grade's "My Quarrel with Hersh Rasseyner."

Although criticism of Western culture is not absent in that response we have called truth-telling (see, for example, Celan's "Death Fugue" and Hecht's "'More Light! More Light!'"), it is likely to appear there in a more detached manner, less frought with anger, pain, and the sense of loss. Czeslaw Milosz observes that it was characteristic of Polish poetry during and after the war to place culture on trial (81–82), but Jewish writers were bound to feel most keenly the collapse of those things we call civilization.

How to Live in the Aftermath

Selections in this anthology show that the modern literature of lamentation can also lead to vexing and painful questions about how to live in the aftermath of the Holocaust. In the face of what has been lost, and in the face of what we have come to know about humankind and God, how are we—Jews as well as non-Jews—to lead our lives? What are we to believe; to what are we to commit ourselves? These questions and a range of answers to them are, we acknowledge, at the periphery of some of the pieces in the truth-telling mode. If, for example, we know the horrific consequences of making "I-them" dichotomies, as illustrated in Denise Levertov's poem "When We Look Up," how do we overcome this tendency? In the lamentation response, however, questions about how one is to live in the aftermath arise with a more intense urgency.

To begin with, what place shall we give in our lives to remembering atrocity and the victims of atrocity? Survivors have little choice but to remember loved ones slain; they are haunted by memory. But what about the rest of us? For Primo Levi in his poem "Shema" the answer is unequivocal: To remember is nothing less than a religious duty, a duty belonging to the sphere of the holy, as the poem's echoes of Deuteronomy 6:4–9 and 11:13–21 imply. Levi's Moses-like speaker admonishes us to think day and night, at home and away, of what has occurred. "Warm houses," "hot food," "friendly faces" can no longer be pleasures we enjoy thoughtlessly. For Levi, there can be no lapses from remembering.

Grandfather Zisskind in "The Name," by the Israeli fiction writer Aharon Megged, thinks and speaks of the Holocaust day and night. An immigrant survivor living in Israel, he mourns the destruction of twenty thousand Jews in his native town in the Ukraine as well as the murder of his brilliant grandson Mendele. He requests that his Israeli-born granddaughter Raya and her husband name their newborn child Mendele. "A ghetto name," exclaims Raya, "ugly, horrible! I wouldn't even be capable of letting it cross my lips. Do you want me to hate my child? . . . I don't always want to remember all those dreadful things." Young citizens of a brave new state, Raya and her husband want to separate themselves from what they believe to be the outmoded piety, narrowness, and passivity of East European Jewish life.

Megged's story was written during the early years of the state of Israel. It was not uncommon for Israelis before the Eichmann trial of 1961 to disassociate themselves from the European tragedy. However, the trial changed the views of many Israelis regarding the alleged passivity of Jewish victims by revealing the full nature of the Nazi terror.

The tension and pathos in Megged's narrative comes from a clash of values of two generations over keeping the memory of the Holocaust alive. Although Megged succeeds in presenting both positions persuasively, his sympathies lie with Grandfather Zisskind. Not to remember, exclaims Zisskind angrily, is "finishing off the work which the enemies of Israel began." To him, there can be no meaningful life without remembering the victims of Eastern Europe and the culture that vanished with them. Unfortunately, he fails to transmit his wisdom to his living grandchildren.

"A Story About Chicken Soup" by the American poet Louis Simpson— flippant on the surface to avoid a moralizing tone—concerns the conflict of an American Jew over whether to put aside the dreadful reality of relatives slain in Eastern Europe or to keep that reality alive. Neither choice feels right. To evade or repress the tragic truth is to feel guilt; the murdered relatives become "eyes": "they have some demand on me— / They want me to be more serious than I want to be." Willingly to remember the slain is to move out of the "painted sunshine"—the world of comfort and pleasure—and "to live in the tragic world forever." Simpson leaves the question of how to live with memory unresolved.

Can we pay homage to the dead and still be open to life's ordinary enjoyments? Or must we, in remembering the past, "live in the tragic world forever"? This question underlies Norma Rosen's fictionalized memoir "The Cheek of the Trout." In the story, a husband and wife from the United States visit Vienna. He is returning after forty years to the city from which he had been rescued as a child shortly after Kristallnacht. That he should have difficulty enjoying the art and beauty of Vienna is understandable. " 'Enjoy the city for me,' he kept saying" to his wife, "as if he *counted* on the difference between them. He had lived there and she had not." But his American-born wife is almost equally handicapped by her knowledge of the past. Not only beauty, but more ordinary, more innocent pleasures— symbolized by the eating of the "cheek of the trout"—are no longer available to them.

Memory of the past is essential, suggests Rosen; it is a mark of sanity and humanity. But how can we remember and yet give ourselves to the present? It is the problem of the survivor, to be sure, yet not only of the survivor. As Norma Rosen has expressed the problem: How do we remember as "an act of homage" without being held "hostage" to memory? (397).

The question of how to live in the aftermath takes another form. How does one live with God after the Holocaust? Equally perplexing, how does one live with the world—a world in which philosophy, religion, law, or ethics fail to prove capable of halting the catastrophe? Does the failure of secular humanism return us to God, or does the seeming failure of God strengthen our resolve to improve the world? In "My Quarrel with Hersh Rasseyner," considered a classic of modern Yiddish literature (Alexander 233), Chaim Grade takes up these questions in a deeply searching way.

Hersh, a zealous member of the Mussarists, an ascetic Jewish sect, experienced the tortures of the concentration camp and is convinced of the total failure of man and of man-made systems to create a humane world. His answer to the murder of six million is more faith in God: "How could I stand it without Him in this murderous world. . . . Father, Father, only You are left to us!" Chaim, the narrator (and the author thinly disguised), a religious skeptic and a writer who wandered through Europe during the war, is more committed than ever to making the world better. If he is to live responsibly, he insists, he must question God's justice; he must ask the Jobian questions about the suffering of the innocent, only multiplied for a million murdered children.

There is no winner in the philosophical debate between the two former yeshiva mates who in 1948 meet in Paris, a city that, because of its history of revolution, symbolizes the tension between secular and religious values. Hersh's words are as moving as Chaim's—perhaps even more so. The intensity and passion with which both positions are presented suggest the conflicting beliefs within the author's own mind.

What shall our relationship be to each other in the post-Holocaust world? How do we conduct our lives so that the indifference to human suffering that contributed to the Holocaust does not persist in the aftermath? This theme is developed in the dreamlike, surrealistic story "The Night" by the Israeli Nobel Prize–winner Samuel Y. Agnon.

Belief and action have no connection for Agnon's narrator. "What is custom worth," he asks, "if you're not ready to disregard it for the sake of another person?" Yet this narrator denies giving his relative Moshele, an Auschwitz survivor who has come to Israel, "his own flesh and blood, who has escaped the fires of cremation," a place to sleep on the floor of his hotel room. Images of the narrator's guilt and remorse appear in the incongruous dreamlike sequences of the story. Whether the change in the narrator at the conclusion is a true movement toward caring is left ambiguous. Agnon's title is evocative. Shall the night of the Holocaust be followed by the night of unconcern? Will we be unchanged by our knowledge?

Like the truth-telling mode, lamentation, then, is a many-leveled, many-faceted response. Its social, ethical, and theological concerns account for its distinctive character. It is more than an expression of grief and scarcely at all an attempt to console or to soothe. The selection of stories and poems reflecting lamentation appears in Part 2 of this volume. Many of these pieces may be regarded as the *kinot* and *s₄lichot* of our terrible time.

Stylistic Diversity

To be sure, neither truth-telling nor lamentation is likely to exist in pure form. As the literature of truth-telling may contain elements of lamentation, so the literature of lamentation may contain elements of truth-telling. Yitzhak Katzenelson's *The Song of the Murdered Jewish People,* Charlotte Delbo's prose poem "Street for Arrivals, Street for Departures," and Ida Fink's short story "A Scrap of Time" are examples of works in which both elements appear. Our arrangement of material in this volume reflects what we consider to be the dominant mode of response within a given work.

Nor do we mean to insist that truth-telling and lamentation are the only patterns of response that one may find in this collection. This volume is organized according to these patterns because they encompass so much in the way of thought and feeling and provide some sense of an order underlying the apparent diversity. The reader may, of course, find other patterns of response in the works we present here. There is the response of ghetto writers compared to that of post-Holocaust writers, the response of writers who experienced the inferno compared to that of writers who did not. Or, if one looks at the short fiction and poetry by such female authors as Sara Nomberg-Przytyk, Cynthia Ozick, Irena Klepfisz, and Malke Heifetz Tussman, or at the way women are characterized in the works of Simcha Bunim Shayevitsh, Miklos Radnoti, and Robert Mezey, different patterns become visible, such as the special vulnerabilities of mothers and of women in general given the sexism of the Nazi system. These patterns are supported by the oral testimonies, memoirs, and novels of female survivors (Heinemann and Ringelheim).

The two modes of literary response to the Holocaust we have described are characterized by considerable stylistic diversity. In the short stories, realism dominates but appears in numerous guises. We encounter, for example, the biting reportorial style of Zelkowicz's "25 Live Hens and One Dead Document"; the stark realism of Borowski's "This Way for the Gas, Ladies and Gentlemen," with its surprising, unprecedented narrative perspective; the leisurely, meditative realism of Gascar's "The Season of the Dead," with its subtle, symbolic overtones; the poetic realism of Ozick's "The Shawl," with its economy and metaphoric density; and the realism that frames a philosophic debate in Grade's "My Quarrel with Hersh Rasseyner." Versions of surrealism appear in Lind's "Journey Through the Night" and Agnon's "The Night," the former combining gallows humor with incidents of an extraordinary kind, the latter presenting more ordinary events but with strange and provocative discontinuities. In "Bertha," Appelfeld moves from realism to a surrealistic conclusion which, paradoxically, deepens the sense of reality.

Diversity is also characteristic of the poetry in this collection. The poetry written in the ghettos of Eastern Europe tends, for the most part, to be public and rhetorical, catering to the needs of the Yiddish-speaking masses. It thus differs from the more personal and reflective poetry written after the war. This difference is apparent if we compare some lines about the plight of children in poems by Yitzhak Katzenelson of the Warsaw Ghetto and American poet Robert Mezey. In Canto VI of *The Song of the Murdered Jewish People*, Katzenelson writes of the orphans in the ghetto:

> The first to perish were the children, abandoned
>   orphans,
> The world's best, the bleak earth's brightest.
> These children from the orphanages might have been our
>   comfort.
> From these sad, mute, bleak faces our new dawn might have
>   risen.
>
> (Stanza 4)

Katzenelson speaks here not only as an individual sufferer, but also as a member of a group: surviving Jews, wherever they are. His identification with this group is reflected in the repetition of the personal pronoun *our* ("our comfort," "our new dawn"). Rhetorical in character is his evocation of communal feeling by means of amplifying a single image or idea (the children are "abandoned orphans, / The world's best, the bleak earth's brightest"). The language is direct and explicit, and the figures of speech, although effective, are conventional ("earth's brightest," "new dawn").

The following lines from Robert Mezey's "Theresienstadt Poem" are addressed to thirteen-year-old Nely Silvinova, whose watercolor painting, created at the concentration camp at Therezin, Czechoslovakia, survived her.

> In your watercolor, Nely Sílvinová
> your heart on fire
> on the gray cover of a sketchbook
> is a dying sun or
> a flower
> youngest of the summer
>
> the sun itself
> the grizzled head of a flower
> throbbing
> in the cold dusk of your last day
> on earth
>
> There are no thorns to be seen
> but the color says
> thorns

Mezey's lines, although addressed to a murdered child, are in reality a meditation, a soliloquy in which the audience is the speaker himself. Mezey broods on the images in the watercolor (is it a sun or a flower?), imagines the painting to have been created on Nely's last day of life, and in general seeks to enter her tragic world through her painting. The utterance is personal and inward, reflected in the relative absence of punctuation and ordinary syntax and in the somewhat ambiguous and evocative figures of speech ("your heart on fire," "the sun itself / the grizzled head of a flower / throbbing," "the color says thorns"). If Katzenelson writes to be heard, Mezey writes to be overheard.

Diversity also appears in the kinds of poems that appear in this anthology. Although the elegiac lyric dominates Holocaust poetry as a whole and is the most prevalent form for survivor poets, our selection includes narrative pieces, for example, the surrealistic "The Death of an Ox" by Abraham Sutzkever and the satiric "The Bird" by Louis Simpson. A number of poems experiment with dramatic form and present speakers other than the poet. "Death Fugue" by Paul Celan and "Chorus of the Rescued" by Nelly Sachs are notable examples, but W. H. Auden, Randall Jarrell, W. D. Snodgrass, Charles Reznikoff, and Adrienne Rich likewise offer inventive uses of dramatic method. Not having firsthand experience of the Holocaust, this latter group might well be turning to dramatic form as a means of entering imaginatively into the minds of victim or executioner.

Diversity characterizes the language of poetry as well. We encounter the explicit, direct expression of Katzenelson and Shayevitsh; the plain, factual style of Reznikoff or Radnoti; the complex, metaphoric style of Sutzkever and Sachs; and the deliberately mutilated syntax of Celan and Jarrell. In tone, too, the poetry is highly varied. We experience the sorrowful and compassionate voice of Sachs's "If I only knew"; the note of quiet amazement in Kovner's "And There You Were"; the satiric, ironic bite of Snodgrass's "Heinrich Himmler Reichsfuehrer"; the reverential feeling of Sutzkever's "1980"; and the overflow of bitter anger of Sexton's "After Auschwitz."

We cannot say that one form or style is more effective than another in rendering the Holocaust experience. This anthology demonstrates that work of high artistic value has been created using a wide variety of forms and approaches. Some writers seek innovative ways to render a reality for which there is no analogue. This is reflected, for example, in a tendency to combine or fuse genres, as in the fictionalized memoir (Nomberg-Przytyk), the poeticized memoir (Delbo), the fictionalized chronicle (Zelkowicz), or the prose poem (Sutzkever). A longer narrative work not included here—*Maus* by Art Spiegelman—actually combines documentary, memoir, and comic-book form. Fusion on another level appears in the joining of grotesque humor with tragic subject matter, as in the fiction of Jacov Lind. Some writers, on the other hand, have been reluctant to give special prominence to stylistic aspects of their art in dealing with the Holocaust, feeling that to do so is irreverent. Such a reluctance, as the critic Samuel Niger points out, is particularly characteristic of postwar Yiddish writers (13, 17).

Obstacles and Challenges

> The Holocaust remains the unconquered
> Everest of our time, its dark mysteries
> summoning the intrepid literary spirit to
> mount its unassailable summit.
>
> —Lawrence L. Langer

As we noted earlier, writers imprisoned in Hitler's ghettos and writing primarily in Hebrew, Yiddish, and Polish were intensely motivated to chronicle all aspects of the Nazi destruction. They had a burning desire to bear witness, to testify against the murderous enemy before the court of the world. They also had a natural need to give voice to their anguish and rage. They had no hesitation in writing about their experience. Clearly, they did not choose silence. "A poet who clothes adversity in poetic form," wrote Chaim Kaplan in *Warsaw Diary*, "immortalizes it in an everlasting monument." Kaplan exhorted poets to write: "Poet of the people, where art thou?" (79).

Before writers perished in the ghettos or death camps, they sought every means to preserve their writings. During preparations for the armed uprising in the Warsaw Ghetto, the Jewish National Committee transmitted to the leadership of the Polish underground a map of the hiding places of the "Oneg Shabbath" Archives (Kermish xxxiii). Yitzhak Katzenelson, who wrote *The Song of the Murdered Jewish People* in Vittel, the German concentration camp for foreigners in France, hid his poem in three glass bottles at Vittel. Fortunately, surviving admirers exhumed his work and published it in 1945, a year after he perished in Auschwitz. Under the Nazi rule, then, authors, whether engaged in expository or creative writing, were determined to give an account of the Nazi destruction. They were also determined that their writings should live.

This perseverance to transmit to future generations all that occurred—this urge to write—was less keen in writers who survived the war, or in writers without direct experience of the events. Artistic expression did not come quickly for these writers; in most cases, it came years later. Partly because post-Holocaust writers had full knowledge of the nature and scope of the devastation, they were stunned initially into silence. It took time to acquire perspective on so huge a destruction. Writers who survived the Nazi oppression also wished to forget, to find oblivion in one form or another even though, as Aharon Appelfeld observes, they had imagined, while in the ghettos and camps, that after the war they would never cease to tell what they witnessed (86).

Post-Holocaust writers were conscious, moreover, of numerous impediments to writing creatively about the Holocaust. Indeed, it is difficult fully to appreciate the achievement of postwar writers without recognizing the obstacles and challenges they had to face. How, to begin with, was one to find words for so vast a destruction? Writers who experienced and survived the inferno have repeatedly expressed the belief that the most carefully crafted words would be inadequate to record the truth. "We become aware that our language lacks words to express this offence, the demolition of man," observes Primo Levi in his memoir *Survival in Auschwitz* (3).

After what the Nazis did to language—resorting to verbal acrobatics to disguise atrocities—how could one trust words even if one could find them? The Nazis devised countless euphemisms for murder: "resettlement," "conscription for labor," "liquidation," "bath houses," "action," "final solution." In her story "A Scrap of Time," Ida Fink tells of a Nazi "action" in her hometown in Poland—a mass shooting and burial. The word *action,* Fink reflects sadly, normally signifies "movement, a word you would use about a novel or a play."

We do not go so far as claiming with George Steiner that the Nazi use of language to dehumanize imposed an enforced silence on artists, but we imagine that these perversions of language contributed to the difficulties writers had rendering their experiences. As Steiner reminds us, under Nazism "words were committed to saying things no human mouth should ever have said and no paper made by man should ever have been inscribed with" (99). When the Jewish victim Lebovitch in Pierre Gascar's story "The Season of the Dead" shifts abruptly from German into English as he describes the ordeals under the German occupation, the astute narrator Peter, a French prisoner of war, understands what the German language has come to represent in Lebovitch's mind. Similarly, in Bernard Malamud's story "The German Refugee," which is not included in this volume, the journalist Oskar Gassner, who fled Hitler, "furiously flung his pen against the wall" after writing the opening pages of his first public lecture in America in German, at the same time shouting that "he could no longer write in that filthy tongue." In short, if the Nazis could pervert the German tongue, would not words in any language be suspect?

How could writers trust words, moreover, when, as the survivor poet and critic Czeslaw Milosz has pointed out, lofty words deceived the world with ideas about good and beauty, ideas about human dignity and the individual's likeness to God—all a cover hiding genocide (81).

And even if trust were possible and words could be found, survivor writers have feared that the world would surely refuse to believe. In the opening passage of *The Drowned and the Saved,* Primo Levi quotes the boast of the S.S. man who asserts that even if a handful of Jews survive, the world will never believe their story. This same thought, Levi tells us, actually arose in the dreams of prisoners. Even if they were to tell the story, would it be believed? As a writer, Levi himself experienced that fear (11–12).

The last words the urbane cannibal addresses to his victim in Jacov Lind's surrealistic story "Journey Through the Night" echo Levi's story about the boasting S.S. man. Taunting his victim by saying that no one will believe his tale of terror, Lind's cannibal then shouts, "See . . . you've made an ass of yourself for life." In simply telling the truth, writers feared they would be taken for liars. Commenting on the obstacles to writing about the horrors right after the war, Aharon Appelfeld has observed: "Everything that happened was so gigantic, so inconceivable, that the witness even seemed like a fabricator to himself" (86)

The Holocaust was a time when values were reversed. The criteria of good and evil disappeared; a crime became a praiseworthy act; an obvious lie was dogma that humans believed. How, as Alvarez asks, does one create "a coherent artistic world out of one which was the deliberate negation of all values? How does one make art out of the forces of anti-art" (25–26)? One recalls, in this connection, the words of the Hungarian poet Miklos Radnoti in "Fragment." Describing in 1944 this incredible inversion of values, Radnoti refers to its silencing effect on poets, silencing even rage:

> I lived on this earth in an age
> when the poets too were silent
> and waited for Isaiah, the scholar
> of terrifying words, to speak again—
> since only he could utter the right curse.

After the war, there was also the feeling among survivors that their experience could not be told, that no one could understand it. How could common ground be established with post-Holocaust readers? Granted, a tradition of treating violence in literature precedes the Holocaust. The violence that World War I unleashed was reflected in the work of such writers as James Joyce, Gertrude Stein, Franz Kafka, T. S. Eliot, and Ezra Pound. But survivor writers would not be likely to see a strong analogy between that tradition of violence and the Holocaust, and hence would not feel that they could draw readily on the collective imagination of readers. In a work like Kafka's *Penal Colony,* for example, survivors would be likely to see an invention, a fictional world and not a reality. The world they experienced was more extreme than any invention.

The creative writer on the Holocaust may also have feared that the artistic imagination would distort the truth. As Sidra Ezrahi points out, the survivor writer experiences a need to "establish the historicity of the subject before admitting it to the imagination" (22). The world, which quickly forgets the past, must know what happened, especially because actual witnesses eventually die out. In the face of so pressing a need to record the truth, writers may have distrusted the artistic impulse they normally valued. Or else, in treating the awesome historical event imaginatively, sensitive writers may have feared that their artistic work would be seen as excessive pride. Following this logic, the most appropriate memorial, again, would seem to be silence. Robert Jay Lifton has identified this fear of writing about certain sacred historical events, like the bombing of Hiroshima or the Holocaust, as "creative guilt" (473).

How is the artistic imagination, furthermore, to deal with metaphor or analogy? The artistic imagination expresses itself naturally through these literary resources, but an inappropriate comparison might trivialize or falsify; it might degrade either the suffering or the courage of victims. In his novel *Blood from the Sky*, Piotr Rawicz, for example, expresses his determination "to kill comparisons, to expunge them all . . . and to engage in mere recounting, mere enumerating" (183–84). Commenting on the danger of metaphorical or analogical discussion of the Holocaust, Robert Skloot observes that "Protecting against the debasement of language is the job of every artist, but artists of the Holocaust must exercise a special kind of vigilance so that the full horrifying power of the word is preserved" (15).

We can better understand writers' anxiety about metaphor when we notice our own dissatisfaction, even indignation, at indiscriminate uses of the Holocaust as a metaphor for other events—floods, fires, accidents of one sort or another, and even economic calamities. We sense in such uses a trivialization of language and a diminishment of the historic event.

For writers who knew the inferno directly, there must have loomed yet another problem of great psychological import. How does one give a full account of the madness of the times without oneself going mad? How does one survive the reopening of wounds? A number of brilliant writers on the Holocaust—Tadeusz Borowski, Paul Celan, and Primo Levi—who dared to deal with the core experience, the death camps, took their own lives. Of the suicide of Borowski and of the young Polish film director Andrzej Munk (*The Passenger* is the title of his film about Auschwitz) Alvarez writes: "The concentration camps are a dangerous topic to handle. They stir mud from the bottom, clouding the mind, rousing dormant self-destructiveness" (28).

In the ghettos and camps themselves, there were debates about whether writing was a moral act. Should the writer simply write while his or her people were dying, or should the writer promote more active resistance (Roskies, *Against the Apocalypse* 201)? In the post-Holocaust period, however, the question became, Should one write at all? Was it morally right to make art out of the unspeakable pain and anguish of the victims? Speaking for himself and for other survivors, Aharon Appelfeld observes, "Artistic expression after the Holocaust seems repugnant, disgusting. . . . Moreover, art, and not without reason, was linked in our minds with a sphere of European culture of which we had been the victims" (89). Many writers in this volume would agree with Theodore Adorno's now-famous statements that, after Auschwitz, to write a poem is "barbaric," that it is "wringing pleasure" from "the so-called artistic representation of naked bodily pain of victims felled by rifle butts" (125–26).

Thus the question is, Why have they written? And the answer is that ultimately, as the impulse to silence lost some of its strength, they could not help but write about what they knew and what they felt. That is true not only with respect to the problem of making art out of horror, but with respect to all the other impediments to writing that we have mentioned earlier. They could not *not* write. It was imperative that they add their testimony, or express their sorrow or rage, or remember the victims—despite the literary, psychological, or moral difficulties or dangers. As Appelfeld puts it, "A religious person will certainly argue in favor of silence, but what can we do? By his very nature . . . man has a kind of inner need for ritualization, not only of his joy, but also, and perhaps essentially, of his pain and grief" (83). And Cynthia Ozick, whose writing has touched on the Holocaust again and again, says "I am not in favor of making fiction of the data, or of mythologizing or poeticizing it. . . . [Yet] I constantly violate this tenet; my brother's blood cries out from the ground, and I am drawn and driven" (Lang 284).

Despite the various apprehensions of postwar writers—especially survivors—about literary treatment of the Holocaust, they have produced since the destruction a rich and diverse body of work. Like writers in the ghettos, they have felt compelled to be witnesses declaring the truth, and they have been unable to suppress indefinitely the grief that needed an outlet. If they feel that their words have not been totally adequate, those words have at least provided an opening to the catastrophe.

Not all the fears and apprehensions of postwar writers on the Holocaust have proven valid. The imagined difficulty of survivors of not having readers who share a firsthand knowledge of the terrible events has not proven to be a major barrier. As it turns out, post-Holocaust readers can have a privileged position that works well for writers. Some works of Holocaust literature, like the story "A Ghetto Dog" by Isaiah Spiegel or the well-known novella *Badenheim 39* by Aharon Appelfeld, for example, are not explicit in rendering the evil, but go only to the threshhold of the darkness. Such works call upon readers—who know the fate of victims—to fill in the missing information. The post-Holocaust reader thus becomes, as Ezrahi points out, a "collaborative witness" to those events (9). Omission becomes an artistic way of handling the aspects of the Holocaust that most defy description. Meanwhile, writers can achieve powerful effects of understatement.

But even works that do not take readers to the threshhold of atrocity depend upon and make use of readers' knowledge of the historical facts. We could not, for example, fully experience the drama and significance of the ideological debate in Grade's "My Quarrel with Hersh Rasseyner" or the meaning of the extraordinary events in Lind's "A Journey Through the Night" without bringing factual knowledge to the stories. Even writers on the Holocaust who are not themselves survivors have seen the value of using readers' knowledge. We could not, for example, enter fully into the conflict of generations in Aharon Megged's story "The Name" or appreciate the moral failure of the narrator of Samuel Agnon's story "The Night" without bringing a knowledge of the Holocaust to our reading.

American writers have been understandably reluctant to present the details of atrocity, primarily because of their lack of firsthand experience. Reliance on the reader's knowledge of fact has worked well for them, too, as can be seen in such poems as Randall Jarrell's "Protocols" and Irving Feldman's "The Pripet Marshes." In each case, prior knowledge elicits irony and pathos because readers know more of the fate of the victims than the victims themselves.

Nor has the fear of using extraordinary suffering for purposes of art, the fear of making the Holocaust an instrument of literary enjoyment, proven to be an insurmountable obstacle. The best writers have succeeded in transmitting truths and lamenting the catastrophe without making pleasure, in the conventional sense, a product of their work. Lawrence L. Langer has pointed out that numerous works treat the atrocities and avoid producing the kind of pleasurable response Adorno and others would see as dishonorable and immoral. Poems by Celan, Sachs, and Hecht and stories by Borowski, Lind, Gascar, and others produce what Langer calls a "disfiguration" of reality that brings the reader into the realm of the "grotesque, senseless, and unimaginable" in a way that militates against conventional aesthetic pleasure (3). "The art of atrocity," observes Langer, "is a stubbornly unsettling art, indifferent to the peace that passeth understanding and intent only on reclaiming for the present not the experience of horror itself, since by common consent of the survivors this is impossible to do vicariously, but a framework for responding to it, for making it imaginatively, if not literally, accessible" (12).

In the lamentation literature, as distinct from the literature that transmits truths, readers may, indeed, experience satisfaction from sympathetic identification with the thoughts and feelings of characters and speakers. But such satisfaction has a humane, moral dimension that cannot be identified with the superficial pleasure that derives from novelties of language, clever rhetoric, sentimentality, or the merely lachrymose or melodramatic. Nor do the pieces in the lamentation approach offer the pleasure of easy consolations and facile ways of imbuing the Holocaust with meaning. The best work in the lamentation mode avoids imparting the pleasure of the hopeful and heroic. It remains, when all is said and done, a painful literature, one that intensifies our sense of what was lost as well as our sense of the incomprehensibility of the catastrophe.

Criteria of Selection

Perhaps in the preceding account we have suggested something of the criteria by which the poems and stories for this collection have been selected. We have avoided works that distort or exploit the historical facts in order to entertain. In recent years, we have observed enough of this tendency in movies, television, the theater, and various works of fiction. Rather, we have favored works that treat the Holocaust with restraint or understatement, or with shrewd forms of indirection that make the reader a participant in the act of creation. We have not always felt comfortable making our selections on the basis of such "literary" standards, especially when choosing from the writings of survivors. At times it has seemed insensitive to focus upon literary considerations when much more than a literary response is appropriate. As David Denby points out, a "literary judgment" of a survivor's work "might be taken as a dismissal of the experience behind the writing," when actually the experience of Holocaust writers "is all on the same level and beyond judgment" (27).

Nevertheless, some works on the Holocaust engage us more fully than others; some call forth our imaginative response more powerfully than others. This fuller response has something to do with linguistic competence or originality—with what is omitted as much as with what is said—in short, with ways of giving shape to experience through language. Ambivalent, then, as we have been about raising questions of literary merit, we have, with few exceptions, made our selections with the quality of the writing in mind.

Given our preference for a more indirect treatment of the subject, we have, for the most part, chosen pieces that tend to be ironic, symbolic, and paradoxical; we have selected those which employ realism in cunning ways or use surrealistic effects to realize their purposes. A few of our selections expose harsh realities through subtle forms of humor. Our preference is for the oblique over the blunt. As Irving Howe points out, "The more sensitive writers on Holocaust themes have apparently felt that their subject cannot be met full-face or head-on. Before the unspeakable, a muteness, a numbed refusal come upon one. If approached at all, the Holocaust must be taken on a tangent, with extreme wariness, through oblique symbols, strategies of indirection, and circuitous narratives" ("How to Write about the Holocaust" 17). We have not included works that are so oblique and indirect as to be accessible only to a small portion of readers (some of the late poems of Paul Celan and Nelly Sachs are cases in point). Nor have we been interested in the restrained or the shrewdly indirect unless accompanied by substance and depth.

An exception to our general preference for the muted and indirect appears in a number of poetic works we have included from the Holocaust itself—works written in the Nazi ghettos and camps and written under physical and psychic conditions that make us wonder how any imaginative writing could have been accomplished at all. We see these works as having unique historical value. Because poems by Katzenelson, Shayevitsh, Sutzkever, Kirman, and

Szlengel, as well as songs by Glik and Kaczerginski, were written in the midst of ordeal and not afterward, they provide a heightened sense of what individuals experienced and felt at the time, while people were starving to death, being cruelly overworked, contemplating or executing some form of resistance, or being deported to death camps.

These poets witnessed the annihilation of their people. Under such conditions, subtlety and indirection are not likely to be prized qualities, and writers are likely to treat their subject—and to give vent to their emotions—in a more head-on fashion. What Noah Rosenbloom says of Katzenelson's *Song of the Murdered Jewish People* is, to a large extent, true of the writings of other ghetto poets we have included in this collection. Those writings are characterized by "authenticity . . . primeval force, unsophisticated veracity-. . . and visceral simplicity" (118).

There is another reason why modernist literary standards cannot be applied to much of the poetry written in the ghettos. This poetry was essentially public in character, reaching the Yiddish-speaking masses through underground presses, theater performances, or public readings. Its purpose was to unify, consolidate, and inspire. Hardly a ghetto work by Katzenelson failed to reach the public in one way or another. This is also true of many of Sutzkever's creations in the Vilna Ghetto and of Hirsh Glik's "Never Say," which became known beyond the confines of the Vilna Ghetto, evolved into a folk song, and became the partisans' anthem. Wladyslaw Szlengel's poem "Counterattack," a song of glory to Jewish heroism written in January 1943 during the first armed resistance in the Warsaw Ghetto, was "on everybody's tongue" (Kermish xvi). Because ghetto poetry tended to be a means of public communication, its language and style were the opposite of subtle and oblique. Ghetto poetry was direct, accessible, even conventional.

Why Read *Truth and Lamentation?*

The stories and poems in this collection are often painful to read. In part, this is because they are about realities and not simply about invented terrors such as may be found in Dante's *Inferno* or in fictions by Poe or Kafka. Like the speaker in Simpson's poem "A Story About Chicken Soup" or the narrator in Agnon's story "The Night," most of us are inclined, in spite of occasional guilt feelings, to turn away from the cruel reality. The painfulness of this literature is also compounded by the fact that in it civilization is on trial; not only did man die at Auschwitz, as Elie Wiesel pointed out, but also "the idea of man" (*Legends of Our Time* 190). The death of our pre-Holocaust conception of man, passionately presented, for example, in Grade's story "My Quarrel with Hersh Rasseyner" and in Sexton's poem "After Auschwitz," is distressing to confront. It is not pleasant to read a body of literature whose message is dark and whose tone is so frequently elegiac.

Why, then, should we read the literature in this volume? What can it do for us? Perhaps we should first remember what it cannot do. It cannot console, for it does not point to compensations for loss or offer a redemptive vision that mitigates the tragedy. We might be suspicious of it if it did, just as we can be suspicious of the heroic uplift offered in some of the popular novels on the Holocaust, for example, Leon Uris's *Mila 18,* John Hersey's *The Wall,* and Jean-Francois Steiner's *Treblinka.* What consolations, after all, can be offered in the face of the almost successful annihilation of European Jewry? In the strongest literature of the Holocaust, there is no binding up the wounds of loss. (Ghetto writers' expressions of faith and hope seem tragically ironic because readers know more about the nature and extent of the annihilation than the writers could know.)

Nor will this literature make us understand the mystery of scientific, bureaucratic extermination at the center of European civilization. How, we often ask, is evil on this scale possible? How could individuals and nations be so indifferent, so complacent? What was God's role in all this? The literature in this volume is not likely to answer such questions. It may, instead, intensify our sense of the incomprehensibility of the Holocaust. Indeed, the best writers on this subject tacitly assume that the Holocaust cannot be comprehended. They seem to share an attitude that Irving Howe expressed so well: "We cannot 'understand' the Holocaust; we can only live with it in a state of numb agitation" ("How to Write about the Holocaust" 16).

Still, this literature has much to offer. It can lead us, as we suggested at the outset, to ponder questions about human nature, the place of God in our lives, the culture we have inherited, and the world in which we now live. Combining historical fact and imagination, this literature can heighten our consciousness of that time of fire and silence; bring us closer to the mind of victim, executioner, and survivor; and give us a fuller sense of the world we inhabit as a consequence of Auschwitz. In addition, stories and poems in this volume, both in their truth-telling and lamentation functions, can remove from our minds the film of abstraction that surrounds the Holocaust and can excite our capacity for compassion. They can make unprecedented sorrow and loss more palpable; they can suggest what it feels like to struggle with unresolved angers and theological dilemmas, what it feels like to be committed to keeping the dead alive through memory. Perhaps such deeper pondering, such heightened consciousness and enlarged sympathy, can be translated into humane action so that the future is without victims and perpetrators.

Readers are likely to come away from these works with sharp, vivid pictures, perhaps unforgettable ones, visual equivalents of suffering and loss:

Ervin in Lustig's "The Lemon" removing the gold teeth from his father's corpse; Rosa in Ozick's "The Shawl" stuffing her throat with Magda's shawl to stifle her scream; Anna, in Spiegel's "A Ghetto Dog," unwilling to give up her dog to the German, twisting the leash onto her arm as if it were the strap of the phylacteries. Or, the reader may be able to envision the crazed mother in Nelly Sachs's "Already embraced by the arm of heavenly solace," twisting her hands into urns so as to bury her child who was reduced to ash; the poet Jacob Glatstein strolling among the graves in his "nighttime / dead garden"; the speaker in Irving Feldman's "The Pripet Marshes" frantically hiding loved ones in a pillowcase, in a shoebox, as the Germans "break their fists on the hollow doors." Images like these, we believe, may have a lasting impact on us—indeed, a deep moral impact—because they engage us as whole persons, our senses, our feelings, our intellect. They translate what seems unreal and mythical into the experience of human beings. The tortured are no longer abstract and anonymous. They have human forms.

Works Cited

Adelson Alan, and Robert Lapidus, eds. *Lodz Ghetto: Inside a Community under Siege.* New York: Viking, 1989.

Adorno, Theodore. "Engagement." In *Noten zur Literatur III,* 125–26. Frankfurt am Mein: Suhrkamp Verlag, 1965.

Alexander, Edward. *The Resonance of Dust: Essays on Holocaust Literature and Jewish Fate.* Columbus: Ohio State University Press, 1979.

Alvarez, A. "The Literature of the Holocaust." In *Beyond All This Fiddle,* 22–33. New York: Random House, 1968.

Appelfeld, Aharon. "After the Holocaust." In *Writing and the Holocaust,* ed. Berel Lang, 83–92. New York: Holmes and Meier, 1988.

Berger, Alan L. *Crisis and Covenant: The Holocaust in American-Jewish Fiction.* Albany: State University of New York Press, 1988.

Denby, David. "The Humanist and the Holocaust." *New Republic,* July 28, 1986, 27–33.

Ezrahi, Sidra DeKoven. *By Words Alone: The Holocaust in Literature.* Chicago: University of Chicago Press, 1982.

Fishman, Charles, ed. *Blood to Remember: American Poets on the Holocaust.* Lubbock: Texas Tech University Press, 1991.

Friedlander, Albert H., ed. *Out of the Whirlwind: A Reader of Holocaust Literature.* New York: Union of American Hebrew Congregations, 1968.

Glatstein, Jacob, Israel Knox, and Samuel Margoshes, eds. *Anthology of Holocaust Literature.* Philadelphia: The Jewish Publication Society, 1969.

Heimler, Eugene. *Night of the Mist.* Translated by Andre Ungar. 1959. New York: Vanguard Press, 1959. Reprint. Westport: Greenwood Press, 1978.

Heinemann, Marlene E. *Gender and Destiny: Women Writers and the Holocaust.* Westport: Greenwood Press, 1986.

Hilberg, Raul. *The Destruction of the European Jews.* 3 vols. Rev. ed. New York: Holmes and Meier, 1985.

Howe, Irving. "How to Write about the Holocaust." *New York Review of Books,* March 28, 1985, 14–17.

—————. "Writing and the Holocaust." *New Republic,* October 27, 1986, 27–39.

Kaplan, Chaim A. *The Warsaw Diary of Chaim A. Kaplan.* Translated by Abraham I. Katsh. New York: Collier, 1973. Previously published as *Scroll of Agony.* New York: Macmillan, 1965.

Kermish, Joseph, ed. *To Live with Honor and Die with Honor: Selected Documents from the Warsaw Ghetto Underground Archives "O.S."* ["Oneg Shabbath"]. Jerusalem: Yad Vashem, 1986.

Krakowski, Shmuel. *The War of the Doomed: Jewish Armed Resistance in Poland, 1942–1944.* Translated by Orah Blaustein. New York: Holmes and Meir, 1984.

Kremer, Lillian. *Witness Through the Imagination: Jewish American Holocaust Literature.* Detroit: Wayne State University Press, 1989.

Lang, Berel, ed. *Writing and the Holocaust.* New York: Holmes and Meier, 1988.

Langer, Lawrence L. *The Holocaust and the Literary Imagination.* New Haven: Yale University Press, 1977.

Laska, Vera, ed. *Women in the Resistance and in the Holocaust: The Voices of Eye Witnesses.* Westport: Greenwood Press, 1983.

Levi, Primo. *The Drowned and the Saved.* Translated by Raymond Rosenthal. New York: Summit Books, 1988.

—————. *The Reawakening.* Translated by Stuart Woolf. New York: Collier Books, 1965.

—————. *Survival in Auschwitz.* Translated by Stuart Woolf. New York: Collier Books, 1973. Previously published as *If This Is a Man.* New York: Orion Press, 1959.

Lifton, Robert Jay. *Death in Life: Survivors of Hiroshima.* New York: Vintage, 1967.

Mark, Ber. *The Uprising in the Warsaw Ghetto.* Translated by Gershon Freidlin. New York: Schocken Books, 1975.

Milosz, Czeslaw. *The Witness of Poetry.* Cambridge: Harvard University Press, 1983.

Niger, Samuel. "Yiddish Poets of the 'Third Destruction.'" *The Reconstructionist,* June 27, 1947, 13–18.

Rawicz, Piotr. *Blood from the Sky.* Translated by Peter Wiles. New York: Harcourt, Brace & World, 1964.

Ringelheim, Joan. "Women and the Holocaust: A Reconsideration of Research." *Signs: Journal of Women in Culture and Society* 10, no. 4 (1985): 741–61.

Rosen, Norma. "Notes Toward a Holocaust Fiction." In *Testimony: Contemporary Writers Make the Holocaust Personal,* ed. David Rosenberg, 392–98. New York: Random House, 1989.

Rosenbloom, Noah H. "The Threnodist and the Threnody of the Holocaust." In Yitzhak Katzenelson, *The Song of the Murdered Jewish People.* Translated and annotated by Noah H. Rosenbloom, 93–132. Israel: Ghetto Fighters' House, Hakibbutz Hameuchad Publishing House, 1980.

Rosenfeld, Alvin H. *A Double Dying: Reflections on Holocaust Literature.* Bloomington: Indiana University Press, 1988.

Roskies, David G. *Against the Apocalypse: Responses to Catastrophe in Modern Jewish Culture.* Cambridge: Harvard University Press, 1984.

———, ed. *The Literature of Destruction: Jewish Responses to Catastrophe.* Philadelphia: The Jewish Publication Society, 1988.

Rossiter, Margaret L. *Women in the Resistance.* New York: Praeger, 1986.

Skloot, Robert, ed. *The Theater of the Holocaust.* Madison: University of Wisconsin Press, 1982.

Steiner, George. *Language and Silence.* New York: Atheneum, 1967.

Trunk, Isaiah. *Jewish Responses to Nazi Persecution: Collective and Individual Behavior in Extremis.* Translated by Gabriel Trunk. New York: Stein and Day, 1979.

Whitman, Ruth. *The Testing of Hanna Senesh.* Detroit: Wayne State University Press, 1986.

Wiesel, Elie. *Legends of Our Time.* New York: Schocken Books, 1982.

PART I

Transmitting Truths

25 Live Hens
And One Dead Document

Such an unimportant, trivial document:

25 live hens were requisitioned this Saturday on Podrzeczna Street and taken to the headquarters of the HIOD [*Hilfs-Ordnungsdienst,* the Auxiliary Order Service]. As agreed to by [Jewish Police Chief] Rozenblat, the hens were distributed as follows:

13 hens were returned.

6 were sent to Drewnowska Street

1 hen—Rozenblat

5 hens, i.e., 20 meals—*Hilfs-Ordnungsdienst.*

Don't throw this paper away, even if it is unsigned, undated and written in pencil.

This dry, insignificant document you've accidentally found among old papers could reveal one of the ghetto's most horrible and tragic stories—if only you knew how to read it.[1]

It's the story of 24 Jews who perished for no reason, none at all.

It's the story of 24 people who lost their lives in the street, like rabid dogs.

This piece of paper you've found by chance in the ghetto archives says nothing about 24 dead Jews. In fact, it speaks only of 25 live hens. But listen to the people, and they'll tell you the story that begins with a Polish ruffian from the city.

A *shaygets* [Yid: Gentile youth] who was born on Zielony Rynek [Green Market], who grew up among Jews and was known by the name Rudy Janek [Red-headed Johnny], decided one day to turn his coat inside out and become a *Volksdeutsch.*

As a *Volksdeutsch* he could grab Jews for forced labor. Some paid him off without a word. Some did not; their pockets were cleaned out by him.

As a *Volksdeutsch* he could enter any Jewish house he wished, and rob Jewish property.

---

1. The Lodz Ghetto in western Poland was created by the Nazis in April 1940. During 1942 and June–July 1944, there were massive deportations from Lodz to the Chelmno extermination camp. In August–September 1944, the ghetto was liquidated, and the remaining sixty thousand Jews were sent to Auschwitz.

A lowly porter from Zielony Rynek, a sack pusher for the Jews, Rudy Janek was transformed into a lord.

Instead of hanging around the market with a rope on his back, the *Volksdeutsch* could walk around in his Sunday suit even on a weekday and, just as he used to on Sundays, get dead drunk.

Before, Janek had to carry a 100-kilogram sack on his back for 20 *groschen*, hiding in his pockets the beans he stole for his pigeons from Jewish stores. And now these pockets were filled with 20-Reichsmark notes.

Before, Janek had to beg for those beans, but more often he stole them. From time to time he was caught and got a slap in the face. Now he is given the 20-mark notes with a friendly smile, and those who don't wish to be friendly have their money taken from them and also get a bashing in the face from Janek.

When they slapped him for theft, they did so with justice and pity. The few beans didn't make a difference, but this redheaded lad should learn not to touch them. So he got off with a few well-meaning slaps. He was happy that it was just that, and they were happy, having taught a thief a lesson. But when Janek hits, he knows no justice or pity. Janek likes blood. Lots of blood.

Bravo, Janek! You possess all the attributes of a real German. You've become a true-to-life German. But woe to you, Janek, for just when you trained yourself to be a stray dog, who takes and grabs and lusts for blood, just then they put you on a leash!

Janek, who was no good for anything any more, not even for lifting a sack, who was no more than a stray dog, a mangy dog, was good enough to be a watchman for the German police, a warden of Jewish lives in the ghetto.

Janek, now the German policeman Johann, was posted at the ghetto border to see that Jews didn't slip into the city looking for food.

Janek did not feel comfortable in the uniform they put on him. A dog does not like his muzzle.

The 20-mark banknotes were all gone. Since all the Jews had been driven into the ghetto, there was no way to get new ones. Janek had to live on the modest wages of a police guard. And he had to stand there and watch—like a chained dog.

Janek was not used to it. He was a stray dog. Stray dogs hate having chains around their necks. He was in a state of rebellion but could not rebel openly, for he could get shot. The gall in him rose to his mouth. His life was bitter, his world oppressively small.

Ever since he was put in uniform, Janek had been thirsty for a drink. His tongue felt glued to his palate like a piece of dried liver. And the only taste he had in his mouth was the taste of gall. Gall and liver.

Janek longed for freedom, longed for the 20-mark banknotes. With his stupid mind, with his piggish-blue eyes he began to look for banknotes right there, at the ghetto border.

Standing there one day, his mouth dry and his tongue out like a thirsty dog, Janek spotted Redhead Leyzer.

They hardly recognized each other. The Janek in uniform looked altogether different. Leyzer, who had had a flour store on Zielony Rynek, remembered Janek as a ragged, shabby *shaygets* who wore torn trousers, walked barefoot, and had a face covered with reddish, pig-stiff bristles. On Sundays Janek used to put on his one and only black suit, which he had bought in the Old Town, and his high-heeled red shoes, shave his face, and make the reddish hair cling to his head. But on Sundays Leyzer's business was closed, so Leyzer never saw Janek in his Sunday incarnation. It never crossed Leyzer's mind, therefore, that that scoundrel, that red-headed Polish ragamuffin might be changed into a German soldier with a gun—and that he would be standing right there, guarding him, Leyzer.

On the other hand, in the old days when he owned a store on Zielony Rynek, Redhead Leyzer was a man with a big belly. In the summer he used to wear a shiny alpaca coat, which glittered like a well-cleaned mirror, and light chamois shoes with soft toes. In the winter, a beaver coat with a wide fur collar, boots lined with felt and galoshes. And in every season he had a shiny, reddish, well-trimmed beard. So Janek could not know that this ragged, shabby Jew, with the worn pants around his sunken belly, with a torn, little excuse for a beard, that this pitiful little Jew was Redhead Leyzer from Zielony Rynek.

So they met but did not recognize each other. Yet they'd been looking for each other so long that they finally understood.

"They'd been looking for each other" does not necessarily mean that Redhead Leyzer was looking specifically for Rudy Janek, or that Rudy Janek was eager to see no one but Redhead Leyzer. In fact, Redhead Leyzer was looking for a German guard corrupt enough to want to live well and let others live too, a guard who, as businessmen used to say, would agree to be "poisoned" and would make deals. At the same time, Rudy Janek was looking for Jews who, like in the good times not so long ago, would fill his pockets with 20-mark banknotes.

Thus, facing each other eye to eye—on either side of the ghetto fence— they looked at one another for a long time without speaking. And when they were finally done with the survey—Leyzer of Janek's grandeur and Janek of

Leyzer's dejection—Janek took another look around to make sure that nobody was watching—and let Leyzer come closer to the fence.

"How are you, Leyzer? Come, don't be afraid."

Just like that. Feeling a sudden exhilaration over Leyzer's downfall, Janek addressed his erstwhile boss informally.

Leyzer did not appear at all shocked. He even liked this intimacy. A *shaygets*, yes, but our *shaygets*. A servant. And so Leyzer came nearer without fear.

Janek, having grown up among Jews and having earned his keep from them, knew a few Yiddish words, such as *mamele, tatele, a kholere, a kaporeh* [Yid: Mama, Papa, cholera, bad bird (the latter two used as curses)]. Now, to find favor with Leyzer, he embedded these words in the speech he directed at him.

"See, Leyzer. *Di kholere hot gekhapt* [Yid: the devil has taken the lot of] you Jews. Your sacks of flour on Zielony Rynek are now ours. Everything is ours. The whole world will be ours. Me now—Johann, a master. And you Leyzer—a lousy Jew, a servant."

Leyzer saw that if Janek went on like that, he would be unable to begin. Answering with an insult was too dangerous. He had to try diplomacy, a little flattery, and a bit of scolding. So he didn't say a word but sighed deeply instead, meaning: "You are right, Janek, we are in trouble." And then he began:

"Nie boj sie, Janek, tam gdzie woda byla, woda bedzie, a gowniarz gowniarzem zostanie" [Pol: Don't worry, Janek; where there was water, there will always be water, and a shithead will always be a shithead]. In other words, Janek, where there was money, there will be money again, and a swine will remain a swine.

After a bit of this small talk, with hints from Leyzer and punches from Janek, they came to the following agreement: Janek would toss over the fence whatever he could get in the city. Leyzer would sell the merchandise, and they'd share the proceeds.

"You know, Janek—live and let live!"

"That's right, Mister Leyzer: where water was, water will always be; money goes to money. You will have and I, too, will have, as in the old days. Remember, Leyzer?"

These were the first days of the ghetto. People did not yet comprehend the evil which had befallen them. The population was, so to speak, in the honeymoon of ghetto life, and behaved therefore like a young, freewheeling bridegroom, eating well and spending one banknote from his dowry after another.

Everything in the ghetto, therefore, was for sale. Everything that could be procured.

After the turmoil in the city, after the killings inside the "planned resettlement," after the grabbing of people on th labor, after the scare about what was going to happen tom few hours, the Jews in the ghetto, among themselves, *niente* [Ital: sweet frivolity]. Crowds gathered in the str good news. Cards were played outdoors, and food was stash

Prices rose by the hour. But the devil had already taken so much, so much Jewish property had been swallowed, the whole wedding was so terribly costly, that these few marks did not matter any more. Thus, exorbitant sums were paid for food, as long as it could be had—which it could, indeed, from the other side of the fence.

These were prosperous times in the ghetto. But it was prosperity turned upside down. People did not earn what they spent. Only a few individuals, who were willing to take the risk and run smuggling operations through the fence, made a profit. The others spent their last money buying everything: soap, sugar, flour, meat, and the greatest of delicacies, live hens! Live hens were capital that increased every day, and there was also the daily bonus—an egg! An egg in the ghetto, God in heaven, it was treasure; two, two and a half marks a day.

Therefore Leyzer urged Janek:

"Janek, by God, remember hens!—not geese, not turkeys, but hens!"

Janek interpreted this in his own way:

"Ha, ha, no more geese and turkeys for them Jews, just hens!"—but since he was "requisitioning" the loot from the peasant women who brought their merchandise to the city, he was not that strict and sometimes added a rooster to the hens he got for Leyzer.

When the ghetto stores all of a sudden began selling eggs for two and a half marks, and on the streets one could buy a plate of poultry meat for 15 marks a quarter, and live hens were seen in the ghetto, the Jewish police became restless.

How come? Hens in the ghetto? Eggs in the ghetto without their knowledge? Merchandise being smuggled into the ghetto, people becoming rich, and they had no share in it? Jewish *chutzpah* [Yid: nerve]! Such Jews should be taught a lesson!

And who could search better than the Jewish police? So they searched until they found Redhead Leyzer and the twenty-five live hens he had gotten from Rudy Janek.

What happened to the twenty-five hens, we learned from the above document: thirteen hens were returned to Leyzer, and let no one say that the Jewish *Hilfs-Ordnungsdienst* resembles the German police, the Kripo, the Schupo, etc., just because they too made an acronym of their name, the HIOD.

Six hens, according to the document, were sent to Drewnowska Street. Since the recipient is not named, we have to assume that it was the hospital on Drewnowska Street. It's hard to believe, however, that it was the patients who got the hens. It would be closer to the truth that the loot was devoured by the managing personnel.

One hen was given to the commander of the Order Service, the overseer of public order in the ghetto, so as to have approval for the remaining 5 hens given to the HIOD, in the form of 20 meals.

And thus it happened that the principle of "one for all" was finally realized in the ghetto. One Redhead Leyzer was able to satisfy an entire hospital, a whole unit of the Jewish police, and even the commander of the Order Service.

A second part of the "one-for-all" principle was executed by Rudy Janek. Janek was irked, not so much by the loss as by the *chutzpah* of those Jews who, without his permission, used his own method of requisitioning merchandise. He was thinking:

Good. The damn Jews took twelve of his hens away. Well, then, he'd take two Jews for each hen. They decided, "Fifty-fifty"; he responded, "Double— 24 Jews for 12 hens. And let the damn Jews know who Janek is!"

Let the ghetto know who Janek is, who—two months and two days after the ghetto was closed off—shot 24 Jews to death, for nothing. Like stray dogs.

On July 2, 1940, he shot a fifteen-year-old girl in the heart.

Three days later, when he was again sent to his post at the ghetto fence, he killed a 29-year-old man and a young woman of 21.

After a pause, on July 10, he shot a 30-year-old woman in the head.

On July 11 a man of 23.

On July 12 he shot the brains out of a 65-year-old man.

On July 16 he hit a 50-year-old woman and a 16-year-old boy.

On July 18 he put a bullet in the heart of a 62-year-old man.

On July 20 he murdered a 20-year-old girl.

With murderous precision he killed five people on one day, July 21: a 17-year-old girl, three young men in their twenties, and a 30-year-old man.

On July 24 two aged women.

On July 26 a 17-year-old boy.

On July 27 a 24-year-old man.

On July 28 his last two victims, a 17-year-old girl and a 50-year-old woman.

A total of thirty-five people were killed by the guards of German justice in the month of July 1940. Rudy Janek killed twenty-four of them. Not one more. Twenty-four—with truly German precision.

But of those twenty-four Jews shot to death, no mention is made in any document. Nor is it mentioned whether the one hen taken by the commander of the Order Service, the guardian of public order in the ghetto, was to his taste or, God forbid, it was not.

In the Ghetto, January 1942
Translated from the Yiddish by Marek Web

Chronicle of a Single Day

How differently my song would sound
If I could let it all resound.
　　　　　—paraphrase of *Monish*[1]

Tired, pale fingers are setting type somewhere in Cracow: "Tik-tak-tak, tik-tak-tak-tak. Rome: the Duce has announced . . . Tokyo: the newspaper *Asahi Shimbun*[2] . . . Tik-tak-tak . . . Stockholm . . . Tik-tik . . . Washington: Secretary Knox has announced . . . Tik-tik-tik-tak . . . And I am hungry."

It's not yet five o'clock. At the door of the room, a new day awaits you. A quiet breeze. A puppy wants to play with you—jumps up at your neck, over your body, behind your back, nuzzles up, wants to tease, to get you to go out and play. A discordant orchestra of sleepers breathing. As one begins, another—a child—interrupts right in the middle. And a third—and a fourth. The conversations in one's sleep are over, complaints satisfied. From time to time someone groans in his sleep. And my brain is bursting, my heart is sick, my mouth is dry. I am hungry. Food, food, food!

The last portion of soup—yesterday at twenty to one. The next will be—today at the same time. The longest half, already endured. How much longer to go? Eight hours, though you can't count the last hour from noon on. By then you're already in the kitchen, surrounded by the smell of food; you're already prepared. You already *see* the soup. So there are really only seven hours to go.

"Only" seven hours to go; it's no joke. Seven hours—and the fool says "only." Very well then; how does one get through the seven hours—or the nearest two? Read? Your brain won't take it in. All the same, you pull the book out from under the pillow. German. Arthur Schnitzler. Publisher so-and-so. Year. Printer. "Eva looked into the mirror." You turn the first page and realize you've understood no more than the first sentence. "Eva looked into the mirror."

You've reached the end of the second page. Didn't understand a single word. Yesterday the soup was thin and almost cold. You sprinkled in some

---

1. A mock-heroic poem by the Yiddish writer I. L. Peretz, published in 1888.
2. A Japanese daily newspaper.

salt, which didn't dissolve properly. And yesterday Friedman died . . . of starvation. Definitely of hunger. You could see he wouldn't last long. And there's a gnawing in my stomach. If you only had a quarter of a loaf now! One of the quarter loaves over there, a square-shaped quarter loaf, like the ones in that display window, by that table. Oh, brother! You realize that you've jumped up, the idea was so delicious. There's some name or other on page four of the novella: Dionisia. Where she's from, and what she wants—you don't know. There! A quarter of a loaf! There! A bowl of soup! You would make it differently. You would warm it through until it began to boil. So that a spoonful could last five minutes at least. So that you would sweat as you ate. So that you would blow at the spoon, not be able to swallow the soup all at once! Like that!

Maybe it isn't nice to think about oneself in this way—only about oneself, oneself. Remember once; preached a thousand times: the century of the masses, of the collective. The individual is nothing. Phrases! It's not me thinking it, it's my stomach. It doesn't think, it yells, it's enough to kill you! It demands, it provokes me. "Intellectual! Where are you, with your theories, your intellectual interests, your dreams, your goals? You educated imbecile! Answer me! Remember: every nuance, every twist of intellectual life used to enchant you, entirely possess you. And now? And now!"

Why are you yelling like that?

"Because I want to. Because I, your stomach, am hungry. Do you realize that by now?"

Who is talking to you in this way? You are two people. Arke. It's a lie. A pose. Don't be conceited. That kind of split was all right at one time when one was full. *Then* one could say, "Two people are battling in me," and one could make a dramatic, martyred face.

Yes, this kind of thing can be found quite often in literature. But today? Don't talk nonsense—it's you and your stomach. It's your stomach and you. It's 90 percent your stomach and a little bit you. A small remnant, an insignificant remnant of the Arke who once was. The one who thought, read, taught, dreamed. Of the one who looked ironically from the dock directly into the eyes of the Prosecutor and smiled directly into his face. Yes, stomach of mine, listen: such an Arke existed once. Once, once, he read a Rolland,[3] lived side by side with a Jean-Christophe, admired an Annette, laughed with a [Colas] Breugnon. Yes, and for a while he was even a Hans Castorp,[4] by some writer . . . Thomas Mann.

3. A French author (1866–1945); Jean-Christophe, Annette, and Breugnon are characters in his novels.

4. A character in Thomas Mann's novel *The Magic Mountain*.

"I don't understand, wise guy. Haven't you eaten?"

Yes, stomach, sure, I ate but I didn't know I had eaten. Didn't think I was eating.

"Do you remember, buddy, the first day in jail? You sat in solitary confinement, bewildered, sad; they had just thrown you, like a piece of old clothing, into a pantry. For two days you didn't eat, but didn't feel the least hunger. And suddenly the peephole opened in the door: 'Good evening, Arke! Keep it up! *Grunt się nie przejmować, dobrze się odżywiać* (keep your spirits up and eat well)! Listen, Arke, in the corner, behind the radiators, there's bread and bacon. The main thing, brother, is to eat—the next installment comes tomorrow, on the walk.' Remember?"

And yesterday Friedman died. Of starvation. Of starvation? When you saw him naked, thrown into the large—the gigantic—mass grave (everyone covered his nose with a handkerchief, except for me and his mother), his throat was cut. Maybe he didn't die of hunger—maybe he took his own life? Yes . . . no. People don't take their own lives nowadays. Suicide is something from the good old days. At one time, if you loved a girl and she didn't reciprocate, you put a bullet through your head or drained a flowered phial of vinegar essence. At one time, if you were sick with consumption, gallstones or syphilis, you threw yourself from a fourth floor window in a back street, leaving behind a stylized note with "It's nobody's fault" and "I'm doing the world a big favor." Why don't we kill ourselves now? The pangs of hunger are far more terrible, more murderous, more choking than any sickness. Well, you see, all sicknesses are human, and some even make a human being of the patient. Make him nobler. While hunger is a bestial, a wild, a rawly primitive—yes, a bestial thing. If you're hungry, you cease to be human, you become a beast. And beasts know nothing of suicide.

"Brilliant, my pet, an excellent theory! So how long is it, wise guy, till twelve o'clock?"

Shut up, it'll soon be six o'clock. Another six hours and you'll get your soup. Did you see the burials yesterday? Like dung—that's how they drop the dead into the grave. Turned the box over and flipped them in. The bystanders get such a livid expression of disgust on their faces, as if death were taking revenge for the aura of secrecy. For the various irrelevant, unnecessary things that had been tied on to him, now, out of spite, he let down his pants and— here! Look at me, kiss my ass. Like a spoiled child, who's sick of endearments. And do you know, Brother Stomach, how I imagined death when I was a child? I remember when I was four and five, I went to kindergarten. They played the piano and split their sides laughing and spoke Hebrew. And I remember there was a funeral in the same courtyard. I only saw the hearse entering the courtyard, and soon after, cries and laments. I fancied that the man in the black coat and stiff hat wanted to drag a woman into the hearse, and she didn't want to go, and in fact it was she who was making the noise, and she threw herself on the ground, and he took hold of both her arms, and she was sitting and sliding along, and shouting and screaming. How do you like that, my little stomach? You don't answer—are you asleep? Well, sleep, sleep, the longer the better. At least until twelve o'clock.

Food, food. It isn't my stomach talking now—it's my palate and my temples. Just a half a quarter loaf, just a little piece of crust, even if it's burnt, black, like coal. I jumped off the bed—a drink of water helps, it provides an interruption. On your way back to bed you fall—your feet are clumsy, swollen. They hurt. But you don't groan. For the last few months you've got used to not groaning, even when you're in pain. At the beginning of the war, when you were lying in bed at night and thinking about the whole thing; or in the morning, when you had to get up, you often emitted a groan. Not now. You're like a robot now. Or maybe, again, like a beast? Perhaps.

Die? So be it. Anything is better than being hungry. Anything is better than suffering. Oh, if only one could use arithmetic to reckon *when* one would breathe one's last! That woman in the courtyard, from No. 37, who died, had been starving for six weeks. Yes, but she ate nothing, not even soup once a day. And I do eat soup. One can go on suffering for years in this way—and maybe kick the bucket tomorrow. Who knows?

I realize the I'm still holding the book. Page seven. Let's see if I can get through it. I turn the pages. Somewhere, on one of the pages, my eye spots the [German] word *Wonne*. Ecstasy. A piquant, magnificent erotic scene. A few pages earlier they were eating in a restaurant. Schnitzler gives you the menu. No, no, don't read it. Your mouth becomes strangely bitter inside, your head spins. Don't read about what they ate. That's right—just as old people skip descriptions of sex. What's the time? Half past six. Oh, how early it still is!

But it's possible that tomorrow or even today I'll give up the ghost. The heart is a sneak—you never can tell. Maybe I'm lying here for the last time and feeling so sluggish for the last time. So slow to get dressed. And handing in a soup ticket for the last time and taking a new one for tomorrow. And the cashier, and the waitress, and the janitor by the door—they will all look at me with indifference, as they do every day, and not know at all, at all, that tomorrow I won't come here anymore, and not the day after tomorrow and not the day after that. But I will know, and I will feel proud of my secret when I am with them. And perhaps in a few months, or after the war is over, if statistics are made of the diners who died, I'll be there, too, and maybe one of the waitresses will say to another: "D'ya know who else died, Zoshe? That redhead who insisted on speaking Yiddish, and whom I teased for an hour and, just to fix him good, didn't give him his soup. He's been put in the box too, I bet."

And Zoshe, of course, *won't* know, as if she would remember such a thing—and then you will have such a high, high [. . .].[5] Maybe it will already have been poured; oh, how magnificently Thomas Mann describes it in *The Magic Mountain*.

I remember his thoughts, the way he delineated them. Never has their brilliant truth appeared so clear to me as it does now. Time—and time. Now it stretches like rubber, and then—it's gone, like a dream, like smoke. Right now, of course, it's stretched out horribly, it's really enough to kill you. The war has been going on for a full two years, and you've eaten nothing but soup for some four months, and those few months are thousands and thousands of times longer for you than the whole of the previous twenty months—no, longer than your whole life until now. From yesterday's soup to today's is an eternity, and I can't imagine that I'll be able to survive another twenty-four hours of this overpowering hunger. But these four months are no more than a dark, empty nightmare. Try to salvage something from them, remember something in particular—it's impossible. One black, dark mass. I remember, in prison, in solitary confinement. Days that stretch like tar. Each day like another yoke on your neck. And in the evenings, lying in the dark, reviewing the day that had passed, I could hardly believe that I had been in the bath-house that day—it seemed that it was at least four or five days ago. The days passed with dreadful slowness. But when I went through the gate on that side of the street, all the days ran together like a pack of dogs on a hunt. Black dogs. Black days. All one black nightmare, like a single black hour.

At the prison gate friends were waiting—I don't remember all of them. But I remember Janek.[6] Yes, Janek. I forgot all about him. Not long ago, last year, I met him. Half naked, in rags, he was tinkering with the gas pipe in a bombed-out house halfway along Marszalkowska Street. He called to me. And out of the blue, as if twelve years hadn't gone by since we met last, he gave me our standard greeting, "Know something?"

"No. And you?"

"Me neither. But it's OK."

Then the supervisor came up and left. So maybe, maybe I should write to Janek. Write to him: Listen, brother, I'm having a hard time. Send me something. Write, then? By all means, write yet more openly: if you could provide

---

5. Ellipses within a bracket here and elsewhere indicate an indecipherable passage in the original manuscript.

6. A Christian Pole.

me with a quarter of a loaf every day—ah, a little quarter loaf. Yes, when I'm dressed I'll write to him. It may be difficult to send the note but I'll write to him—A little quarter loaf. And if you can't, then let it be an eighth.

Somewhere in the world people are eating as much as they want. In America sits Hershel eating his supper—and there is bread on the table, and butter, and sugar and a jar of jam. Eat, Hershele, eat! Eat! Hershel, eat a lot, I tell you. Don't leave the crust, it would be a waste, and eat up the crumbs from the table! It tastes good, you become full—true, dear Hershel?

And somewhere in the world there is still something called love. Girls are kissed. And girls kiss in return. And couples go walking for hours in the gardens and the parks and sit by a river, such a cool river, under a spreading tree; and they talk so politely to each other, and laugh together, and gaze in such a friendly way, so lovingly and passionately, into each other's eyes. And they don't think about food. They may be hungry, but they don't think about it. And they are jealous and become angry with each other—again, not eating. And all this is so true, and it is all happening in the world—far away from here, true, but it is happening, and there are people like me over there. . . .

"Sick fantasies!" interrupts the scoundrel, my stomach; he's woken up, the cynic. "What a dreamer! Instead of looking for a practical solution, he lies there deluding himself with nonsensical stories. There are no good or evil stomachs, no educated or simple ones, none in love and none indifferent. In the whole world, if you're hungry, you want to eat. And by the way, it's all nonsense. There are good providers for their stomachs, and there are unlucky wretches like you. You can groan, you idiot, but as far as filling me up—damnation, what's the time?"

Ten past eight. Four hours to go. Not quite four whole hours, but let's say four, and if less, that's certainly to the good. I slowly draw on my pants. I no longer touch my legs. I touched them until, not long ago, I measured them with my fist, to see how far they'd shrunk. No more. What's the point?

And Friedman has died. Tying my shoelaces reminds me of the dozens of dangling genitalia there in the large common grave. And young girls stood around, holding their noses with handkerchiefs, and looked at the islands of hair. Again—is it because animals have no shame? Yes, so it seems, at the cemetery—funeral notices of rich men, of doctors, of good citizens . . . there is no end of rickshaws, and an easily recognizable crowd gathers—no poor people there. In other words, this kind of person dies too, though they have enough to eat. One doesn't die of hunger alone. Things even themselves out. They'd better get the message.

"Tell me, friend, are you starting up with your stories again? It's already time to go. Maybe the soup will be earlier today. Move, my dear!"

In the air and heat of early fall the street is full of the smell of sweat and the smell of corpses, just as in front of the ritual cleansing room at the cemetery. Bread, bread everywhere. It costs the same as yesterday. You want to go to a stall, feel, pinch the fresh whole-wheat bread, satiate your fingertips with the soft, bakedbrown dough. No, better not. It'll only increase your appetite, that's all. No, no—just as you didn't want to read what the lovers ate in the restaurant on the quiet Viennese street. And fish roe is cheaper. Cheese—the same price. Sour cream is now in season—but it's expensive. Cucumbers are cheaper, and onions are at the same price. But they're bigger today than yesterday.

Cheerful tomatoes, full of joie de vivre, laugh in front of you, greet you. Trips into the mountains, rucksacks, shorts, open shirts, wild, joyous songs of earthly happiness rising into space. When, where? Two years ago, altogether two years. Tanned faces, black hands and feet. And hearty laughter, and brooklets of unexpected spring water, and bread and butter sandwiches with sweet tea; and no armbands on your sleeves, no mark of being a *Jude*.

Bread, bread, bread.[7] *Razowka. Sitkowka. Vayse sitka. Hele sitka. Tunkele sitka. Walcowka.* First-class bread. *Beknbroyt.*

Bread, bread. The abundance of it dazzles your eyes. In the windows, on the stalls, in hands, in baskets. I won't be able to hold out if I can't grab a bite of breadstuff. "Grab? You don't look suspicious," says he, my murderer. "They'll let you near, they'll even put it in your hand. They'll trust you. They can see you aren't one of the grabbers."

Shut up, buddy, you've forgotten that I can't run. Now *you're* the wise guy, hah?

"You're a goner, you are, my breadwinner," says he. "Just take a look at those two having their identity papers[8] checked at the gate. Look at the color of their faces. You can bet they've eaten today, and they'll damn well eat again, soon. But look over there—they're waiting for the car to pick them up. If you were a *mentsh*,[9] you'd have looked after me earlier on, and you'd be eating like a human being, and *not* have swollen legs. And you'd also be able to wheedle yourself in and go along for the ride. They give you half a liter of soup and a loaf of bread a week. Too bad you're such a *shlemazel!*"[10]

Wrong again, you argue with him, your stomach. To begin with, there isn't soup every day. Often enough they come back without eating. And

7. The Polish words that follow are names of breads listed in the order of desirability.
8. Workers would have their identity papers checked at the gates of the ghetto before they were taken to their workplaces outside the ghetto.
9. Yiddish word for a mature, responsible person.
10. Yiddish word for an inept person.

they're not treated with kid gloves either. Sometimes they get pushed around. You take your chances. But now, you're guaranteed the soup in the kitchen, you have a ticket. And for doing nothing, and without working. Well, where could you be more secure?

The secondhand dealers by the gates look at you, at everybody, according to the value of the jacket you're wearing, and expertly value the pants that will be pulled off you tomorrow—whether you're dead or alive. A light breeze carries a torn fragment from the wall: "Four hundred grams of black salt. Chairman of the Judenrat." Go to him, perhaps? Something rises in your memory: a committee, a hall, not very large, a bell, a carafe of water. You recognize him: a tall figure, a fleshy Jewish nose, a bald head. A small bow tie. Yes, *he* is now the chairman. Maybe you really should go to him? Write to him: Honored sir, I do not request much of you. I am hungry—you understand?—hungry. So I request of you (and remind him here of your becoming acquainted, in 1935 I think—does he remember?). Therefore, I request of you, Mr. Chairman, that you see to it that I receive a piece of bread every day. I know, much honored sir, that you have a thousand other things to do—what importance at all can it have for you that such a wreck of a person as I am should kick the bucket. All the same, Mr. Chairman of the Judenrat—[11]

You stumble over something on the ground. You nearly fall. But no, your two feet keep their balance. On the ground, across the sidewalk lies a mound of rags with a . . . a green, hairy lump of wet dirt that was once a face with a beard. Now for the first time you realize that the calls, "Hello, hello," were to you. At first you didn't look around because Jews don't have names anymore—all Jews today are called . . . ; but now one of those secondhand dealers is standing by you. Didn't I see that I nearly stepped on a corpse? Philosopher! As if his jacket hadn't been sufficiently creased and disheveled? Must I add insult to injury? The shoes have been pulled off by someone and sold; at least leave the pants! What use is it to tell him that I was just thinking about the Chairman of the Judenrat. The gatekeeper walks slowly, lazily, from the gate, carrying bricks and an old, excrement stained sheet of newspaper, ties it round the dead body and walks slowly away, and that's it.

According to some clocks, old and crippled, it is already eleven o'clock. You get a liking for the ones that tell you it's later. Those big ones are haughty and not in any hurry, and you hate them. Another hour, no, stand around and wait . . . standing is also a way of passing the time. Another hour. A few

11. The Jewish Council, the official body of Jewish representatives organized by the Nazis in the ghettos to administer the occupied Jewish communities. The Judenrat carried out Nazi orders while attempting, usually in vain, to modify them.

dozen minutes—they count for something too! It's nothing, indeed, but if you were eating a good old piece of bread, eh? What would you do, for example, if you were now to be given a slice of bread—would you eat it right away, or would you keep it for the soup to make it more filling? I think you'd keep it. And if the soup was late, and it came out much later, let's say, would you also wait? Enough stories for the time being, don't make a fool of yourself. You'd devour it like a wolf. Oh, how you'd demolish it!

"Just a little bit of bread . . . ," the refrain of all the criers, from the sidewalks, from the cobbles, a little bit of bread. Oh, you jokers! Don't you know that I too want nothing more than a "little bit of bread"?

"My father's dead, my mother's in hospital, my elder brother's missing—a little bit of bread. . . ."

You've eaten today, you bastard, haven't you?

"Small children at home—a little bit of bread." And I would so gladly add my voice: I'm hungry, hungry, hungry. Another hour till soup, another hour—you understand? "A little bit of bread!!!!"

The soup was *not* late today. The steam is already in the air. Plates are already being rattled. The manager is already shouting at the waitresses, the assistant manager is already measuring the length of the hall with his tiny feet and nodding his plump head from side to side as in a puppet show. The second assistant manager is already shouting at some diners. The day of soup giving is already begun. There are more people here than yesterday, just as yesterday there were more than the day before. Poor fellow! They're starting to hand out the soup from *that* table. So you'll have to sit here until it reaches you. How do you like that—you can eat your heart out.

Time—and more time. You remember the days when the kitchen announced, indifferently, and you thought, vengefully, "There's no meal today," How bitter were the words on the door: "Today's tickets are valid for tomorrow." How hideously long were those days and nights. And yet it seems to you that that pain was nothing compared with the half hour that you still have to wait.

The opposite table is already in a state of grace. Peaceful quietness—they are already eating. And it somehow seems to you that the people at that table feel superior to you, worthier. Someone or other takes from his bosom a quarter sheet of newspaper and unwraps it, uncovering a thin, round piece of bread. Unlike you, they don't gobble the soup directly; first they stir it, wrinkling up their noses in disgust—just as they do every day, because it's thin; start at the side, where it's shallow; chew for a long time, slowly; pretend to be looking around, as if the soup were of secondary importance and the main thing—the ceiling. After the first few spoonfuls they add salt. They play with the soup as a cat plays with a mouse. And after the soup their faces wear an expression of near-religious bliss.

And it hasn't reached your table yet. And—are you only imagining it?—somehow the people sitting here all have such long faces, not-having-eaten faces, with swollen ghetto spots under their eyes, which give the face a Mongolian look. You think of a master of world literature, a Tolstoy, a Balzac, a Wassermann. How they made a fuss over people, they chiseled every feature, every move. "You seem to be somewhat pale today!" one of these geniuses would write, and the world was enraptured. "You seem to be somewhat pale today," and women dabbed their eyes with handkerchiefs, critics interpreted and serious, business-like gentlemen, owners of textile factories or partners in large, comfortable manufacturing businesses beneath white marble signs felt a quiver in their cheeks—reminiscent of the first kiss, fifty years ago. "You seem to be somewhat pale today"—ha, ha! If someone *today* were to read or write, "You seem somewhat pale today," when the whole world is deathly pale, when everyone, everyone has the same white, chalky, lime-white face. Yes, yes it was easy for *them* to write. They ate, and knew that the readers were going to eat and that the critics were going to eat. Let these masters *now* show their true colors and write!

"Why don't you eat?" What is this? Everyone around you is eating; in front of you, too, there is a bowl of steaming soup, glistening and glittering with delicious splendor. You were looking across at the people and saw nothing. And did she take the ticket? No, you're still holding it in your hand. What's going on? Should you call? Turn it in? You've already finished with the helping, while around you people are smacking their lips, spitting, sipping as a cat sips milk, and grumbling, exactly as if they weren't eating. And that scoundrel over there, who has such a full plate, full of fried onions sits there sniveling—you could just faint. It's all right, they're hungry, everyone may eat any way he likes. I'm probably comical too when I eat my soup. And there are some who tilt the plate so convulsively and scrape together the last drops . . . and submerge their whole face in the plate and see nothing else, as if it were the entire earth, the world. Can she possibly have given you the soup without a ticket? You steal a glance—the date is right. She simply didn't notice in the confusion. No, don't give it to her. Revenge. And she will realize it maybe; maybe not. I can't be—maybe, maybe to get another helping? And say nothing? But she did it on purpose. You know what, Arke? If a *man* sits down at your table now to eat his soup, you'll take the risk; if a *woman*, it's a bad omen, and you won't give up the ticket.

You stare hard. On one side a mother is now sitting with a child. A waitress hurries past, the mother says to the child, loudly, with a smiling, ingratiating look: "Wait, wait, the lady will soon bring you some thick soup." The

61

bench squeaks, someone has sat down. That person is hidden from view; you see a bit of white toast. A fragment of a second: man or woman?—man or woman? A woman! Apparently—a pair of eyes—a mummy, eyes without expression. A woman, a woman, damn it. This means not turning in the ticket, not taking another bowl of soup? Too late, that's the way you set it up. But now the soup is better and better, thicker, hotter. How do you know? That's the way it always is. The later the better. Though it's not so certain. But this time—yes. And so once again, from the beginning. Man or woman, man or woman?

There is movement around you. People come and go, sit down, speak. Polish, Yiddish, Hebrew, German. First here, now there, like a rocket, a question flutters with an exclamation: Who, him? I saw him only yesterday! Who, her? She ate here only the day before yesterday! They are talking about those who have died, one of hunger, another from "that" louse and today's sickness. And they whisper so mysteriously in each other's ears: "Don't shout—so, died at home, unannounced." But above all other conversations, one theme—we won't be able to survive it. There's such a winter coming. If the war lasts through the winter. Last year we still had something. Parcels were still arriving, it wasn't sealed so shut. What are they splitting hairs about? Whether we will survive or not. What can people do, when they are sentenced to death and know the exact time of the execution? Thus the French aristocrats in the prisons during the great Revolution gambled at cards, acted in plays, until the man in the tricolor came in and called out the names, and "The guillotine is waiting." Yes, you see? But they weren't hungry and weren't threatened with starvation. Yes, indeed, this is really the main point. Well, and during the more recent Russian Revolution? But why am I getting involved in these great stories—man or woman, man or woman?

At this point she showed up, the waitress, and automatically began taking tickets. Everyone held them out, you as well. It's over. And now you dip your spoon in the bowl, in the second bowl of soup—you understand? It really is thicker than the first. Now you can afford to play with it, to eat graciously, like all the rest, and not gobble. You don't eat in whole spoonfuls. Sometimes you spit out a piece of chaff, like a VIP.

In the street the smell of fresh corpses envelops you. Like an airplane propeller just after it's been started up, which spins and spins, and yet stays in one place—that's what your feet are like. They seem to you to be moving backwards. Pieces of wood.

They were looking, weren't they? Involuntarily, you cover your face with your arm. And what if they find out? They can, as a punishment, take away your soups. Somehow it seems to you that they already know. That man who's walking past looks so insolently into your eyes. He knows. He laughs, and so does that man, and another and another. Hee, hee—they choke back their stinging laughter, and somehow you become so small, so cramped up. That's how you get caught, you fool. A thief? *Only* unlucky. That one soup can cost you all the others.

A burning in your left side. Your arm, your leg, your heart; not for the first time, but this time it's stronger. You must stop moving. You feel someone is watching. It's already too late to respond. A director of social assistance, in a rickshaw, [12] is riding down the street. A former acquaintance. Yes, he looked at you; yes. You notice when someone's looking—it's your nature. Always, when you see him traveling past, you look at him, wanting to catch his eye, and always in vain. Today it's the other way around: *he* noticed *you.* Maybe . . . maybe he already knows.

The director is already far away. Behind him are dozens of rickshaws. But the burning remains. Why the devil did you have to be in the street just *now?* Others go past, actually touch you and don't recognize you, or pretend not to. And he—saw you from up there in his rickshaw and pierced you with a glance. What will happen now?

By a gate, in a narrow crack, a cucumber. A whole one, untouched. It seems that it fell from a housewife's shopping basket. Mechanically, without thinking, you bend down, take it, no disgrace, no joy. You deserve it. Just as a dog deserves a bone. A bittersweet cucumber. From looking at the skin you can already taste the sweetness of the seeds. It's not healthy. Typhus? Dysentery? Nonsense. For thirty centuries, generations of scholars have devoted their brilliant abilities, their youth, their lives to extorting from Nature the secrets of vitamins and calories—in order that you, Arke, by a gate in Leszno Street should munch on a cucumber you found, which someone lost, or threw down for you.

What? It's impossible to [. . .]? Oh, if you only tried . . . if you only tried . . . if you only tried to beg. The first housewife that comes along . . . make a piteous face . . . So what? Better people than you are out begging. Should I list them for you? You don't want to? Then, don't! If you don't want to, you don't have to—he stopped at L[. . .].

You feel that today you have fallen a step lower. Oh, yes, that's how it had to begin. All these people around you, apparently, began like that. You're on your way [. . .] The second soup—what will it be tomorrow?

12. A two-wheeled vehicle used as a means of conveyance in the Warsaw Ghetto, and a symbol of luxury.

It's getting dark. The darkness thickens; you could cut it with a knife. It would be good to buy some bread now, it's cheaper. It would! A round-bellied prostitute gives irises to two of her friends. On their lime-white faces, all skin and bone, the rouge and color on their spear-sharp eyebrows look ghostly.

A small group of people stand on the sidewalk and look across at the other side, from where a long beam of light falls. It's the children's hospital. Low down, on the first floor, in a wide, high window, a large electric lamp hangs over a table. A short woman in a white mask moves something very quickly with her hands. Around her, other women, also in masks. A calm hurry. And everything—to the table, to the one who lies on the table. An operation. You've never seen one before. At the movies, in a book, in the theater, yes, but in life, no. Strange, isn't it? You've lived some thirty-odd years, seen so much—and now you're seeing an operation for the first time; and it has to be in the *ghetto!* But why, why? Why save? Why, to whom, to what is the child being brought back?

And suddenly you remember that dead Jew, whom you nearly tripped over today. What's more, you now see him more clearly than before, when you were actually looking at him. Somewhere, years ago, there was a mother who fed him and, while cleaning his head, knew that her son was the cleverest, the most talented, the most beautiful. Told her aunt, her neighbors his funny sayings. Sought and delighted in every feature in which he resembled his father, his father. And the word *Berishl* was not just a name to her, but an idea, the content of a life, a philosophy. And now the brightest and most beautiful child in the world lies in a strange street, and his name isn't even known; and there's a stink, and instead of his mother, a brick kisses his head and a drizzling rain soaks the well-known newspaper around his face. And over there, they're operating on a child, just as if this hadn't happened, and they save it; and below, in front of the gate stands the mother, who knows that her Berishl is the cleverest and the most beautiful and the most talented—Why? For whom? For whom?

And suddenly (you—a grown, tall man, a male) you feel a quiver in your cheek, in your hands, all over your body. And your eyes become so rigid, so glassy. Yes, that's how it must be. This is the sign—you understand?—the equation, the eternal Law of Life. Maybe you are destined now, of all times, in your last days, to understand the meaning of the meaninglessness that is called life, the *meaning of your hideous, meaninglessly hungry days.* An eternal law, an eternal machine: death. Birth, life. Life. Life. Life. An eternal, eternal law. An eternal, eternal process. And a kind of clarity pours over your neck, your heart. And your two propellers no longer spin round in one spot—they walk, they walk! Your legs carry you, just as in the past! Just as in the past!

Somewhere a clock is striking dully: one, two, half past. Four-thirty, five-thirty? I don't know. Here there is no sunrise. The day comes to the door like a beggar. The days are already shorter. But I—I, like the fall, autumnal, foggy dawns. Everything around you becomes so dreamy, lost in thought, longing, serious, blue-eyed, concentrated in itself. Everything—people, the world, clouds—draws away somewhere, prepares for something responsible that carries a yoke, something that connects everything together. The gray patch that stands in the corner of the room with open arms—that's the *new day.* Yesterday I began to write your experiences. From the courtyard came the shouts of the air-raid wardens telling people to turn out the light. There's a smell of *cholent.* [13] How come? It's Thursday, not the Sabbath [. . .]. A forest, a river, the whistle of a train, an endless golden field. Kuzmir, Tatrn [. . .]. The Lithuanian border. This longing, this wound will never go away, it will stay forever, even if today, tomorrow should once again [. . .]. Let it be in the city itself, go, go—go forever, without stopping, at least see the bank of the Vistula, at least see just the city. The city that you know. The happiness of quickly turning a corner, then [. . .] the hundredth. With an open jacket, with happy, swift steps. *Your city,* your second mother, your great, eternal love. The longing pierces your heart. It remains.

Somewhere they are typing [. . .]. They're reporting. It is reported from Brussels . . . Belgrade, Paris. Yes, yes, we're eating grass. Yes, we're falling in the streets without a word of protest—we wave our hands like this, and fall [. . .]. Each day the profiles of our children, of our wives, acquire the mourning look of foxes, dingoes, kangaroos. Our howls are like the cry of jackals. Our hymn, *papierosy, papierosy* (cigarettes, cigarettes) is like something from a nature reserve, a zoo. But we are not animals. We operate on our infants. It may be pointless or even criminal. But animals do not operate on their young!

Tokyo. Hong Kong. Vichy. Berlin. General number of enemy losses: six thousand eight hundred and forty-nine. Stockholm. Washington. Bangkok. The world's turning upside down. A planet melts in tears. And I—I am hungry, hungry. I am hungry.

Warsaw ghetto, [14] August 1941
(Ringelblum Archive, Part 1, no. 1486)
Translated from the Yiddish by Elinor Robinson

13. Yiddish word for a traditional pot roast with vegetables baked in an oven.

14. Established by the Nazis in November 1940, the Warsaw Ghetto was surrounded by a wall and contained nearly five hundred thousand Jews. In 1941 alone, about forty-five thousand Jews died there due to overcrowding, starvation, disease, and hard labor.

TADEUSZ BOROWSKI

This Way for the Gas,
Ladies and Gentlemen

All of us walk around naked. The delousing is finally over, and our striped suits are back from the tanks of Cyclone B solution, an efficient killer of lice in clothing and of men in gas chambers. Only the inmates in the blocks cut off from ours by the 'Spanish goats'[1] still have nothing to wear. But all the same, all of us walk around naked: the heat is unbearable. The camp has been sealed off tight. Not a single prisoner, not one solitary louse, can sneak through the gate. The labor Kommandos have stopped working. All day, thousands of naked men shuffle up and down the roads, cluster around the squares, or lie against the walls and on top of the roofs. We have been sleeping on plain boards, since our mattresses and blankets are still being disinfected. From the rear blockhouses we have a view of the F.K.L.—*Frauen Konzentration Lager;* there too the delousing is in full swing. Twenty-eight thousand women have been stripped naked and driven out of the barracks. Now they swarm around the large yard between the blockhouses.

The heat rises, the hours are endless. We are without even our usual diversion: the wide roads leading to the crematoria are empty. For several days now, no new transports have come in. Part of "Canada"[2] has been liquidated and detailed to a labor Kommando—one of the very toughest—at Harmenz. For there exists in the camp a special brand of justice based on envy: when the rich and mighty fall, their friends see to it that they fall to the very bottom. And Canada, our Canada, which smells not of maple forests but of French perfume, has amassed great fortunes in diamonds and currency from all over Europe.

Several of us sit on the top bunk, our legs dangling over the edge. We slice the neat loaves of crisp, crunchy bread. It is a bit coarse to the taste, the kind that stays fresh for days. Sent all the way from Warsaw—only a week ago my mother held this white loaf in her hands . . . dear Lord, dear Lord . . .

We unwrap the bacon, the onion, we open a can of evaporated milk. Henri, the fat Frenchman, dreams aloud of the French wine brought by

1. Crossed wooden beams wrapped in barbed wire.—Trans.
2. This term designated wealth and well-being in the camp. More specifically, it referred to the members of the labor gang, or Kommando, who helped to unload the incoming transports of people destined for the gas chambers.—Trans.

the transports from Strasbourg, Paris, Marseille. . . . Sweat streams down his body.

"Listen, *mon ami,* next time we go up on the loading ramp, I'll bring you real champagne. You haven't tried it before, eh?"

"No. But you'll never be able to smuggle it through the gate, so stop teasing. Why not try and 'organize' some shoes for me instead—you know, the perforated kind, with a double sole, and what about that shirt you promised me long ago?"

"*Patience, patience.* When the new transports come, I'll bring all you want. We'll be going on the ramp again!"

"And what if there aren't any more 'cremo' transports?" I say spitefully. "Can't you see how much easier life is becoming around here: no limit on packages, no more beatings? You even write letters home. . . . One hears all kind of talk, and, dammit, they'll run out of people!"

"Stop talking nonsense." Henri's serious fat face moves rhythmically, his mouth is full of sardines. We have been friends for a long time, but I do not even know his last name. "Stop talking nonsense," he repeats, swallowing with effort. "They can't run out of people, or we'll starve to death in this blasted camp. All of us live on what they bring."

"All? We have our packages. . ."

"Sure, you and your friend, and ten other friends of yours. Some of you Poles get packages. But what about us, and the Jews, and the Russkis? And what if we had no food, no 'organization' from the transports, do you think you'd be eating those packages of yours in peace? We wouldn't let you!"

"You would, you'd starve to death like the Greeks. Around here, whoever has grub, has power."

"Anyway, you have enough, we have enough, so why argue?"

Right, why argue? They have enough, I have enough, we eat together and we sleep on the same bunks. Henri slices the bread, he makes a tomato salad. It tastes good with the commissary mustard.

Below us, naked, sweat-drenched men crowd the narrow barracks aisles or lie packed in eights and tens in the lower bunks. Their nude, withered bodies stink of sweat and excrement: their cheeks are hollow. Directly beneath me, in the bottom bunk, lies a rabbi. He has covered his head with a piece of rag torn off a blanket and reads from a Hebrew prayer book (there is no shortage of this type of literature at the camp), wailing loudly, monotonously.

"Can't somebody shut him up? He's been raving as if he'd caught God himself by the feet."

"I don't feel like moving. Let him rave. They'll take him to the oven that much sooner."

"Religion is the opium of the people," Henri, who is a Communist and a *rentier,* says sententiously. "If they didn't believe in God and eternal life, they'd have smashed the crematoria long ago."

"Why haven't you done it then?"

The question is rhetorical; the Frenchman ignores it.

"Idiot," he says simply, and stuffs a tomato in his mouth.

Just as we finish our snack, there is a sudden commotion at the door. The Muslims[3] scurry in fright to the safety of their bunks, a messenger runs into the Block Elder's shack. The Elder, his face solemn, steps out at once.

"Canada! *Antreten!* But fast! There's a transport coming!"

"Great God!" yells Henri, jumping off the bunk. He swallows the rest of his tomato, snatches his coat, screams *"Raus"* at the men below, and in a flash is at the door. We can hear a scramble in the other bunks. Canada is leaving for the ramp.

"Henri, the shoes!" I call after him.

"Keine Angst!" he shouts back, already outside.

I proceed to put away the food. I tie a piece of rope around the suitcase where the onions and the tomatoes from my father's garden in Warsaw mingle with Portuguese sardines, bacon from Lublin (that's from my brother), and authentic sweetmeats from Salonica. I tie it all up, pull on my trousers, and slide off the bunk.

"Platz!" I yell, pushing my way through the Greeks. They step aside. At the door I bump into Henri.

"Was ist los?"

"Want to come with us on the ramp?"

"Sure, why not?"

"Come along then, grab your coat! We're short of a few men. I've already told the Kapo,"[4] and he shoves me out of the barracks door.

We line up. Someone has marked down our numbers, someone up ahead yells, "March, march," and now we are running towards the gate, accompanied by the shouts of a multilingual throng that is already being pushed back to the barracks. Not everybody is lucky enough to be going on the ramp. . . . We have almost reached the gate. *Links, zwei, drei, vier! Mützen ab!* Erect, arms stretched stiffly along our hips, we march past the gate

3. The camp name for a prisoner who had been destroyed physically and spiritually, and who had neither the strength nor the will to go on living—a man ripe for the gas chamber.—Trans.

4. A prisoner who is the foreman of labor detail, responsible to the detail leader. In popular language, *kapo* became the generic term for all inmate functionaries.

briskly, smartly, almost gracefully. A sleepy S.S.[5] man with a large pad in his hand checks us off, waving us ahead in groups of five.

"*Hundert!*" he calls after we have all passed.

"*Stimmt!*" comes a hoarse answer from out front.

We march fast, almost at a run. There are guards all around, young men with automatics. We pass camp II B, then some deserted barracks and a clump of unfamiliar green—apple and pear trees. We cross the circle of watchtowers and, running, burst on to the highway. We have arrived. Just a few more yards. There, surrounded by trees, is the ramp.

A cheerful little station, very much like any other provincial railway stop: a small square framed by tall chestnuts and paved with yellow gravel. Not far off, beside the road, squats a tiny wooden shed, uglier and more flimsy than the ugliest and flimsiest railway shack; farther along lie stacks of old rails, heaps of wooden beams, barracks parts, bricks, paving stones. This is where they load freight for Birkenau:[6] supplies for the construction of the camp, and people for the gas chambers. Trucks drive around, load up lumber, cement, people—a regular daily routine.

And now the guards are being posted along the rails, across the beams, in the green shade of the Silesian chestnuts, to form a tight circle around the ramp. They wipe the sweat from their faces and sip out of their canteens. It is unbearably hot; the sun stands motionless at its zenith.

"Fall out!"

We sit down in the narrow streaks of shade along the stacked rails. The hungry Greeks (several of them managed to come along, God only knows how) rummage underneath the rails. One of them finds some pieces of mildewed bread, another a few half-rotten sardines. They eat.

"*Schweinedreck,*" spits a young, tall guard with corn-coloured hair and dreamy blue eyes. "For God's sake, any minute you'll have so much food to stuff down your guts, you'll bust!" He adjusts his gun, wipes his face with a handkerchief.

"Hey you, fatso!" His boot lightly touches Henri's shoulder. "*Pass mal auf,* want a drink?"

"Sure, but I haven't got any marks," replies the Frenchman with a professional air.

5. Schutzstaffel, or Protection Squad: the Nazi elite guard responsible for destroying anti-Nazis and Jews. Its chief function was the supervision of the camps and ghettos.

6. The extermination center of Auschwitz, one of the most notorious Nazi concentration and death camps, which imprisoned about four million people from June 1941 to December 1944.

"*Schade,* too bad."

"Come, come, Herr Posten, isn't my word good enough any more? Haven't we done business before? How much?"

"One hundred. *Gemacht?*"

"*Gemacht.*"

We drink the water, lukewarm and tasteless. It will be paid for by the people who have not yet arrived.

"Now you be careful," says Henri, turning to me. He tosses away the empty bottle. It strikes the rails and bursts into tiny fragments. "Don't take any money, they might be checking. Anyway, who the hell needs money? You've got enough to eat. Don't take suits, either, or they'll think you're planning to escape. Just get a shirt, silk only, with a collar. And a vest. And if you find something to drink, don't bother calling me. I know how to shift for myself, but you watch your step or they'll let you have it."

"Do they beat you up here?"

"Naturally. You've got to have eyes in your ass. *Arschaugen.*"

Around us sit the Greeks, their jaws working greedily, like huge human insects. They munch on stale lumps of bread. They are restless, wondering what will happen next. The sight of the large beams and the stacks of rails has them worried. They dislike carrying heavy loads.

"*Was wir arbeiten?*" they ask.

"*Niks. Transport kommen, alles Krematorium, compris?*"

"*Alles verstehen,*" they answer in crematorium Esperanto. All is well—they will not have to move the heavy rails or carry the beams.

In the meantime, the ramp has become increasingly alive with activity, increasingly noisy. The crews are being divided into those who will open and unload the arriving cattle cars and those who will be posted by the wooden steps. They receive instructions on how to proceed most efficiently. Motor cycles drive up, delivering S.S. officers, bemedalled, glittering with brass, beefy men with highly polished boots and shiny, brutal faces. Some have brought their briefcases, others hold thin, flexible whips. They walk in and out of the commissary—for the miserable little shack by the road serves as their commissary, where in the summertime they drink mineral water, *Studentenquelle,* and where in winter they can warm up with a glass of hot wine. They greet each other in the state-approved way, raising an arm Roman fashion, then shake hands cordially, exchange warm smiles, discuss mail from home, their children, their families. Some stroll majestically on the ramp. The silver squares on their collars glitter, the gravel crunches under their boots, their bamboo whips snap impatiently.

We lie against the rails in the narrow streaks of shade, breathe unevenly, occasionally exchange a few words in our various tongues, and gaze listlessly at the majestic men in green uniforms, at the green trees, and at the church steeple of a distant village.

"The transport is coming," somebody says. We spring to our feet, all eyes turn in one direction. Around the bend, one after another, the cattle cars begin rolling in. The train backs into the station, a conductor leans out, waves his hand, blows a whistle. The locomotive whistles back with a shrieking noise, puffs, the train rolls slowly alongside the ramp. In the tiny barred windows appear pale, wilted, exhausted human faces, terror-stricken women with tangled hair, unshaven men. They gaze at the station in silence. And then, suddenly, there is a stir inside the cars and a pounding against the wooden boards.

"Water! Air!"—weary, desperate cries.

Heads push through the windows, mouths gasp frantically for air. They draw a few breaths, then disappear; others come in their place, then also disappear. The cries and moans grow louder.

A man in a green uniform covered with more glitter than any of the others jerks his head impatiently, his lips twist in annoyance. He inhales deeply, then with a rapid gesture throws his cigarette away and signals to the guard. The guard removes the automatic from his shoulder, aims, sends a series of shots along the train. All is quiet now. Meanwhile, the trucks have arrived, steps are being drawn up, and the Canada men stand ready at their posts by the train doors. The S.S. officer with the briefcase raises his hand.

"Whoever takes gold, or anything at all besides food, will be shot for stealing Reich property. Understand? *Verstanden?*"

"*Jawohl!*" we answer eagerly.

"*Also los!* Begin!"

The bolts crack, the doors fall open. A wave of fresh air rushes inside the train. People . . . inhumanly crammed, buried under incredible heaps of luggage, suitcases, trunks, packages, crates, bundles of every description (everything that had been their past and was to start their future). Monstrously squeezed together, they have fainted from heat, suffocated, crushed one another. Now they push towards the opened doors, breathing like fish cast out on the sand.

"Attention! Out, and take your luggage with you! Take out everything. Pile all your stuff near the exits. Yes, your coats too. It is summer. March to the left. Understand?"

"Sir, what's going to happen to us?" They jump from the train on to the gravel, anxious, worn-out.

"Where are you people from?"

"Sosnowiec-Będzin. Sir, what's going to happen to us?" They repeat the question stubbornly, gazing into our tired eyes.

"I don't know, I don't understand Polish."

It is the camp law: people going to their death must be deceived to the very end. This is the only permissible form of charity. The heat is tremendous. The sun hangs directly over our heads, the white, hot sky quivers, the air vibrates, an occasional breeze feels like a sizzling blast from a furnace. Our lips are parched, the mouth fills with the salty taste of blood, the body is weak and heavy from lying in the sun. Water!

A huge, multicoloured wave of people loaded down with luggage pours from the train like a blind, mad river trying to find a new bed. But before they have a chance to recover, before they can draw a breath of fresh air and look at the sky, bundles are snatched from their hands, coats ripped off their backs, their purses and umbrellas taken away.

"But please, sir, it's for the sun, I cannot. . . ."

"*Verboten!*" one of us barks through clenched teeth. There is an S.S. man standing behind your back, calm, efficient, watchful.

"*Meine Herrschaften,* this way, ladies and gentlemen, try not to throw your things around, please. Show some goodwill," he says courteously, his restless hands playing with the slender whip.

"Of course, of course," they answer as they pass, and now they walk alongside the train somewhat more cheerfully. A woman reaches down quickly to pick up her handbag. The whip flies, the woman screams, stumbles, and falls under the feet of the surging crowd. Behind her, a child cries in a thin little voice "Mamele!"—a very small girl with tangled black curls.

The heaps grow. Suitcases, bundles, blankets, coats, handbags that open as they fall, spilling coins, gold, watches; mountains of bread pile up at the exits, heaps of marmalade, jams, masses of meat, sausages; sugar spills on the gravel. Trucks, loaded with people, start up with a deafening roar and drive off amidst the wailing and screaming of the women separated from their children, and the stupefied silence of the men left behind. They are the ones who had been ordered to step to the right—the healthy and the young who will go to the camp. In the end, they too will not escape death, but first they must work.

Trucks leave and return, without interruption, as on a monstrous conveyor belt. A Red Cross van drives back and forth, back and forth, incessantly: it transports the gas that will kill these people. The enormous cross on the hood, red as blood, seems to dissolve in the sun.

The Canada men at the trucks cannot stop for a single moment, even to catch their breath. They shove the people up the steps, pack them in tightly, sixty per truck, more or less. Near by stands a young, cleanshaven "gentleman," an S.S. officer with a notebook in his hand. For each departing truck he enters a mark; sixteen gone means one thousand people, more or less. The gentleman is calm, precise. No truck can leave without a signal from him, or a mark in his notebook: *Ordnung muss sein.* The marks swell into thousands, the thousands into whole transports, which afterwards we shall simply call "from Salonica," "from Strasbourg," "from Rotterdam." This one will be called "Sosnowiec-Będzin." The new prisoners from Sosnowiec-Będzin will receive serial numbers 131–2–thousand, of course, though afterwards we shall simply say 131–2, for short.

The transports swell into weeks, months, years. When the war is over, they will count up the marks in their notebooks—all four and a half million of them. The bloodiest battle of the war, the greatest victory of the strong, united Germany. *Ein Reich, ein Volk, ein Führer*—and four crematoria.

The train has been emptied. A thin, pock-marked S.S. man peers inside, shakes his head in disgust and motions to our group, pointing his finger at the door.

"Rein. Clean it up!"

We climb inside. In the corners amid human excrement and abandoned wrist-watches lie squashed, trampled infants, naked little monsters with enormous heads and bloated bellies. We carry them out like chickens, holding several in each hand.

"Don't take them to the trucks, pass them on to the women," says the S.S. man, lighting a cigarette. His cigarette lighter is not working properly; he examines it carefully.

"Take them, for God's sake!" I explode as the women run from me in horror, covering their eyes.

The name of God sounds strangely pointless, since the women and the infants will go on the trucks, every one of them, without exception. We all know what this means, and we look at each other with hate and horror.

"What, you don't want to take them?" asks the pockmarked S.S. man with a note of surprise and reproach in his voice, and reaches for his revolver.

"You mustn't shoot, I'll carry them." A tall, grey-haired woman takes the little corpses out of my hands and for an instant gazes straight into my eyes.

"My poor boy," she whispers and smiles at me. Then she walks away, staggering along the path. I lean against the side of the train. I am terribly tired. Someone pulls at my sleeve.

"En avant, to the rails, come on!"

I look up, but the face swims before my eyes, dissolves, huge and transparent, melts into the motionless trees and the sea of people . . . I blink rapidly: Henri.

"Listen, Henri, are we good people?"

"That's stupid. Why do you ask?"

"You see, my friend, you see, I don't know why, but I am furious, simply furious with these people—furious because I must be here because of them. I feel no pity. I am not sorry they're going to the gas chamber. Damn them all! I could throw myself at them, beat them with my fists. It must be pathological, I just can't understand. . . ."

"Ah, on the contrary, it is natural, predictable, calculated. The ramp exhausts you, you rebel—and the easiest way to relieve your hate is to turn against someone weaker. Why, I'd even call it healthy. It's simple logic, *compris?*" He props himself up comfortably against the heap of rails. "Look at the Greeks, they know how to make the best of it! They stuff their bellies with anything they find. One of them has just devoured a full jar of marmalade."

"Pigs! Tomorrow half of them will die of the shits."

"Pigs? You've been hungry."

"Pigs!" I repeat furiously. I close my eyes. The air is filled with ghastly cries, the earth trembles beneath me, I can feel sticky moisture on my eyelids. My throat is completely dry.

The morbid procession streams on and on—trucks growl like mad dogs. I shut my eyes tight, but I can still see corpses dragged from the train, trampled infants, cripples piled on top of the dead, wave after wave . . . freight cars roll in, the heaps of clothing, suitcases and bundles grow, people climb out, look at the sun, take a few breaths, beg for water, get into the trucks, drive away. And again freight cars roll in, again people. . . . The scenes become confused in my mind—I am not sure if all of this is actually happening, or if I am dreaming. There is a humming inside my head; I feel that I must vomit.

Henri tugs at my arm.

"Don't sleep, we're off to load up the loot."

All the people are gone. In the distance, the last few trucks roll along the road in clouds of dust, the train has left, several S.S. officers promenade up and down the ramp. The silver glitters on their collars. Their boots shine, their red, beefy faces shine. Among them there is a woman—only now I realize she has been there all along—withered, flat-chested, bony, her thin, colourless hair pulled back and tied in a "Nordic" knot; her hands are in the pockets of her wide skirt. With a rat-like, resolute smile glued on her thin lips she sniffs around the corners of the ramp. She detests feminine beauty with the hatred of a woman who is herself repulsive, and knows it. Yes, I have seen her many times before and I know her well: she is the commandant of the F.K.L. She has come to look over the new crop of women, for some of them, instead of going on the trucks, will go on foot—to the concentration camp. There our boys, the barbers from Zauna, will shave their heads and will have a good laugh at their "outside world" modesty.

We proceed to load the loot. We lift huge trunks, heave them on to the trucks. There they are arranged in stacks, packed tightly. Occasionally somebody slashes one open with a knife, for pleasure or in search of vodka and perfume. One of the crates falls open; suits, shirts, books drop out on the ground . . . I pick up a small, heavy package. I unwrap it—gold, about two handfuls, bracelets, rings, brooches, diamonds. . . .

"*Gib heir,*" an S.S. man says calmly, holding up his briefcase already full of gold and colourful foreign currency. He locks the case, hands it to an officer, takes another, an empty one, and stands by the next truck, waiting. The gold will go to the Reich.

It is hot, terribly hot. Our throats are dry, each word hurts. Anything for a sip of water! Faster, faster, so that it is over, so that we may rest. At last we are done, all the trucks have gone. Now we swiftly clean up the remaining dirt: there must be "no trace left of the *Schweinerei.*" But just as the last truck disappears behind the trees and we walk, finally, to rest in the shade, a shrill whistle sounds around the bend. Slowly, terribly slowly, a train rolls in, the engine whistles back with a deafening shriek. Again weary, pale faces at the windows, flat as though cut out of paper, with huge, feverishly burning eyes. Already trucks are pulling up, already the composed gentleman with the notebook is at his post, and the S.S. men emerge from the commissary carrying briefcases for the gold and money. We unseal the train doors.

It is impossible to control oneself any longer. Brutally we tear suitcases from their hands, impatiently pull off their coats. Go on, go on, vanish! They go, they vanish. Men, women, children. Some of them know.

Here is a woman—she walks quickly, but tries to appear calm. A small child with a pink cherub's face runs after her and, unable to keep up, stretches out his little arms and cries: "Mama! Mama!"

"Pick up your child, woman!"

"It's not mine, sir, not mine!" she shouts hysterically and runs on, covering her face with her hands. She wants to hide, she wants to reach those who will not ride the trucks, those who will go on foot, those who will stay alive. She is young, healthy, good-looking, she wants to live.

But the child runs after her, wailing loudly: "Mama, mama, don't leave me!"

"It's not mine, not mine, no!"

Andrei, a sailor from Sevastopol, grabs hold of her. His eyes are glassy from vodka and the heat. With one powerful blow he knocks her off her feet, then, as she falls, takes her by the hair and pulls her up again. His face twitches with rage.

"Ah, you bloody Jewess! So you're running from your own child! I'll show you, you whore!" His huge hand chokes her, he lifts her in the air and heaves her on to the truck like a heavy sack of grain.

"Here! And take this with you, bitch!" and he throws the child at her feet.

"*Gut gemacht,* good work. That's the way to deal with degenerate mothers," says the S.S. man standing at the foot of the truck. "*Gut, gut, Russki.*"

"Shut your mouth," growls Andrei through clenched teeth, and walks away. From under a pile of rags, he pulls out a canteen, unscrews the cork, takes a few deep swallows, passes it to me. The strong vodka burns the throat. My head swims, my legs are shaky, again I feel like throwing up.

And suddenly, above the teeming crowd pushing forward like a river driven by an unseen power, a girl appears. She descends lightly from the train, hops on to the gravel, looks around inquiringly, as if somewhat surprised. Her soft, blonde hair has fallen on her shoulders in a torrent, she throws it back impatiently. With a natural gesture she runs her hands down her blouse, casually straightens her skirt. She stands like this for an instant, gazing at the crowd, then turns and with a gliding look examines our faces, as though searching for someone. Unknowingly, I continue to stare at her, until our eyes meet.

"Listen, tell me, where are they taking us?"

I look at her without saying a word. Here, standing before me, is a girl, a girl with enchanting blonde hair, with beautiful breasts, wearing a little cotton blouse, a girl with a wise, mature look in her eyes. Here she stands, gazing straight into my face, waiting. And over there is the gas chamber: communal death, disgusting and ugly. And over in the other direction is the concentration camp: the shaved head, the heavy Soviet trousers in sweltering heat, the sickening, stale odour of dirty, damp female bodies, the animal hunger, the inhuman labour, and later the same gas chamber, only an even more hideous, more terrible death. . . .

Why did she bring it? I think to myself, noticing a lovely gold watch on her delicate wrist. They'll take it away from her anyway.

"Listen, tell me," she repeats.

I remain silent. Her lips tighten.

"I know," she says with a shade of proud contempt in her voice, tossing her head. She walks off resolutely in the direction of the trucks. Someone tries to stop her; she boldly pushes him aside and runs up the steps. In the distance I can only catch a glimpse of her blonde hair flying in the breeze.

I go back inside the train; I carry out dead infants; I unload luggage. I touch corpses, but I cannot overcome the mounting, uncontrollable terror. I try to escape from the corpses, but they are everywhere: lined up on the gravel, on the cement edge of the ramp, inside the cattle cars. Babies, hideous naked women, men twisted by convulsions. I run off as far as I can go, but immediately a whip slashes across my back. Out of the corner of my eye I see an S.S. man, swearing profusely. I stagger forward and run, lose myself in the Canada group. Now, at last, I can once more rest against the stack of rails. The sun has leaned low over the horizon and illuminates the ramp with a reddish glow; the shadows of the trees have become elongated, ghostlike. In the silence that settles over nature at this time of day, the human cries seem to rise all the way to the sky.

Only from this distance does one have a full view of the inferno on the teeming ramp. I see a pair of human beings who have fallen to the ground locked in a last desperate embrace. The man has dug his fingers into the woman's flesh and has caught her clothing with his teeth. She screams hysterically, swears, cries, until at last a large boot comes down over her throat and she is silent. They are pulled apart and dragged like cattle to the truck. I see four Canada men lugging a corpse: a huge, swollen female corpse. Cursing, dripping wet from the strain, they kick out of their way some stray children who have been running all over the ramp, howling like dogs. The men pick them up by the collars, heads, arms, and toss them inside the trucks, on top of the heaps. The four men have trouble lifting the fat corpse on to the car, they call others for help, and all together they hoist up the mound of meat. Big, swollen, puffed-up corpses are being collected from all over the ramp; on top of them are piled the invalids, the smothered, the sick, the unconscious. The heap seethes, howls, groans. The driver starts the motor, the truck begins rolling.

"Halt! Halt!" an S.S. man yells after them. "Stop, damn you!"

They are dragging to the truck an old man wearing tails and a band around his arm. His head knocks against the gravel and pavement; he moans and wails in an uninterrupted monotone: *"Ich will mit dem Herrn Kommandanten sprechen*—I wish to speak with the commandant. . . ."* With senile stubbornness he keeps repeating these words all the way. Thrown on the truck, trampled by others, choked, he still wails: *"Ich will mit dem. . . ."*

"Look here, old man!" a young S.S. man calls, laughing jovially. "In half an hour you'll be talking with the top commandant! Only don't forget to greet him with a *Heil Hitler!*"

Several other men are carrying a small girl with only one leg. They hold her by the arms and the one leg. Tears are running down her face and she whispers faintly: "Sir, it hurts, it hurts. . . ." They throw her on the truck on top of the corpses. She will burn alive along with them.

The evening has come, cool and clear. The stars are out. We lie against the rails. It is incredibly quiet. Anemic bulbs hang from the top of the high lamp-posts; beyond the circle of light stretches an impenetrable darkness. Just one step, and a man could vanish for ever. But the guards are watching, their automatics ready.

"Did you get the shoes?" asks Henri.

"No."

"Why?"

"My God, man, I am finished, absolutely finished!"

"So soon? After only two transports? Just look at me, I . . . since Christmas, at least a million people have passed through my hands. The worst of all are the transports from around Paris—one is always bumping into friends."

"And what do you say to them?"

"That first they will have a bath, and later we'll meet at the camp. What would you say?"

I do not answer. We drink coffee with vodka; somebody opens a tin of cocoa and mixes it with sugar. We scoop it up by the handful, the cocoa sticks to the lips. Again coffee, again vodka.

"Henri, what are we waiting for?"

"There'll be another transport."

"I'm not going to unload it! I can't take it any more."

"So, it's got you down? Canada is nice, eh?" Henri grins indulgently and disappears into the darkness. In a moment he is back again.

"All right. Just sit here quietly and don't let an S.S. man see you. I'll try to find you your shoes."

"Just leave me alone. Never mind the shoes." I want to sleep. It is very late.

Another whistle, another transport. Freight cars emerge out of the darkness, pass under the lamp-posts, and again vanish in the night. The ramp is small, but the circle of lights is smaller. The unloading will have to be done gradually. Somewhere the trucks are growling. They back up against the steps, black, ghostlike, their searchlights flash across the trees. *Wasser! Luft!* The same all over again, like a late showing of the same film: a volley of shots, the train falls silent. Only this time a little girl pushes herself halfway through the small window and, losing her balance, falls out on to the gravel. Stunned, she lies still for a moment, then stands up and begins walking around in a circle, faster and faster, waving her rigid arms in the air, breathing loudly and spasmodically, whining in a faint voice. Her mind has given way in the inferno inside the train. The whining is hard on the nerves: an S.S. man approaches calmly, his heavy boot strikes between her shoulders. She falls. Holding her down with his foot, he draws his revolver, fires once, then again. She remains face down, kicking the gravel with her feet, until she stiffens. They proceed to unseal the train.

I am back on the ramp, standing by the doors. A warm, sickening smell gushes from inside. The mountain of people filling the car almost halfway up to the ceiling is motionless, horribly tangled, but still steaming.

"Ausladen!" comes the command. An S.S. man steps out from the darkness. Across his chest hangs a portable searchlight. He throws a stream of light inside.

"Why are you standing about like sheep? Start unloading!" His whip flies and falls across our backs. I seize a corpse by the hand; the fingers close tightly around mine. I pull back with a shriek and stagger away. My heart pounds, jumps up to my throat. I can no longer control the nausea. Hunched under the train I begin to vomit. Then, like a drunk, I weave over to the stack of rails.

I lie against the cool, kind metal and dream about returning to the camp, about my bunk, on which there is no mattress, about sleep among comrades who are not going to the gas tonight. Suddenly I see the camp as a haven of peace. It is true, others may be dying, but one is somehow still alive, one has enough food, enough strength to work. . . .

The lights on the ramp flicker with a spectral glow, the wave of people—feverish, agitated, stupefied people—flows on and on, endlessly. They think that now they will have to face a new life in the camp, and they prepare themselves emotionally for the hard struggle ahead. They do not know that in just a few moments they will die, that the gold, money, and diamonds which they have so prudently hidden in their clothing and on their bodies are now useless to them. Experienced professionals will probe into every recess of their flesh, will pull the gold from under the tongue and the diamonds from the uterus and the colon. They will rip out gold teeth. In tightly sealed crates they will ship them to Berlin.

The S.S. men's black figures move about, dignified, businesslike. The gentleman with the notebook puts down his final marks, rounds out the figures: fifteen thousand.

Many, very many, trucks have been driven to the crematoria today.

It is almost over. The dead are being cleared off the ramp and piled into the last truck. The Canada men, weighed down under a load of bread, marmalade and sugar, and smelling of perfume and fresh linen, line up to go. For several days the entire camp will live off this transport. For several days the entire camp will talk about "Sosnowiec-Będzin." "Sosnowiec-Będzin" was a good, rich transport.

The stars are already beginning to pale as we walk back to the camp. The sky grows translucent and opens high about our heads—it is getting light.

Great columns of smoke rise from the crematoria and merge up above into a huge black river which very slowly floats across the sky over Birkenau and disappears beyond the forests in the direction of Trzebinia. The "Sosnowiec-Będzin" transport is already burning.

We pass a heavily armed S.S. detachment on its way to change guard. The men march briskly, in step, shoulder to shoulder, one mass, one will.

"*Und morgen die ganze Welt. . . .*"[7] they sing at the top of their lungs.

"*Rechts ran!* To the right march!" snaps a command from up front. We move out of their way.

Translated from the Polish by Barbara Vedder

7. "And tomorrow the whole world. . . . "

The Block of Death

Rapportführer[1] SS man Taube was famous in Auschwitz[2] for his ability to kill a person in two motions. First he would hit the victim on the head to knock the person unconscious, and then he would put his foot on the person's throat strangling her to death. I remember being a witness to one of his executions on the *zugangen*[3] block. One night Taube was in charge of the evening roll call, and that evening there was a number missing. The *sztubowe*[4] were sent scurrying through the camp to look for the lost woman while I stood there trembling with fear to think what might happen to her when they found her. It turned out that she was in the camp latrine. She could not leave the place because she was suffering from dysentery. She was not yet aware of how important a cog she was in the camp mechanism, that they were not able to finish the roll call unless she was present. She had to be there, and the *sztubowe* had to drag her to appear before the *rapportführer.* It did not matter whether she were dead or alive. When the *sztubowa* hauled her to the roll call area she was half dead with fright. Taube approached her slowly and then snuffed out her life with his usual technique. It took no more than five seconds for Taube to perform the execution. After the execution we were permitted to return to our blocks. All numbers were accounted for, and the roll call was finished.

No one would tell me, and I asked often, why Taube, during the roll call of the first transport of Jews from Slovakia in 1941, should have noticed Cyla and appointed her to be *blokowa*[5] of Number 25, the death block. Rosina, a nurse, and Mancy, a doctor from Bratislawa, told me stories about Cyla.

"Taube must have seen something terrible in Cyla," I said, "something that made her stand out from the other prisoners."

"Nothing of the sort," the girls answered. "She was almost a child when she first came to the camp. She was barely fifteen years old; when she was on

1. Noncommissioned officer in charge of roll call.
2. A complex consisting of concentration, extermination, and labor camps in Upper Silesia. In addition to the main camp (Auschwitz) and the extermination center (Birkenau), there was also a labor camp, Monowitz-Buna.
3. German term for new arrivals.
4. Room leaders, assistants to the *blokowa*, whose job was to maintain order among the prisoners.
5. Female prisoner in charge of a block.

the transport with us she was still wearing a school apron. She was slim, not too tall, and she was pretty. She came from a well-to-do, middle-class Jewish family, religious and highly respected. She had no brothers or sisters. Up to the moment that Taube told her to step out of the line and stand next to him, she was a normal girl, frightened as the rest of us by what was going on around her."

"Listen to how Taube made a criminal of her," Mancy started telling me. "He picked her out of the roll call, while she was dressed in rags, like the rest of the *zugangen*. Her head was shaved and she was wearing wooden shoes. That night she did not return to our block, so we were very worried about what might have happened to her. We did not know where they had taken her or what they were doing to her. Since we were all *zugangen*, it was impossible to find someone who could give us any information. Those first few months in the camp we had no contacts and no organization.

"For a few days Cyla was nowhere to be found. She was not on our block, and she was not with the *komando* working at the construction of the camp. We were sure that Cyla was no longer among the living. We could hardly imagine anything else. The first selection of the *zugangen* took place a few weeks after we arrived at Auschwitz. The murderous work in the swamps, the lack of wholesome drinking water, hunger, and disease knocked even the strongest prisoners off their feet. Young girls who had been the picture of health a few weeks earlier quickly became *mussulmen*,[6] incapable of doing any work. The death camp was just being built at that time. The gas chambers, the crematoria, the *effektenkammer*[7] were all being erected by the hands of the prisoners. Those who were not capable of hard work had to perish. At that time the selections[8] took place at the roll call because the death machinery was not yet in working order. On that fall day of 1941, the day of the first selection, we stood at the roll call and waited for death.

"'Achtung,' barked the *blokowa*. Taube walked into the roll call area, with Cyla following a short distance behind him. At first I did not recognize her. When finally I realized who she was I was so surprised that my eyes almost popped out. Could it really be Cyla? She looked so elegant and so scrubbed and she smelled so good. I looked her over, top to bottom. She wore rubbers on her feet, a beautiful rain coat, and a multi-colored silk scarf on her head. She avoided our gaze, looking straight in front of her. She walked behind the *rapportführer*, step for step. When he stopped she stood at his side. I was so

6. See note for Muslims, page 68.
7. Warehouse where newly confiscated goods were located.
8. Choosing inhabitants of a ghetto or camp for deportation or death.

fascinated at the sight of Cyla that I forgot about the selection. She stood to the side and waited patiently.

"'Now you will stand in line and you will approach the *rapportführer*,' shouted the *blokowa*. The line moved slowly, everybody trying to look her best. Every few minutes Taube picked somebody out of the line and stood her to the side. Then Cyla approached with a notebook in her hand and wrote down the number. The number of those standing off to the side began to swell. But all this time Cyla kept writing down the numbers, making sure that everybody remained in place. She did everything calmly and precisely. When the roll call ended, Cyla lined the women up in ranks of four and took the chosen ones to the new block. That was how the death block was created, and from that day Cyla was functioning as the *blokowa* there. Today she is eighteen years old and has the heart of a criminal capable of committing murder." That was the story Mancy told me.

Block 25 was located on field "A," not far from the block of the *zugangen*. From the outside it looked like any other camp block, except that it was always bolted, and people did not stroll around there. Those who chanced to be sent there left only in the *leichenauto*, the car that transported the dead. Selections were a permanent feature of camp life. There were large selections, which encompassed the whole camp, and there were hospital selections, which Mengele[9] arranged every few months. He always managed to arrange a selection when there was some Jewish holiday. When the holidays approached, we could expect a selection. Sometimes the selections reminded us that it was actually a Jewish holiday, which we would have forgotten otherwise. Mengele, that monster in the body of an Adonis, never forgot.

In addition to the large organized selections, a day did not go by that someone was not condemned to the gas. In our infirmary the SS doctors looked over the sick people who came to the area every day. It did not take long before we were able to tell which of the sick women would be sent to the gas. For example, Dr. Koenig did not like sick people with swollen feet. Mengele, on the other hand, did not like them with sores on their breasts. Since we knew in advance who would be looking over the women, we simply concealed those whom we knew would be vulnerable. Mengele gave us the most trouble. He was so handsome that he inspired trust. He would make himself comfortable in a chair and then become engrossed in conversation. The newly arrived women would forget where they were and start describing all their ailments.

9. Josef Mengele (1911–79?), medical doctor and S.S. captain who at Auschwitz made "selections" and conducted sadistic medical "experiments" on prisoners.

One of them might tell him, "I have been suffering from a heart condition for a long time and I simply can't walk." Another might say, "The camp food doesn't agree with me, because I have liver problems."

These women did not realize that they were signing their own death warrants. Before the doctor's visit we would beg the women to say nothing and to pretend that they did not speak German, but rarely did anyone listen. Sometimes an SS man would write down the number of a prisoner to whom he had taken a dislike. There were times when for no reason at all, and contrary to the regular routine, several German doctors would descend on the block, look over the sick, and write down a few numbers for the gas.

All those whose numbers were listed went to the *blokowa*, whose duty it was to escort them to Block 25. Here Cyla received them, and from that moment forth they were nothing but meat for the oven. Strange as it may seem, the functionaries regarded those in Block 25 as dead already. I was once witness to this phenomenon. On one occasion, the clerk of one of the hospital blocks, a robust, healthy woman, took charge of the sick whose numbers had been written down during the selection. There were about thirty women in the group, all extremely emaciated. She gathered them together in the foyer, dressed only in their slips, then led them barefoot in the snow to the death block. She later explained this brutal procedure as follows: "I wanted to save myself some work. What is the point of taking them to Block 25 fully clothed, and then having to make an extra trip to the warehouse with their clothes. To them it doesn't matter anyway." I can still see the sad walk of those nearly naked women, holding each other up, leaving a trail of bloodstains in the snow. Beside them walked the redcheeked clerk, dressed in a warm sweater, carrying in her hand the card containing the numbers of these corpses.

They stayed on the block until there were enough of them to fill the gas chamber so that the gassing could be carried out with maximum efficiency. Sometimes it took a few days, sometimes more. They waited for death. On Block 25, which it was forbidden to enter, Cyla had a little room. In the camp there were rumors circulated about the goings-on there. In her little apartment Cyla, it was rumored, received Taube, who was said to be her lover. Taube had issued orders that the sick on Block 25 were not to receive any food, thereby conserving the gas it would take to eradicate them. The result was that Cyla received a hefty portion of provisions because the sick were still on the camp register, and she would confiscate their rations for herself. Hot coffee was brought to the block in caldrons. Cyla would kick the caldron over, letting it spill into the drains, and then shout in several languages, "Drink water!" Her shouting could be heard all over field "A." Cyla exchanged margarine, bread, and salami for cigarettes. She would then exchange the cigarettes for luxuries that were brought into the camp by prisoners who worked outside the camp.

Cyla came to our infirmary very often. She was happy and very self-satisfied. She used to bring us chocolates, and once she even brought me a dress as a present. In spite of her cordiality I feared her greatly. To put it bluntly, she was a monster. I avoided getting into discussions with her. I remember that I once let my curiosity get the better of me, and I asked her the question that had been on my mind for a long time: "Tell me, Cyla, how can you act this way? Aren't you afraid that the people will never forgive you?"

We were alone in the in the infirmary, and no sooner had I popped the question than fear overwhelmed me. But she answered me calmly: "You probably know that I put my own mother in the car that took her to the gas. You should understand that there remains for me nothing so terrible that I could not do it. The world is a terrible place. This is how I take my revenge on it."

I did not see Cyla when the prisoners were evacuated from Auschwitz. I do not know what happened to her, but I am convinced that there can be no place for her among normal human beings.

Translated from the Polish by Roslyn Hirsch

Esther's First Born

April 1944 was unusually sunny. In the air you could feel the warm breezes of spring. This year, in the neighborhood of the railroad tracks that led straight to the crematorium, the women were at work laying sidewalks and arranging bunches of flowers. The earth, which smelled of freedom, was freshly dug, and hope entered our hearts. Not far from the fence, new earth was piled up and topped with a floor. This was where the camp orchestra gave concerts and singers sang famous solos. Once a week, after lunch, those concerts took place in the area. Anyone who could drag his feet came. Benches were taken out of the barracks. The healthier people stood or sat on the ground. Those who were able to get to the concert listened, and their thoughts would escape far beyond the present stinking, sordid life.

The orchestra consisted of many instruments. The conductors were a Russian woman and a Hungarian woman. A beautiful Hungarian woman was the soloist. The members of the orchestra wore identical outfits, and the soloist even wore an evening gown. I can remember one of those red, low-cut dresses in which she did not hesitate to appear for the performance. The Russian girl was young—very poised and calm. As soon as she tapped with her baton, the Strauss waltzes started flowing immediately. Everything looked so innocent, but we who knew how much human misery, degradation, and suffering were being covered by this curtain of music, and how many shattered dreams were there, were startled by this seeming innocence. The second conductor was dark and fiery. She also played the violin, and as she played she turned one way and another, setting the rhythm of a czardas for the orchestra, which accompanied her as she played the longing notes of a gypsy melody.

Sometimes, near the barbed wire, a train would go by, carrying Jews from the west in Pullman cars. The people tried to get to the window to wave to us. They took in the ideal picture, which calmed them and allowed them to believe that they were really going to work and that there would even be time for play. I lowered my head, realizing that I was taking part in this deception that was helping the Germans to send millions of people, without difficulty, to a tortuous death.

One warm April day Esther came to the infirmary. She approached me and said very quietly, "I have a very important matter to discuss with you. Can we discuss it privately?"

I knew Esther from the Bialystok Ghetto. On 16 August 1943, the Bialystok Ghetto had been liquidated. For three months Esther, her husband, her mother, and a five-year-old niece who perished in Slonim,[1] hid with me in a bunker built in my apartment. At the time she was a young woman. I doubt that she was even twenty years old. She had a pretty face but it was not an interesting one. I remember that in the bunker we had a lot of trouble with her, because she had no talents and could not be counted on to help out. When the German gendarmes discovered our bunker they shot her husband on the spot. As soon as the three females arrived at Auschwitz, the Germans took away the little girl whom she had cared for affectionately, and a few months later her mother was taken at a selection. Esther was alone in Auschwitz.

She stood before me, now, peculiarly thick, red in the face and a little embarrassed. Maybe she was pregnant.

"As you can see for yourself," she blurted out, "I am going to give birth any day now. All this time I've been going to work, but now I want to stay in the hospital. I want to give birth to this baby. It's my first baby. It moves. It kicks me. It will probably be a son. My husband is not here anymore. That's his son. Please help me," she ended her pleading.

I turned to stone. Didn't she know what Mengele did to women who had babies in the camp? I looked into her happy eyes and at her enraptured features. For the first minute I really did not know what to tell her. Could I extinguish the happiness that emanated from her whole body? Or maybe I should just say nothing. Maybe I should let her live through her great love for her first baby and let the worst come later.

Orli had told me once how Mengele explained to her why he killed Jewish women together with their children. "When a Jewish child is born, or when a woman comes to the camp with a child already," he had explained, "I don't know what to do with the child. I can't set the child free because there are no longer any Jews who live in freedom. I can't let the child stay in the camp because there are no facilities in the camp that would enable the child to develop normally. It would not be humanitarian to send a child to the ovens without permitting the mother to be there to witness the child's death. That is why I send the mother and the child to the gas ovens together."

Imagine that cynical criminal justifying his hideous crimes in the name of humanitarianism, making a mockery of the tenderest of all feelings, a mother's love for her children.

---

1. Small city in eastern Poland with a substantial but fluctuating Jewish population before World War II. Ruled by Poland between World War I and World War II, it was captured by the Germans on 17 July 1941.—Trans.

I had seen the conditions under which Jewish women gave birth in the camp. A doctor from the infirmary took me to one of the births. "Come with me," she said. "Join me in witnessing the crimes of Auschwitz and the depth of human suffering."

On our way to the block in field "B" Mancy told me that the women who were due to deliver were not taken to the infirmary. The delivery took place in the block where the woman lived. "You see," she said, "the birth has to take place in secrecy. Nobody is supposed to know about it. In the hospital block it is impossible to conceal the birth of a child from the Germans. Our procedure now is to kill the baby after birth in such a way that the mother doesn't know about it."

"What? You kill it?" I stopped in the middle of the path.

"It's very simple," Mancy continued. "We give the baby an injection. After that, the baby dies. The mother is told that the baby was born dead. After dark, the baby is thrown on a pile of corpses, and in that manner we save the mother. I want so much for the babies to be born dead, but out of spite they are born healthy. I simply don't know why the children are healthy. The pregnant women do heavy work till the last day; there is no food; and in spite of it all, the children are healthy. My worry now is that I don't have any injections left."

It was already dark when we arrived at the block. The women took us to the woman in labor. Mancy told her to lie on the ground under the board bed. She herself hid there too. "Remember," she said to her quietly, "you are forbidden to utter a sound. Everything has to take place in complete silence. Nobody should know that you are giving birth." She told me to bring her a bucket of cold water. She put it next to her.

"Sit next to me. You will be my helper," she said to me.

Two women stood near the bed. One of them was guarding the entrance to the block.

The birth started. The woman bit her lips in pain until she drew blood. But she did not utter even one sound. She held my hands so tightly that afterwards I had black and blue marks. Finally, the baby was born. Mancy put her hand over his mouth so he would not cry, and then she put his head in the bucket of cold water. She was drowning him like a blind kitten. I felt faint. I had to get out from under the bed.

"The baby was born dead," Mancy said. Later, she wrapped the dead baby in an old shirt, and the woman who was guarding the entrance took the baby and left to put it on a pile of corpses. The mother was saved.

Right then Esther, who knew nothing, was standing in front of me, wanting to go to the hospital to give birth to a baby like thousands of other women in the world. She was listening to the movements of her baby and was happy.

She did not know that if a German doctor found out she would die with her baby. I decided to tell her everything.

"You see, Esther," I started, "you can't give birth to a living baby. It must die before anybody finds out about it. Otherwise, you will die with it."

"What? A dead baby? I want to have a live baby. I am sure that when Mengele sees it he will let me raise it in the camp. It is going to be a beauty because my husband was very handsome. You knew him. I want to have it in the infirmary."

Mancy and Marusia talked to her, but without success. The same day she went to the infirmary, and that night she gave birth to a beautiful baby boy.

She lay there in bed with the baby, very happy. The attendants tried to convince her not to feed the baby so that it would die of hunger. Esther would not hear of it. She gave the baby her breast and talked with wonder about how beautifully it suckled. The supervisor of the infirmary had a duty to report all births, but somehow she delayed. She had pity on Esther.

On the third day of Esther's stay in the hospital block, the first day of the Passover holiday, a big selection took place. I was on the block when Mengele and an SS man came in. They both stood on the stove. The gate was bolted, and every sick woman was paraded naked in front of them. In his tightly closed fist Mengele held a pencil whose point stuck out a little way from his palm. The SS man read, and at the same time, wrote down the numbers, while Mengele pushed the pencil into his fist with a slow movement of his thumb. This meant death. The red-headed SS man put down a cross next to the designated number. Finally, Esther's turn came. She went naked, and in her arms she held the baby. She held it up high as though she wanted to show them what a beautiful and healthy son she had. Mengele slowly pushed the pencil into his clenched fist.

Translated from the Polish by Roslyn Hirsch

The Lemon

Ervin was scowling. His feline eyes, set in a narrow skull, shifted nervously and his lips were pressed angrily into a thin blue arch. He hardly answered Chicky's greeting. Under his arm he was clutching a pair of pants rolled into a bundle.

"What'll you give me for these?" he demanded, unrolling the trousers, which were made of a thin nut-brown cloth. The seat and knees were shiny.

Chicky grinned. "Ye gods, where did you pick those up?" He inspected the cuffs and seams. "Jesus Christ himself wouldn't be caught dead in such a low-class shroud."

Ervin ignored the sneer. "I'm only interested in one thing, Chicky, and that's what I can get for them." He spoke fast.

"Listen, not even a resurrected Jesus Christ on the crummiest street in Lodz would wear a pair of pants like that," Chicky went on with the air of an expert.

He noticed the twitching in Ervin's jaw. "Well, the knees still look pretty good, though," he reconsidered. "Where did you get them?"

It was cloudy and the sun was like a big translucent ball. The barn swallows were flying low. Ervin looked up at the sky and at the swallows swooping toward unseen nests. He'd been expecting Chicky to ask that and he'd prepared himself on the way.

He displayed his rather unimpressive wares again. He knew he had to go through with it now, even if the pants were full of holes. The skin on Chicky's face was thin, almost transparent; he had a small chin and rheumy eyes.

A member of the local security force came around the corner.

"Hey, you little brats," he snapped, casting a quick glance at their skinny bodies, "go on, get out of here!"

They turned around. Fortunately, a battered yellow Jewish streetcar came along just then and diverted the security guard's attention.

"Don't tell me it's a big secret," Chicky said. "Anybody can easily see those pants belonged to some grown-up. What're you so scared of?"

"What should I be scared of?" Ervin retorted, clutching the trousers close. "I've got to cash in on them, that's all."

"They're rags."

"They're English material, they're no rags."

"Well, I might see what I can do for you," Chicky relented. "But on a fifty-fifty basis."

Ervin handed over the bundle, and Chicky took a piece of twine from his pocket and tied up the trousers to suit himself, making a fancy knot. He looked up and down the street.

The security guard was at the other end of the street with his back to the boys. They were on the corner of an alley which hadn't had a name for a long time. It was intermittently paved with cobblestones. People hurried on; Ervin and Chicky moved closer to the wall. The streetcar now took a different route. The next stop was out of sight.

Chicky, the smaller of the two, the one with the shaved head, was clutching the brown checkered pants under his arm as Ervin had done.

"But don't you go having second thoughts, Ervin. Don't let me go ahead and work my ass off and then. . . ."

"My dad died," Ervin said.

"Hm . . . well," Chicky remarked. "It's taken a lot of people these last few weeks," he observed.

"Now there's only one important thing, and that's how you're going to cash in on those pants."

It occurred to Chicky that Ervin might want a bigger share of the take because the pants had been his father's.

"Who's your customer, Chicky?"

"Old Moses," Chicky lied.

"Do I know him?"

"Little short guy."

"First time I've heard of him."

"He just comes up as high as my waist. He's absolutely the biggest bastard in town. But he kind of likes me. Maybe it's because I remind him of somebody."

"He's interested in pants?"

"He's interested in absolutely everything, Ervin."

"Funny I never heard of him."

"Well, I guess I'd better be going," Chicky said.

"What do you suppose your friend would give me for these pants?" Ervin asked.

"Give *us*, you mean," Chicky corrected.

"Anyway, go on and see what you can do," said Ervin, dodging a direct answer.

"He might cough up some bread in exchange for these pants. Or a couple ounces of flour." He unrolled the trousers again. "Like I told you, the knees are still pretty good and the lining's passable. The fly isn't stained yellow like it is in old men's pants. In that respect, these trousers are in good shape and that tells you something about the person who wore them. I'll try to get as much as I can for them, Ervin." He bared his teeth in a tiger grin.

"I need a lemon, Chicky."

"What about a big hunk of nothing?"

"I'm not joking," Ervin said curtly. "All right, then half a lemon, if you can't get a whole one." The expression on Chicky's face changed.

"You know what *I* need, Ervin?" he began. "I need an uncle in Florida where the sun shines all year long and trained fish dance in the water. I need an uncle who would send me an affidavit and money for my boat ticket so I could go over there and see those fish and talk to them." He paused. "A *lemon!* Listen, Ervin, where do you get those ideas, huh, tell me, will you?"

Chicky gazed up into the sky and imagined a blue and white ocean liner and elegant fish poking their noses up out of the silver water, smiling at him, wishing him bon voyage.

Swallows, white-breasted and sharp-winged, darted across the sullen sky. Chicky whistled at them, noticing that Ervin didn't smile.

"That lemon's not for me," said Ervin.

"Where do you think you are? Where do you think Old Moses'd get a lemon? It's harder to find a lemon in this place than. . . ."

But he couldn't think of a comparison.

Chicky's expression changed to one of mute refusal. He thought to himself, Ervin is something better than I am. His father died, Ervin took his trousers, so now he can talk big about lemons. Chicky's mouth dropped sourly.

"It's for Miriam," Ervin said flatly. "If she doesn't get a lemon, she's finished."

"What's wrong with her?"

"I'm not sure. . . ."

"Just in general. I know you're no doctor."

"Some kind of vitamin deficiency, but it's real bad."

"Are her teeth falling out?"

"The doctor examined her this morning when he came to see my mother. The old man was already out in the hall. There's no point talking about it."

"It's better to be healthy, I grant you that," Chicky agreed. He rolled up the pants again. "At best, I may be able to get you a piece of bread." He tied the twine into a bow again. "If there were four of us getting a share of this rag, Ervin—your mom, your sister, and you and me, nobody would get anything out of it in the end."

"If I didn't need it, I'd keep my mouth shut," Ervin repeated.

"I can tell we won't see eye to eye, even on Judgment Day."

A Polish streetcar rattled and wheezed along behind them. The town was divided into Polish and Jewish sectors. The streetcar line always reminded Ervin that there were still people who could move around and take a streetcar ride through the ghetto, even if it was just along a corridor of barbed wire with sentries in German uniforms so nobody would get any ideas about jumping off—or on.

"It's got to be something more than that. Everybody's got a vitamin deficiency here. What if it's something contagious, Ervin, and here I am fussing around with these pants of yours?" He gulped back his words. "And I've already caught whatever it is?"

"Nobody knows *what* it is," said Ervin.

"Well, I'm going, Ervin. . . ."

"When are you coming back?"

"What if we both went to see what we could do?"

"No," said Ervin quietly.

"Why not?"

Ervin knew what it was he had been carrying around inside him on his way to meet Chicky. *It was everything that had happened when he'd stripped off those trousers. His father's body had begun to stiffen and it felt strange. He kept telling himself it was all right, that it didn't matter.* Instead, he kept reciting the alphabet and jingles.

This was your father, a living person. And now he's dead. Chicky was the only one he could have talked to.

"I haven't got a dad or a mother even," Chicky said suddenly. A grin flickered. "That's my tough luck. They went up the chimney long ago."

The sky above the low rooftops was like a shallow, stagnant sea.

Chicky lingered, uncertain.

It was just his body, Ervin told himself. *Maybe memory is like the earth and sky and ocean, like all the seashores and the mountains, like a fish swimming up out of the water to some island, poking out its big glassy eyes just to see how things look. Like that fish Chicky had been talking about. Nobody knows, not even the smartest rabbi in the world. And not the bad rabbis either. But while he was taking his father's trousers off, he knew what he was doing. He wasn't thinking about his father, but about an old Italian tune he used to sing and which Miriam loved. Father sang off key, but it sounded pretty. Prettier than a lot of other things. It was about love and flowers and his father had learned it during the war when he fought in the Piave campaign.*

He already had the trousers halfway off. And he knew the reasons he loved his father would never go away.

The swallows flew quietly in low, skidding arches. Ervin looked around to see how the weather was, and finally his gaze dropped. The rounded cobblestones melted away.

"All right then, I'll bring it around to your place later," Chicky said.

"By when do you think you can do it?"

"In two or three hours."

"But, Chicky. . . ."

Chicky turned and disappeared around the corner as another streetcar came clanging along.

Now Ervin could think ahead, instead of going back to what had been on his mind before. He set off down the alley in the opposite direction, toward the house where he and his family had been living for two years.

The tiny shops upstairs and in the basement had been hardly more than market stalls which had been converted into apartments for several families.

He remembered how he discovered that his father no longer wore underpants. The stringy thighs. The darkened penis, the reddish pubic hair. Rigid legs. Scars on the shin bone. His father had gotten those scars when he was wounded fighting in Italy.

Then that old tune came back to him, sung off key again, the song from somewhere around Trieste that he and Miriam had liked so much.

Hell, who needed those pants more than they did? Father had probably traded in his underpants long ago. Who knows for what?

So Father died, he is no more, Ervin thought to himself.

He reached home, one of the dwarfish shops where he and his mother and sister lived.

The corrugated iron shutter over the entry had broken a spring, so it wouldn't go all the way up or down. He could see a mouse.

He squeezed through a crack in the wall. Mother was scared of mice, so he'd repaired the wall boards through which the mice came in and out. Pressing against the wall, Ervin was suddenly aware of his body, and that reminded him of his father again.

"It's me," he called out.

It had occurred to him that there was nothing to be proud of, being unable to cash in on the trousers *himself*. (Even so, his mother must have known what he had done.) He had to take a deep breath and adjust to the musty smell in the room. It was easier to get used to the difference between the light outside and the darkness inside.

Mother greeted him with a snore. She had long since lost any resemblance to the woman who had come here with him. He peered around him. He had been almost proud of having such a pretty mother. On top of everything else, her legs had swollen. She hadn't been able to get out of bed for the past eight weeks. She'd waited on everything for Father, and now for him.

"Where've you been?" his mother asked.

"Out," he answered.

He crawled into his corner where he could turn his back on everything, including his father who lay out in the hall wrapped in a blanket. Miriam, too, was curled up next to the wall, so he couldn't see her face. He heard her coughing.

He bundled his legs into the tattered rug that used to be his father's. *He'd always had the worst covers. He didn't want to admit he was a loser, and as long as he was able to give up something for them, maybe it wasn't so obvious. The dim light made its way through the thin fabric of dust and dampness and the breath of all three of them. When he lost, he put on the smile of a beautiful woman. He was making a point of being a graceful loser. As if it made any difference to anybody except himself.*

"Did you find anything?" his mother asked.

"No. . . ."

"What are we going to do?"

"Maybe this afternoon," he said, his face to the wall.

"Miriam," his mother called out to his sister. "Don't cough. It wears you out."

"Mirrie," Ervin said. "Miriam." She didn't answer.

"Can't she speak?" he asked his mother.

"It wears her out," she repeated. "You really ought to look around and see if you can't scrape up something."

"There's no point so early in the afternoon."

"You ought to try at least," his mother insisted.

"That's how it used to be with Father, Ervin recalled. *She always kept sending him somewhere. But Father had gone out just as he'd done now, and, like him, he almost felt better outside; he also may have believed that just by going out he was getting back in shape, that he'd be able to do what he used to do in the beginning. Then Mother started saying things couldn't get any worse. She never went wrong about that. That's because there is no limit to what's "worse." The limit was in his father. And now Ervin had to find it, just like his father.*

"I already told you, I can't find anything just now." he said.

"You ought to go out and try, dear," his mother went on. *This was what Father had had to put up with.* "You see how Miriam looks, don't you?" his mother persisted.

"I can see her," he answered. "But I can't find anything now."

"This can't help but finish badly."

"Oh, cut it out. I'm not going anywhere," Ervin declared flatly. "I've already tried. There's nothing to be had."

"For God's sake, listen to me," his mother cried sharply. "Go on out and *try.* Miriam hasn't had a thing to eat today."

The stains on the plaster were close to his eyes. The room was damp, and it almost swallowed up the sound of his mother's voice and his own. The dampness didn't bother him, though. He could hear faint scratching noises in the walls.

The boards he'd put up didn't help much. He almost envied mice. Just as he'd felt envy for trees when he was outside. Ervin suddenly wished he could catch one of those little animals. Pet it, then kill it. Father had told them about the time they were besieged during the First World War and the soldiers ate mice.

To kill and caress. Or simply kill, so you're not always bothered by something or somebody. So it is—to be killed or to kill.

But if Chicky was right, a trained mouse should get along great.

"I wonder if I shouldn't air out the room a bit," he said into the silence.

"Have they been here already?" he asked after a while.

"No."

"They're taking their time about it."

Now, in her turn, his mother was silent. "Who knows how many calls they have to make today?"

"Why don't you want to go out, child?"

"I will. In a while," he answered. "It doesn't make any sense now, though."

"Ervin, child. . . ."

The room was quiet, the silence broken only by Miriam's coughing.

Ervin put his head between his knees, trying to guess where the mouse was and what it was doing. He stuck his fingers in his ears. The scratching continued. *So Father's still lying out there in the hall. He doesn't have any pants and Mother doesn't even know it. He's naked, but that doesn't bother his old Piave scars. Mother could use that extra blanket now,* he thought to himself. *But he left it around his father for some reason which he didn't know himself. So I don't have the feeling that I've stolen everything from him, including our second tattered blanket,* he thought to himself. *It was lucky she couldn't get out of bed now, even if she wanted to. Her legs wouldn't support her. She'd see that Father had no pants. They'll probably take him along with the blanket. What the hell? They were certainly taking their time. They should have been here an hour ago. It was a regulation of the commanding officer and the self-government committee that corpses must be removed promptly. Everybody was scared of infection. The corpse collectors were kept busy. They probably didn't miss a chance to take anything they could get. Everybody knew they stole like bluejays.*

Miriam would probably have been afraid to sleep with a dead person in the same room, even if it was Father, Ervin decided.

"There's some rabbi here who works miracles, I heard," his mother said. "Why don't you go and see him?"

"What would I say to him?"

"Tell him that I'm your mother."

"I don't have any idea where he lives. And even if he could perform a miracle, he certainly won't put himself out to come over here. He waits for people to come to him."

"I feel so weak," his mother told him.

Suddenly it occurred to him that maybe his mother would have been better off lying out in the hall beside his father. It would be better for Miriam too. Mother's gestures and the things she told him were getting more and more indecisive.

"Why don't you want to go anywhere?" Mother said.

"Because there's no point," he replied. "I'd be wearing myself out in vain. I'll find something, but not until this afternoon."

"Miriam won't last long. She can hardly talk anymore."

"Miriam?" Ervin called out.

Miriam was silent and his mother added: "You know how it was with Daddy."

"He'd been sick for a long time."

And when her son said nothing, she tried again. "Ervin. . . ."

"It doesn't make any sense," he growled. "I'm not going anywhere now. Not till later."

He sat quite still for a while, staring at the blotches and shadows moving on the wall. Rabbis say your soul is in your blood, but some kids and old people say it's in your shadow. There are a lot of lies around. Who cares where your soul is? Maybe under your dirty fingernails? Maybe when you have diarrhea? He could hear mice scampering across the floor toward the mattress where Mother and Miriam were lying. Mother screeched, then Miriam.

Ervin was bored.

It might be more comfortable and pleasant to wait outside. But there was something in here that made him stay. He remembered how he and Chicky used to play poker. They always pretended there was some stake. That made it more interesting. You could bluff and pretend to have a full house when you didn't even have a pair. But there was always the chance—which they'd invented—that you might win something.

He remembered how he and Miriam used to go ice-skating. She was little and her knees were wobbly. He'd drag her around the rink for a while, then take her into the restaurant where you could have a cup of tea for ten hellers. Miriam's nose would be running, and she'd stay there for an hour with her tea so he could have a good time out on the ice. Once his mother had given them money to buy two ham sandwiches. His arches always ached when he'd been skating. So did Miriam's.

If they'd come for Father—and he wished it were over with—he wouldn't have to worry that the body would start to decay or that his mother would find out he didn't have any pants on.

"Why don't you go out and see that miracle rabbi?"

"Because it doesn't make any sense."

At first, Mother only had trouble with her legs. And Miriam hadn't coughed *quite* as much.

The sentries along the streetcar line always looked comfortably well-fed, with nice round bellies, as though they had everything they needed. When these sentries passed through the ghetto, they acted as though victory was already theirs, even if they might lose this little skirmish with the Jews. *Daddy once said that this was their world, whether they won or lost.*

Ervin's stomach growled. It was like the noise the mice made. He stretched and waited for his mother to start nagging him again. But she didn't, and it was almost as though something were missing. *He didn't want to think about his father's body wrapped in that blanket out in the hall. Daddy had been sick long enough. He was certainly better off this way.*

After a while, he wasn't sure whether his stomach was making the noise or the mice. His mother groaned. He thought about a nap. Just then he heard someone banging on the iron shutter. He got up.

"Well, I'll be on my way," he said.

"Come back soon," his mother replied. "Come back safe and sound."

"Sure," he answered. As he approached the shutter, he asked, "Is that you, Chicky?"

"No," a voice replied. "It's the miracle-working rabbi with a pitcher of milk."

Ervin pushed the broken shutter and slipped through. It was easy. His body was nothing but skin and bones now. He had a long narrow skull, with bulging greenish blue eyes. He could feel his mother's eyes on him as he squeezed out. Outside in the courtyard he pulled down his shirt and his bones cracked. Chicky was waiting on the sidewalk.

"So?" asked Ervin.

"Even with those stains on the seat," Chicky started.

"What're you trying to tell me?"

"He gave me more than I expected." He smiled slyly and happily.

Chicky produced a piece of bread, carefully wrapped in a dirty scarf. He handed it to Ervin. "This is for you. I already ate my share on the way, like we agreed."

"Just this measly piece?"

"Maybe you forgot those stains on the seat of those pants."

"Such a little hunk?"

"What else did you expect, hm? Or maybe you think I ought to come back with a whole moving van full of stuff for one pair of pants?"

Chicky wiped his nose, offended.

"You just better not forget about those stains on the seat. Besides, almost everybody's selling off clothes now."

Ervin took the bread. Neither one mentioned the lemon. Ervin hesitated before crawling back into the room, half-hoping Chicky was going to surprise him. Chicky liked to show off.

"Wait here for me," he blurted. "I'll be right back."

Ervin squinted through the dimness to where his mother lay on the mattress.

"Here, catch," he said maliciously. He threw the bread at her. It struck her face, bounced, and slid away. He could hear her groping anxiously over the blanket and across the floor. As soon as she had grabbed it, she began to wheeze loudly.

She broke the bread into three pieces in the dark.

"Here, this is for you," she said.

"I don't want it."

"Why not?" she asked. He heard something else in her voice. "Ervin?"

He stared at the cracks in the wall where the mice crawled through. He was afraid his mother was going to ask him again.

"My God, Ervin, don't you hear me?"

"I've already had mine," he said.

"How much did you take?"

"Don't worry, just my share." He felt mice paws pattering across the tops of his shoes. Again, he had the urge to catch one and throw it on the bed.

"Miriam," his mother called.

Ervin left before he could hear his sister's reply. He knew what his mother was thinking.

Chicky was waiting, his hands in his pockets, leaning against the wall. He was picking his teeth. He was looking up at the sky trying to guess which way the clouds were going. There must be wind currents that kept changing.

For a while the two boys strolled along in silence. Then just for something to say, Chicky remarked: "You know what that little crook told me? He says you can't take everything away from everybody."

Everything melted together: father, bread, mother, sister, the moment he was imagining what Chicky might bring back for them. Mice.

"He says we can *hope* without *believing*." Chicky laughed, remembering something else.

"Do you feel like bragging all day?"

"If you could see into me the way I can see into you, you could afford to talk. When my dad went up the chimney, I told myself I was still lucky to have my mother. And when I lost Mother, I told myself that at least I was lucky to have a brother left. He was weaker than a fly. And I said to myself, it's great to have your health at least."

Ervin was silent, so Chicky continued: "Still, we're pretty lucky, Ervin. Even if that's what my little businessman says too. Don't get the idea the world's going to stop turning just because one person in it is feeling miserable at this particular moment. You'd be exaggerating."

They didn't talk about it anymore. They could walk along like this together, so close their elbows or shoulders almost touched, and sometimes as they took a step together, their hips. The mice and the chameleon were gone; Chicky was really more like a barn swallow. Chicky was just slightly crooked. The thought suddenly put him in a better mood. Like when the sun came out or when he looked at a tree or the blue sky.

"He's full of wise sayings," Chicky resumed. "According to him, we have to pay for everything. And money and *things* aren't the worst way to pay."

"Aw, forget it. You're sticking as close to me as a fag."

"What about you?" Chicky's little face stretched.

"They haven't come to get him yet, the bastards."

"I can probably tell you why," Chicky declared. "Would you believe it, my dad's beard grew for two days after he was already dead?"

"Do you ever think you might have been a swallow?"

"Say, you're really outdoing yourself today," Chicky remarked. "But if you want to know something, I *have* thought about it."

Ervin looked up into the sky again. He might have known Chicky would have ideas like that. Ervin himself sometimes had the feeling that he was up there being blown around among the raindrops when there was a thunderstorm. The sky looked like an iron shutter. Sometimes he could also imagine himself jumping through the sky, using his arms and legs to steer with.

"Ervin. . . ." Chicky interrupted.

"What?"

"That old guy gave me a tremendous piece of advice."

"So be glad."

"No, Ervin, I mean it."

"Who's arguing?"

"Aren't you interested? He asked me if your old man had anything else."

"What else could he have?"

"He was just hinting."

"These have been hungry days for us. That crooked second-hand man of yours, his brains are going soft. I hope he can tell the difference between dogs and cats."

"Considering we're not their people, Ervin, what he told me wasn't just talk."

"My dad was the cleanest person in this whole dump," said Ervin.

"He didn't mean that and neither did I, Ervin."

"What's with all this suspense?"

"Just say you're not interested and we'll drop it," Chicky said.

"Come on, spill it, will you? What *did* he mean then?"

"Maybe there was a ring or something?"

"Do you really think he'd have let Mother and Miriam die right in front of his eyes if he'd had anything like a *ring?*"

"He wasn't talking only about a ring. He meant gold."

"Dad had to turn over everything he had that was even gilded."

"He hinted at it only after I tried to explain to him about the lemon."

"You know how it was. Mother doesn't have anything either."

"He only hinted at it when I told him how important it was for you to have that lemon, Ervin."

"Well, what was it he hinted, then?" Ervin noticed the expectant look on Chicky's face.

"He hinted that it wasn't impossible, but only in exchange for something made of pure gold. And that he didn't care what it was."

"Don't be a bastard," said Ervin slowly. "Forget it. My dad didn't have anything like that. Go on, get lost."

"He even indicated exactly *what* and *how.*"

"Look, come on—kindly spill it," Ervin said with irritation. *Once again, he saw his father lying there wrapped in the blanket. It flooded through him in a dark tide, like when his mother didn't believe that he hadn't taken more than his share of the bread. He'd known right from the start what Chicky was talking about.*

Ervin didn't say anything.

"Gold teeth, for instance. It's simply something in the mouth he doesn't need anymore, something nobody needs except maybe you and me."

Ervin remained silent.

"Well, I wasn't the one who said anything about a lemon," he concluded.

Ervin stopped and so did Chicky. Then Ervin turned and looked him up and down, eyes bulging.

"Aw, cut it out," Chicky said wearily. "Don't look at me as though I killed your dad."

Suddenly Ervin slapped him. Chicky's face was small and triangular, tapering off crookedly at the top. It was very obvious because his head was shaved. Then Ervin slapped him again and began to punch his face and chest.

When his fist struck Chicky's Adam's apple, Ervin could feel how fragile everything about him was.

Again he saw himself stripping those brown checkered trousers off his father's body. The undertakers would be coming along any minute. {They should have been here long ago.} He thought of how he'd managed to do that before they came and how he'd probably manage to do even this if he wanted to. And he knew that he couldn't have swallowed that piece of bread even if his mother had given it to him without those second thoughts of hers. He kept pounding his fists into Chicky, and it was as if he were striking at himself and his mother. *He kept telling himself that his father was dead anyway and that it didn't matter much and that it didn't have any bearing on the future either.*

Then he felt everything slowing down. Chicky began to fight back. Ervin got in two fast punches, one on the chin, the other in the belly. Chicky hit Ervin twice before people gathered and tried to break it up, threatening to call the security guards.

Ervin picked himself up off the sidewalk as fast as he could. He shook himself like a dog and went home through the courtyard.

"Ervin?" his mother called out. "Is that you?"

"Yeah," he answered.

"Did you find anything else?"

He was shivering as he sometimes did when he was cold because he'd loaned his blanket to his mother or Miriam.

"Mirrie. . . ." he tried.

He bundled himself up into the rug. He was glad Chicky had hit him back. It was hard to explain why. It was different from wanting to catch a mouse and kill it. He touched his cheek and chin, fingering the swollen places. Again he waited for his mother to say something. But she didn't. Mother only knows as much as I tell her, he said to himself. Mother's quite innocent, Ervin decided. Despite everything she's still innocent. Would she have been able to do what she had criticized him for? He wished she'd say something, give at least an echo. He thought of Miriam. For a moment he could see her, tall and slender, her breasts and blond hair.

The twilight began to melt into the dampness of the cellar. The spider webs disappeared in the darkness. He wished they'd muffle the edge of his mother's voice. He waited for Miriam's cough. The silence was like a muddy path where nobody wants to walk. *And his father was still lying out there in the hall.*

When someone dies, Ervin thought to himself, *it means not expecting, not worrying about anything, not hoping for something that turns out to be futile. It means not forcing yourself into something you don't really want, while you go on behaving as though you did. It means not being dependent on anybody or anything. It means being rid of what's bothering you. It's like when you close your eyes and see things and people in your own way.*

That idea of a path leading from the dead to the living and back again is just a lot of foolishness I thought up by myself. To be dead means to expect nothing, not to expect somebody to say something, not to wait for someone's voice. Not to stare enviously after a streetcar going somewhere from somewhere else.

He looked around. Miriam had begun to cough again. She's coughing almost gently, he thought to himself. She probably doesn't have enough strength left to cough anymore.

My God, that lying, thieving, sly old man, that bastard who's fed for six thousand years on Jewish wisdom and maybe would for another half an hour—but maybe not even that long. That dirty louse, full of phony maxims and dreams as complicated as clockwork, lofty as a rose, rank as an onion, who perhaps wasn't quite as imaginary as I wanted to think he was, judging from Chicky's descriptions which made him sound as though he'd swallowed all the holy books. That slimy crook with his miserable messages, that you have to pay for everything and that money and things aren't the most precious currency. But he also said you can't take everything away from everybody, as though he wanted to confuse you by contradicting himself in the same breath. Where did he get those ideas?

"No, I don't have anything," he said suddenly, as if he knew his mother was still waiting for an answer.

He heard her sigh. From his sister's bed he heard a stifled cough. (She's probably ashamed of coughing by now.)

Nothing's plaguing Father anymore either. Not even the craving for a bowl of soup. He wasn't looking forward anymore to seeing Ervin dash out onto the field in a freshly laundered uniform and shiny football boots, which he took care of, in front of crowds of people waiting for entertainment and thrills and a chance to yell their lungs out. If they come for Father now, they'll do just what Chicky said they would. Anyway, the undertakers themselves do it to the old people. He remembered his father's smile which got on his mother's nerves.

He stared into the darkness. His mother was bandaging her swollen legs. Her eyes were very bright. She's probably feverish, he thought. She made a few inexplicable gestures. *What if the rabbis are right and there is some afterwards? Then his father must be able to see him. Where do you suppose he really is,* Ervin wondered, *and where am I? Does anybody know? Inwardly he tried to smile at his father. It would be nice if I could really smile at him. To be on the safe side,* Ervin tried smiling at his father again.

"I'm going out and take another look around," he said.

Mother ceased her strange movements. "Where do you want to go in the dark?"

"I want to have a look at something."

"Be careful, child."

He went out into the hall and the place he had avoided before, so he wouldn't have to look at the wall beside which his father's body was still lying. He was squeezing through the crack in the wall. For a short while an insurance agent had lived in the corner shop. *But this isn't your father anymore,* he told himself; *he was only until yesterday. Now there is nothing but a weight and the task of carrying it away,* he reminded himself immediately. *But I'll think of him only in good ways. And Mother and Miriam will think about him as if nothing's happened.*

He threw off the old blanket. He closed his eyes for a second. I won't be able to eat very much, he realized, as though he wanted to convince himself that this was the only difference it would make. Everything moved stiffly. He had to turn the head and open its mouth. He grabbed it by the chin and hair and that was how he managed. He couldn't remember exactly which tooth it was. He tried one after another. He was hurrying. He didn't want Chicky and the men with the coffins to catch him at it. Instead, he tried to imagine that lemon. It was like a yellow sphere at the end of the hall. Suddenly he couldn't remember where lemons came from, except that it was somewhere in the south, and whether they grew on trees or bushes. He'd never really known anyway.

He picked up a sharp stone. He had a sticky feeling as though he were robbing somebody. He tried to decide which was the best way to knock it out. He tried several times without success. Then he stopped trying to get at just that one tooth. There is no other way, he kept repeating to himself. Do it. Do it fast. The faster the better.

Finally something in the jaw loosened. Ervin could smell his own breath. He tossed the stone away. He was glad nobody had seen him. Into the palm of his hand he scooped what he'd been seeking. (He was squatting and the head dropped back to the floor.)

Ervin stood up slowly. He felt as though his body and thoughts were flowing into a dark river, and he didn't know where it came from and where it was going. He wiped his hands on his pants. The cellar was dark, like the last place a person can retreat to. For a moment he closed his eyes. He had to take it out into the light. He headed for the other end of the corridor.

He'd hardly stepped out into the street when he saw Chicky's face in the twilight. There, you see, Ervin said to himself. He was keeping watch after all. Chicky would have done what he'd just done if he'd had the chance.

"Hello, kid," Chicky began. "Hello, you Jew bastard." Then Chicky exploded: "You lousy hyena. You son of a bitch. I suppose you've come to apologize. At least I hope so."

Ervin was clutching the thing tightly in his fist. He stared at Chicky for a long time.

"But I got in two good punches, didn't I? Like Max Schmeling." Chicky sounded pleased with himself. His eyes shone.

But then he noticed that the skin under Ervin's eyes was bluer than any bruise could have made it. He noticed, too, the pale blotches on Ervin's face. And how he kept his hand in his pocket.

"No hard feelings," Chicky said.

"I have it."

"I was sure you'd manage. . . ."

Ervin pulled his hand out of his pocket and Chicky's glance shifted swiftly.

"Bring me that lemon, Chicky, but the whole thing." He unclenched his fist. It lay there cupped in his palm, a rather unattractive shell of gold the color of old copper, and very dirty.

"You won't take the tiniest slice for yourself."

"If it's pure, Ervin, you're in luck," Chicky said.

When Ervin did not respond he continued: "Sometimes it's just iron or some ersatz. Then it's worn through on top. The old man warned me about that in advance. But if it isn't, then you're damned lucky, Ervin, honest."

"When will you bring me that lemon?" Ervin asked, getting to the point.

"First hand it over and let me take a look."

Impatiently, Chicky inspected the crown, acting as though he hadn't heard Ervin. He scraped away the blood that had dried around the root and removed bits of cement. He blew on it and rubbed the dull gold between his fingers, then let it rest in his palm again.

"For this, the old runt will jump like a toad."

"I hope so."

"But first, Ervin, it's fifty-fifty."

"The hell it is," he answered firmly.

"I'll only do it for half."

"If Miriam doesn't get that lemon, she won't even last out till evening."

"Why shouldn't she last out? I'm keeping half."

"You're not keeping anything," repeated Ervin. "Now get going before it's too late."

Ervin glared at him, but there was a question in his eyes. Chicky acted calm. None of his self-satisfaction had filtered through to Ervin. His throat tightened. He began to shiver. He could feel the goose pimples on his neck and arms. It wasn't the way he wanted to think it was, *that his father had died and otherwise everything was just the same as before.* And when Chicky looked at him, Ervin could read in his eyes that instead of bringing a lemon or some kind of pills that have the same effect as lemons, Chicky would probably bring another piece of bread.

Ervin heard the quiet gurgle rising in his throat. He tried thinking about that runty second-hand dealer.

"I'd be crazy to do it for nothing," said Chicky slowly. He squinted warily and his nostrils flared. He bared his teeth. There were big gaps between them.

"Either we go halves or I tell your mom how you're treating me."

"You're not such a bastard, Chicky, are you?"

"Well, I'd have to be," replied Chicky.

"Get going," Ervin said.

"That sounds more like it."

"I'll wait at home."

"All right."

"And hurry up. Honestly, it's very important."

"Fast as a dog can do you know what," grinned Chicky.

Small and nimble, he dodged among the pedestrians. In the meantime, two men with tubs had appeared. Chicky must have passed them. The tubs were covered with tattered sheets and something bulged underneath. Everybody stepped aside as the porters passed. They knew what they were carrying.

Ervin didn't feel like going back home. He crawled into the opening of a cement culvert pipe. His long skinny head stuck out as he sat there watching the sun set behind the clouds. It dropped slowly. The barn swallows were flying lower now than they had been earlier that afternoon, flying in flocks, suddenly soaring up, then back toward earth.

He kept looking up and down the alley so he wouldn't miss Chicky when he came back.

It all began to melt together before his eyes: the silhouettes of the buildings and the cobblestones that had been pounded into the earth and then washed loose by long-gone rains. He watched the sky which was full of barn swallows and the sun disappeared. Rain was gathering in the clouds as their colors changed.

I ought to be like a rock, he told himself. Even harder than a rock. He forced his eyes up to the sky where the swallows were wheeling. Maybe swallows are happy, free, without guilt. He tried to swallow the distance, the wet air and the disappearing light, the flowing wind.

And he wept, quietly and without tears, in some little crevice which was inside.

Translated from the Czech by Jeanne Nemcova

The Shawl

Stella, cold, cold, the coldness of hell. How they walked on the roads together, Rosa with Magda curled up between sore breasts, Magda wound up in the shawl. Sometimes Stella carried Magda. But she was jealous of Magda. A thin girl of fourteen, too small, with thin breasts of her own, Stella wanted to be wrapped in a shawl, hidden away, asleep, rocked by the march, a baby, a round infant in arms. Magda took Rosa's nipple, and Rosa never stopped walking, a walking cradle. There was not enough milk; sometimes Magda sucked air; then she screamed. Stella was ravenous. Her knees were tumors on sticks, her elbows chicken bones.

Rosa did not feel hunger; she felt light, not like someone walking but like someone in a faint, in trance, arrested in a fit, someone who is already a floating angel, alert and seeing everything, but in the air, not there, not touching the road. As if teetering on the tips of her fingernails. She looked into Magda's face through a gap in the shawl: a squirrel in a nest, safe, no one could reach her inside the little house of the shawl's windings. The face, very round, a pocket mirror of a face: but it was not Rosa's bleak complexion, dark like cholera, it was another kind of face altogether, eyes blue as air, smooth feathers of hair nearly as yellow as the Star sewn into Rosa's coat. You could think she was one of *their* babies.

Rosa, floating, dreamed of giving Magda away in one of the villages. She could leave the line for a minute and push Magda into the hands of any woman on the side of the road. But if she moved out of line they might shoot. And even if she fled the line for half a second and pushed the shawl-bundle at a stranger, would the woman take it? She might be surprised, or afraid; she might drop the shawl, and Magda would fall out and strike her head and die. The little round head. Such a good child, she gave up screaming, and sucked now only for the taste of the drying nipple itself. The neat grip of the tiny gums. One mite of a tooth tip sticking up in the bottom gum, how shining, an elfin tombstone of white marble gleaming there. Without complaining, Magda relinquished Rosa's teats, first the left, then the right; both were cracked, not a sniff of milk. The duct-crevice extinct, a dead volcano, blind eye, chill hole, so Magda took the corner of the shawl and milked it instead. She sucked and sucked, flooding the threads with wetness. The shawl's good flavor, milk of linen.

It was a magic shawl, it could nourish an infant for three days and three nights. Magda did not die, she stayed alive, although very quiet. A peculiar smell, of cinnamon and almonds, lifted out of her mouth. She held her eyes open every moment, forgetting how to blink or nap, and Rosa and sometimes Stella studied their blueness. On the road they raised one burden of a leg after another and studied Magda's face. "Aryan,"[1] Stella said, in a voice grown as thin as a string; and Rosa thought how Stella gazed at Magda like a young cannibal. And the time that Stella said "Aryan," it sounded to Rosa as if Stella had really said "Let us devour her."

But Magda lived to walk. She lived that long, but she did not walk very well, partly because she was only fifteen months old, and partly because the spindles of her legs could not hold up her fat belly. It was fat with air, full and round. Rosa gave almost all her food to Magda, Stella gave nothing; Stella was ravenous, a growing child herself, but not growing much. Stella did not menstruate. Rosa did not menstruate. Rosa was ravenous, but also not; she learned from Magda how to drink the taste of a finger in one's mouth. They were in a place without pity, all pity was annihilated in Rosa, she looked at Stella's bones without pity. She was sure that Stella was waiting for Magda to die so she could put her teeth into the little thighs.

Rosa knew Magda was going to die very soon; she should have been dead already, but she had been buried away deep inside the magic shawl, mistaken there for the shivering mound of Rosa's breasts; Rosa clung to the shawl as if it covered only herself. No one took it away from her. Magda was mute. She never cried. Rosa hid her in the barracks, under the shawl, but she knew that one day someone would inform; or one day someone, not even Stella, would steal Magda to eat her. When Magda began to walk Rosa knew that Magda was going to die very soon, something would happen. She was afraid to fall asleep; she slept with the weight of her thigh on Magda's body; she was afraid she would smother Magda under her thigh. The weight of Rosa was becoming less and less; Rosa and Stella were slowly turning into air.

Magda was quiet, but her eyes were horribly alive, like blue tigers. She watched. Sometimes she laughed—it seemed a laugh, but how could it be? Magda had never seen anyone laugh. Still, Magda laughed at her shawl when the wind blew its corners, the bad wind with pieces of black in it, that made Stella's and Rosa's eyes tear. Magda's eyes were always clear and tearless. She watched like a tiger. She guarded her shawl. No one could touch it; only Rosa

1. Literally, the peoples speaking Indo-European languages. The Nazis distorted the term by considering Aryans to be superior to all other racial groups and by referring to those of Teutonic or Germanic background as model Aryan stock. To the Nazis, the typical Aryan was fair-skinned, blue-eyed, and tall.

could touch it. Stella was not allowed. The shawl was Magda's own baby, her pet, her little sister. She tangled herself up in it and sucked on one of the corners when she wanted to be very still.

Then Stella took the shawl away and made Magda die.

Afterward Stella said: "I was cold."

And afterward she was always cold, always. The cold went into her heart: Rosa saw that Stella's heart was cold. Magda flopped onward with her little pencil legs scribbling this way and that, in search of the shawl; the pencils faltered at the barracks opening, where the light began. Rosa saw and pursued. But already Magda was in the square outside the barracks, in the jolly light. It was the roll-call arena. Every morning Rosa had to conceal Magda under the shawl against a wall of the barracks and go out and stand in the arena with Stella and hundreds of others, sometimes for hours, and Magda, deserted, was quiet under the shawl, sucking on her corner. Every day Magda was silent, and so she did not die. Rosa saw that today Magda was going to die, and at the same time a fearful joy ran in Rosa's two palms, her fingers were on fire, she was astonished, febrile: Magda, in the sunlight, swaying on her pencil legs, was howling. Ever since the drying up of Rosa's nipples, ever since Magda's last scream on the road, Magda had been devoid of any syllable; Magda was a mute. Rosa believed that something had gone wrong with her vocal cords, with her windpipe, with the cave of her larynx; Magda was defective, without a voice; perhaps she was deaf; there might be something amiss with her intelligence; Magda was dumb. Even the laugh that came when the ash-stippled wind made a clown out of Magda's shawl was only the air-blown showing of her teeth. Even when the lice, head lice and body lice, crazed her so that she became as wild as one of the big rats that plundered the barracks at daybreak looking for carrion, she rubbed and scratched and kicked and bit and rolled without a whimper. But now Magda's mouth was spilling a long viscous rope of clamor.

"Maaaa—"

It was the first noise Magda had ever sent out from her throat since the drying up of Rosa's nipples.

"Maaaa . . . aaa!"

Again! Magda was wavering in the perilous sunlight of the arena, scribbling on such pitiful little bent shins. Rosa saw. She saw that Magda was grieving for the loss of her shawl, she saw that Magda was going to die. A tide of commands hammered in Rosa's nipples: Fetch, get, bring! But she did not know which to go after first, Magda or the shawl. If she jumped out into the arena to snatch Magda up, the howling would not stop, because Magda would still not have the shawl; but if she ran back into the barracks to find the shawl, and if she found it, and if she came after Magda holding it and shaking it, then she would get Magda back, Magda would put the shawl in her mouth and turn dumb again.

Rosa entered the dark. It was easy to discover the shawl. Stella was heaped under it, asleep in her thin bones. Rosa tore the shawl free and flew— she could fly, she was only air—into the arena. The sunheat murmured of another life, of butterflies in summer. The light was placid, mellow. On the other side of the steel fence, far away, there were green meadows speckled with dandelions and deep-colored violets; beyond them, even farther, inno- cent tiger lilies, tall, lifting their orange bonnets. In the barracks they spoke of "flowers," of "rain": excrement, thick turd-braids, and the slow stinking maroon waterfall that slunk down from the upper bunks, the stink mixed with a bitter fatty floating smoke that greased Rosa's skin. She stood for an instant at the margin of the arena. Sometimes the electricity inside the fence would seem to hum; even Stella said it was only an imag- ining, but Rosa heard real sounds in the wire: grainy sad voices. The farther she was from the fence, the more clearly the voices crowded at her. The la- menting voices strummed so convincingly, so passionately, it was impos- sible to suspect them of being phantoms. The voices told her to hold up the shawl, high; the voices told her to shake it, to whip with it, to unfurl it like a flag. Rosa lifted, shook, whipped, unfurled. Far off, very far, Magda leaned across her air-fed belly, reaching out with the rods of her arms. She was high up, elevated, riding someone's shoulder. But the shoulder that carried Magda was not coming toward Rosa and the shawl, it was drifting away, the speck of Magda was moving more and more into the smoky distance. Above the shoulder a helmet glinted. The light tapped the helmet and sparkled it into a goblet. Below the helmet a black body like a domino and a pair of black boots hurled themselves in the direction of the electrified fence. The electric voices began to chatter wildly. "Maamaa, maaa-maaa," they all hummed together. How far Magda was from Rosa now, across the whole square, past a dozen barracks, all the way on the other side! She was no bigger than a moth.

All at once Magda was swimming through the air. The whole of Magda traveled through loftiness. She looked like a butterfly touching a silver vine. And the moment Magda's feathered round head and her pencil legs and bal- loonish belly and zigzag arms splashed against the fence, the steel voices went mad in their growling, urging Rosa to run and run to the spot where Magda had fallen from her flight against the electrified fence; but of course Rosa did not obey them. She only stood, because if she ran they would shoot, and if she tried to pick up the sticks of Magda's body they would shoot, and if she let the wolf's screech ascending now through the ladder of her skeleton break out, they would shoot; so she took Magda's shawl and filled her own mouth with it, stuffed it in and stuffed it in, until she was swallowing up the wolf's screech and tasting the cinnamon and almond depth of Magda's saliva; and Rosa drank Magda's shawl until it dried.

An Old Acquaintance

In a bus, one summer evening, in Tel Aviv. The sultriness of the day, instead of lessening, leaves behind a heavy stagnant heat which insinuates itself into every pore, weighs on every gesture and breath, blurs every image. People doze on their feet, about to drop into the void. Breathing, even looking, requires immense effort.

We are hardly moving. As we make our way up the principal thoroughfare, Allenby Boulevard, toward the center of town, traffic moves slower and slower and soon it will come to a standstill. Used to this kind of adversity, the passengers demonstrate their wisdom. Some read the newspaper, others chat or scan the advertisements for wines, shaving creams, cigarettes. The driver whistles the latest hit tune. Too bad, I will have to get off at the next stop. I have an appointment. I shall make it faster on foot.

But it is a long way to the next stop. We do not seem to be moving. One bottleneck after another. As if three lanes of cars had broken down. I want to get off: the doors do not open until the bus comes to a complete stop. Useless to argue: the driver's nerves are up to anything. Not mine. Irritated, I curse myself for not having foreseen this. I made a mistake to take the bus. And to think we are in the land of the prophets!

To pass the time I play my favorite game. I pick someone at random and, without his knowing it, establish a mute exchange. Seated across from me is a middle-aged man with a lost look. I examine him thoroughly from head to toe. Easy to classify. Office worker, government clerk, foreman. The anonymous type. Avoiding extremes, responsibilities. He takes orders only to transmit them. Neat, punctual, efficient. He is not at the top of the ladder nor is he at the bottom. Neither rich nor poor, happy or unhappy. He just makes a living. He holds his own. Against everybody.

I put myself in his place: I think and dream like him. I am the one his wife will greet with love or rancor; the one who will drown my resentment in sleep or in solitary drinking; the one my friends betray and my subordinates detest; the one who has wasted my life and now it is too late to begin again.

Caught up in the game, I suddenly realize the passenger looks familiar. I have seen before that bald head, that hard chin, that thin nose. I have seen before that wrinkled forehead, those drooping ears. He turns around to glance outside, I see his neck: red, naked, enormous. I have seen that neck before. A shudder runs through me. It is no longer a matter of curiosity or game. The time changes pace, country. The present is in the grip of all the years black and buried. Now I am glad I accepted the engagement for this evening, and that I decided against going by taxi.

The passenger does not suspect a thing. He has just lost his anonymity, returned to his prison, but he does not know it yet. Now that I have him, I will not let him get away again. What is he thinking about? Probably nothing. Thinking frightens him. Talking frightens him. Memories, words frighten him: that can be read on his lifeless face. This passenger, I am trying to place him, I know him; I used to practice that same defense myself. The best way to keep from attracting the executioner's attention was not to see him. In order not to be noticed, you must murder imagination: dissolve, blend into the frightened mass, reduce yourself to an object. Go under in order to survive. But the man still does not realize my growing interest in him. Were a hundred of us looking him over, he would not notice any the more.

I leave my seat and stand up directly in front of him. I brush up against him, my knees touch his, but his eyes keep their distance. In a very low voice I say: "I think I know you."

He does not hear. He is playing deaf, blind, dead. Just the way I used to do. He is taking refuge in absence, but tenaciously I track him. I repeat my sentence. Slowly, warily, he comes to life. He raises his tired eyes toward me.

"Were you speaking to me?"

"To you."

"You were saying?"

"I think I have met you somewhere before."

He shrugs his shoulders. "You're mistaken, I don't know you."

The bus starts up, then stops again. I lean over the passenger, who is pretending to ignore me, as if the incident were closed. I admire him: he acts well, he does not even blink. We are so close to one another that our breaths mingle, a drop of my sweat falls onto his shirt. He still does not react. If I were to slap him, he would say nothing. A matter of habit, of discipline. The lesson: conceal pain, because it excites the executioner much more than it appeases him. With me, this technique will not be of any help to him: I know the routine.

"You're not from around here," I say.

"Leave me alone."

"You're from somewhere else. From Europe."

"You're disturbing me. I'd appreciate it if you would stop pestering me."

"But you interest me."

"Too bad. You don't interest me at all. I haven't the slightest desire to talk or listen to you. Go back to your seat before I get angry. You hear me? Beat it!"

The tone of his voice startles me. For an instant, our glances meet. Nothing more is needed: I see myself twenty years ago, a tin plate in my hand, before this all-powerful master who was distributing the evening soup to a pack of starved corpses. My humiliation gives way to a somber joy which I can scarcely contain. According to the Talmud, only the mountains never meet: for the men who climb them, no circle is closed, no experience unique, no loss of memory definitive.

"I have some questions to ask you," I say.

"I don't give a damn about you or your questions."

"Where were you during the war?"

"That's none of your business."

"In Europe—right?"

"Leave me alone."

"In an occupied country, right?"

"Stop annoying me."

"In Germany perhaps?"

The bus stops at last at a station and the man takes advantage of the opportunity: he leaps up and rushes toward the exit; I follow him.

"How odd, we're getting off at the same place."

He steps back quickly to let me pass. "I made a mistake, my stop is further on."

I too pretend to step down and immediately turn back. "How odd, so is mine."

We remain standing near the door. Two women have already taken our places.

"May I go on with our conversation?"

"I don't know who you are or what you could want of me," he says, his teeth clenched. "Your questions are uncalled for, your manners disagreeable and out of place. I don't know what game you're playing, but I refuse any part of it. You do not amuse me."

"You don't remember me. It is understandable. I've changed, I've grown up, I've gained weight, I'm better dressed, I feel well, I walk without fear of collapsing, I lack neither food nor friendship. What about you? How do you feel? Answer me, it interests me. Well, what do you say? No insomnia at night, no pangs of anxiety in the morning?"

Once again he takes shelter behind a mask of indifference, a state of nonbeing. He thinks himself secure, unattackable. But I pursue him relentlessly:

"Let's start again, shall we? We've established your place of residence during the war: somewhere in Germany. Where, exactly? In a camp. Naturally. With other Jews. You are Jewish, aren't you?"

He answers me with lips so thin they are almost nonexistent, in a tone which still has lost nothing of its assurance:

"Go to hell, I tell you. Shut up. There's a limit to my patience. I would not like to cause a scene, but if you force me. . . ."

I pay no attention to his threat. I know he will do nothing, he will not complain, he will not use his fists, not he, not here, not in public: he is more afraid than I of the police. So I proceed:

"What camp were you in? Come on, help me, it's important. Let's see: Buchenwald? No, Maidanek? No, not there either. Bergen-Belsen? Treblinka? Ponar? No, no. Auschwitz? Yes? Yes, Auschwitz.[1] More precisely, in a camp which was part of Auschwitz, Javischowitz? Gleivitz? Monovitz? Yes, that's it—there we are—Monovitz-Buna. Or am I mistaken?"

He performs well, he knows his lesson thoroughly. Not a shiver, not the slightest reaction. As if I weren't speaking to him, as if my questions were addressed to someone else, dead a long time. Still, his efforts not to betray himself are becoming visible now. He controls his hands poorly, clasping and unclasping them; clenching his fingers which he hides behind his back.

"Let's get down to specifics. What did you do there? You weren't just a simple inmate? Not you. You are one of those who knew neither hunger nor weariness nor sickness. You are not one of those who lived in expectation of death, hoping it would not be too long in coming so that they could still die like men and not like unwanted beasts—unwanted even by death itself. Not you, you were head of a barracks, you had jurisdiction over the life and death of hundreds of human beings who never dared watch as you ate the dishes prepared specially for you. It was a sin, a crime of high treason, to catch you unawares during one of your meals. And what about now? Tell me, do you eat well? With appetite?"

He moistens his lips with his tongue. An almost imperceptible sigh escapes him. He has to redouble his efforts not to answer, not to take up the challenge. His muscles stiffen, he will not hold out much longer. The trap is closing on him, he is beginning to understand that.

"What about the barracks number? The seat of your kingdom? Do you remember it? Fifty-seven. Barracks fifty-seven. It was right in the center of

1. Buchenwald was one of the first major Nazi concentration camps, opened in 1937 near Weimar, Germany. Maidanek was a Nazi camp and killing center opened for men and women near Lublin in eastern Poland in late 1941. Bergen-Belsen opened in 1940 as a prisoner-of-war camp and by March 1944 was a concentration camp. Treblinka, opened in July 1942, was the largest of the killing centers. Treblinka was destroyed in a prisoners' revolt on August 2, 1943. Ponar, a wooded area six miles from Vilna, was used by the Nazis for the mass shooting of Jews and Soviet POWs.

the camp, two steps away from the gallows. I've a good memory, haven't I? And you? Is your memory still alive? Or did it bury us all a second time?"

The conductor announces a stop; the barracks-chief does not move: it seems all the same to him. The door opens, a couple gets off, a young mother gets on pushing her little boy in front of her. The driver calls out, "Hey, lady, you owe me a *groosh* or a smile!" She gives him both. We start off again. My prisoner no longer notices: he has lost touch with reality. Outside is the city, so close, so unreal, the city with its lights and its sounds, its joys, its laughter, its hates, its furies, its futile intrigues; outside is freedom, forgetfulness if not forgiveness. At the next stop the prisoner could take flight. He will not, I am sure. He prefers to let me act, decide for him. I know what he is feeling: a mixture of fear, resignation, and also relief. He too has returned to the world of barbed wire: as in the past, he prefers anything whatsoever to the unknown. Here, in the bus, he knows what places him in jeopardy and that reassures him: he knows my face, my voice. To provoke a break would be to choose a danger the nature of which escapes him. In the camp, we settled into a situation this way and for as long as possible did anything to keep from changing it. We dreaded disturbances, surprises. Thus, with me, the accused knows where he stands: I speak to him without hate, almost without anger. In the street, the throng might not be so understanding. The country is bursting with former deportees who refuse to reason.

"Look at me. Do you remember me?"

He does not answer. Impassive, unyielding, he continues to look into the emptiness above the heads of the passengers, but I know his eyes and mine are seeing the same emaciated, exhausted bodies, the same lighted yard, the same scaffold.

"I was in your barracks. I used to tremble before you. You were the ally of evil, of hunger, of cruelty. I used to curse you."

He still does not flinch. The law of the camp: make yourself invisible behind your own death mask. I whisper: "My father was also in your barracks. But he didn't curse you."

Outside, the traffic starts to move, the driver picks up speed. Soon he will shout, "Last stop, everybody off!" I have passed my stop, no matter. The appointment no longer seems important. What am I going to do with my prisoner? Hand him over to the police? "Collaboration" is a crime punishable by law. Let someone else finish the interrogation. I shall appear as a witness for the prosecution. I have already attended several trials of this kind: a former Kapo, a former member of the *Judenrat,* a former ghetto policeman—all accused of having survived by choosing cowardice.

PROSECUTION: "You have rejected your people, betrayed your brothers, given aid to the enemy."

DEFENSE: "We didn't know, we couldn't foresee what would happen. We thought we were doing the right thing, especially at the beginning; we hoped to alleviate the suffering of the community, especially during the first weeks. But then it was too late, we no longer had a choice, we couldn't simply go back and declare ourselves victim among victims."

PROSECUTION: "In the Ghetto of Krilov, the Germans named a certain Ephraim to the post of president of the Jewish council. One day they demanded he submit a list of thirty persons for slave labor. He presented it to them with the same name written thirty times: his own. But you, to save your skin, you sold your soul."

DEFENSE: "Neither was worth very much. In the end, suffering shrinks them and obliterates them, not together but separately: there is a split on every level. Body and mind, heart and soul, take different directions; in this way, people die a dozen deaths even before resigning themselves or accepting a bargain with the devil, which is also a way of dying. I beg of you, therefore: do not judge the dead."

PROSECUTION: "You are forgetting the others, the innocent, those who refused the bargain. Not to condemn the cowards is to wrong those whom they abandoned and sometimes sacrificed."

DEFENSE: "To judge without understanding is a power, not a virtue. You must understand that the accused, more alone and therefore more unhappy than the others, are also victims; more than the others, they need your indulgence, your generosity."

I often left the courtroom depressed, disheartened, wavering between pity and shame. The prosecutor told the truth, so did the defense. Whether for the prosecution or for the defense, all witnesses were right. The verdict sounded just and yet a flagrant injustice emerged from these confused and painful trials; one had the impression that no one had told the truth, that the truth lay somewhere else—with the dead. And who knows if the truth did not die with them. I often used to think: "Luckily, I am witness and not judge: I would condemn myself." Now I have become judge. Without wanting it, without expecting it. That is the trap: I am at the point where I cannot go back. I must pass sentence. From now on, whatever my attitude may be, it will have the weight of a verdict.

The smell of the sea rises to my nostrils, I hear the whisper of the waves, we are leaving the center of the city and its lights. We are coming to the end of the line. I must hurry and make a decision, try my former barracks-chief. I will take on all the roles: first, the witnesses, then the judge, then the attorney for the defense. Will the prisoner play only one role, the accused—the victim? Full powers will be conferred upon me, my sentence will be without appeal. Facing the accused, I will be God.

Let us begin at the beginning. With the customary questions. Last name, first name, occupation, age, address. The accused does not recognize the legitimacy of this procedure, or of the court; he refuses to take part in the trial. It is noted. His crimes are what interest us, not his identity. Let us open the dossier, examine the charges leveled against him. Once again I see the scene of the crime, the uniform face of suffering; I hear the sound of the whip on emaciated bodies. At night, surrounded by his sturdy protégés, the accused shows he is skilled in doing two things at once: with one hand he distributes the soup, with the other he beats the inmates to impose silence. Whether the tears and moaning touch him or irritate him does not matter. He hits harder to make them stop. The sight of the sick enrages him: he senses in them a bad omen for himself. He is particularly cruel with the aged: "Why are you hanging on to this disgusting, filthy life? Hurry up and die, you won't suffer anymore! Give your bread to the young, at least do one good deed before you croak!"

One day he saw my father and me near the barracks. As he always did, my father was handing me his half-full bowl and ordering me to eat. "I'm not hungry anymore," he explained and I knew he was lying. I refused: "Me neither, Father, really, I'm not hungry anymore." I was lying and he knew it, too. This same discussion went on day after day. This time the barracks-chief came over and turned to my father: "This your son?"—Yes.—"And you aren't ashamed to take away his soup?"—But . . . —"Shut up! Give him back that bowl or I'll teach you a lesson you won't soon forget!"

To keep him from carrying out that threat, I grabbed the bowl and started eating. At first I wanted to vomit but soon I felt an immense well-being spread through my limbs. I ate slowly to make this pleasure, stronger than my shame, last longer. Finally, the barracks-chief moved on. I hated him, and yet, down deep, I was glad that he had intervened. My father murmured, "He's a good man, charitable." He was lying, and I lied too: "Yes, Father, charitable."

How do you plead: guilty or not guilty?

My father did not conceal his pride: his son had obeyed him. As in the past. Even better than in the past. So there was, in the camp, in the midst of this organized insanity, someone who depended on him and in whose eyes he was not a servile rag. He did not realize that it had not been his will I had been performing, but yours. I was aware of that, and so were you, but I refused to think of it; you did not. I also knew that by obeying you both as your slave and your accomplice, I was cutting short my father's life by one breath, by one awakening. I buried my remorse in the yellowish soup. But you were wiser and certainly shrewder than my father; you were not deceived. As you moved away, you had an air of assurance, as if to say: "That's the way it is, that's life, the boy will learn, he'll find his way and who knows? someday maybe he'll succeed me." And I did not give the soup back to my father. I did not hurl myself at you and tear from you your eyes and your tongue and your victory. Yes, I was afraid, I was a coward. And hunger was gnawing at me: that's what you had counted on. And you won.

Has the accused anything to say in his defense?

You always won, and sometimes, at night, I thought that maybe you were the one who was right. For us, you were not just the whip or the ax in the murderer's hand: you were the prince who played the game of death, you were its prophet, its spokesman. You alone knew how to interpret the rages of the executioner, the silences of the earth; you were the guide to follow; whoever imitated you, lived; the others would perish. Your truth was the only valid truth, the only truth possible, the only truth that conformed to the wishes and designs of the gods.

Guilty or not guilty?

Instead of rejoining the ranks of the victims, of suffering like us and with us, instead of weeping without tears and trembling before the incandescent clouds, instead of dying like us and with us, perhaps even for us, you chose to reign over the work of darkness, proclaiming to whomever wanted to hear that pity was criminal, generosity fruitless, senseless, inhumane. One day after the roll-call you gave us a long lecture on the philosophy of the concentration camp: every man for himself, every man the enemy of the next man, for each lived at the other's expense. And you concluded: "What I am telling you is true and immutable. For know that God has descended from heaven and decided to make himself visible: I am God."

How do you plead?

The judge hears the stifled moans of the witnesses, living and dead; he sees the accused beat up one old man who was too slow in taking off his cap, and another because he did not like his face. "You, you look healthy to me," says the accused, and punches him in the stomach. "And you, you look sick to me, you're pale," and he slaps his face. Itzik has a heavy shirt: the accused takes it away from him. Itzik protests and he is already writhing in pain. Izso has held onto his old shoes: the accused claims them. Izso, clever, hands them over without saying a word. The accused takes them with a contemptuous smile: look at this imbecile, he does not even resist, he does not deserve to live.

Well, then? Guilty or not guilty?

And what if everything could be done over again? What are you now compared to what you were then? Tell us about your repentance, your expiation. What do you tell your wife when she offers you her pride, when she speaks of the future of your children? What do you see in the eyes of the passerby who says to you "good morning," "good evening," and "*shalom,*" "peace be with you"?

"Well?" yells the driver. "How many times do I have to tell you we're here?"

He looks at us in his rear-view mirror, shouts louder. Our inertia is too much for him. He turns around in his seat and shouts again: "Boy, you must be deaf! Don't you understand Hebrew?"

My prisoner pretends not to understand any language. He sleeps, he dreams, transported somewhere else, in another time, the end of another line. He is waiting for me to make the first move, to break the curse that separates us from other men. As in the past with his masters, he will follow, he will obey.

The driver is getting angry. These two speechless and immobile phantoms apparently want to spend the night in his bus. Do they think they are in a hotel? He gets up, grumbling, "I'll show you, you'll see." He moves toward us, looking furious. My prisoner waits for him without flinching, indifferent to whatever may happen. I touch his arm.

"Come on, let's go."

He complies mechanically. Once down, he stands stationary, and wisely waits for me on the sidewalk. He could make a dash for the dark little streets that lead to the ocean. He does not. His will has defaulted. He is not about to upset the order of things, to speculate on an uncertain future. Above all, no initiative, that was the golden rule at camp.

The bus starts up and leaves: here we are alone. I have nothing more to say to him. A vague feeling of embarrassment comes over me, as if I had just done something foolish. All of a sudden, I become timid again. And in a weak voice I ask him: "You really don't remember me?"

In the darkness I can no longer make out his face. I no longer recognize him. Doubt chokes me: and what if it was not he?

"No," he says, after a long silence, "I don't remember you."

I no longer recognize the sound of his voice. It used to be gruff, cutting. It has become clear, humane.

"And yourself? Do you remember who you were?"

"That is my business."

"No. It is my business, too."

I suddenly think I must put an end to this: but how? If he whimpers and justifies himself and begs my forgiveness, I will have him arrested. And if he keeps on denying everything? What would he have to say for me to let him go? I do not know. It is up to him to know.

Abruptly he stiffens. I know his eyes have regained their coldness, their hardness. He is going to speak. At last. In defending himself he is going to throw all the light on this mystery to which we remain chained forever. I know he will speak without altering the thin line of his lips. At last he is speaking. No: he is shouting. No! he is yelling! Without preparation, without warning. He insults me, he is offensive. Not in Hebrew—in German. We are no longer in Israel but somewhere in the universe of hate. He is the barracks-chief who, his hands clasped behind his back, "advises" one of his slaves to leave at once or he will regret the day he was born. Will he hit me, break my bones, make me eat dirt, as he is threatening to do? No one would come to my aid: in camp it is the strongest and most brutal who is in the right. Is he going to crush me in his claws, murder me? If he does, I will carry his secret with me. Can one die in Auschwitz, after Auschwitz?

The barracks-chief is lecturing me the way he used to and I do not hear what he is saying. His voice engulfs me, I let myself drown in it. I am no longer afraid. Not of dying nor even of killing. It is something else, something worse. I am suddenly aware of my impotence, of my defeat. I know I am going to let him go free, but I will never know if I am doing this out of courage or out of cowardice. I will never know if, face to face with the executioner, I behaved like a judge or a victim. But I will have acquired the certitude that the man who measures himself against the reality of evil always emerges beaten and humiliated. If someday I encounter the Angel of Death himself in my path, I will not kill him, I will not torture him. On the contrary. I will speak to him politely, as humanely as possible. I will try to understand him, to divine his evil; even at the risk of being contaminated.

The barracks-chief is shouting obscenities and threats; I do not listen. I stare at him one last time without managing to distinguish his features in the night. My hands in my pockets, I turn around and begin to walk, slowly at first, then faster and faster, until I am running. Is he following me?

He let me go. He granted me freedom.

A Plaque on Via Mazzini

Et j'ai vu quelquefois ce que
l'homme a cru voir. [1]

Rimbaud

I

In August 1945, when Geo Josz reappeared in Ferrara, sole survivor of the hundred and eighty-three members of the Jewish Community whom the Germans had deported in the autumn of '43 and whom most people not without reason considered long since exterminated in the gas chambers, at first nobody in the city recognized him.

They didn't remember who he was, to tell the truth. Unless, some added in a dubious tone, unless he could be a son of that Angelo Josz, well-known cloth wholesaler, who though exempted for patriotic reasons (these were the terms of the decree of '39; and after all it had been only human, on the part of the late Consul Bolognesi, at that time already the Fascist Party Secretary of Ferrara and always a good friend of old Josz, to adopt, in memory of their common enterprises with the Fascist squads of their youth, a language that was so generic) had been unable, despite this distinction, to keep himself and his family out of the great roundup of Jews in '43.

Yes, one of those withdrawn young people, they began to recall, pursing their lips and frowning, no more than ten in all, who after '38 had perforce broken off all relations with their former schoolmates and had also, in consequence, stopped visiting their homes, and had been seen about only rarely, growing up with strange faces, frightened, wild, contemptuous, so that when people saw them every now and then, rushing off, bent over the handlebars of a bicycle, speeding along Corso Giovecca or Corso Roma, they became upset and preferred to forget about them.

But apart from that: in this man of indefinable age, so fat he seemed swollen, with an old lambskin hat on his shaven head, wearing a kind of sampler of all the known and unknown uniforms of the time, who could have recognized the frail boy of seven years ago, or the nervous, thin, shy adolescent of four years later? And if a Geo Josz had ever been born and had existed, if he too, as he asserted, had belonged to that band of a hundred and eighty-three

---

1. "What man has imagined, I have witnessed." From the poem "The Drunken Boat" (1871) by French poet Arthur Rimbaud.

shadows devoured by Buchenwald, Auschwitz, Mauthausen, Dachau, etc.;[2] was it possible that he, only he, should come back from there now, and present himself, oddly dressed, true, but very much alive, to tell about himself and about the others who hadn't come back and would never, surely, come back again? After all this time, after so much suffering which all had more or less shared, without distinction of political belief, social position, religion or race, what did he want, Geo, at this moment? Even Signor Cohen the engineer, the President of the Jewish Community, who had insisted on dedicating, the moment he got back from Switzerland, in memory of the victims, a large marble plaque which now stood out, rigid, enormous, brand-new, on the red brick façade of the Temple (and then the plaque had to be done over, naturally, to the satisfaction of those who had reproached Signor Cohen for his commemorative haste, since dirty linen—as love of Fatherland teaches us—can always be washed without causing scandal), even he, at first, had raised a host of objections; in short, he wanted nothing to do with it.

But we must proceed in an orderly fashion; and before going any further, we must linger for a moment on the episode of the plaque set in the façade of the Temple thanks to Signor Cohen's rash initiative: an episode which is, properly speaking, the beginning of the story of Geo Josz's return to Ferrara.

To tell it now, the scene might appear scarcely credible. And, to doubt it, you have only to picture it taking place against the background—so normal, so familiar to us—of Via Mazzini (not even the war touched the street: as if to signify that nothing, ever, can happen there!): the street, that is, which from Piazza delle Erbe, flanking the old ghetto—with the Oratorio of San Maurelio at the beginning, the narrow fissure of Via Vittoria at the halfway point, the red brick façade of the Temple a bit farther on, and the double line of its hundred warehouses and shops, each harboring, in the semidarkness steeped in odors, a cautious little soul, imbued with mercantile skepticism and irony—connects the winding, decrepit little streets of Ferrara's medieval core with the splendid Renaissance avenues, so damaged by bombardments, and the modern section of the city.

Immersed in the glare and silence of the August afternoon, a silence interrupted at long intervals by the echoes of distant shooting, Via Mazzini lay empty, deserted, intact. And so it had appeared also to the young workman wearing a paper hat, who at half past one, climbing onto a little scaffold, had

2. Mauthausen was a concentration camp for male prisoners near Linz in Austria opened by the Nazis in August 1943. Dachau was the first and largest Nazi concentration camp; it was established in March 1933 near Munich, Germany.

started working on the marble slab that they had given him to put in place, six feet from the ground, against the dusty bricks of the synagogue. His presence there, a peasant forced to the city by the war and obliged to turn himself into a mason (he was slowly filled by the sense of his own solitude and by a vague fear, because this was a commemorative plaque, surely; but he had taken good care not to read what was written on it!), had been erased from the beginning by the light, and he was unable to cancel the deserted quality of the place and the hour. Nor had it been canceled, this emptiness, by the little group of passers-by who, gathering later, apparently without his being aware of them, had come gradually to cover, in their various attitudes and colors, a good part of the cobbled pavement behind his back.

The first to stop were two youths: two bearded, bespectacled partisans, with knee-length shorts, red kerchiefs tied around their throats, automatic rifles slung over their shoulders: students, young gentlemen of the city, the young mason-peasant had thought, hearing them speak and turning slightly just to glance at them. A little later they were joined by a priest, unperturbed despite the heat, wearing his black cassock, but with its sleeves rolled up— he had a strange, battlelike manner, as if defiant—over his hairy white forearms. And then, afterward, a civilian, a man of sixty with a grizzled beard, an excited manner, his shirt open over his scrawny chest and his bobbing Adam's apple: this man, after beginning to read in a low voice what was presumably written on the plaque (and this was names and names; but not all Italian, or so it seemed), had broken off at a certain point to cry, emphatically: "A hundred and eighty-three out of four hundred!" as if he too, Aristide Podetti of Bosco Mesola, by chance in Ferrara, where he had no intention of staying longer than strictly necessary, a man who stuck to his work and nothing else, could be stirred by those names and those numbers to unknown memories, as if they aroused unknown emotions in him. What did it matter, to him, whose names those were and why they had been carved in marble? The remarks of the people who had instead been attracted precisely by them, and who were becoming more and more numerous, made a tiresome buzzing in the mason's ears. Jews, yes, all right, a hundred and eighty-three out of four hundred. A hundred and eighty-three out of the four hundred who lived in Ferrara before the war. But what were they, after all, these Jews? What did they mean, they and the *others*, the Fascists, by that word? Ah, the Fascists! From his very village, in the Po plain, which in the winter of '44 they had made a kind of headquarters, they had sown terror through the countryside for months and months. The people called them *tupin*, mice, because of the color of their shirts; and exactly like mice, when the time had come for settling scores, they quickly found holes to hide in. They stayed hidden, now. But who could guarantee they wouldn't come back? Who could swear they weren't still walking around the streets, also wearing red kerchiefs at their throats, waiting for the moment of revenge? At the right moment, as quickly as they had hidden, they would jump out again with their black shirts, their death's-heads; and then, the less a man knew, the better off he was.

And he, the poor boy, was so determined not to know anything, because all he needed was work, nothing else interested him; so unaware and distrustful of everything and everybody, as, locked in his rough dialect of the Po delta, he turned his stubborn back to the sun, that when, all of a sudden, he felt a light touch on his ankle ("Geo Josz?" a mocking voice said at the same time) he wheeled around promptly with a nasty look.

A short, square man, with a strange fur hat on his head, stood before him. Raising his arm, the man pointed to the plaque behind the boy's shoulders. How fat he was! He seemed swollen with water, like a drowned man. And there was nothing to be afraid of; because he was laughing, surely to make himself agreeable.

"Geo Josz?" the man repeated, still pointing to the plaque, but now serious.

He laughed again. But at once, as if repentant, and dotting his words frequently with "please" like the Germans (he spoke with the polish of a gifted salon conversationalist; and Aristide Podetti, since he was the one being addressed, listened openmouthed), he declared that he was sorry, "believe me," to spoil everything with his interruption, which, as he was ready to admit, bore all the earmarks of a *faux pas*. Ah, yes, he sighed, the plaque would have to be done over again, since that Geo Josz, to whom it was partly dedicated, was none other than himself, in person. Unless (and, saying this, his pale blue eyes looked around, as if to seize an image of the Via Mazzini from which the little crowd, surrounding him, holding its breath, was excluded; not a head, meanwhile, had peered out of the many shops nearby), unless the Committee which sponsored the commemoration, accepting this event as a hint from fate, were to give up entirely the idea of the memorial plaque: which, he sneered, though it offered the unquestionable advantage of being set in that place where there was so much traffic that it had to be read almost perforce ("You aren't bearing in mind the dust, however, my dear friend; in a few years no one will notice it any more!"), had also the serious defect of unsuitably altering the straightforward, homely façade of "our dear old Temple": one of the few things, including also Via Mazzini—which the war, thank God, had spared completely, and which had remained exactly as "before"—the few things on which (". . . yes, dear friend, I mean this for you also, though I imagine you are not Jewish . . .") one could still count.

"It's a bit as if you—for example—were obliged with that face, with those hands, to put on a dinner jacket."

And, at the same time, he displayed his own hands, calloused beyond all belief, but with white backs where a registration number, tattooed a bit above the right wrist in the skin so flabby it seemed boiled, could be read distinctly, all five numbers, preceded by the letter *J*.

II

And so, with a look that was not menacing but rather ironic and amused (his eyes, a watery blue, peered up coldly from below, as if he were emerging, pale and swollen as he was, from the depths of the sea), Geo Josz reappeared in Ferrara, among us.

He came from afar, from much farther than the place he actually had come from! And to find himself again suddenly here, in the city where he had been born. . . .

Things had gone more or less like this:

The military truck, on which he had been able to travel in a few hours from the Brenner Pass to the Po Valley, after driving off the ferry at Pontelagoscuro had slowly climbed up the right bank of the river. And then, having reached the top, after a final, almost reluctant jolt, it offered to his gaze the immense, forgotten plain of his childhood and adolescence. Down there, a bit to the left, should lie Ferrara. But was Ferrara, he had asked himself, and had asked, also, the driver sitting at his side—was Ferrara that dark polygon of dusty stone, reduced, except for the Castle's four towers which rose airy and unreal in the center, to a kind of lugubrious flatiron which weighed, heavy, on the fields? Where were the green, luminous, ancient trees that once rose along the crest of the maimed walls? The truck was rapidly approaching the city, as if, gradually accelerating along the intact asphalt of the straight highway, it were going to plunge on Ferrara from above; and through the wide breaches here and there in the bastions, he could already see the streets, once so familiar, now made unrecognizable by the bombings. Less than two years had gone by since he was taken away. But they were two years that counted for twenty, or two hundred.

He had come back when no one expected him any longer. What did he want, now?

To answer calmly a question like this—with the calm necessary to understand and sympathize with what, at first, had probably been only a simple, if unexpressed, desire to live—perhaps other times, perhaps another city was required.

It required, in any case, people a bit less frightened by those certain gentlemen who set the norm, again as always, for the city's public opinion (there were, in that group, along with some big merchants and landowners, several of the most authoritative professional men of Ferrara: the sinew, in short, of what had been, before the war, our so-called leading class): the people who, having been forced to "support," more or less in a body, the defunct Fascist Social Republic, and who couldn't resign themselves to step down even for a short while, now saw traps, enemies, and even political rivals on all sides. They had accepted Party cards, the infamous card, true. But out of pure civic duty. And, in any case, not before that fatal December 15th of 1943, when fully eleven fellow citizens had been shot at once, the date which had marked the beginning, in Italy, of the never sufficiently deplored "fratricidal struggle." Riddled with bullets across the street from the portico of the Caffè della Borsa, they had lain for a whole day, guarded by troops with guns at the ready; and the others had seen them, with their own eyes, the bodies of those "poor wretches," flung in the filthy snow like so many bundles! And so, continuing in this tone, all caught up as they were in their effort to convince others and themselves that, though they may have erred, they had erred more from generosity than fear (for this reason, having removed all other badges, they began to appear with every possible military decoration stuck in the buttonhole of their jacket), they surely couldn't be considered the ideal sort to recognize in others that simplicity and normality of intentions, that famous "purity" of action and ideas which, in themselves, they were unable to give up. As for the specific case of the man in the old fur hat: even assuming he was Geo Josz—and they weren't entirely convinced of that, however—assuming he was, he still could not be trusted. That fat of his, all that fat made them suspicious. Oh yes, starvation edema! But who besides Geo could have started such a story circulating, in a clumsy attempt to justify a corpulence in singular contradiction to what was said about German concentration camps? Starvation edema didn't exist, it was an outright invention. And Geo's fat meant two things: either in those *Lagers* one didn't suffer the great hunger that propaganda insisted on, or else Geo had enjoyed conditions of special favor there. One thing was sure: under that fur hat, behind that lip curled in a perpetual smile, there was room, they would have sworn, only for hostile thoughts and plans.

And what of the others—a minority, to tell the truth—who remained shut up in their houses, ears alert to the slightest noise from outside, the very image of fear and hate?

Among the latter there was the man who had offered to preside, a tricolor-sash across his chest, at the public auction of the Jewish Community's confiscated possessions, including the silver chandeliers of the Temple and the ancient vellum Scriptures; and those who, pulling black caps with the Brigade's death's-head over their white hair, had been members of the special tribunal responsible for various executions: almost always respectable people, for that matter, who perhaps before then had never shown any sign of being interested in politics, and who, in the majority of cases, had led a largely retired life, devoted to the family, to their profession, their studies. . . . But they feared greatly for themselves, these people; they had, on their own account, such a fear of dying that even if Geo Josz had wanted only to live (and this was the least, really, that he could want)—well, even in such a simple and elementary request, they would have found some personal threat. The thought that one of them, any night of the week, could be seized quietly by the "reds" and carried off to be slaughtered in some unknown place in the country: this terrifying thought returned, constantly, to drive them mad with anxiety. To live, to stay alive, no matter how! It was a violent demand, exclusive, desperate.

If at least that man in the fur hat, "that wreck," would make up his mind to leave Ferrara!

Unconcerned that the partisans, having taken over the command post of the Black Brigade,[3] were using the house on Via Campofranco, his father's property, as their barracks and prison, he was clearly content, on the other hand, to carry around that obsessive, ill-omened face of his: surely to add new fuel to the wrath of those who would make it their business to avenge him and all his people. The greatest scandal, in any case, was that the new authorities put up with such a state of things. It was no good appealing to the Prefect, Doctor Herzen, installed in office just after the "so-called" Liberation, by the same National Committee of Liberation of which, after the events of December '43, he had been the underground President, if it was true, and it was, that they compiled black lists every evening in his office, in the Castle. Ah yes, they knew him well, they did, that character who in '39 had allowed his property to be confiscated, almost smiling at the loss of the big shoe factory he owned at the gates of the city, and whose possession now, if Allied bombers hadn't reduced it to rubble, he would surely demand again! A man of about forty, bald, tortoise-shell spectacles, he had the typically peaceful and inoffensive look (except for the "Jewish" name, Herzen, and the stiff, inflexible back which seemed fastened to the seat of his inseparable bicycle) of all those who are seriously to be feared. What about the Archbishopric? And the English military government? Was it, unfortunately, a sign of the times that even from these offices no better answer came than a sigh of desolate solidarity or, worse, a mocking grin?

3. Band of men in the Fascist party, not in the military service. With little military experience, they were bandits who robbed, raped, and murdered civilians at will. They were feared by Jews and antifascists.

There's no reasoning with fear and hate. For if they had wanted, getting back to Geo Josz himself, to understand something of what was really going on in his spirit, they had only to begin, after all, with his extraordinary reappearance in Ferrara; and specially with the sequel of that singular scene which, just by the entrance to the Temple on Via Mazzini, at a certain point had led him to extend his hands, not without sarcasm, to a young mason's stunned examination.

Perhaps the man of sixty, with the sparse grizzled beard, will recall it, he who was among the first to stop before the marble slab, the memorial plaque desired by Signor Cohen, the man who at a given moment had raised his shrill voice ("A hundred and eighty-three out of four hundred!" he had shouted proudly) to remark on its content.

Well, after silently following with the others what happened in the next minutes, when he pushed his way awkwardly through the little crowd and fell on the neck of the man in the fur hat, kissing him noisily on the cheeks and showing that, first of all, he had recognized in him Geo Josz, the latter, his hands still outstretched, remarked coldly: "With that ridiculous beard, dear Uncle Daniele, I hardly knew you"—a remark that was truly revealing, not only of the kinship between him and one of the city's surviving representatives of the Josz family (a brother of his father's, to be precise, who having miraculously eluded the great roundup of November '43 had returned to the city the end of last April), but also the deep, sharp intolerance that he, Geo, felt for any sign that spoke to him, in Ferrara, of the passage of time and of the changes, even the tiny ones, that it had wrought in things.

And so he asked: "Why the beard?"

"Do you think perhaps that beard is becoming?"

It honestly seemed he could think of nothing but observing, with critical eye, all the beards of various form and shape that the war, and the notorious forged papers, had caused to become common usage; and this was his way, since he could hardly be called a talkative type, of expressing his disagreement.

In what had been before the war the Josz house, where uncle and nephew appeared that same afternoon, there were, naturally, plenty of beards; and the little, low, red-stone building surmounted by a slender Ghibelline tower, so long that it covered almost a whole side of the brief and secluded Via Campofranco, assumed a military, feudal air, perhaps suitable for evoking the ancient lords of the palace, the Marquesses Del Sale, from whom Angelo Josz had bought it in 1910 for a few thousand lire, but it hardly evoked Angelo, the Jewish cloth wholesaler who had vanished with his wife and children in the ovens of Buchenwald.

The main door was wide open. Outside, seated on the steps of the entrance with guns between their bare legs, or lying on the seats of a jeep pulled up by the high wall that, opposite, separated Via Campofranco from a vast private garden, about a dozen partisans were loafing. But others, in greater numbers, some with voluminous files under their arms, and all with faces marked by energy and resolution, came and went constantly despite the sultry air of the late afternoon. And so, between the street half in shadow and half in the sun and the breached door of the old aristocratic palazzo, there was an intense bustle, lively, gay, in perfect harmony with the cries of the swallows that dipped low, grazing the cobbles, and with the typewriters' clicking that came steadily through the enormous seventeenth-century grilles of the ground floor.

The strange couple—one tall, thin, perky, the other fat, slow, sweating— came in the door then, and immediately attracted the attention of those present: mostly armed men, generally with long hair and flowing beards, sitting, waiting on the rough benches set along the walls. They gathered around; and Daniele Josz, who evidently wanted to demonstrate to his nephew his own familiarity with this environment, was already willingly answering their questions, for himself and for his companion.

But he, Geo, examined, one by one, those tanned, flushed faces that pressed around him, as if through the beards he wanted to investigate some secret, some hidden corruption.

Ah, you can't fool me! his smile said.

He seemed reassured only for a moment, discovering that beyond the gate of the portico, right in the center of the bare little garden that stretched beyond, there still shone, dark and flourishing, a large magnolia. But not sufficiently reassured to prevent him, a little later, upstairs, in the office of the young Provincial Secretary of the Partisans Association (the same man who two years later was to become the most brilliant Communist member of the Italian Parliament, so polite, reserved, and reassuring that he made not a few of our most worthy *meres de famille* sigh with regret, since he also belonged to one of the finest middle-class families of Ferrara, the Bottecchiaris, and, what's more, was a bachelor) from repeating his now time-worn remark:

"That beard isn't at all becoming to you, do you know that?"

So, in the frozen embarrassment that fell immediately on what until then, thanks entirely to Uncle Daniele, had been a fairly cordial conversation, in the course of which the future Deputy had acted as if he didn't notice the formal *Lei* which Geo on his part had maintained, while the other man insisted on the affectionate *tu* used among those of the same age and the same Party, it was suddenly clear what Geo Josz really wanted, the reason why he was there (and if only those who, on the contrary, were so afraid of him could have been present!). That house where *they*, like the *others*, the blacks, had made their headquarters before them, was his, didn't they remember that? By what right had they taken possession of it? He looked threateningly at the typist, who jumped and suddenly left off striking the keys, as if he meant to tell even her, especially her, that he wouldn't be at all satisfied with a single room, even if it were this one, so handsome and sunny—once a salon for receiving, of course, even if the parquet had been torn from the floor probably for fire-wood—which was nice and comfortable, wasn't it, from dawn to dusk, and perhaps even after dusk, working with the young partisan commander who seemed so determined, out of the goodness of his heart, to remake the world.

Down in the street they were singing:

The wind is whistling, the tempest screams,
Our shoes have holes, and yet we must march on. . . .

and the song, impetuous and absurd, came through the window, open to the sky, which was a tender, very gentle pink.

But the house was his, they should have no illusions. Sooner or later he would take it back, all of it.

III

This was to happen, in fact, though obviously not at once.

For the moment, Geo seemed to be satisfied with only one room—and it wasn't, of course, the office of Nino Bottecchiari! Instead, it was a kind of attic at the very top of the tower that dominated the house, and to reach it he had to climb at least a hundred steps, then, at the end, some worm-eaten little wooden stairs which led directly from a space below once used as a store-room. It was Geo himself, in the disgusted tone of one resigned to the worst, who first spoke of this "makeshift." As to the storeroom below, that too, he added, would be rather useful, since he could put, as he meant to, his Uncle Daniele there. . . .

But it was soon clear that Geo could follow from that height, through a wide glass window, whatever happened in the garden, on one side, and in Via Campofranco, on the other. And since he hardly ever left the house, presum-ably spending a great part of his day looking at the vast landscape of dark tiles, gardens, and green countryside that stretched out below him (an im-mense view, now that the leafy trees of the city wall were no longer there to cut it off!), for the occupants of the lower floors, his constant presence soon became a troublesome, nagging thought. The cellars of the Josz house, which all opened onto the garden, since the time of the Black Brigade had been transformed into secret prisons, about which many sinister stories had been told in the city even after the Liberation. But now, subjected to the probable, untrustworthy control of the guest in the tower, they no longer served, naturally, those purposes of summary and clandestine justice for which they had been set up. Now, with Geo Josz installed in that sort of observatory, there was no being sure even for a moment, since the kerosene lamp he kept burning all night long—and you could see its faint glow through the panes, up there, until dawn—led everyone to suppose he was always alert, he never slept. It must have been two or three in the morning after the evening Geo first appeared on Via Campofranco, when Nino Bottecchiari, who had stayed working in his office until that hour and was finally about to allow himself some rest, stepping out into the street, happened to raise his eyes to the tower. "Watch yourself!" Geo's lamp warned, suspended in the starry sky. And the young future Deputy was bitterly reproaching himself for guilty carelessness and his acquiescence—but at the same time, as a good politician, preparing to take the new circumstances into account—as he decided, with a sigh, to climb into the jeep.

But it was also possible for him to turn up at any hour of the day, as he soon began to do, from one moment to the next, on the stairs or down in the entrance: passing before the eyes of the partisans permanently gathered there, dressed in his impeccable civilian suit of olive gabardine which had almost immediately replaced the fur hat, the leather jacket, and the tight trousers of his arrival in Ferrara. He walked among the mute partisans without greeting anyone, elegant, perfectly shaven, with the brim of his brown felt turned down at one side of his brow, over a cold, icy eye; and in the vague uneasiness that followed each of his apparitions, he was from the beginning the authoritative landlord of the house: too polite to quarrel, but strong in his right, he needs only to show himself to the vandal tenant in arrears, who has to leave. The tenant grumbles, pretends not to notice the silent, insistent protest of the owner of the building, who for the present is saying nothing though, at the right moment, will surely ask for an accounting of the ruined floors, the stained walls; so, from month to month, the situation worsens, becomes more and more embarrassing and precarious. It was late, after the elections of '48, when so many things in Ferrara had by then changed, or rather had gone back to their prewar state (but meanwhile young Bottecchiari's candidacy for Parliament had had time to be crowned with the most complete success)—it was then that the Partisans Association decided to move its headquarters elsewhere, specifically to three rooms in the former Casa del Fascio on Viale Cavour, where in 1945 the Provincial Labor Council had established its offices. It is true, all the same, that the silent, implacable action of Geo Josz made that move seem long overdue.

He hardly ever left the house, then, as if he wanted them not to forget him there, not even for a moment. But this didn't prevent him from showing up every so often on Via Mazzini, where in September he had arranged for his father's storehouse, in which the Community had collected all it could recover of the possessions confiscated from the Jews during the period of the Fascist Republic, to be cleared out in view of the "more than necessary"—as he said to Signor Cohen in person—"work of restoration and reopening of the business"; or, more rarely, along Corso Giovecca, with the uncertain tread of one advancing in prohibited territory, his spirit torn between the fear of unpleasant encounters and the sharp, conflicting desire for them, joining the evening promenade that had already begun once more, animated and lively as always; or at the apéritif hour, sitting abruptly at a little table—because he arrived each time breathless, dripping sweat—at the Caffè della Borsa on Corso Roma, which had remained the political center of the city. Nor did the ironic, contemptuous attitude habitual with him, which had persuaded even the expansive Uncle Daniele, so electrified by the early postwar atmosphere, to renounce quickly all conversation through the trapdoor above his head, show any signs of being disarmed by the show of cordial welcome, the affectionate cries of "Good to have you back!" which now, after the uncertainty of the first moment, began to be addressed to him from every direction.

People came from the shops near the one that had been his father's and was now his, with the outstretched hand of those offering help and advice or even promising, in a hyperbole of generosity, honest competition forever; or they crossed the Giovecca on purpose, broad as it was, with excessive enthusiasm, made even more hysterical by the fact that, as a rule, they knew him only by name, and they flung their arms around his neck: or else they left the counter of the bar, still immersed in that turbulent darkness where, in the past, every day at 1 P.M. the radio's announcements of defeat had come (announcements that could just reach, as it passed, the fleeting bicycle of the young Geo), to come and sit beside him, under the yellow awning that offered such slight protection from the blinding sun and the dust of the rubble. He had been in Buchenwald and had come back from there, the only one, after having undergone God only knows what physical and moral torments, after having witnessed unknown horrors. And they were there, at his disposal, all ears, ready to listen. He should tell them; and they would never grow tired, prepared to sacrifice, for him, even the dinner to which the Castle clock, with two strokes, was already summoning them. In general these seemed so many pathetic apologies for having delayed recognizing him, for having tried to reject him, to exclude him once again. It was as if, in chorus, they said: "You've changed, you know? A full-grown man, by God, and then, you've put on so much weight! But, you see, we've changed too, time's gone by for us as well. . . .";

and as if to testify to their sincerity, supporting the development, they displayed their trousers of rough canvas, their rolled-up sleeves, the military bush jackets, the collars without ties, the sandals without socks, as well as, naturally, their beards, since nobody was without one now. . . . And they were sincere in submitting themselves, each time, to Geo's examination and judgment, and sincere, afterward, in lamenting his inflexible repulsion: just as, in their way, just about everybody in the city after April of '45—including those who had most to fear from the present and to distrust of the future—was sincere in the conviction that, for better or worse, a new period was about to begin, better in any event than the other, which, like a long slumber filled with atrocious nightmares, was ending in bloodshed.

As for Uncle Daniele, who for three months had been living hand-to-mouth and without a fixed address, the stifling storeroom in the tower had immediately appeared, in his incurable optimism, a marvelous acquisition, and nobody was more convinced than he that, with the end of the war, the happy age of democracy and of universal brotherhood had begun.

"At last we can breathe freely!" he had ventured to say, the first night he had taken possession of his stairwell—and he spoke, lying supine on his straw mattress, his hands clasped behind his head.

"Aah, at last we can breathe freely," he repeated, in a louder voice. And then:

"Don't you feel, too, Geo, that the air in the city is different from what it was before? Things have changed, believe me: inside, in people's bones, not just on the outside. These are the miracles of liberty. For myself, I am profoundly convinced. . . ."

What had profoundly convinced Daniele Josz must have seemed of quite dubious interest to Geo, since the only reply he ever let fall from the aperture toward which the wooden ladder and his uncle's impassioned exclamations rose was an occasional "Hmm!" or a "Really?" which didn't encourage the other man to continue. What can he be doing? the old man would ask himself then, falling silent, as his eyes went to the ceiling, scraped back and forth by a pair of tireless slippers; and he didn't know what to think.

To him, it seemed impossible that Geo didn't share his enthusiasm.

After fleeing Ferrara in the days of the armistice, he had spent almost two years as the guest of some peasants, hidden in a remote village of the Tuscan-Emilian Apennines. And up there, after the death of his wife, who, poor thing, devout as she was, had to be buried under a false name in consecrated ground, he had joined a partisan brigade as political commissar. He had been among the first, tanned and bearded on top of a truck, to enter liberated Ferrara. What unforgettable days! To find the city half destroyed, true, almost unrecognizable, but completely clear of Fascists, of those from *before* and the last-ditch Salò ones[4]—all those faces, in short, many of which Geo should also recall: this, for him, had been such a complete, such an extraordinary joy! To sit calmly at the Caffè della Borsa, which, as soon as he returned, he immediately made the base of his operations in his old, modest activity as an insurance agent, where no frowning eye ordered him to leave but, on the contrary, where he felt the center of universal affection; now, after the fulfillment of such a wish, he was ready even to die. But Geo? Was it possible Geo felt none of all this? Was it possible that, after having descended into hell, and having miraculously risen from it, there was no impulse in him except the desire to evoke the static past, as was demonstrated somehow by the ghastly array of photographs of his dead family (poor Angelo, poor Luce, and little Pietruccio born ten years after Geo, when nobody in the family was expecting him, born to know only violence and anguish and to end at Buchenwald!): the photographs which, one day when he had secretly climbed into the room above, his nephew's room, he had found papering all four walls? Was it possible, finally, that the only beard in the whole city to which Geo had raised no objection was the beard of that old Fascist Geremia Tabet, poor Angelo's brother-in-law, who even after 1938, despite the racial laws and the consequent ostracism imposed against Jews everywhere, had still been able to frequent the Merchants Club for the afternoon bridge, though not officially? The very evening of Geo's return, he, Daniele Josz, had had reluctantly to accompany his nephew to the Tabet house on Via Roversella, where he had never set foot since his return to the city. Well, wasn't it inconceivable, the former political commissar kept repeating to himself, the sixty-year-old ex-partisan, as his nephew, in the room above, never stopped pacing heavily up and down—wasn't it inconceivable that, the minute the Fascist uncle peered out of a second-floor window, Geo should let out a shrill cry, ridiculously, hysterically passionate, almost savage? Why that shout? What did it mean? Did it mean perhaps that the boy, despite Buchenwald and the massacre of all his family, had grown up like his father Angelo, who in his ingenuousness had been to the last, perhaps even to the door of the gas chamber, a "patriot," as he had heard Angelo proclaim himself so many times with foolish pride?

"Who is it?" a worried voice asked, from above.

"It's me, Uncle Geremia; it's Geo!"

They were down below, outside the closed front door of the Tabet house. It was ten o'clock by then, and at the end of the narrow street you couldn't see more than a foot ahead. Geo's cry, Daniele Josz recalled, had made him start with surprise. It had been a kind of strange howl, choked by the most

4. Ones belonging to the Republic of Salo, the new Fascist state established in Italy in September 1943.

violent and inexplicable emotion. Surprise and embarrassment: impossible to say anything. In silence, bumping into each other, stumbling over the steps, they had groped their way, in the most total darkness, up two steep flights of stairs.

Finally, at the top of the stairs, half in and half out of the door, the lawyer Geremia Tabet, wearing his pajamas, had appeared, in person. In his right hand he was holding a little dish, with a candle erect in it, whose wavering light cast vague, greenish glints over the natural pallor of his face, framed by the beard which hadn't even become very gray. As soon as he saw him, he, Daniele Josz, stopped short. It was the first time he had seen him since the end of the war; and if he was there now, on the point of visiting him, he had been induced into it only to please Geo, who, on the contrary, after his examination of the house on Via Campofranco a few hours earlier, seemed to have thoughts only for "Uncle Geremia." Setting the candle on the floor, Lawyer Tabet clasped his nephew to his bosom, in a long embrace; and this sufficed to make the outsider, who had remained on the lower landing to observe the scene, forgotten down there like a stranger, feel once more the poor relation that all of them—his brother Angelo agreeing, in this, with the Tabets—had always avoided and scorned for his "subversive" ideas. He should go away. Go away without a word of good-by. Never set foot in that house again. What a pity he had resisted that temptation! Actually, he had been stopped by a hope, an absurd hope. After all, he had thought, poor Luce, Geo's mother, was a Tabet, Geremia's sister. Perhaps it was only his mother's memory which, at first, kept Geo from behaving toward his maternal uncle with the coldness the old Fascist deserved. . . .

But he had been mistaken, unfortunately, and for the rest of the evening, indeed until late in the night, as Geo seemed never to make up his mind to leave, Daniele had to sit in a corner of the dining room and witness displays of affection and intimacy which were little short of disgusting.

It was as if a kind of instinctive understanding had been established between the two, and with equally immediate promptness the other members of the family had fallen in with it: Tania Tabet, so aged and worn, and hanging always, with those dazed eyes, from her husband's lips; and also the three children, Alda, Gilberta, and Romano, though, like their mother, they soon went off to bed. The pact was this: Geo would not refer, not even indirectly, to his uncle's political past, and his uncle, for his part, would avoid asking his nephew to tell about what he had seen and undergone in Germany, where he too, for that matter—and this should have been recalled also by those who wanted to throw some of his little youthful errors in his face, some only human mistakes in political choices—had lost a sister, a brother-in-law, and a nephew whom he loved very much. What a misfortune, to be sure, what a calamity! But a sense of proportion and discretion (the past was past, no use digging it up again!) should now prevail over every other impulse. It was better to look ahead, to the future. And in fact, while they were on the subject of the future, what—Geremia Tabet asked at one point, assuming the serious but kindly tones of the head of the family, who looks ahead and can deal with many things—what were Geo's plans? He was surely thinking of reopening his father's shop: a very noble ambition, which his uncle could only approve, since the storehouse, *at least,* was still there. But to make a success of it, he would need money, a lot of money; he would have to have the backing of some bank. Could he help him, in this last matter? He hoped he could, he really did. But if, in the meanwhile, in any case, seeing that the Via Campofranco house had been occupied by "the reds," he would like to come and live temporarily with them, a cot, if not a proper bed, could always be found!

It was exactly at this point, Daniele Josz recalled, that he, looking up with more lively attention, had tried once more, though in vain, to understand.

Sweating profusely, even in his pajamas, old Tabet sat with his elbows propped on the great black "refectory" table in the center of which the candle was guttering, about to die; and at the same time, puzzled, Geremia twisted with his fingertips the little gray beard, the classical Fascist goatee which, alone among the old Fascists of Ferrara, he had had the courage, or the effrontery, or—who knows?—perhaps the cleverness not to cut off. As for Geo, while he shook his head and, smiling, declined the invitation, that now-graying goatee and the pudgy hand toying with it were the object of his attention, from the other side of the table, as his pale-blue eyes looked at them with a stubborn, fanatical stare.

IV

The autumn ended. Winter came, the long, cold winter of our region. Then spring returned. And slowly, with the spring, but still as if only Geo's examining gaze were evoking it, the past also returned.

Strange, isn't it? And yet time was arranging things in such a way that between Geo and Ferrara—between Geo and us—you might say a kind of secret dynamic relationship seemed to exist. It's hard, I know, to explain clearly. On the one hand, there was the progressive reabsorption by Geo's body of those unhealthy humors, that fat which, at his first appearance on Via Mazzini in August of the previous year, had given rise to so much argument and perplexity. On the other hand, there was the simultaneous reappearance, first timid, then more and more evident and determined, of an image of Ferrara and of ourselves, moral and physical, which no one, in his heart, had ever wanted, at a certain point, to forget. Slowly Geo grew thinner, as the months went by; he regained, except for his sparse hair prematurely gray at the temples, a face whose glabrous cheeks made it even more youthful. But also the city, after the highest piles of rubble were removed, and an initial rage for superficial changes had died down, also the city was slowly settling into its sleepy, decrepit lines, which centuries of clerical decadence, suddenly at history's malicious decree, following the remote and ferocious and glorious times of the Ghibelline Seigniory, had by now fixed for any possible future in an unchangeable mask. Everything in Geo spoke of his desire, or rather of his determination, to be a boy again, the boy he had been, yes, but also, plunged as he was into the timeless hell of Buchenwald, the boy he had never been able to be. And so we too, his fellow citizens, who had been the witnesses of his childhood and adolescence, and yet recalled him as a boy only vaguely (but he recalled us, to be sure, so different from what we were today!), we became what we had once been, our prewar selves, our selves of forever. Why resist? If *he* wanted us like that, and if, especially, that's how we were, why not satisfy him? We thought with sudden indulgence and weariness. But our will, one could feel clearly, had little or nothing to do with it. We had the impression that we were all involved, Geo Josz on one side and the rest of us on the other, in a vast, slow, fatal motion, which it was impossible to evade. A motion so slow—synchronized, like that of little connected wheels, gears operated by a single, invisible pivot—that only the growing of the little plane trees replanted along the city's bastions as early as the summer of '45, or the gradual accumulation of dust on the big commemorative plaque on Via Mazzini, could have furnished an adequate measurement of it.

We came to May.

So that was the reason! we said to ourselves, smiling. So it was only in order that an absurd nostalgia wouldn't seem so absurd, so that *his* illusion could be perfect, that, at the beginning of the month, along the Via Mazzini, their bicycles' handlebars spilling wild flowers, flocks of pretty girls, their arms enlaced, came pedaling by, returning from excursions to the nearby countryside and heading for the center of the city. And it was, moreover, for the same reason that, at the same time, coming from God knows what hiding place and resting his back against the marble shaft that for centuries had supported one of the three gates of the ghetto, there appeared again down at the corner, unchanged, like a little stone idol, a symbol for all of us, without exception, of the truly blissful *entre deux guerres,* the enigmatic little figure of the notorious Count Scocca. ("Look, the old madman's back again!" people muttered, spontaneously, as soon as they recognized in the distance the unmistakable yellowish boater tilted over one ear, the toothpick clenched between thin lips, the fat sensual nose raised to sniff the odor of the hemp-macerating vats that the little evening breeze carried with it.)

And since, in the meanwhile, Ferrara's latest generation of beautiful girls, inspiring open exclamations of praise from the narrow sidewalks, and more secret glances of admiration from the darkness of the shops beyond, had almost finished, one of those evenings, their lazy ride back down Via Mazzini and, indeed, was about to debouch in Piazza delle Erbe and go by, laughing: thus, facing the spectacle of life eternally renewing itself, and yet always the same, and indifferent to the problems and passions of mankind, no grudge, no matter how stubborn, could at this point continue to put up resistance. The little stage of Via Mazzini displayed, to the left, emerging against the sun from the end of the street, the close and radiant ranks of the cycling girls; and to the right, motionless and gray against the wall where he was leaning, Count Lionello Scocca. How could you help but smile at such a spectacle, and at the light that enfolded it, as if of posterity? How could you not be moved at the sight of that kind of wise allegory that suddenly reconciled everything: the anguished, atrocious yesterday, with the today so much more serene and rich in promises? Certainly, on seeing the aged, penniless nobleman openly resume his former observation post, where a man with sharp eyesight and keen hearing, like his, could observe the whole extent of Via Mazzini and, at the same time, the adjacent Piazza delle Erbe, you suddenly lost the heart to reproach him for having been a paid informer of the Secret Police for years or for having directed, from 1939 to 1943, the local bureau of the Italo-German Cultural Institute. He had allowed that little Hitler mustache to grow for the occasion, and he kept it still; now didn't it lead you to considerations tinged with fondness, and even—why not?—even with gratitude?

It seemed scandalous therefore that, with Count Scocca—a harmless eccentric, after all—Geo Josz, on the contrary, behaved in a way that not only showed no fondness or gratitude, but had to be considered lacking in even the most elementary humanity and discretion. And the surprise was all the greater because for some time it had become customary to smile benevolently, understandably at him and his own oddities, including his dislike of the so-called "war beards." To speak of Geo and his famous whims ("He's against beards! Well, if that's all it amounts to. . . .") and to assume the resigned air of one, harassed, who prepares to give in "just to make him happy," above all "to please him": this was the custom and this was, also, the profound truth. Though at the same time the city's beards fell one by one beneath the barber's scissors and, for this, much of the credit was his—since, I repeat, everything was done "to let him have his way," above all "to make him happy"—as so many gentlemen's faces dared finally reappear, naked, in the naked light of the sun. And it was true, entirely true, on this score, that Geremia Tabet, Lawyer Tabet, Geo's maternal uncle, hadn't yet cut off his beard, nor in all likelihood would he ever cut it off. But his case might have represented a valid exception only for those who couldn't mentally associate that poor little white goatee with the black wool tunic, the shiny black boots, the black fez, in which every Sunday morning, until the late summer of '38, to the very end of the "good old days," Geremia had gloriously displayed himself, between noon and one o'clock, at the Caffè della Borsa.

At first the incident seemed unlikely. Nobody believed it. It was positively impossible to picture the scene: Geo, coming without surprise, with his languid walk, into the eyeshot of Count Scocca, leaning against the wall; Geo, striking the old, resuscitated spy's parchment cheeks, with two sharp, peremptory slaps, "like a real Fascist bully." The event, however, actually did take place: dozens of people saw it. But, on the other hand, wasn't it fairly strange that various, even contradictory, versions immediately started circulating, about the course events had taken? One was almost tempted to doubt not only the authenticity of each version, but even the true, objective reality of that double slap, itself, *smack-smack,* so full and resounding, according to the general report, that it had been heard for a good part of Via Mazzini: from the Oratorio di San Maurelio, a few yards from where the Count was standing, all the way to the Temple and even beyond.

For many people Geo's act remained unmotivated, without any possible explanation. A few moments before he had been seen walking slowly in the same direction as the bicycling girls, letting them pass him. He never turned his face from the center of the street; and nothing in his face, where a mixed emotion of joy and amazement was legible, could have led anybody to imagine what was to happen a moment later. So when he came up to Count Scocca, and looked away from a trio of girls about to turn from Via Mazzini into Piazza delle Erbe, Geo, all of a sudden, stopped abruptly, as if the Count's presence, at that spot and at that hour, seemed, to say the least, inconceivable to him. His hesitation, in any case, had been minimal. Just long enough for him to frown, purse his lips, clench his fists convulsively, mutter some broken, incoherent words. After which, as if operated by a spring, he had literally flown at the poor Count, who, for his part, had until then shown no sign of having noticed him.

Is that all? And yet there was a reason, there had to be, others insisted, pulling down their lips, dubiously. Count Scocca hadn't noticed Geo's arrival; and that, though in itself might seem strange, found all more or less in agreement. But how could one think that Geo became aware of the Count at the very moment when the three girls, at whom his eyes were greedily staring, were about to disappear on their bicycles into the golden mist of Piazza delle Erbe?

According to those others, the Count, instead of standing motionless and silent to watch the passers-by, concerned only with remaining absolutely identical to the image that he and the city, in a united emotion of fondness, both wanted, was doing something. And this something, which nobody who went by at a distance greater than two yards could have noticed—also because his lips, in spite of everything, persisted in shifting the toothpick from one side of his mouth to the other—this something was a soft whistling, so faint that it seemed not so much timid as accidental: a lazy, random little whistle, which would certainly have remained unobserved if the tune he was indicating had been something other than "Lili Marlene." (But wasn't this, after all, the final, the really toothsome detail, for which one should be most grateful to the old informer?)

Underneath the lamplight, by the barracks gate. . . .

Count Scocca whistled, softly but distinctly, his eyes also lost, despite his seventy-odd years, in pursuit of the cycling girls. Perhaps he too, breaking off his whistling for an instant, had briefly joined his voice to the unanimous chorus of praise that rose from the sidewalks of Via Mazzini, murmuring in dialect, following the goodhearted, sensual custom of the Emilian province: "Blessed by God!" or "Blessed are you and the mothers that bore you!" But as bad luck would have it, that idle, peaceful, innocent whistling—innocent to anyone, that is, except Geo—came at once to his lips. Needless to say, from this point on, the second version of the incident coincided with the first.

There was, nevertheless, a third version: and this, like the first made no mention of "Lili Marlene" nor of any other whistling, innocent or not, provocative or not.

If this last report was to be believed, it was the Count himself who stopped Geo. "Hey there!" he exclaimed, seeing him go by. Abruptly Geo stopped. And then the Count immediately started speaking to him, starting right off with his full name ("Why, look here, you aren't by chance Geo Josz, son of my friend Angiolino?"), because he, Lionello Scocca, knew everything about everybody, and the years he had been forced to spend in hiding, God knows how or where, hadn't in the least befuddled his memory or diminished his ability to recognize a face among thousands—even when it was a face like Geo's, which at Buchenwald, not in Ferrara, had become the face of a man! And so, long before Geo flung himself on the old spy and, heedless of his age and of everything else, slapped him violently, for a few minutes the two had gone on talking between themselves with great affability, Count Scocca questioning Geo about the end of Angelo Josz, of whom, he said, he had *always* been so fond, inquiring closely into the fate that had befallen the other members of the family, including Pietruccio, deploring those "horrible excesses" and at the same time congratulating him, Geo, on his return; and Geo, answering, with a certain embarrassed reluctance, true, but answering all the same: to look at, they were not unlike a normal couple of citizens, stopping on a sidewalk to talk of this and that, waiting for night to fall. What had driven Geo, then, suddenly to attack the Count, whom it was logical to credit with having said nothing to offend or in any way hurt his interlocutor, and, in particular, with not having hinted at even the slightest whistle: all the oddness of Geo's character lay there, in the opinion of those who told such things, it all lay in this "enigma"; and the gossip and the suppositions on the subject were to continue for a long while still.

V

No matter what really took place, one thing is sure: after that May evening many things changed. If anybody chose to understand, he understood. The others, the majority, were allowed at least to know that a turning point had been reached, that something serious had happened, something irreparable.

It was on the very next day, for example, that people could really become aware of how much weight Geo had lost.

Absurd as a scarecrow, to the wonder, the uneasiness and alarm of all, he reappeared, wearing the same clothes he had been wearing when he came back from Germany, in August of '45, fur hat and leather jerkin included. They were so loose on him, now—and, obviously, he had done nothing to make them fit better—that they seemed to droop from a clothes hanger. People saw him coming along Corso Giovecca, in the morning sun that shone happily and peacefully on his rags, and they could hardly believe their own eyes. So, during those months he had done nothing but grow thin, dry himself out! Slowly, he had shrunk to the rind! But nobody managed to laugh. Seeing him cross the Corso at the Teatro Communale, and then take Corso Roma (he crossed, looking out for the cars and the bicycles, with an old man's caution), there were very few who, in their hearts, didn't feel a shudder.

And so, from that morning on, never changing his dress, Geo installed himself, so to speak, permanently at the Caffè della Borsa, on Corso Roma, where, one by one, excepting the recent torturers and slaughterers of the Black Brigade, who were still kept hidden, distant, by sentences already "out of date," the old Fascist bullies showed up again, the remote dispensers of castor oil of '22 and '24, whom the last war had scattered and swept into oblivion. Covered with rags, he, from his little table, stared at the groups of them with a manner that lay between defiance and supplication. And his attitude contrasted, entirely to his own disadvantage, of course, with the shyness, the wish not to be too noticeable, that every gesture of the former tyrants betrayed. Old now, harmless, with the ruinous marks that the years of misfortune had multiplied on their faces and their bodies; and yet reserved, polite, well dressed: these men appeared far more human, more moving and deserving of pity than the other, than Geo. What did he want, this Geo Josz? many began to ask themselves once again. But the time of uncertainty and puzzlement, the time—which now seemed almost heroic!—when, before making the slightest decision, one paused and, as they say, split hairs: that time full of romanticism just after the war, so suited to moral questions and examinations of conscience, unfortunately, could not be called back. What did he want, Geo Josz? It was the old question, yes, but uttered without secret trembling, with the impatient brutality that life, eager to assert its rights, now forced one to adopt.

For this reason, except for Uncle Daniele, in whom the presence at those same tables, "so in the public eye," of some of the leading members of the local Fascist bands, former Consuls of the Militia, former Provincial Secretaries, former Mayors, etc. always aroused indignation and an argumentative streak (but his loyalty was too natural, too obvious: who could feel it was a real exception, a true consolation?)—for this reason, I say, the frequenters of the Caffè della Borsa still able to make the effort to rise from their wicker chairs, cover the few necessary yards, finally sit down beside Geo had become few.

There were some, in any case, more unwilling than the others to surrender to their inner repugnance. But the embarrassment they brought back each time from those voluntary *corvées* was always the same. It was impossible, they would cry, to converse with a man in costume! And, on the other hand, if they let him do the talking, he immediately started telling about Fòssoli, about Germany, Buchenwald, the end of all his relatives; and he went on like that for whole hours, until you didn't know how to get away from him. There, at the café, under the yellow awning which, whipped obliquely by the sirocco, had a devilishly hard time protecting the little tables and the chairs from the fury of the noonday sun, there was nothing to do, while Geo narrated, but follow with one eye the movements of the workman opposite, busy filling with plaster the holes made in the parapet of the Castle's moat by the shooting of December 15, 1943. (By the way, the new Acting Prefect, sent from Rome after Doctor Herzen's sudden flight abroad, must have issued precise instructions in this matter!) And meanwhile Geo repeated the words that his father had murmured in a whisper, before dropping exhausted in the path from the *Lager* to the salt mine where they worked together; and then, still not satisfied, he imitated with his hand the little gesture of farewell his mother had made to him, at the grim station of their arrival, in the midst of the forest, as she was pushed aside with the other women; and then, going on, he told about Pietruccio, his little brother, seated beside him, in the dark, in the truck transporting them from the station through the fir trees to the huts of the camp, and how all of a sudden he vanished, like that, without a cry, without a moan, and nobody could find out anything more about him, then or ever. . . . Horrible, of course, heart-rending. But in all this there was something excessive, everyone declared, in agreement, returning from those too-long and depressing sessions, not without frank amazement, it's only fair to say, at their own coldness—there was something false, forced. It's the fault of all this propaganda, perhaps, they added, excusing themselves. It's true that countless stories of that sort had been heard, *at the proper time,* and to hear them thrust on one now, when the Castle's clock was probably striking the hour of dinner or supper, one simply couldn't fend off, honestly, a certain feeling of boredom and incredulity. As if, after all, to make people listen with greater attention, it was enough to put on a leather jerkin and stick a fur hat on your head!

During the rest of '46, all of '47, and a good part of '48, the more and more tattered and desolate figure of Geo Josz never stopped appearing before our eyes. In the streets, in the squares, at the movies, in the theaters, by the playing fields, at public ceremonies: you would look around and there he would be, tireless, always with that hint of saddened wonder in his gaze, as if he asked only to start a conversation. But all avoided him like the plague. Nobody understood. Nobody wanted to understand.

When he was just back from Buchenwald, his soul still tortured by dread and anguish, it was completely understandable, everyone admitted, that he would preferably stay in his house, or, on coming out, instead of streets like Corso Giovecca, so broad and open that at times it made even the most normal people feel a bit dizzy, he would instinctively turn to the winding alleys of the old city, the narrow and dark little streets of the ghetto. But afterward, removing the gabardine suit that Squarcia, the best tailor in the city, had made to order for him, and taking out again his lugubrious deportee's uniform, if he planned to turn up wherever there were people with a desire to enjoy themselves or, simply, a healthy wish to emerge from the shoals of that dirty postwar period, to go forward somehow, to "reconstruct," what excuse could be found for such outlandish and offensive conduct? And what should he care, he, who one August evening in '46 had had the bad taste to appear, in this guise, and extinguish the laughter on all lips, what should he care, for God's sake, if more than a year after the war's end they had decided to open a new outdoor dance hall, the one just beyond Porta San Benedetto, in fact, in the bend of the Doro! It wasn't one of the usual places, after all! As anyone had to admit, it was a very modern establishment, in the American style, with magnificent neon lighting, a fine bar and restaurant permanently open, kitchen always ready, which could provoke no more serious criticism (according to the article in the *Gazzetta del Po* written by that poor dreamer, the young Bottecchiari) than that it was located less than a hundred yards from the place where, in '44, five leaders of the underground National Liberation Committee had been shot in reprisal. Well, apart from the fact that the dance hall in the bend of the Doro was, as the crow flies, not a hundred, but at least two hundred yards from the little marble column commemorating the execution, only a maniac, a hater of life, could think of venting his wrath on such a pleasant and jolly place. What harm was there? The first months everyone went there, more or less, coming out of the movies after midnight, with the idea of a late snack. But often people ended by having supper there; and then they danced to the radio, perhaps, among transient groups of truck drivers, making merry and enjoying the good company until dawn. It was only natural. Society, shattered by the war, was trying to pick up again. Life was resuming. And when it does, of course, it pays no attention to anyone.

Suddenly, faces, bitterly interrogatory until a moment before, without a ray of hope, brightened with malicious certitude. And what if Geo's disguise and self-exhibition, so insistent and irritating, had a political aim? What—and they winked—if he were a Communist?

That evening at the dance hall, for example, when he started displaying left and right the photographs of his relatives who had died in Buchenwald, he reached such an excess of arrogance that he tried to grasp the lapels of some young people who wanted only, at that moment—since the orchestra, meanwhile, had started playing again—to fling themselves, embracing, onto the dance floor. These weren't tales, hundreds of people saw him. And then, what could he be getting at, with those gestures, those honeyed grins, those imploring—ironically imploring!—grimaces, that bizarre and macabre pantomime of his, in short, unless he and Nino Bottecchiari, having recently come to an agreement about the house on Via Campofranco, were now, *also in other matters and namely Communism,* hand in glove? And if that's how things stood, if he was only a useful idiot, wasn't it right, after all, that the Friends of America Club, where in the chaos and enthusiasm of the immediate postwar period somebody had officially signed up Geo also, should now arrange to drop him, as a measure of obvious prudence, from its list of members? Probably no one, to tell the truth, at least for the moment, dreamed of thinking about him, about Geo Josz. But he *wanted* a scandal, that was clear: on that notorious evening when he had forcibly demanded entrance to the Club (it was in '47, in February), the waiters had seen appear before them not a decently dressed gentleman, but a strange character in the condition of a beggar, with a shaved neck like a prisoner—something, considering also the filth and the stink, very similar to Tugnín, the poor city beggar—who, from the vestibule full of overcoats and furs hanging in full view from the racks, had started proclaiming in a loud voice that he, being, as then proved quite correct, a regularly inscribed member of the Club, could visit it when he liked. And on what grounds, anyway, could the Club itself seriously be criticized, for having made such a radical decision toward Geo, when in the autumn of the preceding year the assembly of members had expressed a unanimous desire for the organization to return as soon as possible to its former, glorious name, the Circolo dei Concordi, again restricting the membership to the aristocracy—the Costabili, Del Sale, Maffei, Scroffa, Scocca families, and others of the sort—and to the most select members of the bourgeoisie? If the Friends of America, *pro temporum calamitatibus,* had been wise to accept anybody at all without fuss, the Circolo dei Concordi had certain standards, certain long-established customs, certain natural exclusions—and politics had nothing to do with this—and, really, there was no reason to fear restoring them. Why? What was odd about it? Even old Maria, Maria Ludargnani, who in that same winter of '46–'47 had reopened her house of ill-fame in Via Arianuova (it had remained the only place, after all, where people could foregather, without political opinions cropping up to spoil friendly relations; and evenings were spent there as in the old days, mostly limited to gossip or to playing rummy with the girls . . .)—even she would have nothing to do with Geo, that night he came to knock at her door; she wouldn't let him in, nor would she move away from the peephole, her eye glued to it observing him for a long time, until she saw him go off in the fog. In short, if on that occasion nobody thought for a moment that Geo had been deprived of some right; then all the more reason to recognize that the Circolo dei Concordi had behaved toward him in the most correct and sensible fashion. Democracy, if the word had a meaning, had to safeguard *all* citizens: the lower ranks, of course, but also the upper ones!

It was only in '48, after the elections of April 18th, after the Provincial Office of the Partisans Association was forced to move into three rooms of the former Casa del Fascio on Viale Cavour (and this proved, belatedly, that the rumors about the owner of the house on Via Campofranco and his Communism were purely imaginary), it was only in the summer of that year that Geo Josz decided to leave the city. He disappeared suddenly, leaving not the slightest trace after him, like a character in a novel; and immediately some people said he had emigrated to Palestine, following the example of Doctor Herzen; others said to South America; others, to an unknown country "behind the curtain."

They went on talking about him for a few months more: at the Caffè della Borsa, at the Doro, in Maria Ludargnani's house, and in many other places. Daniele Josz was able to hold forth publicly on the subject many times. Geremia Tabet, the lawyer, stepped in as administrator of the disappeared man's not inconsiderable possessions. And meanwhile:

"What a madman!" one heard repeated on all sides.

They would shake their heads good-naturedly, purse their lips, silently raise their eyes to heaven.

"If he had only been a bit more patient!" they would add, with a sigh; and they were again sincere, now, sincerely grieved.

They said time, which adjusts all things in this world, and thanks to which also Ferrara, luckily, was rising, identical, from its ruins, time would finally have calmed even him, would have helped him to return to the fold, fit in once more, in short—because, when you got down to it, this was his problem. But no. He had preferred to go away. Vanish. Act the tragic hero. Just when, by renting properly the now empty palazzo on Via Campofranco, and giving a good push to his father's business, he could have lived comfortably, like a gentleman, and, among other things, devoted himself to building a family again. Marrying, naturally; since there wouldn't have been a young lady in Ferrara, of the class to which he belonged, who, in the event, would have bothered about the religious difference (the years, on this score, had not passed in vain; in these matters people everywhere were much less strict than in the past!), no one would have considered it an insuperable obstacle. Odd as he was, he couldn't know that; but, with a 99 percent probability, this is how things would have gone. Time would have settled everything, as if absolutely nothing had ever happened. To be sure, you had to wait. You had to be able to control your nerves. But, instead, had a more illogical way of behaving ever been seen? A more inscrutable character? Ah, but to realize the sort of person he was, the kind of living enigma who had turned up in their midst, the Count Scocca episode, without waiting for all the rest, was really more than enough. . . .

VI

An enigma, yes.

Still, on closer examination, when, lacking surer clues, we fell back on that sense of the absurd and, at once, of revealed truth, which at the approach of the evening any encounter can arouse in us, that very episode with Count Scocca revealed nothing enigmatic, nothing that couldn't be understood by a slightly sympathetic heart.

Oh, it is really true! Daylight is boredom, the deaf sleep of the spirit, "boring hilarity!" as the poet says. But let, finally, the twilight hour descend, the hour equally steeped in shadow and in light, a calm May dusk; and then things and people who a moment before seemed utterly normal, indifferent, can suddenly show themselves for what they truly are, they can suddenly speak to you—and at that point it is as if you've been struck by lightning—for the first time of themselves and of you.

"What am I doing here, I, with this man? Who is he? And I, who answer his questions, and at the same time lend myself to his game, who am I?"

The two slaps, after a few moments of mute wonder, answered like lightning the insistent though polite questions of Lionello Scocca. But those questions could also have been answered by a furious, inhuman scream: so loud that the whole city, as much as was still contained beyond the intact, deceitful scenery of Via Mazzini to the distant, breached walls, would have heard it with horror.

Translated from the Italian by William Weaver

Bertha

In winter, he would return. Perspiring, a knapsack on his back, he would bring with him the fresh scent of worlds unknown here. His comings and goings were quiet. You never knew whether he was happy to leave or happy to return.

Inside, in the small room, life remained unchanged. Bertha would sit on the floor, knitting. It seemed as if the passing of years did not touch her. She remained just as he had left her in summer, small, dwarfish even, and quite unaltered.

"Maxie," she would exclaim, as a crack of light came through the door. Throughout the long months she had waited for this light. As the door opened her gaze would fall on him, helplessly.

Very slowly, with studied caution, he would unpack the knapsack. There were clothes and household articles that he had brought with him from his travels. At the sight of them, tears of joy welled up in Bertha's eyes. "That's for you, for you," Max would say, stroking her hair.

The first days after his return were delightful. Bertha sat beside Max, talking. She told him the various details that had accumulated in her memory, trivial experiences, which in this dark room became objects of childlike admiration. Max also talked. He had little to say; what had happened had frozen somewhere on the way. Of course, it was not possible to tell her everything. During the long summer months, on the floor among the skeins of wool, the gaps that he had left between the stories provided her with food for fantasy with which to amuse herself.

Bertha would light the stove, and Max, like a weary traveler, would sink into a long slumber that lasted through the winter. Only in early spring would he stretch himself, saying, "Well, Bertha, it's time I was on my way."

Between naps he would try, half maliciously, half affectionately, to discuss his plans for her. The conversations were full of tears and laughter, and in the end everything remained as before. Max would leave on his travels and Bertha remained behind. And so, the seasons changed, one year followed another, a sprinkling of white appeared at Max's temples, stomach pains began to trouble him, dysentery, a harsh cough, but Bertha remained as she was, small and dwarfish, these qualities becoming more pronounced, perfected as it were.

At first, he had tried, firmly enough, to put her into an institution for girls. He had even had a few preliminary meetings with the headmistress of the institution, who had turned out to be a strong woman with piercing eyes whom he couldn't stand from the very first meeting. The plan, of course, came to nothing. For several days she roamed the streets, until they found her desolate, and brought her back. No amount of persuasion on his part did any good, he did not have the courage to force her to go, and so she stayed on. There had been one other serious attempt to find her what might be called a suitable living arrangement. This was with a woman, an old woman whose children wanted to find her a companion. Bertha returned the next day, her eyes full of tears, and the matter was closed.

Soon afterward, he began to travel.

Max left, hoping that within a year people would make some arrangement for her, or that she herself would find some way out, but when after a year, upon returning to his room, he found her sitting on the floor among the skeins of wool, half knitting, half playing, he simply couldn't be angry with her.

Several years passed—five years, or more. The passage of time became blurred, especially since there were no innovations. Life went on its lazy routine, devouring time. The coming of winter left a stale taste, something like the sourness of a cigarette. Little by little he began to take the fact of her being there for granted. Even when he made far-reaching plans for her, he made them good-humoredly, for he knew with growing certainty that he would never be able to get rid of her.

Between naps he would sit and watch her, as if he were observing his own life.

Sometimes, he went haunted by the old question of his purpose in life. What was he to do with her, or what was she going to do? It was her duty to think of it—she must not be a perpetual burden on him.

Bertha would stand up, looking at him helplessly with her big eyes, unable to understand. When he nagged her, she would burst into tears. This weeping was deep and bitter. It wasn't she that wept; some sleeping animal wept inside her. Sometimes it was a high-pitched wail. After words of reconciliation, everything returned to normal. Bertha would go back to her knitting and Max would cover his head with the blanket.

Sometimes he teased her with riddles. "Don't you ever feel any change; don't things weigh upon you?" Or, in another direction, "What would you like to be someday?" The questions were venomous, aimed at her most vulnerable feelings, but she did not react. Closed, encased in a hard shell, she dragged after him like a dead weight, and sometimes like a mirror wherein his life was reflected.

She was stubbornly loyal, another quality that was not quite human. All summer long she would sit and knit fantastic patterns in strange colors. "I'm knitting for Maxie," she would say. They were not sweaters. A dumb smile would appear on her face at the sight of the patterns. In the end she would unravel them and then the same wool would appear again on the needles, year after year. The tape measure he brought her was no help, since she did not seem to understand what it was for.

But sometimes she, too, asked questions.

They were not the sort of questions that one person asks another, but a sort of eruption, not entirely irrational, that would claim his complete attention. These questions drove him out of his mind; at those moments he was ready to throw her out, to hand her over to the welfare authorities, to denounce her, even to beat her, something that he, incidentally, never did. At these moments, he felt the whole weight of this human burden that had been thrust upon him.

Sometimes he would let her ask her questions and she would sit and drift along with them, like a ship tossing in the wind. Then came the time when he reconciled himself to his fate. Now he knew that he would not leave Bertha, and Bertha knew that she was to stay with him.

Bertha would remain with him . . . some day she might change . . . medical care might cure her . . . she was a girl like all other girls. They were great thoughts, and they surged up within him. At those times everything seemed pleasantly near. "I'll wind up my affairs, Bertha, and I'll come." The feeling was powerful, leaving no room for doubts. "Isn't it so, Bertha?" he would ask suddenly.

At the moment she was that same Bertha who had been handed to him during the big escape when the others couldn't take her, when the only thing they could do was to give her to him. He hadn't been able to carry her either, but he couldn't throw her into the snow.

At the same moment, he conjured up the snow, those thick flakes falling from the skies, soft as a caress, but sometimes swooping down on you, hard, like the beating of hooves.

From the day that they had reached this country, oblivion had overcome her. Her memory froze at a certain point. You couldn't make her disclose anything from the past, nor was she capable of absorbing anything new. "Some pipe is stopped up." This feeling, oversimplified as it might be, remained a sort of certainty that he could not doubt, feeling as he did that something was clogged up in him, too. This had been so several years ago, but perhaps now as well.

When spring came he didn't go out to work. He took Bertha with him to the Valley of the Crucifixion, opposite the monastery. At that moment they were close to each other as they had never been before.

"The sun is good," said Bertha.

"It's a beautiful spring," said Max.

And there was a feeling that the pipe had become unstopped; there was communication, they weren't suspicious of one another any more, they had left their experiences behind them. Now the words, half-syllables, groped toward their hearts. Something was happening to her as well.

The future became misty and sweet. The way it had been in the first day of the liberation. Open roads and many wagons full of refugees, and an inexplicable desire to walk, to take Bertha and to walk with her to the end of the world, just the two of them, and to swallow up the beautiful distances.

"Isn't it beautiful today. . ." he tried.

"Beautiful," she said.

"Isn't it beautiful today. . ." he tried again.

"Beautiful," she said.

Exposed to the spring, to the good sun, the thoughts welled up in him until he could almost feel their physical movement. He was only slightly annoyed with Bertha for not feeling the change.

He bought food; as long as he had enough money, no one could force him to go out traveling. It was a moment of sweet abandonment that would sooner or later bring some sort of whiplash in its wake. Soon he would have to go back to work, but in the meantime, there was something festive about this walk, in the glittering olive trees, the comfortable warmth, the light playing on his shirt.

This sweet indolence lasted a few days. Not many. A letter arrived reminding him that he must be on his way. The letter was brief and unequivocal, with a sufficiently firm conclusion and certain threatening overtones.

Now he didn't know how these months of his vacation had gone by—or perhaps they had never existed at all. The cars, the refrigerator, the workers, the whole atmosphere of busy commerce suddenly came to life and seemed so near that you could smell them. The signboards flashed vividly before his eyes.

His pity was aroused: pity for himself, for the room, for Bertha, for his belongings, and for a small body that made him, too, bend his head a bit, surrender, and also love a little.

The parting was difficult for Bertha this time; promises did no good. She begged him to take her with him. The next day he saw her packing her belongings.

"Where are you going, Bertha?"

"With you."

In the evening he managed to get away. At the station, when he turned his head, he saw the flickering of lights on the road. A car was being towed to the garage. The trip was slow, as if they wanted to delay him, to prolong that which cannot be prolonged, perhaps even to bring him back. He saw that he was mean, so mean, that he felt the heaviness of his shoes, even the dirt at the roots of his hair, the sweat in his armpits. "It's not the first time I've left her, but I have always found her again—I left her enough to live on." Thus he stifled his thoughts.

That night, when he arrived at work, Frost greeted him warmly. "Well, how was the vacation, Max?" He was glad that he could go out with the first truck, unloading the cold drinks all over the city, feeling the cases on his back, full of good foaming beer. For some reason, he didn't feel like any now. He felt fresh and vigorous, ready for any load.

Late that night, after two whole rounds, he was still as fresh as he had been at the beginning. Only his thoughts pounded inside him, as if they had disengaged themselves from him, leaving him incapable of directing them. He didn't really grasp what they demanded of him, he only felt them revolving in his head.

"You've left Bertha again"—he heard this clearly; the voice resounded like the ceaseless ringing of a bell.

Then came the time that seemed ordained to bring this feeling to a head; a decision had to be taken. His fellow workers saw the need to interfere. Max needed a wife. It started, as these things usually do, as a joke. Later they fixed up a date for him—with a typist at the plant.

He didn't have much to offer her. They didn't speak about Bertha. But with her feminine intuition she discovered it in a roundabout way.

He could have said that she was retarded, that she would soon be put in an institution. This was an accepted way of speaking, even to Mitzi. But he couldn't put it that way; something stopped him from saying the words. Sometimes your cunning betrays you, and you are suddenly left naked and ashamed. At those moments you are as vulnerable as a bare neck at the change of the seasons. Mitzi delved deeply into the matter; she too, had been hurt enough in her life.

Max was called upon to clarify matters, so that, for the time being, her own affairs were pushed aside.

"This Bertha," she said, "I don't understand why she hasn't been put into an institution by now."

What could he answer? Her questions were direct, going straight to the heart of the matter; they showed up all the contradictions, and even contained an element of mild reproach.

"She didn't want to." Max tried to shake off his embarrassment.

"What do you mean, she didn't want to?"

They met every evening; it was as if she were trying to exhaust the matter completely. In order to ease the confession, she invited him to her room.

The problem was not dismissed in her room. It kept floating up to the surface like a buoy.

"It's only a question of making the arrangements," he tried to defend himself.

"Then why has it been going on for so long?"

One day he felt that something had happened to him, something physical—something that had to do with the way he handled the crates. He moved differently, and once he even dropped a crate of bottles. "Take it easy there!" cried the foreman, who liked him.

His thoughts fumbled, as though he were tipsy. Late at night he felt the fire burning in his head.

He tried to clarify the matter to himself logically, drawing the thread of Mitzi's questions to himself. In his dreams, the stark mystery took hold of him—Bertha's knitting needles, toys, hell and paradise, a strange combination of rudimentary symbols and objects.

"Does Bertha dream of me, too?"—Now he did not doubt it.

If she knew how to read, he would write her a letter. He would clarify, explain, enumerate all the reasons, one by one. Distance made it easier to hide one's facial expression. One day during the noon break, between loading, he tried to write, but in the end, when he was about to fold the letter, he realized how idiotic it was.

Mitzi asked him no further questions, as if waiting to see the impact of her words. The silence was hard for him, since he knew that it would only lead to new questions.

The movies became his most comfortable refuge.

But the secret weighed on him. Was it still a secret? He had told everything. He thought he had exhausted the matter. That is how it seemed to him as they sat in a small café once, after the movies.

Late at night, during the second shift when the storehouse was empty, he suddenly felt that he was still carrying the secret within him. If only he could give it a name, he would feel easier; but the name eluded him.

The days were as flat as the cement floor of the storehouse. He felt that the light that protected him was being taken away. Sometimes a feeling of nakedness overcame him. He tried in vain to glean something from Mitzi's eyes; they were watery eyes, the color seemed to melt in them; something was melting in him, too, but he didn't know what it was.

If there were a starting point, it would make things a great deal easier—to say, "I will begin from here," to take a day off and go up to Jerusalem, to Bertha, even to bring Mitzi, to show her. How complicated the possibilities seemed, and in the meantime all he saw were the bottles; in the darkness of the warehouse the alcohol was fermenting. He had to make a decision; Mitzi's moderate tone demanded it.

"When was Bertha entrusted to me?" The question arose from some dark depth. "Fifteen years ago." The event seemed so near to him, as if it had taken place during his last vacation.

Mitzi did not tell him what to do. She wanted to see what he would do himself. Only once did she say to him in passing, as she always did: "Maybe she's yours; you can tell me, I won't blame you; things like that happened during the war." She had thought it all out beforehand.

Now he had to act, to prove to Bertha if not to himself, to finish once and for all, to get rid of the nuisance. How close he felt at that moment to Mitzi.

He asked for his quarterly vacation. "To take care of something," he said to Frost.

He wore his good suit, and in the evening he came to Mitzi. "Very nice, very nice," said Mitzi, like a merchant who leaves the way open for negotiations, not over-eager but never refusing an offer.

"Aren't you pleased I'm going to finish it?"

"Of course, of course."

For some reason he was reminded of the headmistress of the institution with whom he had negotiated—the long corridor, girls dressed in blue.

"The institutions here in this country are fine," he said.

"Of course."

"Maybe you'll come with me."

"Better not. . . ." she said, as if shaking off some unpleasantness.

The next day he got up early. It was a nice day, mild after the first rains. There was an air of simple festivity on this weekday, little traffic. He thought he would get there quickly by taxi, but meanwhile he was attracted by the shop windows. He never came emptyhanded, and he was angry with himself for leaving her so little cash.

First he bought her a short winter coat, then a woolen blouse. In the next shop he bought shoes; the colors matched, colors that he liked. Then he was drawn to the central shops. A sudden fit of spending took hold of him. He ended up with two large packages. In the taxi he started a conversation with a man, telling him that he worked for Frost, and the man in the blue suit said that he also knew Frost.

Suddenly he felt the cool mountain air in his shirt.

"On vacation?" asked the man.

"Have to arrange something," said Max.

It wasn't clear to him what he would do. The certainty started to fall apart. The chill wrapped itself around his neck. He was exposed to the cutting air. He just wanted the journey to go on, to take as long as possible.

"Aren't you afraid of catching cold?" asked the man.

Jerusalem was as beautiful as on the day he had first arrived with Bertha. Lights glittered in the city. For some reason he was slow in his movements. It turned out that the man who had traveled with him was still standing next to him. "I've come to arrange something," apologized Max. They parted.

His head was empty of all thoughts. He wasn't sure for what he had come. His feet drew him to the slope. He caught a glimpse of Bertha's head. Simple indifference was written on her face. She was sitting outside, knitting.

"Bertha," he said. It was the biggest word that he could cut out of his heart; it seemed that only once had he called that way, once at a Gentile woman's in Zivorka, after the big hunt when he was forced to leave her. It was the same head with the same tangled hair. A small, warm body that needed nothing, that was beyond patience, beyond any change that might come. It asked for nothing except to be left here, among these skeins of wool, to sit and knit thus, like a spider, like a bee; you couldn't call it stupidity, idiocy, or any similar names called to mind by that strangeness. It was something different, something that a man like Max couldn't give a name to, but could feel.

"Max!" she said. Not a muscle moved in her face.

"I came early this time." He too was unable to utter another word.

He got down on his knees. "This coat," he said, starting to take apart the package, "this coat will suit you. It's warm; at this time of year you have to be careful."

Bertha put down the knitting needles without saying a word. Supreme indifference froze her face. Now he had no doubt she knew everything. But he could not detect any signs of anger in her. She was a princess, a devil, a gypsy, something that could not be contained in any human measure. She was not a girl to whom he could say "I couldn't, I was forced, I never loved Mitzi, it was only a blind incident." But again he repeated: "Bertha"—as if trying to suggest everything in this one word.

He tried to explain to her in the vocabulary that he had carried with him all these years, that had ripened within him.

"Max!" said Bertha, as if cutting short his confession. A deep flush suffused her face.

At that moment, he could not guess how near the solution was. Sometimes catastrophe wears festive garb.

Bertha wanted to put on her new clothes and go to town. She had matured during these months, or perhaps she had just acquired some of the gestures of a woman. She was different.

"Let's go!" she said. This was a new tone that was unfamiliar to him.

They passed by the institution. In the corridor there was confusion. Girls in blue were running around and the headmistress appeared in the entrance. It was an old Arab house that was disproportionately tall. No one noticed them.

Again he didn't know how he had got here; Bertha's cheeks were burning, and they were already in the center of town. The traffic was very heavy. Max suddenly realized why he had come and he said, "You must understand, Bertha, you're already grown up; one must marry, set up a household. You too, you too!"

Bertha turned her head and looked at him.

He wanted to say something else, but the noise in the street prevented it. Afterward, when they came to the quiet side streets, to Ibn Gabirol Street and Rambam Boulevard, it was too quiet for them to speak.

Their walk continued for some time. It was as solemn as a ceremony, as a farewell, as a simple never-to-be-forgotten occasion. You are not in control of yourself, other powers dominate you, lead you as in a procession. Oaths are broken, but another oath, greater than all, takes their place. Your eyes glisten with tears. The lights begin to dance.

Now he was already in the realm of mystery.

A smile lit up Bertha's face, and there was something sharp in her eyes like an inanimate object unexpectedly changing its form. Darkness rose up from the streets, and above them was light. Among the trees there were dark shadows.

When they returned home, her face was very flushed—a fire burned in her. Her eyes were open, but you could see nothing in them. Toward morning she began to shiver.

In the morning, the ambulance came.

She was as light and small as on the day when he had received her; the years had added no weight. He asked permission to go along with her.

The casualty ward in the hospital was full, but they made room for her. A man wheeled her carefully through the corridor on a low bed, as if trying to smooth her passage, as if he did not want to break the silence.

They told him that he must leave. The gate closed behind him.

At that moment he could remember nothing. His eyes saw, his heart fumbled, the tips of his fingers were tingling. Inside the cavity of his skull, something floated as in a heavy fluid.

"Now, my load is lighter," he said naïvely, failing to understand the situation.

The cars crept slowly down the slope, the traffic was heavy, everything flowed as through blocked pipes. He remembered nothing. The sky was clear without a trace of cloud, like glass that had been well polished in order to see through to its depths. Each object was unique: the traffic signs, the posters, and the two people coming toward him.

"Can't I remember anything at all? My memory is gone."

The landscape was bathed in bright sunshine, as if it wanted to exhibit every detail to him slightly more enlarged than usual and brought closer to the eye.

"But I must remember," he said to himself. "Forgetting won't release me."

There was no connection between one thought and another. It was as if they had frozen in one of his arteries. His body was working properly, and you could hear the gentle pulse within it.

The neighborhood began to empty as if it wanted to hide the traffic from him, to illustrate the paralysis of the inanimate landscape.

"I must choose a starting point; from now on I will try to reconstruct. One detail will bring another in its wake, and in this way I can reconstruct all the events to myself."

Nothing came to him, not a single detail that would lead him on or connect anything. His eyes saw, and he could make out everything, still enlarged, as it had seemed to him before. But he couldn't remember a thing.

If some sort of guilt erupted within him; it would make him feel easier. But no feeling of this sort existed in him at that moment. Everything was just more enlarged than usual, everything seemed so close that it made him dizzy.

He turned toward the slope, trying to thaw the solidity, and suddenly he began to feel a current of warmth in his knees. He was still in the grounds of the hospital; a bluish light flickered at the windows, something like the light in Frost's warehouses.

He felt lighter in weight; only something outside him made his walk heavy. Thus he walked around and around the hospital, unable to tear himself away from the circle.

Slowly, like a sharp stimulus, memory started ebbing back, around the thin tubes of his temples. He clutched his head, afraid that it would burst.

A slight chill met him at the entrance to the yard, and he drew his short coat closer around his body. There was a warm light in the streets. Low pinkish clouds stretched across the skies. The copper-colored rooftops glistened in the light. The street was long and exposed; one could see the remarkably straight rows of trees and the white, almost transparent, traffic signs. Then the redness descended, intertwining itself with the roads, and Max tried to submerge his eyes in it.

The street gradually filled with rich colors. The shadows, dumb and cautious, passed across. Dark circles whirled at its end. When he turned his head back, he saw the thick redness strangled by damp powerful arms.

The street emptied and you could see how the mist was being absorbed by the tree trunks.

His vacation permit was in his pocket.

A pain, a kind of stimulus, stabbed him in the ankles, pricking his toes. He remembered that from here he used to leave for work, a long journey that always began with an attack of nausea.

Now, he was already in the realm of forms. Reality, as it were, shed its skin; all he felt was a kind of familiarity, as if he were being drawn—he did not know toward what; to the blue color, to the trees or to the stray dog that chanced to be there. He did not see Bertha. She had become something that could no longer be called Bertha.

He entered the hospital. The nurse told him that the girl had amazed the ward. That was all she said, and the other nurses said nothing.

He became a regular visitor there; the attendants soon recognized him, and let him in as if he belonged there. Most of the day he would sit on the bench, looking at the tiled walls. If they had let him remain at night, he would have stayed. The dream became full of ceremonies. Sometimes she was handed over to him and sometimes a delegation came to claim her from him; sometimes it was in a forest and sometimes in Frost's warehouse.

Was it Bertha, or only a vision? Again details rose up, denying it. The shoes, the beads, the knitting needles, the blue wool—was this Bertha?

Again you went out to search for her the way you searched for her in the forest, the way you searched for yourself in the street. You just found details; you couldn't see her, just as you couldn't see yourself.

The nurse came out again. She kept her distance as if he were a stranger; she didn't trust him. Nurses trailed behind her.

The doctor came over to him, ready to start a conversation.

"Yours?" asked the doctor.

"Mine," he said.

The next day they didn't let him enter. The walls grew higher and the gate was locked. A blue light twinkled in the windows, that familiar blue, the color of a bruise.

Silence descended; it touched his body, slithered through the hair on his head, and was still.

Opposite, there were girls dressed in blue on the pavement, near the side entrance to the institution.

The evening light rested on his shoulders.

Suddenly he saw that Bertha's clothes lay in his hands. He didn't dare to open them—or perhaps these were no longer his hands, but iron rings. . . .

Translated from the Hebrew by T. Zandbank

The Season of the Dead

Dead though they be, the dead do not immediately become ageless. Theirs is not the only memory involved; they enter into a seasonal cycle, with an unfamiliar rhythm—ternary perhaps, slow in any case, with widely spaced oscillations and pauses; they hang for a while nailed to a great wheel, sinking and rising by turns; they have become, far beyond the horizons of memory, rays of a skeleton sun.

We had reached the first stage. We were opening up the graveyard—in the sense in which one speaks of opening up a trench; in this place, there had only been life before there was death. And this freshness was to persist for a long time, before the teeming dust of the charnel should dim it, before, eventually, when all the earth was trodden down, oblivion should spread with couch-grass and darnel, and the writing on the tombstones should have lost its meaning; and the arable land should regain what we had taken from it.

For a graveyard to become a real graveyard, many dead must be buried there, many years must pass. Many feet must tread on it; the dead, in short, must make the ground their own. We were certainly far from that point. Our dead would be war dead, for whom we had to break open a grassy mound. It was all, in short, brimful of newness.

War dead. The formula had lost its heroic sense without becoming obsolete. The war had lately moved away from this spot. These men would die a belated and, as it were, accidental death, in silence and captivity, yielding up their arms for a second time. But could one still use the word "arms"?

From the slope of the mound where the new graveyard lay I could see them walking round and round within the barbed wire enclosure of the camp, looking less like soldiers than like people of every sort and condition brought together by their common look of sleeplessness, their unshaven cheeks and the cynical complicity of gangsters the morning after a raid. Following several abortive escapes through Germany, some thousand French soldiers had just been transferred to the disciplinary camp of Brodno in Volynia. It was a second captivity for them, a new imprisonment that was more bewilderingly outlandish and also more romantic. That word gives us a clue: it was an imprisonment for death.

I had been granted the title of gravedigger in advance of the functions. When you dig a ditch, it's because you have already found water. Just now there was nothing of that sort. The ditch we were digging was too long to have a tree planted in it, too deep to be one of those individual holes in which, at that time, throughout Europe, men in helmets were burrowing, forming the base of a monolithic monument which was hard to imagine, particularly here. It could only be a grave. Now we strengthened it with props, we covered it with planks. Nobody was dead. The grave was becoming a sort of snare, a trap in which Fate would finally be caught, into which a dead man would eventually creep. He would thus have been forestalled and would glide into the darkness through wide-open doors, while we would shrink back as he passed, hiding our earth-stained hands behind our backs.

The German N.C.O. had rounded us up in the camp. He needed six men. When he had got that number he took us to the gate and handed us over to an armed sentry. We skirted the wall outside the camp until we came to a small rough road which, a little farther on, led over the side of a hill. At this point a track took us to the verge of the forest. The N.C.O., riding a bicycle, had caught up with us. He went to cut a few switches from an elm tree.

"Who knows German?" he asked without turning round.

"I do."

He called me to him. He was trimming the leaves from the switches with vigorous strokes of his penknife. I disliked the sight: swift-working fingers, pursed lips, and at the end of the supple, swaying branch a ridiculous tuft of leaves dancing as though before an imminent storm. There is no wretchedness like that of flogged men.

"There's to be a graveyard here. . . ." he said to me, suddenly handing me the trimmed branches. "These are yours. Follow me and tell your mates to pull off some more branches."

I passed on the order and followed the N.C.O. to a place where the skirt of the wood dipped down into a narrow valley at the end of which lay a round pond like a hand mirror. The German dug the heel of his boot into the grass: "Here." As carefully as a gardener I planted a branch at the spot he showed me. Then he straightened his back and made a half-turn; staring straight in front of him, he walked forward, stopped and dug his heel into the grass, started off again and stopped again. My companions came up with their arms loaded with leafy branches. The task of planting began, and soon the branches stood lined up there in the still morning, marking the footsteps of the man as he doggedly staked his theoretical claim.

When the enclosure was thus demarcated, the German called me. We had to mark the site of the first grave. When this was set out, my companions, in a fit of zeal, immediately began to lift up clods of turf. Then the earth suddenly appeared as it really was; it lay there against the grass like a garment ready to be put on.

"That's enough, you can dig it tomorrow," the German told us. "We must always have one ready. Death comes quickly these days. War's a shocking thing."

He collected us together and the sentry took us back to the camp. As we were going through the gate one of us got from him, after some pleading, a leaf from his notebook with his signature. We rushed to the kitchens where extra rations of soup were sometimes distributed to the men who were working in gangs about the camp.

"Graveyard!" cried the prisoner who held the voucher, waving it. The man with the soup-ladle looked at us uncertainly for a moment, as though trying to remember to what burial ground this irregular privilege could suddenly have been allotted.

"Camp graveyard!" someone else repeated. The man took the can that was held out to him and filled it. Death had spoken; moreover, death's voucher was in order.

From that day, and still more from the following day when the first grave had been dug and shored up, I began to look out for death in the faces of my comrades, in the weight of the hour, the color of the sky, the lines of the landscape. Here, the great spaces of Russia were already suggested; I had never known a sky under which one had such a sense of surrender.

Sometimes the earth, dried by the early spring sunshine, was blown so high by the wind that the horizon was darkened by a brown cloud, a storm cloud which would break up into impalpable dust, and under which the sunflowers glowed so luminously and appeared suddenly at such distances that you felt you were witnessing the brief, noisy revenge of a whole nation of pensive plants, condemned for the rest of their days to the dull quietness of sunshine.

Close to us, the town was shut in with a white wall above which rose a bulbous church spire, some roofs, and the white plume of smoke from a train, rising for a long time in the same spot, with a far-off whistle like a slaughtered factory.

We had reached Brodno one April morning. The melting snows and the rain had washed away so much earth from the unpaved streets that planks and duckboards had been thrown down everywhere to let people cross, haphazard and usually crooked, looking like wreckage left after a flood subsides. The sentries could no longer keep the column in order and we were all running from one plank to another, mingled with women wearing scarves on their heads and boots on their feet, with German soldiers, with men in threadbare caftans; and here and there jostling one of those strange villagers who stood motionless with rigid faces, their feet in the mud, idle as mourners, with white armlets on their arms as though in some plague-stricken city.

It might have been market day, and the animation in the main street of the village might have been merely the good-humored bustle of the population between a couple of showers, such as one sees also on certain snowy mornings, or on the eve of a holiday. . . . In any case, that first day, the star of David, drawn in blue ink on the armlets of those painfully deferential villagers who looked oddly Sundayfied in their dark threadbare town clothes amongst that crowd of peasants, seemed to me a symbol of penitence, somewhat mitigated, however, by its traditional character.

It was not until later on that their destiny was clearly revealed to me. Then, when I saw them in a group away from the crowd, they ceased to be mere landmarks; exposed to solitude as to a fire, that which had been diluted among so many and had passed almost unnoticed acquired sudden solidity. All at once, they became the mourners at a Passion: a procession of tortured victims, a mute delegation about to appeal to God.

A certain number of Jews had been detailed by the Germans to get the camp ready before our arrival. When we entered the gates they were still there, carefully putting the last touches to the fences, finishing the installation of our sordid equipment, and thus implacably imprisoning themselves, by virtue of some premonitory knowledge, within a universe with which they were soon to become wholly familiar.

The camp consisted of cavalry barracks built by the Red Army shortly after the occupation of Eastern Poland at the end of 1939. A huge bare space separated the three large brick-built main buildings from the whitewashed stables which housed the overflow of our column, according to that mode of military occupation that disdains all hierarchy of places—thus identifying itself with the bursting of dams, the blind and inexorable progress of disasters.

Inside every building, whether stable or barracks, wooden platforms, superimposed on one another, had been set up the whole length of the huge rooms, leaving only a narrow passage along the walls and another across the middle of the structure: tiered bunks like shelves in a department store, where the men were to sleep side by side. Our captivity thus disclosed that homicidal trend which (for practical rather than moral reasons) it usually refused to admit: for the Germans, the unit of spatial measurement was "a man's length."

The great typhus season was barely over at Brodno. It had decimated the thousands of Russian prisoners who had occupied the place before us and who had left their marks on the whitewashed walls—the print of abnormally filthy hands, bloodstains and splashed excrement—messages from those immured men jostling one another in the silent winter night, while death and frost exchanged rings: faintly heard calls from far away. Because of the lingering typhus and the risk of propagating lice, we were given no straw.

We were given little of anything that first day. The Germans, except for a few sentries established in their watchtowers, had retired no one knew whither, as though it were understood that at the end of our trying journey we must be granted a day's truce, an unwonted Sunday that found us standing helpless, leaning against the typhus-ridden bunks with our meager bundles at our feet. A louse crawled up one's spine like a drop of sweat running the wrong way, and within one there was that great echoing vault, hunger.

In the afternoon, however, a few pots full of soup were thrust through the kitchen door. A thousand men lined up on the path of planks that led to it. Hardly any of us had a mess-tin, but a great rubbish dump full of empty food cans supplied our needs. When the cans were all used up we unscrewed the clouded glass globes covering the electric lamps in the building, and made empty flower-pots water tight by plugging the holes with bits of wood. When these uncouth vessels appeared in the queue they were greeted with shouts of envy, provoked rather by their capacity than by their grotesque character. A sort of carnival procession in search of soup took place, and the owner of an empty sardine-can might be seen gauging a piece of hollow brick half-buried in the mud, wondering if those four holes like organ-pipes might perhaps be stopped up at the base, and turning over the problem with his foot while the column moved on a few yards. Fine rain was falling.

"It's millet!" shouted a man coming towards us from the kitchens, clasping his brimming can in both hands.

A cry of joy, in an unknown voice: a fragmentary phrase, as though cut out of its context, which, uttered in the dying afternoon in the heart of the Volynian plain, seemed to have escaped from a speech begun very far away, many years earlier, and to have returned now—just as, in the hour of death, words half-heard long ago, neglected then and despised, recur to one's memory, suddenly whispering out their plaintive revenge, suddenly gleaming with a prodigious sheen because they hold the last drops of life.

It was not until much later that somebody died.

From the time of that first burial I felt certain that death would never move far from our threshold. A dead body is never buried as deep as one thinks; when a grave is dug, each blow of the pickax consolidates the boundaries of the underground world. Though you lie sepulchred in the earth, like a vessel sunk in quicksands, and the waves of darkness beat against you from below, your bones remain like an anchor cast.

That day a group of German soldiers accompanied the convoy. They were armed and helmeted. They fell into step with the handful of Frenchmen—the chaplain, the medical orderly, the *homme de confiance*[1]—who were walking behind the *tarantass* on which the coffin was laid. They moved very fast and they seemed to be upon us in a few minutes, as we stood watching from the graveyard on the side of the hill (had they remembered to bring the cross and the ropes?); they were charging on us, a crowd of them, two by two, clad from head to foot; they were coming for us, making us realize in a flash what a terrible responsibility we had accepted when we dug that hole, what echoes our solitary toil had roused over there.

We had to face them, to lay the ropes down side by side on the spot where the coffin would be placed, to put down the two logs at the bottom of the grave on which it would lie so that we might afterwards haul up the cords, the ends of which would flap against the coffin for a minute like the pattering footsteps of a last animal escaping. The chaplain recited prayers. The medical orderly sounded Taps on a bugle, picked up somewhere or other. We grasped our ropes and, leaning over the grave, began to slacken them. At an order from their N.C.O. the German soldiers, who were presenting arms, raised the barrels of their guns towards the sky and fired a salvo.

There is always somebody there behind the target of silence. A shout or a word uttered too loud or too soon, and you hear a distant bush crying out with a human voice—you run towards a sort of dark animal only to see it clasp a white, human hand to its bleeding side; it's the tragedy of those hunting accidents where the victims, emerging from silence, are the friend or stranger—equally innocent—who happened to be passing by; there's always somebody passing just there, and we are never sufficiently aware of it.

The German's salvo re-echoed for a long time. We had lifted our heads again. Lower down, on the little road, some peasants and their women, coming back from the town, who had not witnessed the beginning of the ceremony (at that distance, in any case, they could not have observed its details) began to walk suddenly faster, casting a quick look back at us. Some women drew closer together and took each other's arms, a man stumbled in his haste, and all of them swiftly bowed their heads and refused to look at what was happening in our direction.

They seemed possessed not so much by anxiety as by a kind of shuddering anticipation, making them shun a spectacle which they dreaded as though it were contagious and hurry slightly despite their assumed indifference. They betrayed that tendency to deliberate withdrawal which, at that time, was making the whole region more deserted than any exodus could have done.

1. One of the French prisoners chosen by the rest to represent their interests in dealing with the Germans.—Trans.

Had we run towards them, clasped their hands, gazed into their faces crying "It's all right, we're alive!" they would no doubt still have turned away from us, terrified by fresh suspicions, feeling themselves irremediably compromised. . . . Now they had vanished. The Germans slung their rifles. We stood upright round the grave, like a row of shot puppets.

This incident and others less remarkable gave us a feeling of solidarity. We tried to secure official recognition for our team from the camp authorities by presenting a list of our names to every new sentry—to those that kept guard over the gates, those that supervised the kitchens, those that inspected our block. Every week we made out several lists, in case the camp administration should prove forgetful. We gave notice of our existence to remoter authorities, to prisoners' representatives, shock brigade headquarters, divisional commanders, with the stubborn persistence of minorities ceaselessly tormented by the nightmare of illegality.

We guessed that our proceedings met with secret opposition from the Germans, who were unwilling to give public recognition to this peculiar team, the granting of legal status to which would, for them, have been equivalent to admitting criminal premeditation—and from the prisoners too, since they did not need so realistic a reminder of the gruesome truth.

Between two deaths, it was only owing to the force of habit and the routinist mentality of the guardroom officer that we found a couple of sentries waiting each morning to take us to the graveyard. This, lying on the side of the hill amongst long grass, was in such sharp contrast to the almost African aridity of the camp as to enhance the feeling of separateness and even of exclusion which the failure of our advances to the administration had fostered in us. We belonged to another world, we were a team of ghosts returning every morning to a green peaceful place, we were workers in death's garden, characters in a long preparatory dream through which, from time to time, a man would suddenly break, leaping into his last sleep.

In the graveyard we led that orderly existence depicted in old paintings and, even more, in old tapestries and mosaics. A man sitting beside a clump of anemones, another cutting grass with a scythe; water, and somebody lying flat on his belly drinking, and somebody else with his eyes turned skyward, drawing water in a yellow jug. . . . The water was for me and Cordonat. We had chosen the job of watering the flowers and turf transplanted on to the first grave and amongst the clumps of shrubs that we had arranged within our enclosure.

Its boundaries were imaginary but real enough. We had no need to step outside them to fill our vessels at the pond which, from the graveside, could be seen between the branches, a little lower down; there, the radiance of the sky reflected in the water enfolded us so vividly, lit up both our faces so clearly, that any thought of flight could have been read on them from a distance, before we had made the slightest movement, before—risking everything to win everything—we had set the light quivering, like bells.

The only flight left to us was the flight of our eyes towards the wooded valley at the end of which the pond lay. The leaves and grass and tree trunks glowed in the shadow, through which sunbeams filtered and in which, far off, a single leaf, lit by the sun's direct fire, gleamed transparently, an evanescent landmark whose mysterious significance faded quickly as a cloud appeared.

Flowers grew at the very brink of the pond: violets, buttercups, dwarf forget-me-nots, reviving memories of old herbals; only the ladybug's carapace and the red umbrella of the toadstool were lacking to link up the springtime of the world with one's own childhood. When we had filled our bottles, Cordonat and I would linger there gazing at our surroundings, moved by our memories, and in an impulse of greedy sentimentality guessing at the beechnut under the beech leaf, the young acorn under the oak leaf, the mushroom under the toadstool and the snail under the moss.

Sometimes the sun hid. But we could not stir, for we had fallen down out of our dream to such a depth that our task—watering a few clumps of woodsorrel in a remote corner of Volynia—appeared absurd to the point of unreality, like some purgatorial penance where the victims, expiating their own guilt or original sin, are forced to draw unending pails of water from a bottomless well, in a green landscape, tending death like a dwarf tree—just as we were doing here.

Actually, I did not know whether Cordonat's dream followed the same lines as my own. I had lately grown very fond of Cordonat, but he was so deeply consumed by nostalgia that maybe I only loved the shadow of the man. He was ten years older than I, married, with two children; home consists of what you miss most. This vineyard worker from Languedoc showed his Catalan ancestry in his lean, tanned face, with the look of an old torero relegated to the rear rank of a *cuadrilla*,[2] his delicate aquiline nose and wrinkled forehead with white hair over the temples which predestined him for the loneliness of captivity.

It so happened that, with the exception of myself, all the men of our graveyard team, who belonged to the most recent call-up, were natives of the South of France, and all showed a tendency to nostalgic melancholy which was highly appropriate not only to their new duties but to our peculiar isolation on the fringe of camp life. This distinction enhanced a characteristic which was common to all the prisoners of Brodno, who, by their repeated attempts

2. The team assisting the matador in the bullring.

to escape from Germany, had in effect escaped from their own kind. At a time when under cover of captivity countless acts of treachery were taking place, they had set up on the Ukrainian border, in a corner of Europe where the rules of war were easily forgotten, a defiant Resistance movement, a group of "desert rats" whose most seditious song was the Marseillaise.

Homesickness creates its own mirages, which can supersede many a landscape. But that amidst which we were living now was becoming so cruelly vivid that it pierced through all illusory images; it underlay my companions' dreams like a sharp-pointed harrow. This became clear only by slow degrees.

When Cordonat and I were sitting by the pond, we would look up and see peasants and their wives on their way back from the town, passing along the path through the trees and bushes at the end of our valley. We would stand up to see them better and immediately they would hurry on and vanish from sight, imperceptibly accentuating the furtiveness of their way of walking, stooping a little and averting their eyes as though they were eager to avoid the sight of something unlucky or, more precisely, something compromising.

As we stood at the foot of this hillock, somewhat apart from the other prisoners, we must have seemed to be in one of those irregular situations which were not uncommon here, like cases of some infectious disease. Were we escaped prisoners, obdurate rebels? Were we in quarantine, or about to be shot? In any case we were obviously trying to make them our accomplices, determined to betray them into a word or a look and thus involve them in that contamination that always ended with a shower of bullets and blood splashed against a wall. And the forest in which, only a minute before, spring flowers had awakened childhood memories, now emerged as though from some Hercynian flexure, darker and denser, more mysterious and more ominous, because of the fear and hunger of men. Fear can blast reality.

But it was when we left the skirt of the forest and reached the plain where the town lay that this devastating power of fear seemed actually to color the whole landscape. The white road, the far-off white house fronts, the lack of shadows, all this was deprived of radiance by the subdued quality of the light; but it exuded a kind of stupor. At first, you noticed nothing.

But when we drew near we would suddenly catch sight of a man or a woman standing motionless between two houses or two hedges, and turning towards us in an attitude of submission, like people who have been warned to prepare for any danger. The man or woman would stare at us as we passed with eyes that revealed neither curiosity nor envy nor dread: a gaze that was not dreamy, but enigmatically watchful. A few men, also dressed in threadbare town clothes, were filling up the holes in the pavement. They did not raise their heads as we went by; they kept on with their work, but performed only secondary, inessential tasks, like factory hands waiting for the bell to release them from work and staying at their posts only because they have to.

In every case we were aware that, as we approached (or more precisely as our sentries approached), some final inner process of preparation was taking place (but maybe it had long since been completed?) and that one of the Germans had only to say "Come on!," load his gun or raise the butt to strike, for everything to take its inevitable, unaltering course. The tension of waiting was extreme.

They had long ago passed the stage when your pulse beats faster, spots dance before your eyes and sweat breaks out on your back; they had not left fear behind, but they had been married to it for so long that it had lost its original power. Fear shared their lives, and when we walked past with our sentries beside us it was Fear, that tireless companion, that began, in a burst of lunatic lucidity, to count the pebbles dropping into the hole in the pavement, the trees along the road, or the days dividing that instant from some past event or other—the fête at Tarnopol, or Easter 1933, or the day little Chaim passed his exam: some other spring day, some dateless day, some distant day that seemed to collect and hold all the happiness in life.

Sometimes, in the depth of their night, fear would flare up and wake them, like the suddenly remembered passion that throws husband and wife into each other's arms; then they would embrace their fear, foreseeing the coming of their death like the birth of a child, and their thoughts would set out in the next room the oblong covered cradle in which it would be laid. Morning would bring back their long lonely wait, tête-à-tête with fear. They tied round their arms the strip of white material with the star of David drawn on it. Often the armlet slipped down below the elbow, and hung round the forearm slack and rumpled and soiled like an old dressing that has grown loose and needs renewing. The wound is unhealed, but dry. But why should I speak of wounds? Hunger, cold, humiliation and fear leave corpses without stigmata. One morning we saw a man lying dead by the roadside on the way to the graveyard. There was no face; it was hidden in the grass. There was no distinguishing mark, save the armlet with the star of David. There was no blood. There is practically no blood in the whole of this tale of death.

One Monday morning two new sentries came up to join us at the camp gates. They belonged to a nondescript battalion in shabby uniforms which had been sent from somewhere in Poland by way of relief, and had arrived at Brodno a few days earlier; one of those nomadic divisions to which only inglorious duties are assigned, and whose soldiers get killed only in defeats.

Our two new sentries were a perfect example of the contrasts, exaggerated to the point of grotesqueness, which are always to be found among any group of belatedly conscripted men, since neither regulation dress nor *esprit de corps* nor conviction can replace the uniformity of youth. One of the two soldiers was long and thin, with a high-colored face; the other, short and squat, was pale.

Each morning, when we went into the enclosure, we would quickly dismiss and, one after the other, go and stand before the graves giving a military salute; it was the only solemn moment of the day. That morning, as I was walking after my comrades to pay my homage to the dead, I heard a click behind me: the taller of the two soldiers was loading his gun. We had been running rather quickly towards our dead, because it was Monday and we felt lively. He had been afraid we were trying to escape or mutiny. But we were merely hurrying towards the graves like workmen to the factory cloakroom, discarding discipline and, at the same time, hanging up our jackets on the crosses.

There were only three graves at this time. We made up for this by working on the flowerbeds, those other plots of consecrated, cultivated ground. Cordonat and I were already grasping our bottles, eager to resume our reveries beside the pond, at the bottom of which could be seen a rifle and a hand grenade thrown there by a fugitive Russian soldier. This filthy panoply, sunk deep in the mud, mingled with our reflected images when we bent over the water, as though we had not been haunted enough for the past two years by the memory of our discarded arms.

I went up to the short German soldier (the other had alarmed me by that performance with his rifle a little while before) and explained to him that it was our custom to go and draw water from the pond. He nodded, smiling but silent; then, before I went off, he said to me in French: *"Je suis curé."*

The word, uttered with an accent that was in itself slightly ridiculous, had a kind of popular simplicity that, far from conferring any grandeur on it, seemed to relegate it to the vocabulary of anticlericalism, made it sound like the admission of a comic anomaly. Such a statement, made by this embarrassed little man wearing a dreaded uniform in the depth of that nameless country, suggested the depressing exhibitionism of hermaphrodites, the sudden surprise of their disclosure. I could find nothing to reply.

"Protestant," he went on in his own language. "In France, you're mostly Catholics."

So he was a pastor. The rights of reason were restored—so were those of the field-gray uniform, since I found it easier to associate the Protestant religion with the military profession. I acquiesced: we were, apparently, Catholics. Generously, the Germans granted us this valid historical qualification; we might graze on this reprieve. The little pastor, however, did not try to stop us from going to draw water for our flowers; he encouraged us to do so and walked along with us down the path leading to the pond.

Without giving me time to answer, he chattered in his own language, of which Cordonat understood barely a word. I had never before heard German spoken so volubly; it poured forth like a long-repressed confession, like a flood breaking the old barriers of prejudice and rationalism, and the clear waters rushed freely over me, carrying the harsh syllables like loose pebbles. He was a pastor at Marburg. His family came from the Rhineland and one of his ancestors was French. In the Rhineland they grew vines; the country was beautiful there. Marburg lay farther east; and there they still remembered Schiller and Goethe and Lessing (nowadays people seldom talk about Lessing). The pastor's wife was an invalid. On summer evenings he would go into the town cafés with his elder daughter. They were often taken for man and wife.

He went on talking. It was a sunny June morning. The Ukrainian wheat was springing up. By the side of the sandy roads, you could sometimes see sunflower blossoms thrown away by travelers after eating the seeds. And we carried on our Franco-Rhenish colloquy, squatting at the foot of the hillock, beside the pond, in the shade of the trees, while the peasant women, suspecting some fresh conflict, some subtle and wordy form of bullying, hurriedly passed by higher up, with a rustle of leaves under their bare feet.

In order to keep our hands occupied and to justify our long halt by the pond in the eyes of the other sentry, Cordonat and I had begun to scour our mess-tins. We always carried them about with us. I had fixed a small wire handle to mine so as to hook it to my belt. This habit was partly due to the constant hope of some windfall, some unexpected distribution of food, but also no doubt it expressed a sort of fetishistic attachment to the object that symbolized our age's exclusive concern with the search for food. These mess-tins, which had only been handed out to us on our second day in camp, were like little zinc bowls; we went about with barbers' basins hanging from our waists. As part of this instinctive cult, we felt bound to polish them scrupulously. Cordonat and I were particular about this, to the point of mania. It was largely because of the fine sand on the edge of the pond and also because we were waiting—waiting for better days to come.

"*Ydiom! Ydiom!*" ("Come on!") we heard a peasant woman on the hill above us calling to one of her companions, who must have been lingering in the exposed zone.

The little pastor kept on talking.

"What d'you think of all this?" I asked him.

"It's terrible," he said. "Yes, what's happening here is terrible."

That simple word assumed the value of a confession, of a dangerous secret shared. It was enough in those days (a look, a gesture, a change of expression would have been enough) to lift the hostile mask and reveal the pact beneath. However, I dared not venture further and I began pleading our cause, describing our destitution, making no major charge but only such obvious complaints as could give no serious offense to the Germans. The petty sufferings we endured acted as a convenient salve for one's conscience; I realized this as I spoke and I resented it. Even this graveyard, so sparsely populated and so lavishly decorated, had begun to look like "a nice place for a picnic," with its green turf overlying the great banqueting-halls of death.

"Terrible, terrible," the little pastor kept saying. It was the word he had used earlier. But it had lost its original beauty.

Back in camp, after the midday meal of soup, I waited impatiently for the two sentries to come and take us to the graveyard. I looked forward to seeing Ernst, the pastor (he had told me his name), with a feeling of mingled sympathy and curiosity that was practically friendship; it only needed to be called so.

I was not surprised when, on reaching the graveyard, Ernst took me into the forest, explaining to his mate that we were going to look for violet plants. It was high time, the last violets were fading. The other German appeared quite satisfied with this explanation. Since the morning, he had been so good-humored that I felt inclined to think that that sudden business with the rifle had been an automatic gesture; a gun never lets your hands stay idle. He had a long shrewd face.

"I'm a Socialist," he told my friends while I walked away with Ernst.

Cordonat watched me go; was he envying me or disowning me? He sat there beside the pond like some lonely mythological figure.

But now the forest was opening up in front of me: that forest which hitherto I had known only in imagination, which had existed for me by virtue not of its copious foliage or its stalwart tree-trunks but of its contrasting gloom, the powerful way it shouldered the horizon and above all its secret contribution to the darkness that weighed me down. We walked on amidst serried plants; he carried his rifle in its sling, looking less like an armed soldier than like a tired huntsman, glad to have picked up a companion along the homeward road. But already the forest and its dangerous shadows had begun to suggest that the journey home would be an endless one, that our companionship was forever; once more, in the midst of a primeval forest, we were shackled together like those countless lonely damned couples—the prisoner and his guard, the body and its conscience, the hound and its prey, the wound and the knife, oneself and one's shadow.

"Well, when you're not too hungry in camp, what d'you like doing? You must have some sort of leisure. Oh, I know you don't like that word. But I don't know any other way to express the situation where I'd hope to find your real self—for hunger isn't really you, Peter. Well, what else is there?"

He pushed back from his hip the butt of his rifle, which kept swinging between us.

"I walk round the camp beside the barbed wire, or else I sleep, and when I find a book I read it. . . ."

"And sometimes you write, too. . . ."

I looked at Ernst suspiciously.

"A few days ago," he went on, " I was on guard in one of the watchtowers. I noticed you. You stopped to write something in a little note book. This morning I recognized you at once."

This disclosure irritated me.

"You see, I can't even be alone!" I cried. "Isn't that inhuman?"

"But you were alone. You were alone because at that moment I didn't know you, and you didn't know me. Really, nothing was happening at all."

He was beginning to sound a little too self-confident. It was a tone that did not seem natural to him; there was a sort of strained excitement about it. I did not pursue the matter; without answering I bent down to pick up my violet plants. Ernst stood in silence for a while then, returning to the words I had spoken a few minutes earlier, as though his mind had dwelt on them in spite of what had followed:

"Books," he repeated with a schoolmasterish air of satisfaction and longing. "They were my great refuge too, when I spent a few months in a concentration camp two years ago. I'd been appointed librarian, thank Heaven. . . . Look here," he went on in a livelier tone, as though what had been said previously was of no importance, "put down your violet plants. Come and I'll show you something."

He was giving me line enough, as fishermen say; but I was well and truly caught this time. I stood up. He had started off ahead of me along a path that led to the right. I caught up with him: "I suppose the camp was on account of your political ideas?"

"Political . . . well, that's a word we don't much care for. Rather on account of my moral views. However, they did let me out of that camp. It was just a warning. I need hardly tell you that I haven't changed. . . . You see that wall?"

I saw the wall. It was decrepit, overgrown with moss and briars, its stones falling apart, and it enclosed a space in which the forest seemed to go on, to judge by the treetops that appeared above it. We walked some way round the outside and came to a gap in the wall. Within the enclosure gray stones stood among trees which were slighter than those of the surrounding forest, contrary to my previous impression. Here and there, pale grass was growing; it had begun to take possession of the ground again. The upright stones marked Jewish graves, a hundred years old no doubt. Eastern religions lay their dead at the foot of slabs of slate, stumbling blocks for the encroaching wilderness. Time had jostled many and overthrown a few of these old battlements of death, monoliths on which Heaven had written its reckoning in the only tongue it has ever spoken.

Ernst knew a little Hebrew. His small plump hand was soon moving over the stone, beginning on the right as in fortune-telling by cards. He read out some long-distant date, lazily coiled up now with a caterpillar of moss lying in the concavity of the figures, some name, with the knowledgeable curiosity of an accountant who has discovered old statements, bills yellow with age that have been settled once and for all. His religion was based on the belief that death belongs to the past and, when he looked at a grave, whether worn down by time or black with leaf-mold, he would say to himself with visible gladness that "all that's over and done with." Meanwhile I was overwhelmed by the symbolism of these graves; on most of the stones there was carved a breaking branch—you could see the sharp points at the break and the two fragments about to separate forming an angle, a gaping angle like an elbow. It was like the sudden rending that takes place high up in the tree of life, its imminence revealed by the flight of a bird, of that other soul which has hitherto deafened us by its ceaseless twittering, whereas our real life lay in the roots. On the stone, the branch was endlessly breaking, it would never break; when death has come, has one finished dying? Ernst raised his head and straightened his back.

"I've been rereading your classics," he said to me with a smile.

I did not understand.

"I mean that this ancient, traditional burial ground, close by your own fresh and improvised one, is rather like the upper shelf in a library. . . ." He laid his hand on a carved stone. "The preceding words in the great book. . . ."

"Who can tell? Perhaps the moment of death is never over," I replied, thinking of the symbol of the broken branch. "Perhaps we are doomed to a perpetual leavetaking from that which was life and which lies in the depth of night, as eternal as the patient stars. Perhaps there is no more identity in death than in life. Each man dies in his own corner, each man stays dead in his own corner, alone and friendless. Every death invents death anew."

"But I believe in Heaven and in the communities of Heaven, where no echo of life is heard," replied Ernst joyfully. "In the peace of the Lord."

"I cannot and will not believe that those who are murdered here cease their cries the moment after. . . ."

"Their cries have been heard before," said Ernst. "What do you mean? Do you need to hear dead men's cries? Isn't it enough that God remembers them, that we remember them? I will tell you something: they are sleeping peacefully in the light, all in the same light."

"That's too easy an answer!" I cried. "That's just to make us feel at peace."

"Don't torture yourself," Ernst replied. "In any case, neither you nor I is to blame."

We were not to blame. I had taken up my violets again from the place where I had left them a short while before and, with this badge of innocence, my flowers refuting what Ernst's rifle might suggest, we made our way to the graveyard through the silent forest.

"Tomorrow we'll go for another walk," Ernst said. "We might take the others too. We'll find some pretext."

But next day we were deprived of any pretext. Two men had died in the camp. Graves had to be dug; the dead had to be buried.

Ernst directed our labors skillfully and with pensive dignity. It was he who taught us that in this part of Europe they lined the inside of graves with fir-branches. Not to lag behind in the matter of symbolism we decided to bury the dead facing towards France. As France happened to be on the farther side of the forest against which the first row of graves had been dug, we were obliged to lay the dead men the wrong way round, with their feet under the crosses.

These two deaths occurring simultaneously aroused our anxiety. Sanitary conditions within the camp had worsened; underfed and weakened by their sufferings during the escape, and the subsequent journeys from camp to camp, the men gathered in daily increasing numbers in a huge sickroom. A few French doctors had been sent to Brodno by way of reprisal; lacking any sort of medicaments, they went from one straw mattress to the next making useless diagnoses, reduced to the passive role of witnesses in this overcrowded world whose rhythm was the gallop of feverish pulses and where delirious ravings mingled in a crazy arabesque, while men sat coughing their lungs out.

We buried four men in the same week. June was nearly over; it was already summer. By now, the white roads of the invasion spread like a network over the Russian land, far east of Brodno, right up to the Don, then to the Volga, to the Kuban, milestoned with poisoned wells. The woods were full of hurriedly filled graves, and the smoke rose up straight and still from the countryside, while the front page of German illustrated papers showed bareheaded soldiers, with their sleeves rolled up, munching apples as they set off to conquer the world. Hope dried up suddenly, like a well.

The Germans' victorious summer, as it rolled eastward, left us stranded on that floor formed by the hardened sediments of their violence, their extortions, their acts of murder, which already disfigured the whole of Europe. The drift of war away from us had only removed the unusualness of these things; the things themselves remained, only instead of seeming improvised they had assumed a workmanlike character; ruins were now handmade, homes became prisons, murder was premeditated.

The Jews of Brodno had practically stopped working inside the camp, where everything was now in order. Those who were road menders spent their time vainly searching the roads for other holes to fill; the sawmill workers, whom we used to see on our way to the graveyard, kept on moving the same planks to and fro, with gestures that had become ominously slow. More and more frequently you could see men and women, wearers of the white armlet, standing motionless between houses or against a hedge, driven there by the somnambulism of fear.

Inside the camp the same fatal idleness impelled the French to line up against the barbed wire, with their empty knapsacks slung across their back and clogs on their bare feet. To Jews and Frenchmen alike (to the former particularly) going and staying were equally intolerable fates, and they would advance timidly towards the edge of the road or of the barbed wire, take one step back and move a little to one side, as though seeking some state intermediary between departure and immobility. They would stand on the verge of imagined flight, and in their thoughts would dig illusory tunnels through time.

The tunnels we were digging might well have served them as models. Only ours had no outlet.

"Indeed, yes, Peter, graves have outlets," Ernst told me.

He had just brought me the stories of Klemens von Brentano.[3] Death having left us a brief respite, we had gone off for a walk in the forest. A little way behind us, my comrades were gathered round Otto, the other sentry.

"What's he saying?" they shouted to me. I turned round. Otto repeated the words he had just uttered.

"He says that at home he was the best marksman in the district," I translated.

"Yes, we got that, he won some competitions. But he said something about birds. . . ."

"He can kill a bird on a branch fifty meters off with one shot. He's ready to prove it to us presently."

Otto was smiling, his neck wrinkling. His boast sounded like a public tribute when repeated as an aside by somebody else. I went back to Ernst.

"He's a nuisance with his stories of good marksmanship! Shots would make too much noise in the forest and in these parts they mean only one

3. German poet (1778–1842) of the Romantic school. Brentano wrote plays, lyric poems, fairy tales, and novellas.

thing. I was going to take you to see the girls who work where the new road's being made. If he shoots we shall find them all terrified. . . ."

The project had a frivolous ring but Ernst forestalled my questions:

"They are young Jewish girls, unfortunate creatures. I've made friends with one of them. Every evening I take her some bread—a little bread; it's my own bread—at least, part of my own bread," he added in some confusion, recalling the daily agony of sharing it, his hunger and his weakness.

"Why are we going to see them?" I asked him. "We can't do anything for them. You know that."

"You are French, and the point is this: these are girls from the cultured classes of Brodno. They are better dressed than the peasants, they don't speak the same language, they had relations in various other countries, and now they are isolated, as though by some terrible curse. Nothing can save them from their isolation. Even if tomorrow the peasants round here were to be persecuted, the girls would find no support amongst them, no sense of kinship, no co-operation. Believe me, they've always been exiles in the East, even before the Germans settled here. And perhaps only you and I share what they've got, what makes them different. So don't run away."

"How could I run away?" I pointed to his gun. Ernst reddened with anger and shook his head. Behind us, big Otto had seen my gesture: "Don't talk to the pastor about his gun," he called out to me. "He thinks it's a fishing rod."

I turned round. "Please note that I'm just as much a pacifist as he is," Otto said. "Only I know how to shoot!"

He burst out laughing. Cordonat was near him and beckoned to me. "Ask him to choose a biggish target," he said as I came up, "a rabbit, for instance, or a jay or a crow. Let's at least have something to get our teeth into!"

I passed on the request to Otto.

"But then it wouldn't be a demonstration," he cried. "It's got to be quite a tiny animal."

I tried to explain to him that he could still keep to the rules of the game if he stood farther away from his living target. The argument seemed likely to go on indefinitely.

Ernst walked on ahead of us, indifferent to our conversation, with his back a little bent, like a recluse, and in addition that pathetic look that small men have when they are unhappy. He was going forward through the forest without keeping to the paths, and the forest was growing thicker. Already, we felt cut off from the outside world here, just because the shadows were a little deeper and the ground was carpeted with dead leaves, moss, myrtles and nameless plants. For us, as for millions of others, war meant "the fear of roads." These enslaved men looked at you sometimes with eyes like horses'.

There was still the sky, the sky between the branches when you raised your head, an unyielding sky, still heavy with threats. Daylight is up there. I must be dreaming. It was as if when you pushed open the shutters after a night full of bad dreams the influx of light proved powerless to dispel the terrifying visions of the darkness from your eyes. And yet everything is there, quite real. You need a second or third awakening, the maneuvering of a whole set of sluice-gates, before the morning light yields what you expect of it—not so much truth as justice.

After a few minutes I caught up with Ernst. I was afraid of disappointing him by showing so little interest in the visit he had suggested to me. Perhaps he had given it up; the thought caused me no remorse, for he was a man with too clear a conscience, too easily moved to compassion. But even if I had interfered with the execution of his plans, I did not want him to think me indifferent or insensitive.

"I'm hungry," I said as I drew near him, so as to avoid further explanations.

"So am I. But we shall soon find these girls, and they'll give us some coffee—they make it out of roasted grain. That'll help to appease our hunger. Afterwards we'll go and fell the trees. And then Otto will have plenty of time to fire his shots."

The trees that we were to fell were intended to build a fence round the graveyard. Ernst had discovered this excuse to justify our walks. We were now on a path that led down to the verge of the forest. The new road that was being made skirted it at this point and the workmen had set up a few huts for their gear and for the canteen. Eight Jewish girls worked here under German orders on various tasks, and two of them kept the canteen.

These were the girls we saw first when Ernst, telling his mate we were going to get some coffee, led me towards the hut. The two girls had come out over the threshold. They were wearing faded summer dresses whose original colors suggested Western fashions and cheap mass production. That was enough to introduce into this woodland setting an urban note which would have struck one as strange even without the added impression of bewilderment and weariness conveyed by the pale faces and wild eyes of the two girls. In spite of their youth, their features were devoid of charm. Beautiful faces were rare in this war; those faces which were daily taken from one were like commonplace relatives full of modest virtues, known intimately and loved and now gone into the night, unforgettable faces with their freckles and their tear-stained eyes.

When they recognized Ernst the two girls nodded gently. They stayed close together on the doorstep. Ernst spoke to them, calling them by their names. We were Frenchmen, he told them, prisoners too, hungry and unhappy. "Nothing was happening." We looked at each other, helplessly. What conversation could we hold? Everything has been said before we opened our mouths. It was not to one another that we must listen but to the far-off heavens, to which someday perhaps would rise the noise of our deliverance.

"We can't give you coffee," said one of the girls to Ernst. "The *Meister* hasn't given us any grain today."

Ernst had poked his head inside the hut to peer around. "Who's that?" he asked in a whisper. I looked too. In a corner of the room a man in black was leaning over a basin, with his back towards us. He was dipping a rag in water and from time to time raising it to his face. One could guess from the stiff hunching of his shoulders and the timidity betrayed by his slow awkward gestures that he felt our eyes upon him.

"It's a man from the sawmill," quickly replied one of the girls. "He hurt his face at work."

"But he doesn't work up here," said Ernst. "If the *Meister* finds him here there'll be a row."

"He'll go away when you've gone," said the smaller of the two girls, speaking for the first time and with an ill-disguised nervousness. She was dirty, with untidy red hair hanging down each side of her face. "The other sentinel mustn't see him," she went on in a low voice. "Please, Herr Pastor, be kind and take your Frenchman farther off."

"Where is Lidia?" asked Ernst.

"She's working on the dump trucks," said the other girl. "She's being punished because she broke the cord of the siren this morning."

"It's not fair!" went on the smaller girl, with bitterness. "The cord was rotten. When she tried to stop the siren, at seven o'clock, the cord broke off in her hand. The siren went on wailing long after everybody was at work. All the steam was being wasted. The *Meister* called it insubordination. It's not fair. . . . Yesterday they hanged four more men at Tarnopol."

"The way that siren went on wailing," said her friend. "There was something sinister about it—it was like a warning. But what was the use of warning us? How could we move? What could we do?" she added anxiously.

Ernst did not answer. He stood with downcast eyes.

"Perhaps I'll come back tonight," he said after a while. "Tell Lidia. God be with you."

We joined the group of prisoners who were waiting for us, guarded by Otto, and plunged once more into the forest.

"Somebody must have hit him," muttered Ernst as I walked at his side. "I'm speaking of that man we saw in the hut," he added, with a look at me. "He didn't want us to see the blood."

"Why not?"

"Because they feel that to let their blood be seen is not only a confession of weakness, of impotence, but moreover it marks them out as belonging to the scattered herd of blood-stained victims who are being ruthlessly hunted down. While they are whole, they'll carry on as long as their luck holds; when they're wounded, they go out to meet their own death. The order of things that has been established here is all-embracing, Peter. If a civilian—if one of these civilians is found with blood on him, the authorities think the worst. Where did he get it, who gave him leave to move about? Why is he branded with that mark, and why is he not with the herd of the dead? There's something suspicious about it. That man was well aware of this. He was hiding. He'd 'stolen' a beating. . . ."

"Do you think those girls are really in danger?"

While I was asking Ernst this question I realized that I had no wish to learn from him whether their danger was great or small. For the last few minutes I had experienced that slight nausea which, at the time, was more effective than any outward sign in warning me of imminent peril. Before Ernst could answer me a shot rang out behind us. Otto lowered his rifle and Cordonat ran towards a bush: "It's a jay!" he called out to me.

But I was observing the amazement created all around us, in the lonely forest, by the sudden report. I thought I caught sight of a gray figure disappearing swiftly between distant tree trunks. Then everything was as it had been, unmoving. I did not want to talk any more, and Ernst seemed not to want to either. That rifleshot had been like a blow struck with a clenched fist on a table, a call to order, silencing all chatter, even the private chatter of the heart. Otto was looking at us with a smile. He was looking at Ernst and myself. The bullet had passed just over our heads. He stopped smiling just as I was about to speak, to try and break out of that clear-cut circle which henceforward would enclose the three of us and within which we were now bound to one another by the dangerous silence that followed our commonplace words.

The dead used to be brought to us in the morning, like mail that comes with habitual irregularity and provides no surprises; their belongings had to be classified, bills of lading for ships that have long since put out to sea; a cross had to be provided, with a name and a date. Now the coffins no longer showed those once ever-present wooden faces like those of eyeless suits of armor. Now a dead man in his coffin was no longer a human being wrapped in a door.

All we knew of the dead was their weight. However, this varied enough to arouse in us occasionally a sort of suspicion that somehow seemed to rarefy this inert merchandise. Unconsciously one was led to think in terms of a soul.

A dead body that felt exceptionally heavy or, on the other hand, too light, reassumed some semblance of personality, smuggled in, as it were, in that unexpected gap between the weight of an "average" corpse and that of this particular corpse.

Things had begun to take their course. We might have been tempted to open the coffin, to examine the inscrutable face, to question the dead man's friends and search out his past history. But it was too late; the coffin was being lowered on its ropes, it lay at the bottom of the grave on the two supports we had placed there; the body was laid down, laid on its andirons and already more than half consumed with oblivion, loaded with ashes.

By now our burial ground comprised seventeen graves. The flowers had grown and we were preparing to open a new section. It would be another row of graves set below the first, which lay alongside the edge of the forest. We were thus tackling the second third of the graveyard, for its limits had been strictly set from the beginning. Hardly two months had passed since our arrival at Brodno and we were already beginning to wonder if the graveyard would last out as long as we did, or if it would be full before we left the camp, so that someday we might find ourselves confronted with an overflow of dead bodies which would have to be disposed of in a hasty, slapdash, sacrilegious way.

We foresaw that times would have changed by then; we might have a snowy winter, for instance, full of urgent tasks, and the fortunes of war would be drooping like a bent head. The limits of the burial ground, in a word, were those of our future, of our hope; all summer was contained within them. This summer had begun radiantly.

Fed by marshlands, fanned by the great wind blowing off the plain, the forest was aglow with its thousands of tree trunks—beeches and birches for the most part—and its millions of leaves; carpeted with monkshood and borage, it projected into the middle of the wide wilderness, somewhat like a mirage no doubt, but above all like a narrow concession made to the surrounding landscape, to the past, and, in a more practical sense, to the dead.

We had gone through it now in all directions. As soon as a funeral was over Ernst and Otto would take us off to the hamlets that lay on the other side of the forest. There we would buy food from the peasants in exchange for linen and military garments from our Red Cross parcels; the barter took place swiftly and in silence, as though between thieves. We brought home a few fowls or rabbits, which we hurriedly slaughtered in the forest, using our knees and cursing one another, while the sentries guarded the paths.

We would wipe our hands with leaves. Then the dead creature had to be slipped inside one's trousers, between one's legs, held up by strings tied round the head and feet and wound round one's waist. The volume of the body, the feel of fur or feather, the temporary invasion of the lice they harbored, the smell of blood and a lingering warmth made us feel as though we were saddled with some ludicrous female sexual appendage, as though we had given birth to something hairy and shapeless that obliged us to walk clumsily, with straddled legs.

This stratagem enabled us to get back into the camp safely; I had no hesitation about resorting to it under the eyes of Ernst, since the very vulgarity of my movements, my grotesque gait, freed me from the mental complicity that bound me to him. It was a sort of revenge against despair. Sometimes, on the way back, we would catch a distant glimpse of the men and women at work on the new road. Ernst pointed out Lidia to me; she was wearing a light-colored dress and pushing a dump truck full of earth. Rain was threatening: "She's going to get soaked to the skin," Ernst muttered.

"Why Lidia?" I asked.

"Yes, why Lidia. . . ." he echoed, in torment, his head downcast.

"I meant why are you particularly interested in her?" It was hard to keep up this tone with a barely dead fowl stuck between your thighs.

"One has to make a choice, Peter," Ernst murmured. "One can't suffer tortures on every side at once. Mind you, that doesn't mean. . . ."

Otto was behind us, though far enough not to catch our words. I felt sure that if we went on talking like this he would soon shoot a jay, a magpie, the first bird he saw. There's always one ready to fly off from an empty branch over your head, a little way in front of you or to one side. At every word, like involuntary beaters, we "put up" a covey of pretexts, birds with strange plumage and taunting cries. I turned round; Otto was smiling. Since I had begun carrying slaughtered animals between my legs his smile had grown broader; I was a fellow. Suddenly his smile froze: "Halt!" he called to me, pointing into the depths of the forest. Two figures were rapidly disappearing between the trees.

"Partisans," he said, hurriedly smiling again.

The word "partisans," as he spoke it, seemed to indicate some species of big game, rare and practically invulnerable, some solitary stag or boar shaking the unmysterious undergrowth with its startled gallop. Yet my heart had leaped. One morning, when we reached the burial ground, we caught sight of black smoke drifting over a hamlet in the plain. Otto explained to me that some partisans, having been given a poor reception there in the night, had burned it by way of reprisal. After that the open German cars that drove through Brodno assumed a warlike aspect, despite their gleaming nickel and brightly polished bodies. For beside the officers they were carrying sat two helmeted soldiers armed with Tommy guns.

We did not see them for long; the partisans seemed to have disappeared. In the villages, the Germans had distributed arms and formed militias. A watchman blew a bugle at the first alarm; it was a sort of long wail in the depth of the night which, generally without cause, made those who had taken refuge in treachery stir in their uneasy sleep. During the day Ukrainian policemen passed along the little path below the graveyard. They wore a black uniform with pink, yellow or white braid and badges of the same colors in checks, circles or triangles, like the gaudy signals of some obscure code hung out on the semaphores of terror.

The Germans acknowledged the stiff salutes of these liveried men with a nonchalant air. The Jews shrank back when they drew near: the Ukrainian policemen had the wild cruelty of certain sheep dogs, and above all their eyes and their voices recalled traditional pogroms.[4] A few days earlier they had killed three prisoners who had escaped from the camp, shooting them down in the wood.

When they passed near us Cordonat would taunt them under his breath in the patois of Languedoc. These muttered insults showed the total disconnectedness of everything; what mazes of recent history one would have to explore to account for this absurd conflict between a Ukrainian peasant dressed in a stage uniform and a *vigneron*[5] from the South of France who, before the war, used to vote anti-Communist and who was now talking, in his patois, about joining the Volynian partisans.

Otto made fun of the Ukrainian policemen out loud when they had gone past us, and embarked on a conversation with Cordonat in which gestures to a large extent filled the gaps in their vocabulary; after a lengthy exchange of naïvely pacifist opinions, they had ended by discussing hunting, poaching and mushrooms.

Ernst appeared to be growing somewhat mistrustful of his companion. In order to be able to speak freely to me he evolved the plan of taking me almost every day to the sawmill to get our woodcutting tools sharpened. I had never expressed any wish for these tête-à-tête conversations. They only lasted, actually, during the time we took to walk from the burial ground to the sawmill. This sawmill was worked on behalf of the Germans by a Jewish employer and his men. I met there the man with the wounded face of whom we had caught sight a few days earlier in the girls' hut.

4. A violent, government-condoned attack perpetrated against Russian Jews. Such attacks, backed by official anti-Semitism, occurred in numerous towns and cities between 1881 and the Russian Revolution.
5. Workers in the vineyards.

I had asked the boss of the sawmill for a glass of water, as he stood talking to us in front of the workshop door. He turned round and asked someone inside, whom I could not see, to bring me one. A few minutes later Isaac Lebovitch came up to me carrying a glass of water. It was a glass of fine quality, patterned with a double ring, the remnant of a set no doubt, and its fragility and bourgeois origin made me uneasy. In this token of hospitality I recognized an object which might have been a family heirloom of my own.

Isaac Lebovitch (he was soon to tell me his name) seemed to be about thirty years old. He had a long face with a lean beak of a nose. His dark curly hair, already sparse, grew low on his forehead. He stood beside us while I was emptying my glass.

"It may be that our hour has struck," the master of the sawmill was saying to Ernst. "It may be that the end of our race is in sight. There are things written up there," he added, pointing to the sky which was empty of birds, empty of hope.

I noticed a vine climbing round the door of the sawmill. In that region where vines had never been cultivated it looked strange, like a Biblical symbol.

"And yet," the sawmill boss was saying, "I myself fought during the last war in the Austro-Hungarian army. I was an N.C.O. and I won a medal. That means I was on your side, doesn't it?"

I felt embarrassed as I listened to his words. He was quite an old man, no sort of rebel against order or established authority, ready to accept a strict social hierarchy and even a certain degree of victimization to which his religion exposed him. . . . But not this, not what was happening now! These things were on the scale of a cosmogony. Or worse: they took you into a universe which perhaps had always existed behind the solid rampart of the dead, and of which the metaphors of traditional rhetoric only gave you superficial glimpses: where the bread was, literally, snatched from one's mouth, where one could not keep body and soul together, where one really was bled white and died like a dog.

Like novice sorcerers inexpert in the magic of words, we now beheld the essential realities of hell, escaping from the dry husks of their formulae, come crowding towards us and over us: the black death of the plague, the bread of affliction, the pride of a louse. . . . Seeing that Ernst was listening, with a look of deep distress, to the old man's words, Lebovitch plucked up courage to speak to me. He first addressed me in German, asking me whereabouts in France I lived, what sort of job I had, whether my relatives over there suffered as much from the German occupation as the people here did; then he suddenly spoke a sentence in English.

It was quite an ordinary sentence like "Life isn't good here." There was really no need to wrap it up in the secrecy of another language, since it was no more compromising than the words that had preceded it; and no doubt he had only had recourse to these English words for the sake of their foreignness. A language does not always remain intact; when it had been forced to express monstrous orders, bitter curses and the mutterings of murderers, it retains for a long time those insidious distortions, those sheer slopes of speech from the top of which one looks down dizzily. In those days the German language was like a landscape full of ravines, from the depths of which rose tragic echoes.

"No, life isn't good here," I answered in German. "But out there in the forest. . . ."

"I don't go there any more. The other day. . . ." Lebovitch showed me the dry wound on his forehead. "Besides, you saw. . . ."

"Probably you didn't go far enough, you didn't venture into the depths. . . ."

"I had just gone to see Lidia," said Lebovitch, surprised by my remark. "I have no reason to go farther. You're liable to meet the partisans. . . ."

"That's just what I meant."

He stayed silent for a moment. We had moved a little farther off and had turned our backs on Ernst and the old man. Lebovitch stepped still farther to one side and, realizing that he wanted me to come away from the other two, I went up beside him.

"The partisans," he said with an anxious air. "I'll tell you this: we don't know much about them. If they saw me coming up to them they might shoot me down. And how could I live in that forest? I've got no strength left," he gasped, striking his thin chest with his fist. "And then there's so much violence, so much bloodshed every day, and all those farms set on fire. . . . After all, we're managing to hold out here. I've held out up till now. Perhaps we've been through the hardest part now. Listen, I may perhaps be dead to-morrow but I think it's better for me to save my strength. Don't you think that's best for you too?"

It would have been cruel to tell him that the dangers that threatened us seemed less terrible than his own, and I left him to his patience.

"That girl you call Lidia, who works on the new road," I remarked, "isn't she the one my sentry knows?"

"He ought to stop trying to see her. She told me so. It's likely do her a lot of harm. I think she's had herself sent to the dump trucks on purpose because of him, so that he can't try to see her during the daytime. What's he want with her, anyway? He knows that relations of that sort are forbidden. He'll only get her hanged, and himself after her."

"He wants to help her."

Lebovitch grasped me by the arm, after making sure that the other two could not see him: "Let me tell you this, Frenchman: the Germans can help nobody, d'you understand, nobody. They couldn't if they wanted to, they couldn't any longer. Imagine a hedgehog struggling to stop being a hedgehog; you wouldn't want to go near him then!"

Ernst called me. The tools were ready. We had to get back to the graveyard. As I left Lebovitch I was careful not to tell him that we would soon be back. It was no doubt bad for him and his friends for us to be seen at the sawmill too often. We must each keep to his own solitude; fraternization had become conspiracy.

As we walked back. I spoke to Ernst about Lebovitch. "He's a friend of your Lidia's," I told him. "He's afraid that your interest in her may compromise her in the eyes of the German authorities."

"He's wrong," replied Ernst in an offhand manner. "You know I'm a pastor, and although I'm not a chaplain, the Commandant, who comes from my home town (only yesterday he was asking me for news of my family), gives me tacit permission to make some approaches to these people in a priestly capacity; to behave with a little more humanity, in other words. . . ."

"Humanity," I echoed.

"I know what you're thinking, Peter," murmured Ernst. "Well, even if your thoughts correspond to the reality, what about it? Won't you ever understand?" he cried, appealing, far beyond me, to some unknown body of critics. "We are all lost. There's nothing for us to fall back on; there never will be. Even the earth has begun to fail us. In such conditions, who can forbid me to love in whatever way I can? Who can forbid me? This is the last form of priesthood open to me, Peter—the last power I've got. It's inadequate and clumsy, it needs to be exercised upon a living object, a single object. . . ."

His lips went on moving. I said nothing. I would not have known what to say. And then Otto was already watching us come, from the top of the burial ground; the evening sun was behind his back and we could not see his face. He was standing motionless with his rifle on his shoulder. Behind him the graves were casting their shadows to one side, like beasts of burden relieved of their packs.

From that time on, discovering into what abysses I might be dragged if I followed Ernst, I fell back on the position of safety provided by the graveyard. Here was the only innocent place. Here we seemed to find a sort of immunity. When an officer came to inspect us we each bent as low as possible over a grave, assiduously weeding it as though pressed for time, without raising our heads, and the visitor refrained from speaking to us, wondering (probably for the first time in his life) if we were acting thus in response to some urgent appeal from the dead, such as he himself might perhaps have heard (it suddenly came back to him) in the middle of the night, in the days when he still felt remorse.

"The weeds are the white hair of the dead," Cordonat would say, and his words savored of that senile cult whose hold on us grew in proportion to the dangers that threatened us.

These dangers now assumed the shapes and sunburned faces of S.S. men and military policemen, a few detachments of whom had recently arrived in the region of Brodno. But it was above all the growing silence of that summer, the pallor of the sun at certain hours, the oppressive heat that secretly frightened us. Our religion, which had never actually been a cult of the dead, was becoming a cult of the grave. As we dug and then filled up our pits, we appeased some haunting dream of underground.

With our twenty-two dead, we had already opened up and explored a real labyrinth. We were familiar with its passages, its detours, its angles. It was a sort of deep-down landscape. We knew just where a tangle of hanging roots clutched clods of earth, where you could catch the smell of a distant spring, where you passed over a slab of granite. In the course of our work of excavation we had grown used to the coolness of this universe of the dead and we found our way about it mentally with the help of these particularities of structure rather than with the help of the names of the dead men who had drifted there accidentally, like foreign bodies.

This longing for the depths, unsatisfied by our task of weeding on the surface of the graves, impelled Cordonat and myself to try and open up a trench which would run a few yards into the forest and drain away the rain water that poured down on to the graves and scored deep furrows in their unstable earth. Since we now no longer left the burial ground to walk in the forest, which was patrolled by the soldiers who had recently come to Brodno, I was looking for an occupation.

Digging this trench had another very different result; it was through this narrow channel that I happened on something that I had been anxiously anticipating for many months. It began under my feet, like a forest fire. Right at the start, we had got on fairly fast with our trench and were now digging in the sandy soil of the forest, among the live roots of the trees. Below us our comrades were lying beside the graves, plucking the weeds from off the dead with one hand. Otto and Ernst were sitting in the shade of the trees, Ernst reading *Louis Lambert*,[6] which had just been sent to me and which I had lent

6. A novel by Honore de Balzac (1799–1850).

him. As we worked, Cordonat was telling me about his *landes*.[7] When we stopped to change tools, for we used pick and spade in turn, we divided up a little tobacco. The war seemed endless but here, at this precise moment, under this white silent sky, it had a flavor of patience, a flavor of sand; it bore the same relation to life as a fine sand to a coarser sand.

It was not with the pickax but with the sharp edge of the spade that I cut open the arm of the corpse. It was lying flush with the side of the trench and as I was leveling the walls I struck right into the flesh. It was pink, like certain roots, like a thick root covered with black cloth instead of bark. My blow had ripped off a bit of the sleeve. I started back, spellbound with horror. Cordonat came up and then called the sentries. Everybody was soon gathered round the unknown corpse. A little earth had crumbled away and his elbow and wounded arm were now projecting into the void; he was literally emerging from a wall.

"Cover it up with earth," said Otto.

"We'll make a cross of branches," murmured Ernst.

They went back into the graveyard with our comrades; the problem of burying this corpse was beyond them. It is easy, it is even tempting to throw earth on a dead body. Often, after our burials, we managed, using boards and spades, to push into the hole at one go most of the heaped-up earth that lay at its brink. Here, one would have had to cover over the arm that projected from the wall of earth, to enclose it in an overhanging recess. We therefore decided to fill up our trench and start it again lower down, skirting round the corpse. I did not know what name to give it. But all the indications (the color of the clothes, their "civilian" appearance) suggested that the body was that of a Jew who had been killed there before our arrival or during one night, or maybe on a Sunday, very hurriedly no doubt, in a hush like that of a suicide.

I felt slightly sick. It was very hot. We were working with fierce concentration now, in silence. A few hours later, when we were digging our trench at some distance from the corpse, Cordonat, who was wielding his pickax ahead of me, suddenly started back. A sickly, intolerable smell arose; he had just uncovered a second body. This one was lying at the bottom of the trench, slightly askew and concealed by a thin layer of earth, so that Cordonat had trodden on it before—surprised by the elasticity of the soil—he exposed its clothing and upper part of a moldering face.

I was overwhelmed by the somber horror of it and the truth it revealed. This was death—these liquefying muscles, this half-eaten eye, those teeth like a dead sheep's; death, no longer decked with grasses, no longer ensconced

7. Sandy moors.

in the coolness of a vault, no longer lying sepulchred in stone, but sprawling in a bog full of bones, wrapped in a drowned man's clothes, with its hair caught in the earth.

And it was as though, looking beyond the idealized dead with whom I had hitherto populated my labyrinths, my underground retreats, I had discovered the state of insane desolation to which we are reduced when life is done. Death had become "a dead thing," no more; just as some being once endowed with great dignity and feminine mystery may, after a slow degeneration, surrender to the grossest drunkenness and fall asleep on the bare ground, wrapped in rags; here, the rags were flesh. Death was this: a dead mole, a mass of putrefaction sleeping, its scalp covered with hair or maybe with fur: wreckage stranded in the cul-de-sac of an unfinished tunnel: surrender at the end of a blind alley.

Cordonat discovered three more bodies. We had struck the middle of a charnel, a heap of corpses lying side by side in all directions, in the middle of the wood; a sort of subterranean bivouac which even now, when he had exposed it to the light, lost none of its clandestine character. We shouted, but in vain; this time nobody came to us. We turned over the earth till we were exhausted in an effort to cover up the bodies. We were practicing our craft of gravediggers in sudden isolation. And now it had assumed a wildly excessive character; we were gravediggers possessed by feverish delirium. Night was falling. We had ceased to care who these men were, who had killed them or when; they were irregular troops on the fringe of the army of the dead, they were "partisans" of another sort. We should never have finished burying them.

Their very position close by our own graveyard cruelly emphasized its prudent orderliness. Our dead, meekly laid out in rows, suddenly seemed to exude servility and treachery, wearing their coffins like a wooden livery.

The appalling stench of these accidentally exhumed corpses persisted for a long time in the forest, and spread over our graveyard. It was as though our own dead had awakened for a moment, had turned over in their graves, like wild animals hazily glimpsed in the sultry torpor that precedes a storm. There could be no doubt that something was going to happen. The smell warned one that the tide was about to turn.

The thundery heat and the horror of my discoveries made me feverish. Back in camp, I lay prostrate for several days on the wooden bed. Myriads of fleas had invaded the barrack-rooms and were frenziedly attacking us, while in the shadow of my clothes I traced the searing passage of my lice. Towards evening Cordonat brought me a little water. This was so scarce that at the slightest shower all the men would rush outside clutching vessels, bareheaded, like ecstatic beggars, and when the rain stopped they sprawled on the ground, still jostling one another, round the spitting gutters. Then my fever dropped. When I went back to the burial ground the first trains had begun to pass.

A railway line ran over the plain that we overlooked from our mound. It was only a few hundred yards away. Until then we had paid little attention to it, for the traffic was slight or nonexistent. During my absence it had increased without my noticing it; these trains sounded no whistles. If they had, I should have heard them from my bed in the camp; I should have questioned my comrades and they could have enlightened me, for from certain windows in the building you could see a section of the line, beyond the station which was hidden by houses.

The first trains had gone past behind us, full of stifled cries and shouts, like those trains that pass all lit up, crammed with human destinies and snatched out of the night with a howl while, framed in the window of a little house near the railway, a man in his shirt sleeves stands talking under a lamp, with his back turned, and then walks off to the other end of the room. And now, from the graveyard, I could see them coming, panting in the heat of the day, interminable convoys that had started a long time ago, long freight trains trickling slowly through the summer marshaling-yards, collecting men on leave and refugees like a herd of lowing cattle.

I could hear their rumbling long before they appeared past the tip of the forest, and then when they were in sight (sometimes almost before) I could hear another sound, superimposed and as elusive as a singing in one's ears, a buzzing in one's head, or the murmur in a sea shell: the sound of people calling and weeping.

The trains consisted of some twenty freight cars sandwiched between two passenger coaches, one next the engine and one at the rear. At the windows of these two coaches (they were old ones, green, with bulging bodywork) stood uniformed Germans smoking cigars. All the rest of the train was an inferno.

The cries seemed transparent against the silence, like flames in the blaze of summer. What they were shouting, these men and women and children heaped together in the closed vans, I could not tell. The cries were wordless. The human voice, hovering over the infinite expanse of suffering like a bird over the infinite sea, rose or fell, ran through the whole gamut of the wind before it faded into the distance, leaving behind it that same serene sky, that store of blue that bewildered birds and dying men can never exhaust. On the side of each van a narrow panel was open near the roof, framing four or five faces pressed close together, with other halves and quarters of faces visible between them and at the edges, the clusters of eyes expressing terror.

But it was more than terror, it was a sort of death-agony of fear; the time for beating their breasts was over and now they watched the interminable unrolling of that luminous landscape which they were seeing for the last time, where there was a man standing free and motionless in the middle of a field, and trees, and a harvester, and the impartial summer sun, while your child was suffocating, pressed between your legs in the overcrowded van and weeping with thirst and fright. Here and there a child was hoisted up to the narrow opening. When its head projected the German guards in the first carriage would fire shots. You had to stand still there in front of the opening and bear silent witness to what was going on in the dense darkness of the van: women fainting, old men unable to lie down, newborn babies turning blue, crazed mothers howling—while you watched the symbols of peace slowly filing past.

The trains followed one another at short intervals. Empty trains came back. Beside the narrow openings the deported victims had hung vessels in the hope of collecting water—mess-tins, blue enamel mugs—like pathetic domestic talismans which a mocking Fate kept jingling hollowly as the train disappeared in the dusty distance. They had no thought of displaying sacred draperies or waving oriflammes at this window; death was yet another journey, and they set out armed with water bottles.

Empty trains came back. I recognized them by the sound of the engine's panting.

"Now then, get busy, boys," Otto would tell us.

We had been given a third sentry. Brodno was crammed with troops and they had to be made use of. Ernst was some distance away from us, pale, his lips tight.

"Do you know why they're being taken off and where they're being taken to?" I asked the sentry, whom I did not know.

"Delousing," he answered calmly, "Got to make an end of this Jewish vermin. It's quickly done. It happens some thirty miles away. I'm told it's with electricity or gas. Oh, they don't suffer anything. In one second they're in Heaven."

This man, as I learned later, was an accountant from Dresden. He might just as well have been a blacksmith from Brunswick, a cobbler from Rostock, a peasant from Malchin, a professor from Ingolstadt, a postman from Cuxhaven or a navvy from Bayreuth; he would have used the same language. And he did use the same language under all these different aspects, shifting from one to another like an agile actor impelled by Evil, altering his voice to suit each of these thousands of masks, imbuing it with the atmosphere of profound calm appropriate to Ingolstadt, Malchin, Bayreuth and countless other equally human cities, and repeating, "Oh, they don't suffer, they don't suffer!"

Trains came down from the far depths of Volynia and the Ukraine, loaded with death agonies, with tears and lamentations. At one stop, farther up, the German guards had tossed dead children onto the roofs of the vans; nothing had to be left by the way, for each train was like the tooth of a rake. High up in the wall of the van, a little to the left in the narrow opening, there was a face; it seemed not living, but painted—painted white, with yellow hair, with a mouth that moved feebly and eyes that did not move at all: the face of a woman whose dead child was lying above her head; and beside the opening the little blue enamel mug, useless henceforward, shaken by every jolt of the train. Death can never appease this pain; this stream of black grief will flow for ever.

Towards the end of the morning I succeeded in drawing near to Ernst, who had moved away from the other two soldiers.

"It had started three months ago, at Brest Litovsk, when I was there," he told me in a low, tense voice. "But it wasn't on this scale. In a few days, tomorrow maybe, they'll begin on the people of this place. Do you think she ought to go away? To take refuge in the woods?"

He was looking at me bewilderedly, seeming more like a priest than ever with his smooth, babyish face, his indirect glance.

"It's probably the only chance they've got left," I muttered, bending towards the turf on the grave, since the new sentry was slowly coming towards us.

"But you've seen her: she's not strong, she'll never stand up to such an ordeal!" cried Ernst, without noticing that the soldier was now standing quite close to him.

The soldier looked at Ernst in some surprise and then went off, humming. I stood silent.

"Won't you speak to me, Peter?" asked Ernst humbly. "You're saying to yourself: He thinks only of her. . . ."

"I mistrust the other sentry," I answered. "You're exposing yourself unnecessarily. If you're willing to run the risk, throw away your gun and go off into the forest with her."

"I've thought of that," said Ernst, hanging his head. "I've thought of that. And then nothing gets done. You're horrified and you stay where you are. In this war, every man looks after himself. But we ought to realize that there can't be any true life afterwards for us, who have endured these sights. For me, there'll be no more life, Peter, do you hear, no more life. . . ."

His two companions called him and he went off abruptly. I lifted my head. Down below, there were only empty trains passing along the line. Towards evening all traffic ceased. Ernst did not speak another word to me as we went back to the camp. And I never saw him again.

Next day, when our gang turned up at the guardhouse, the Germans sent us back to our barracks. Soon rumors reached us: the Jews of Brodno were going to be taken away in their turn. Towards noon, looking out of the windows of our building, we saw the first procession of doomed victims appear on the little road leading to the station. Many of them—nursing what hopes, trusting in what promises?—had brought bundles and suitcases. The hastily knotted bundles frequently let drop underclothes or scraps of cloth that nobody had time to pick up, since the soldiers were continually hurrying on the procession, with curses on their lips and rifle butts raised. Other victims, arriving later, thus found themselves confronted with a scene of dispossession whose causes were as yet unknown to them, with the signs of ominous disorder.

The same signs were visible within their own group, where old men, children and adults were mingled; clearly there had been no attempt to sort them out, as had always happened hitherto before the removal of groups of workers or some other utilitarian deportation. The German soldiers from time to time struck at the sides of the column, but as we could only see them from a distance their gestures seemed to be slowed down: silent, clumsy blows, aimed low, more like stealthy misdeeds than like acts of violence. I had turned away from the window.

"Here are more of them!" somebody cried behind me.

Should I see Lidia, her friends, Lebovitch or the old man from the sawmill in this group, or the man who mended the road, or the fair woman who often stood waiting between two houses? Their packs made their silhouettes misshapen. Some of the women hugged them against their stomachs like bundles of washing. The dust was rising and I could not make them out clearly.

Somebody said: "It's their children they're carrying. . . ."

Somebody said: "One of them has fallen. The guards are hitting him. . . . Now he's up; he's starting off again. . . ." Somebody said: "Oh, look at that woman running to catch up with the group!"

The untiring commentaries, despite transient notes of pity, disclosed a sort of detachment, for passionate feeling will not allow you to see things through to the end, whereas these men followed the whole business with the mournful eagerness of witnesses. Evening drew on. I lay stretched out on the wooden bunk. At my side Cordonat was smoking in silence. Later on, flickering lights and distant rumblings rent the night. It was a stifling night, tense with anguish, and you could not tell whether those distant flares came from thunderclouds or from armed men on the march, carrying torches.

The arrests went on all next day. We were told by sentries that the cottage doors had been smashed in with axes and the inhabitants cleared out. Towards noon stifled cries were heard from the direction of the station. The victims, who had spent all night packed together in the vans standing in the sidings, were clamoring for water. By evening not a single train was left in the station. One man was walking along the track, bending down from time to time to check the rails. He went off into the distance, till he was almost invisible. Beyond, the pure sky grew deeper.

It was not until three days later that we set out once more on the road to the burial ground. Two new sentries accompanied us. The road was empty, and most of the houses shut up. In one of them some Poles were setting up a canteen. A few men were working in front of the sawmill. I recognized none of them.

At least we still had our dead, that faithful flock, each of whom we could call by his name without raising up a murdered man's face staring wide-eyed in the darkness. Our dead were already beginning to get used to their earth. After each of our absences they had "put on green," as we said when the grass had once more invaded the graves. Our cult of the dead consisted in wiping away the shadow of a meadow, day by day. And once more the sentries surrendered.

They had come to the graveyard armed with mistrust. But here, amongst the dead, we got the better of them. In front of our tidy graves, so tirelessly tended, their antagonism dropped: our accounts were in order. The liquidations (in the business sense of the word) which the Germans were carrying on all round us took place only spasmodically, as though at an auction, in an atmosphere of anger and excess which, once the payment had been exacted, increased the insatiable credit of the murderers with a debt of bitter resentment; they found it hard to forgive their victims. Our dead, on the other hand, had needed no dunning. Although the Germans were never paid fast enough, these had not worn out their patience like the others; nobody was conscious of having forced them to die.

Then, too, they seemed to be lying at attention under their three feet of earth in properly dressed lines, whereas the others, who had been shot point-blank, hid their heads in the crook of their arms; they had to be pulled by the hair, in fact it was an endless business bringing them to heel.

When the charm of the graveyard had worked, I plucked up courage to ask one of the two soldiers if he knew what had become of Ernst.

"Oh, the little pastor!" he replied. "He got punished. He's been sent to a disciplinary company. He knew a Jewess. They even say he burst out crying in the Commandant's office. Oh, don't talk to me about such people! Anyhow, I'm a Bavarian myself, so you see I'm of the same religion as you. I'm a Catholic, yes, but one's country comes first! Now get along and see to your graves."

I had not had time to inquire about the fate of Otto. In any case I was not deeply concerned about it. I felt calmer; the punishment inflicted on Ernst seemed a light one. Moreover, it cemented our friendship more firmly. He stood beside me now in the rebels' camp, like those guests at a party whom you've expected for a long time, wondering whether they'll come, and who suddenly appear, all made up and grotesquely disguised, with their familiar kindly, serious eyes looking at you from under their hats, when the music has already started and the dark wine is being poured out all round you.

All this was happening in 1942. Our friendship needed some discipline, imposed from without, naturally. I was thinking of Lidia, too. Her relations with Ernst seemed to me solid ground, but there were stars, too. They still wheel round in my dreams. I do not know what became of them on earth, but in the map of heaven, and in the map of my heart, I know where to look for the distant glimmer of that unattainable love.

We never went back to the new road. Our kingdom grew narrower. No more walks in the forest; we went down to the pond only with sentries on either side of us, and we were forbidden to linger there; we were more than ever confined to the burial ground. Otto and Ernst had already passed into a previous existence, threatened with oblivion, when we got news of the former: he sent us a corpse.

This was a fellow that I knew fairly well, a sullen-faced lad from Lyons obsessed by the urge to escape. Seeking an opportunity, he had asked me a few days earlier to let him take the place of a member of our gang who was too sick to leave the camp. He hoped to be able to make an easy getaway from the graveyard. I managed to get him accepted by our sentries. Underneath his uniform he was wearing some sort of escape outfit, and round his ankles there dangled long white laces belonging presumably to the linen trousers formerly issued to the French army. These were only too obvious. Silent, his jaws stiff with anxiety or determination, he thus attracted the guards' attention immediately. They never took their eyes off him and, that evening, he came back to the camp with us.

A few days later he got himself engaged in a gang of "road commandos" (prisoners employed on road-mending at some distance from the town) guarded by several sentries, among whom was Otto. Otto, being indirectly involved in Ernst's punishment, had been posted in charge of this detachment, which performed the duties of a gang of convicts and was rated as such. One evening, as the group was about to pass through the town on its way back to the camp, the young Lyonnais broke ranks abruptly and began to run off into the fields. Otto promptly shouldered his gun and fired. The fugitive dropped; the bullet had gone in through his back and pierced his heart.

It was our first violent death. On the day of the funeral the Germans sent a wreath of fir-branches tied with a red ribbon. The wooden cross bore the inscription FALLEN instead of DIED. Our graveyard had been sorely in need of this heroic note, as I suddenly realized; it was as though it had received the Military Cross.

"You shall soon have some stones, too," a sentry told me. "I know that in the camp they've been asking for a stonemason. It's the Jews' tombstones you're going to get; their graveyard's full of them, down there in the forest. We shall use them for the roads too. You people can't complain, your grave-yard's much finer than the one where our own men are buried. . . ."

It was quite true. With its always green turf, its flowerbeds, its carefully sanded paths edged with small black fir trees which we had transplanted, with its rustic fence of birch boughs, against the dark background of the for-est edge, our graveyard seemed an "idyllic" place, as the Germans put it. On Sunday the soldiers from the garrison used to come and photograph it. The more we adorned it the greater grew its fame, and it aroused a wave of cu-riosity like that which carries crowds to gaze at certain baroque works of art or at others which, devoid of any art, are yet prodigies of patience and skill: houses built of bottle ends, ships made of matches, walking sticks carved to fantastic excess—monstrous triumphs of persistence and time.

On the fringe of the war, on the fringe of the massacres, on the fringe of Europe, sheltering behind our prodigious burial-ground, we seemed like hollow-eyed gardeners, sitters in the sun, fanatical weeders, busily working over the dead as over some piece of embroidery.

But the thought of those stones horrified us. We did not want to rob the Jews of their gravestones; that savored of sacrilege, and also of an incipient complicity with the Germans; and anyhow it "wasn't playing fair." We had made our graveyard out of earth and grass and to bring in marble would have been cheating. I went to lay the problem before the prisoners' French repre-sentative, the *homme de confiance* as we called him. He promised me to protest to the Germans.

A few days later, in one corner of the camp, I saw a man sitting on the ground sawing and planing a tombstone on which was carved a breaking branch.

He seemed in some doubt. Should each of the slabs of marble or granite intended for the graves (merely for epitaphs, not for funerary flagstones) rep-resent an open book, a cushion (he could quite well picture a cushion slightly hollowed out by the weight of an absent head) or a coat of arms? He asked for my opinion. I told him angrily that I wasn't interested in his stones, and that they should never cross the threshold of the graveyard. However, he went on cutting them, full of delight at getting back to his trade, heaping them one on the other when they were ready, although the Germans were now busy with something else and never came to ask for them. In any case, he could not have handed them over as they were, for the essential part of the inscription was missing.

Though my ill-will discouraged him at first, he soon tried to get from one of us the names of the dead and the dates which he needed. He met with the same refusal. Besides ourselves, only the Germans possessed these essential facts, but no prisoner had access to their offices. Thenceforward, he began a patient investigation, going from one building to the next, questioning the men on the deaths that had taken place there. I soon got wind of this. It made me angry. The stonemason's obstinacy, although of a purely professional character, had begun to look like an intrusion into our field. For the last few months we had managed to keep our tasks secret, and now I felt this secrecy threatened by the publicity that he was causing by his noisy investigation of our past.

One day I saw him turn up at the graveyard, following a funeral. The man we were burying that day had come most opportunely in the nick of time, after the lad from Lyons, who, having introduced an appropriately heroic note into the place, had since seemed to be inaugurating a sequence of violent deaths. For here the latest corpse set the tone; it was in front of the latest corpse that we made our military salutes each morning; it was his bare, sparsely sown grave that attracted the attention (albeit vacuous) of visitors. It seemed important therefore that the tone thus set should not be, for too long, that of violent death: after all, a habit is easily acquired. And so I should have been quite glad to welcome this newcomer who restored order to things, had I not perceived, among the handful of Frenchmen walking behind the cart, the stonemason, sporting a swordbelt.

He had probably managed to slip into the procession by posing as one of the dead man's friends; he may even have been one really. . . . But we were already convinced of one thing: he had come to the graveyard to take measurements and pick up names. We decided to keep an eye on him, and we buried the corpse in a state of nervous tension although, in the depths of our innocent hearts, we had longed for it. We did not take our eyes off the man during the whole ceremony which, with its dying bugle-call and the report of arms fired into the sky, was like that which marks the close of a war. When the burial was over the Germans and the Frenchmen who had formed the procession hung about. As the fame of our graveyard increased, funerals had tended to become, for those who were able to attend them, a sort of summer excursion, a trip into the country from which you might well picture yourself returning with armfuls of flowers picked on the spot. The stonemason had moved towards the first row of graves. I followed him. He was already taking a notebook out of his pocket.

"What are you doing there?" I asked him, my voice distorted with anger.

"I've been told to make tombstones!" he said, very loud. "You shan't prevent me! They don't belong to you, after all!" he added, indicating the graves of the dead.

"More than to you, anyhow!" I answered. "We wouldn't go and put stolen stones on their graves. . . ."

"Stolen?" He shook his head. "They're given to us and it's not our business to ask where they come from. . . . Well, I know, of course!" he went on, seeing that I was about to answer. "And so what? Would you rather see them laid on the roads?"

"Yes, I'd rather see them laid on the roads. I suppose you get soup and bread from the Germans for doing this job?"

"Oh, don't you talk about that!" cried the stonemason. He brought his angry face close to mine. "Everybody in the camp knows what you've wangled with your famous graveyard!" He stopped suddenly.

"Well then, tell me! Tell me!" I cried.

"Listen to me," went on the stonemason in a quieter voice, "Can't we make peace?"

Everything seemed conducive to this. The heat of the hour had led Frenchmen and Germans, in separate groups, to sit down beside the graves, where the forest trees cast their shade. Only our words disturbed the silence.

"Don't expect to get the names of the dead, whatever happens," I answered.

"You can keep them," said the stonemason, sitting down. He was a thin-faced man a little older than myself, with short grayish hair. "We're an obstinate pair. After all, I understand your feelings; you don't want it to be said that those stones had names taken off them in order to carve these on. Well, I'd never have had the courage to take them off myself if they hadn't been written in Hebrew. But in Hebrew they mean nothing! I'm not even sure that they were names and dates. And then the stones were there in the camp, without anybody lying beneath them. Put yourself in my place! I'm bored, I need to keep my hand in for after the war, and I'm presented with tools and stones! But it's all right; I give up the names," he added, pulling out his tobacco pouch and handing it to me.

I rolled a cigarette and he did the same.

"I give up the names," he went on, puffing at his cigarette, "but all the same, something really ought to be done with those stones—they're not all in good condition, you know, some of them are molding away. Besides, the dead people or their relations, if there are any left, wouldn't see any harm in our making use of these stones now that the Germans have pulled them up. They'd surely like that better than to see them crushed and scattered on the roads. . . . After all, we're on the same side as they are, aren't we? . . . So this is what I thought. Let's not talk of carving names on them, but let's make them into little ornaments, cornerstones for instance. We must think of our own dead too. I needn't comment on what you've done for them; it's quite unbelievable. But after all, there's nothing permanent about it. Suppose they take us off into Germany next month; after a single winter there'll be no sign of your graves. The rains and the melting snows will have washed all the earth away, and grass and briars will have grown over it. But with stones. . . . Oh, I'm not suggesting making monuments," he cried, raising his hand to forestall objections. "I assure you, very little is needed. And I'm speaking from experience—I'm in the trade. A little pyramid at each corner of the grave for instance, or a ball on a little pedestal if you prefer, although that's much harder to make, or else carved corners joined together with chains, only unluckily we haven't any chains . . . well, you get the idea, something not very high, firmly fastened into the ground, preferably with cement, and above all something decently made. . . ."

But I was no longer listening to him. For the last few minutes I had been listening to the rumble of a train and now it was growing louder. The train was about to emerge round the tip of the wood. I could tell, without waiting for it to roll past before my eyes, what sort of freight it carried. Its slow, jolting sound warned me of the other sounds that would follow although for the moment a contrary wind delayed them. I should soon hear the weeping, the cries of despair. The silence, no doubt, was due to the wind; but perhaps, too, those who were being transported, knowing what fate awaited them, had deliberately refrained from sending out their lamentations into that empty, sun-baked plain, in which the great migrations of death had never yet awakened any lasting echo.

And so it all began again. Every day one or two convoys crossed the plain, and then were no more to be seen; and when night fell a train would rumble, too slowly, through the silence. New processions appeared on the little road that led to the station. They were smaller and more infrequent than the previous ones and seemed to be made up of belated recruits, of survivors from some ancient and now almost forgotten disaster, of beggars or vagrants rounded up in the middle of their wasted summer. Nothing rolled out of the bundles this time; nobody seemed to be in a hurry now, and the soldiers who struck at the sides of the column did so with the lazy indifference of cowherds.

The massacre was drawing to a close, but it lingered interminably like the raw gleam of a lurid sunset on walls, between patches of shadow. We said to ourselves: "Surely this must be the end of these torments." The plain seemed to have nothing left to offer death save its quota of vagrants. We were wrong.

On the contrary, those whom the Germans were now dispatching to be slaughtered had been taken from the ranks of a scattered resistance movement which, up till now, without our knowledge, had been fighting to the last ditch for the right to live.

If they seemed wearier than those who had gone before them along the same road that led between darkly gleaming slagheaps and through engine-sheds to Calvary, it was because they had suffered a twofold defeat. They had been surrounded in the forest, they had been arrested at night on the roads or among the brambles in the ravines, where for so long they had been wandering round and round in dazed despair. Now, in the evenings near the grave-yard, we often caught sight of nonchalant armed soldiers making their way in extended line into the forest, and bending down from time to time to pick a strawberry. Brodno was encircled with a military cordon, and the whole region was being combed step by step.

This state of siege, of which we shortly felt the oppressive effects, brought back a certain animation around the camp and around our graveyard. The inhabitants—Poles, Ukrainians and Ruthenians—realizing that for the moment the Germans had no designs on them, suddenly felt the need to move around in all directions within the circle that hemmed them in. They came to look at the graveyard, the fame of which had reached them. They stood still at some distance from it, motionless, communicating with one another by gestures.

One evening two girls came forward as far as the verge of the forest, close to the spot where we had discovered the charnel.

One of them was plain and awkward; the other was slender and seemed younger. The brightness of her blue-green eyes disturbed me. They shouted to the soldiers that they were Polish. The setting, the gathering dusk and my own troubled heart made the younger girl's smile seem like that of a vision. To the German who, with one foot on a grave, asked them their names and ages, she called out "Maria!" and there was still joy in her voice. I had gone up to the sentry; the girl looked at me and waved to me as she went off. Next day as we made our way to the graveyard I caught sight of her at the door of the new canteen and we made signs of greeting to each other.

From that time on I clung to her image. The first rains of autumn had begun; the graveyard had ceased to be a garden and was once more a burial ground. The earth sank under one's feet; it was deep again, and heavy, like a morass. Autumn promised to be a season rich in deaths. More trains came through from the further end of the plain, with white faces framed in the narrow windows, trains full of condemned creatures who, this time, uttered no cries of thirst but stood motionless, clutching their despair between their hands like a twisted handkerchief. My mind was fixed on her image.

I turned to it again when new processions appeared on the road leading to the station or when, towards evening, groups of soldiers made their way into the forest with more speed than usual. Three or four times a day, whether we were going to the graveyard or coming away from it, Maria, standing at the door of the Polish canteen, would watch me thoughtfully and smile at me. My friends nudged one another but let fall no word. From their dealings with the dead they had learned to respect mysteries. And this was undoubtedly a mystery—my devotion to the image of this girl about whom I knew nothing to suggest that she was worthy of it surprised me more than it surprised them. I pushed back my hair from my forehead—it was damp from the drizzling rain—and stood upright; there were still many things to which I should have to bear witness later, many sufferings to be shared, many hopes to be nurtured, many steps to be taken which would add up to something someday. But as soon as I had reached the graveyard and was standing under the branches at the edge of the forest, where raindrops rustled, the image recurred.

One morning I was sunk in this sort of reverie when Cordonat called me. He led me to the end of the last row of graves where, covered with planks and with an old tarpaulin to keep off the rain water, the spare grave lay empty, awaiting its corpse. He had just been inspecting it and had found there, besides more subtle traces which, as an expert poacher, he had picked out, a cigarette end of unfamiliar origin. It was rolled in a scrap of paper from a child's exercise book and made of coarse unripe tobacco, presumably taken from one of the plants which, in those penurious times, the peasants used to grow outside their houses.

"It wasn't there last night," Cordonat told me. "For several days I'd noticed that somebody had been taking up and putting back the planks and the tarpaulin during the night. So I began to keep an eye on the grave. The other proofs are more tricky, you might not believe them. But this one! There's no possible doubt about it: a man comes to sleep in our grave at night."

"Well, what then?" I asked.

"Well, so much the better," he cried. "It must be a hunted man. For once, let this graveyard be some use to a living man!" (Cordonat had never been really enthusiastic about the graveyard.) "Only we ought to help him. This evening, for instance, we might leave him some provisions."

I did not doubt Cordonat's charitable intentions, but I also suspected that he was anxious to secure a further proof by this method. We had lately been receiving a little food from France and we were able, without too great a sacrifice, to deposit in the grave for the benefit of the stranger who inhabited it a handful of sugar, a piece of chocolate or a few army biscuits deducted from our store of provisions, which were meticulously arranged and counted, dry and crumbly as rats' provender. When evening came, before leaving the graveyard we slipped a parcel between the planks and then replaced them as before. Next day the parcel had disappeared. Cordonat found at the bottom of the grave a scrap of paper on which a message of thanks was penciled, in English. The two words had been written with a trembling hand, no doubt by the first light that filtered through the parted planks as dawn brought back panic.

That evening our gift was made up merely of a few cigarettes. I added a message: "Who are you?" Although the answer consisted only of two initials, it was clear and it did not surprise me. It was written on a piece of packing paper: I. L. An arrow invited me to turn over the page: "You know me Peter = [the arithmetical sign *equals*] I know you. Keep quiet, both of you, keep quiet. Thank You." I had recognized Lebovitch. But how could he know that it was I who had put the cigarettes there and that only one other knew the secret?

"During the day he must stay hidden by the edge of the forest and watch us," said Cordonat.

It would have been madly imprudent, and the Germans would have discovered him long ago; Cordonat admitted it. These communications through the trap door of a grave, these notes with their anguished laconicism, the condition of "semi-survival" in which Lebovitch existed and the second sight with which he seemed to be endowed—all these things concurred to give me the impression that our continual contact with death was beginning to open for us a sort of wicket gate into its domain. I almost forgot Maria. Sometimes, in the evening, she would walk a little way along the road below the graveyard just as we had slipped a few provisions into the grave and were replacing the planks, the tarpaulin and the stones that held it down with furtive care, as though we were laying snares. Cordonat rediscovered the pleasures of his poaching days. I would stand up and wave to Maria. The sentries were amused by my performance and it distracted their attention from the mysterious tasks which we were performing over the empty grave.

"How do you live?" I wrote to Lebovitch, leaving him a few sheets of blank paper. His answers grew longer but also more obscure. He lived with difficulty. During the day he remained hidden, no doubt, in the high branches of a tree, for he wrote: "I am very high up. Do not look for me. A glance might betray me. I see them come to and fro. Please tell me what is happening about the dogs [these last words were underlined]. How soon will autumn be here? Have I the right to try and escape from God's will? Anyhow all this is unendurable and I shall not hold out much longer! If only they would let me speak! I should be exempted. Yes, they should let me speak! Have you heard tell in the village of anyone being exempted! Keep quiet! Thank you."

During the days that followed I had difficulty in preventing Cordonat from staring up at the tree tops on the forest border; he would have attracted the guards' attention. Instinctively, as one accustomed to roaming the woods and starting animals from their lair, he found it an exciting game to hunt for Lebovitch's aerial shelter. One morning I surprised him sitting down with his back turned to the forest and staring into a pocket mirror concealed in his hand which he was slowly turning in all directions.

"I tell you he's not found a perch in any of these trees," he told me, putting back his little mirror into his pocket. "Even if he'd been well camouflaged I'd have discovered him. There's no foliage thick enough to conceal a man. He'd have been obliged to surround himself with other branches, cut off from other parts of the tree; and believe me, I know from experience that the color of leaves changes as soon as they're cut. Ask him about it, once and for all. . . ."

I wrote a note to Lebovitch to this effect, accompanying it with a handful of army biscuits.

"I can't tell you where I am," replied Lebovitch, "You haven't told me anything about the dogs. And the exemptions? Do they ever exempt anybody? Yesterday three more trains went past. During the night there were luminous things drawn on the carriages! You can have *no idea of it*. [The last words were underlined.] This morning I vomited because of all the raw mushrooms I'd eaten. God rises early just now. So does the wind! Couldn't they have pity on me? Tell me if it's humanly possible?"

"We shan't learn anything more," said Cordonat when I had read him this letter.

The incoherence of these notes depressed him. We were too close to the world beyond death not to be aware of its dank breath when speech became so sparing and sibylline, when a human being's presence proved so elusive, while these brief messages expressed a tortured silence pierced by a thousand exclamation marks, like nails. We continued to offer food to this Egyptian tomb, which a couple of days later had to remove farther off; death provided Lebovitch with a new neighbor.

Cordonat offered to dig the spare grave into which, that same evening, Lebovitch would creep to rest, and at the bottom of the grave he arranged a little pile of earth for the sleeper to lay his head on. I helped him in this task which, as we soon admitted to one another, filled us with a strange uneasiness; we had the feeling that we were preparing to bury an unseen friend. The present that we left in the grave that evening was more generous than usual. I avoided putting any message with it, however. The tone of the answers distressed me.

Lebovitch broke silence only on the second morning (he must have written his notes during the day, up in his tree or inside some unknown retreat). He had been deeply touched by Cordonat's thoughtfulness in providing the earthen pillow. Perhaps, also, by the nearness of a newly dead Frenchman, whose burial he must have watched, since he never took his eyes off the graveyard. He wrote: "I know that one day there will be no morning. Last night I went on knocking for an hour against the earth, on the side where all the others are lying. I say an hour, but my watch has stopped. I wanted to go on knocking all night. As long as I'm knocking I'm alive. Even here, where I am now, at this moment, I'm knocking. And I keep saying: have mercy, have mercy! They've killed them all, Peter, killed them all! What is loneliness?"

I could no longer keep up this dialogue, and I could hardly bear the abstract presence that now filled my narrow universe. I could no longer look with confidence at the forest trees or into the hollow grave, nor gaze out over the plain where one of those trains was always dawdling. Like those tireless birds that drop to the ground like stones and as soon as they have touched it dart back to perch on one of a hundred quivering branches, then dizzily gravitate to the ground once more and once more rebound upward, as though in avid quest not of earthly or aerial prey but of pure trajectories, of secretly deliberate flights, of prophetic tangents, or as though irrevocably doomed to this endless to-and-fro, Lebovitch moved between the grave and the treetops every day; he was only fit for shooting down.

Yet I would have liked to save him. His talk of exemptions, although I had at first put it down to insanity (and I was beginning to find out how rich and full was insanity's account compared with the meager bankbooks of reason), had made an impression on my mind. I felt I must sound the Germans, or Maria, who doubtless knew what was happening in the village now.

The Germans told me that the fate of the Jews of Brodno (and elsewhere too) was old history now. "Let's talk of Maria instead," they said to me. "You're keen on her, aren't you, you rascal?"

I endured their mockery. As it happened I was anxious to speak to Maria. If she passed along the road tomorrow, might I not beckon to her to come? I'd only want a couple of minutes with her. I felt infinitely sorry for myself. Evening with its swift black clouds was falling over Volynia and its crowd of dead, over the distant fires of war, and I was standing there, eager to strike my pitiful bargain—two minutes of that time!—I was standing there with Lebovitch at my back, weighing me down, his hard hands against my shoulders. The Germans made fun of my anxiety. "Maybe," they said, sending me back to my graves. I slipped a note into the pit: "In two days I'll know for sure about the exemptions."

Next evening Maria appeared on the road with her friend. "You can call her," cried the sentries, laughing. I called her. She saw me. I beckoned to her to meet me at the graveyard gate. But she shook her head with a smile. She walked away. I had turned white with vexation to which, in the depths of my heart, I gave a bitter name. On the new message that I found in the grave Lebovitch wrote: "I'm knocking harder than ever, Peter. It's the only thing to do: knock, knock, knock!" He said nothing more about the exemptions.

A few trains full of condemned victims still passed through the plain. When the sound of them had faded away I still seemed to hear behind me the dull persistent rhythm of blows hammered against the earth, against a tree trunk, mingled with the throbbing of my temples, the tapping of summer's last woodpecker, a far-off woodcutter's blows and the rumble of a passing cart, in a soothing confusion.

Summer drew to a close. In the darkened countryside all life was slowed down; even the great convoys of death became more infrequent—those harvests, too, had been gathered in. But the dawn of a new season was less like the morning after a bad dream or the lucid astonishment of life than the final draining away of all blood, the last stage of a slow hemorrhage behind which a few tears of lymph trickle, like mourners at life's funeral. Autumn brought a prospect of exhausted silence, of a world pruned of living sounds, of the reign of total death. What had I left to delay this consummation, when every gust of wind in the branches of the trees, every leaf blown away, every corner of the naked sky, reminded me of its imminence?

It was from that moment that the life of Lebovitch, his dwindled, precarious existence, became for me the last remaining symbol of a denial of death—of that death which was so visibly being consummated all around me. I renewed our dialogue. I sent him urgent messages: "Where were the rest? What had happened to him? and indeed, who was he?" I urged him to tell me about his own past and that of all the others.

For nothing makes you feel so impoverished as the death of strangers; dying, they testify to death without yielding anything of their lives that might compensate for the enhanced importance of darkness. Thus what did he know of Lidia's fate? He must tell me; the survival of all my hopes depended on it.

These questions remained unanswered. Lidia sank in her turn, with all the others, like them consecrated to death, behind those distant horizons of memory where, even after we have forgotten everything, there lingers a pale light, an endless comforting twilight, a thin streak of radiance which will perhaps serve us for eyes when our eyes are closed in death. Lebovitch soon caught up with Lidia on that dark slope where never, not in all eternity, should I be able to reach them.

One morning on arriving at the graveyard we found that the planks covering the empty grave had been thrown to one side. At the bottom of the grave there lay a black jacket without an armlet. One of its pockets was full of acorns. I knew then that Lebovitch would never come back. Had he been surprised in his sleep, or, in a fit of madness, had he suddenly rushed out into the forest to meet his murderers? I raised my head. Clouds were rising towards the west. The wind had got up. My companions were taking away the dead leaves that fell on the graves. In the flowerbeds the summer flowers had turned black. Soon no more convoys passed along the railway over the plain, which in the mornings was drowned in mist. There were no more soldiers to be seen patrolling the woods, where the trees were growing bare. Autumn was really there now.

Maria chose this time to visit the burial-ground. I had been waiting for her there for a long time, secretly convinced that she would come. One evening she came along the ill-paved road, her thin summer dress clinging to her in the wind. She walked slowly, her face uplifted, quietly resolute, and her fair hair was fluttering over her brow. A violent fit of trembling possessed me. I turned towards the single sentry who now guarded us. He was a prematurely old man, full of melancholy resignation. He knew about my romance, and nodded his head.

I darted towards Maria like a dog let off the leash. Seeing me come, she hurried forward without taking her eyes off me and, passing the gate of the graveyard, quickly made for the edge of the forest. The sky had grown dark and the wind was blowing stronger. I only caught up with her under the trees. I seized hold of her arm, and she drew me on involuntarily while I spoke to her in breathless tones. I did not know what I was saying; I was in a sort of ecstasy. Suddenly I drew her to me and pressed her closely. My face groped feverishly for the hollow of her shoulder. For so long I had been waiting for this moment of blindness, of oblivion, this ultimate salvation! It was the only refuge within which to break the heavy, clipped wings that thought had set growing on one's temples, the only place where the mind, like a heavy-furred moth dazzled by the great light of death, could for an instant assuage its longing to return to the warm, original darkness of its chrysalis. . . . Frightened by the desperate wildness of my movement, Maria sharply withdrew from my arms, kissed me on the lips and fled. For a moment I tried to follow her. Then I leaned against a tree. Within me and about me a great silence had fallen. After a moment I wiped away my tears and went back to my dead.

Translated from the French by Jean Stewart

Journey through the Night

What do you see when you look back? Not a thing. And when you look ahead? Even less. That's right. That's how it is.

It was three o'clock in the morning and raining. The train didn't stop anywhere. There were lights somewhere in the countryside, but you couldn't be sure if they were windows or stars.

The tracks were tracks—but why shouldn't there be tracks in the clouds?

Paris was somewhere at the end of the trip. Which Paris? The earthly Paris—with cafés, green buses, fountains, and grimy whitewashed walls? Or the heavenly Paris? Carpeted bathrooms with a view of the Bois de Boulogne?

The fellow-passenger looked still paler in the bluish light. His nose was straight, his lips thin, his teeth uncommonly small. He had slick hair like a seal. A moustache, that's what he needs. He could do a balancing act on his nose. Under his clothes he is wet. Why doesn't he show his tusks?

After "that's how it is" he said nothing. That settled everything. Now he is smoking.

His skin is grey, that's obvious—it's taut, too. If he scratches himself it will tear. What else is there to look at? He has only one face and his suitcase. What has he got in the suitcase? Tools? Saw, hammer and chisel? Maybe a drill? What does he need a drill for? To bore holes in skulls? Some people drink beer that way. When empty, they can be painted. Will he paint my face? What colours? Water-colour or oil? And what for? Children at Easter-time play with empty eggshells. His play with skulls.

Well, he said non-committally, putting out his cigarette. He crushed it against the aluminium, making a scratching sound. Well, how about it?

I don't know, I said. I can't make up my mind. Doesn't the fellow understand a joke?

Maybe you need a little more spunk, he said. Now's the time to make up your mind; in half an hour you'll be asleep anyway, then I'll do what I want with you.

I won't sleep tonight, I said. You've given me fair warning.

Warning won't do you any good, he said. Between three and four everybody falls into a dead sleep. You're educated, you should know that.

Yes, I know. But I got self-control.

Between three and four, said the man, rubbing the moustache that was yet to grow, all of us get locked away in our little cubicles, don't hear nothing, don't see nothing. We die, every last one of us. Dying restores us, after four we wake up and life goes on. Without that people couldn't stick it out so long.

I don't believe a word of it. You can't saw me up.

I can't eat you as you are, he said. Sawing's the only way. First the legs, then the arms, then the head. Everything in its proper order.

What do you do with the eyes?

Suck'em.

Can the ears be digested or have they got bones in them?

No bones, but they're tough. Anyway, I don't eat everything, do you think I'm a pig?

A seal is what I thought.

That's more like it. So he admitted it. A seal, I knew it. How come he speaks German? Seals speak Danish and nobody can understand them.

How is it you don't speak Danish?

I was born in Sankt Pölten, he said. We didn't speak Danish in our family. He's being evasive. What would you expect? But maybe he is from Sankt Pölten; I've heard there are such people in the region.

And you live in France?

What's it to you? In half an hour you'll be gone. It's useful to know things when you've a future ahead of you, but in your situation. . . .

Of course he's insane, but what can I do? He has locked the compartment (where did he get the keys?), Paris will never come. He's picked the right kind of weather. You can't see a thing and it's raining; of course he can kill me. When you're scared you've got to talk fast. Would you kindly describe it again. Kindly will flatter his vanity. Murderers are sick. Sick people are vain. The kindly is getting results.

Well, first comes the wooden mallet, he said, exactly like a schoolteacher . . . you always have to explain everything twice to stupid pupils; stupidity is a kind of fear, teachers give out cuffs or marks.

. . . then after the mallet comes the razor, you've got to let the blood out, most of it at least, even so you always mess up your chin on the liver; well, and then, as we were saying, comes the saw.

Do you take off the leg at the hip or the knee?

Usually at the hip, sometimes the knee. At the knee when I have time.

And the arms?

The arms? Never at the elbow, always at the shoulder.

Why?

Maybe it's just a habit, don't ask me. There isn't much meat on the fore-arm, in your case there's none at all, but when it's attached, it looks like something. How do you eat the leg of a roast chicken?

He was right.

If you want pointers about eating people, ask a cannibal.

Do you use spices?

Only salt. Human flesh is sweet, you know that yourself. Who likes sweet meat?

He opened the suitcase. No, I screamed, I'm not asleep yet.

Don't be afraid, you scarecat, I just wanted to show you I wasn't kidding. He fished about among the tools. There were only five implements in the suit-case, but they were lying around loose. It was a small suitcase, rather like a doctor's bag. But a doctor's instruments are strapped to the velvet lid. Here they were lying around loose. Hammer, saw, drill, chisel and pliers. Ordinary carpenter's tools. There was also a rag. Wrapped in the rag was the salt-cellar. A common glass salt-cellar such as you find on the tables in cheap restaurants. He's stolen it somewhere, I said to myself. He's a thief.

He held the salt-cellar under my nose. There was salt in it. He shook some out on my hand. Taste it, he said, first-class salt. He saw the rage in my face, I was speechless. He laughed. Those little teeth revolted me.

Yes, he said and laughed again, I bet you'd rather be salted alive than eaten dead.

He shut the suitcase and lit another cigarette. It was half past three. The train was flying over the rails, but there won't be any Paris at the end. Neither earthly nor heavenly. I was in a trap. Death comes to every man. Does it really matter how you die? You can get run over, you can get shot by acci-dent, at a certain age your heart is likely to give out, or you can die of lung cancer, which is very common nowadays. One way or another you kick the bucket. Why not be eaten by a madman in the Nice-Paris express?

All is vanity, what else. You've got to die, only you don't want to. You don't have to live, but you want to. Only necessary things are important. Big fish eat little ones, the lark eats the worm and yet how sweetly he sings, cats eat mice and no one ever killed a cat for it—every animal eats every other just to stay alive, men eat men, what's unnatural about that? Is it more natural to eat pigs or calves? Does it hurt more when you can say "it hurts"? Animals don't cry, human beings cry when a relative dies, but how can anybody cry over his own death? Am I so fond of myself? So it must be vanity. Nobody's heart breaks over his own death. That's the way it is.

A feeling of warmth and well-being came over me. Here is a madman, he wants to eat me. But at least he wants something. What do I want? Not to eat anybody. Is that so noble? What's left when you don't want to do what you certainly ought to do?

If you don't do that which disgusts you, what becomes of your disgust? It sticks in your throat. Nothing sticks in the throat of the man from Sankt Pölten. He swallows all.

A voice spoke very softly, it sounded almost affectionate: There, you see you're getting sleepy, that comes from thinking. What have you got to look forward to in Paris? Paris is only a city. Whom do you need anyway, and who needs you? You're going to Paris. Well, what of it? Sex and drinking won't make you any happier. And certainly working won't. Money won't do you a particle of good. What are you getting out of life? Just go to sleep. You won't wake up, I can promise you.

But I don't want to die, I whispered. Not yet. I want . . . to go for a walk in Paris.

Go for a walk in Paris? Big deal. It will only make you tired. There are enough people taking walks and looking at the shop windows. The restaurants are overcrowded. So are the whore-houses. Nobody needs you in Paris. Just do me a favour, go to sleep. The night won't go on for ever; I'll have to gobble everything down so fast you'll give me a belly-ache.

I've got to eat you. In the first place I'm hungry, and in the second place I like you. I told you right off that I liked you and you thought, the guy is a queer. But now you know. I'm a simple cannibal. It's not a profession, it's a need. Good Lord, man, try to understand: now you've got an aim in life. Your life has purpose, thanks to me. You think it was by accident you came into my compartment? There's no such thing as an accident. I watched you all along the platform in Nice. And then you came into my compartment. Why mine and not someone else's? Because I'm so good-looking? Don't make me laugh. Is a seal good-looking? You came in here because you knew there'd be something doing.

Very slowly he opened the little suitcase. He took out the mallet and closed the suitcase. He held the mallet in his hand.

Well, how about it? he said.

Just a minute, I said. Just a minute. And suddenly I stood up. God only knows how I did it, but I stood up on my two feet and stretched out my hand. The little wire snapped, the lead seal fell, the train hissed and screeched. Screams came from next door. Then the train stopped. The man from Sankt Pölten stowed the mallet quickly in his suitcase and took his coat; he was at the door in a flash. He opened the door and looked around: I pity you, he said. This bit of foolishness is going to cost you a ten-thousand-franc fine, you nitwit, now you'll have to take your walk in Paris.

People crowded into the compartment, a conductor and a policeman appeared. Two soldiers and a pregnant woman shook their fists at me.

Already the seal from Sankt Pölten was outside, right under my window. He shouted something, I opened the window: See, he shouted, you've made an ass of yourself for life. Look who wants to live. He spat and shrugged his shoulders. Carrying his suitcase in his right hand, he stepped cautiously down the embankment and vanished in the dark. Like a country doctor on his way to deliver a baby.

Translated from the German by Ralph Manheim

Doves on Wires

. . . My child, on a cold and frosty day, with an evil wind blowing and shaking man and earth, your father dragged himself along, tired, in search of himself. He wandered through the streets, past buildings and people.

Instead of himself, he found wires—barbed wires that cut through the street and cut it to pieces. On both sides of the wire people walked up and down. Poverty and hunger drove them towards the fence through which one could see what went on on the other side. Jews, the badge of shame on their arms, walked on one side and Christian boys and girls on the other. When from the other side a loaf of bread was thrown over the fence, boys on this side tried to catch. Police in jack-boots, armed with rubber truncheons, beat up a child. The child cried and German soldiers, looking on, shook with laughter. When a Jewish girl sang a song, begging, pleading—"I am hungry and cold," policemen drove her away, and the soldiers smiled, when they saw the loaf of bread, rolling on the ground.

People walked up and down. And your father stood there and looked over the fence. Suddenly a flight of doves came down, driven from somewhere out of the blue. Silently they settled on the wires and began quietly to coo. I felt the pain of their sadness and sorrow, I listened to their weeping hearts and understood the anguish of the freezing doves.

And yet, my child, how greedy man is! With his heart he feels sympathy, while his eyes are filled with envy. The doves have wings, and if they want to, they can fly, onto wires or up to rooftops, off and away!

Your father stood there, dreaming. And a policeman came and knocked him on the head. Ashamed he began to move on, but he wanted to look once more at the doves. And, then, my child, your father saw something terrible:

The doves were still there, on the barbed wires, but . . . they were eating crumbs, out of the hands of the soldiers! . . .

My child, your father grew very sad, and sad he still is: not about the doves on the freezing wires, and not because they have wings and he has not, but because now he hates the doves, too, and he warns you: Keep away from them, as long as the innocence allows itself to be fed by murderous hands. . . .

It Will Be as in Our Dream . . .

My son! You should not regret it that you have been with me in the locked-up streets of the Ghetto—Dzika, Stavki and Mila.

My son, you should not regret your crying today. It does not matter that, when you look up to the sun, tears come into your eyes.

For you will see, my child, you will see: where today there is wailing and sadness hovers in homes; and the Angel of Death reigns supreme like a drunken madman; and people in rags, heaps of shattered hopes, cower along old, dark and smoky walls; and bodies of old men rot away in doorways or on bare floors, covered with newspapers or pieces of stone; and children shiver and whisper: "We are starving" and like rats stir in piles of refuse; and worn-out women hold up their hands, thin as ribbons in their last barren consumptive prayers; and frost and disease close in on dying eyes that, in their last agony crave for a crust of bread—

> There, my dear, my sunny child,
> there will yet come
> that great,
> that greatest of days,
> that last, the very last day—
> and it will be as in our dream. . . .

Both poems by Kirman
appeared in the Warsaw ghetto,
February—March 1942
Published in the Bundist *Yugnt-shtime*
[Voice of Youth], no. 2/3

Translated from the Yiddish by Jacob Sontag

In the Camp

Those who walk about here are but bodies
And have no longer any soul,
Are only names in books,
Imprisoned: Men and boys and women,
And their eyes stare emptily.

With crumbling, ruined gazes
For hours when in a gloomy cell,
When strangled, trampled, beaten blind,
Their tortured groan, their fear insane,
A creature crept on hands and feet . . .

They all have ears and hear
No longer their own cries.
The prison walls press in, destroy:
No heart, no heart remains to rage!
The soft alarm-clock shrills until it breaks.

Insensate, gray, degenerate they toil,
Cut off from human life,
Stiff, wounded, branded with official stamps,
They wait like slaughter cattle for the knife,
And still remember dimly trough and herd.

And only fear remains, a trembling face,
When late at night a gunshot strikes its mark . . .
And no one sees the man appear
Who, silently, within their midst,
Conveys his barren cross towards the hill.

Translated from the German by Henry A. Smith

This poem is part of Gertrud Kolmar's 1933 poem cycle *Das Wort der Stummen*
[Words of the silent people], in which she describes the human tragedy implied
by the Nazi takeover. Although written before *Kristallnacht* or the mass extermi-
nations, "In the Camp" evokes the horror of the first concentration camps.

The Seventh Eclogue

Do you see night, the wild oakwood fence lined with barbed wire,
and the barracks, so flimsy that the night swallowed them?
Slowly the eye passes the limits of captivity
and only the mind, the mind knows how tight the wire is.
You see, dear, this is how we set our imaginations free.
Dream, the beautiful savior, dissolves our broken bodies
and the prison camp leaves for home.

Ragged, bald, snoring, the prisoners fly
from the black heights of Serbia to the hidden lands of home.
Hidden lands of home! Are there still homes there?
Maybe the bombs didn't hit, and they *are,* just like when we were
  "drafted"?
Next to me, on my right, a man whines, another one lies on my
  left. Will they go home?
Tell me, is there still a home where they understand all this?

Without commas, one line touching the other,
I write poems the way I live, in darkness,
blind, crossing the paper like a worm.
Flashlights, books—the guards took everything.
There's no mail, only fog drifts over the barracks.

Frenchmen, Poles, loud Italians, heretic Serbs, and dreamy
Jews live here in the mountains, among frightening rumors.

Radnoti wrote this poem in the prison camp near the German-controlled copper
mines at Bor in Yugoslavia. With other prisoners, he worked on the construction
of a railway line between Bor and Belgrade. At the Bor camp he wrote many of
his finest poems. When the camp was evacuated in the autumn of 1944, Radnoti
and fellow laborers began the forced march toward Germany that was to end in
his death.

   The poem is addressed to Fanni Gyarmati, whom he married in 1935 and
whose love was a source of comfort during the suffering of his last years.

One feverish body cut into many pieces but still living the same life,
it waits for good news, the sweet voices of women, a free, a
    human fate.
It waits for the end, the fall into thick darkness, miracles.

I lie on the plank, like a trapped animal, among worms. The fleas
attack again and again, but the flies have quieted down.
Look. It's evening, captivity is one day shorter.
And so is life. The camp sleeps. The moon shines
over the land and in its light the wires are tighter.
Through the window you can see the shadows of the armed guards
thrown on the wall, walking among the noises of the night.

The camp sleeps. Do you see it? Dreams fly.
Frightened, someone wakes up. He grunts, then turns in the
    tight space
and sleeps again. His face shines. I sit up awake.
The taste of a half-smoked cigarette in my mouth instead of the taste
of your kisses and the calmness of dreams doesn't come.
I can't die, I can't live without you now.

Lager Heidenau, in the mountains above Žagubica
July 1944
Translated from the Hungarian by Steven Polgar,
Stephen Berg, and S. J. Marks

Fragment

I lived on this earth in an age
when man fell so low
he killed willingly, for pleasure, without orders.
Mad obsessions threaded his life,
he believed in false gods. Deluded, he foamed at the mouth.

I lived on this earth in an age
when it was honor to betray and to murder,
the traitor and the thief were heroes—
those who were silent, unwilling to rejoice,
were hated as if they had the plague

I lived on this earth in an age
when if a man spoke out, he had to go into hiding
and could only chew his fists in shame—
drunk on blood and scum, the nation went mad
and grinned at its horrible fate.

I lived on this earth in an age
when a curse was the mother of a child,
when women were happy if they miscarried,
a glass of thick poison foamed on the table,
and the living envied the rotting silence of the dead.

I lived on this earth in an age
when the poets too were silent
and waited for Isaiah, the scholar
of terrifying words, to speak again—
since only he could utter the right curse.

May 19, 1944
Translated from the Hungarian by Steven Polgar,
Stephen Berg, and S. J. Marks

Written after the German occupation of Hungary in March 1944, when the deportation of Hungarian Jews began.

from "Street for Arrivals,
Street for Departures"

There are people arriving. They scan the crowd of those who wait seeking those who wait for them. They kiss them and they say that they are tired from the journey.

There are people leaving. They say good-by to those who are not leaving and they kiss the children.

There is a street for people arriving and a street for people leaving.

There is a café called "Arrivals" and a café called "Departures."

There are people arriving and there are people leaving.

But there is a station where those arriving are the same as those leaving

a station at which those arriving have never arrived, to which those leaving have never returned

it is the biggest station in the world.

This is the station at which they arrive, wherever they come from.

They arrive here after days and nights

after crossing whole countries

they arrive here with children, even babies, who were not supposed to have been taken

They have brought their children because you do not part with children for this journey.

Those who had gold brought it along because they thought that gold might be useful.

Everyone brought his dearest possession because you must not leave what is dear to you when you go far away.

Everyone has brought his life along, above all it was his life that he had to bring along.

And when they arrive

they think they have arrived

in Hell

possibly. Still they did not believe it.

They did not know that you could take a train to Hell but since they are here, they steel themselves and feel ready to face it

with women, children, aged parents
with family keepsakes and family documents.

*   *   *   *

There are those who come from Warsaw with big shawls and knotted bundles
those who come from Zagreb, women with kerchiefs on their heads
those who come from the Danube with garments knitted by the hearth in multicolored yarns
those who come from Greece, bringing black olives and Turkish Delight
those who come from Monte Carlo
they were in the casino
they are in white tie with shirt fronts that the journey has completely ruined
pot-bellied and bald
they are bankers who played at banking
newlyweds who were leaving the synagogue with the bride dressed in white, wearing a veil, all wrinkled from lying on the floor of the boxcar
the bridegroom dressed in black and top hat with soiled gloves
the relatives and guests, women with beaded bags
who all regret that they were not able to stop off at their homes and change into something less fragile.

The rabbi holds his head up high and walks first. He has always set an example for the others.

There are little girls from boarding school with their identical pleated skirts and their hats with blue streamers. They pull up their stockings carefully as they alight. They walk demurely five by five as though on a Thursday outing, holding one another by the hand and not knowing. What can they do to little girls from boarding school who are with their teacher. The teacher tells them: "Be good, children." They have no wish not to be good.

*   *   *   *

In ranks of five they move along the street for arrivals. They do not know it is the street for departures. You only pass this way once.

They move in strict order—so that you cannot fault them for anything.

They come to a building and they sigh. At last they have arrived.

And when the soldiers shout to the women to strip they undress the children first taking care not to wake them up completely. After days and nights of travel they are fretful and cross

and they begin to get undressed in front of their children, it can't be helped

and when the soldiers hand each one of them a towel they worry if the water in the shower will be warm because the children might catch cold

and when the men come in to the shower room through another door naked too the women hide their children against their bodies.

And then perhaps they understand.

*   *   *   *

And all day and all night

every day and every night the chimneys smoke with this fuel from all the countries of Europe

men assigned to the chimneys spend their days sifting the ashes to recover melted gold from gold teeth. They all have gold in their mouths these Jews and they are so many that it makes tons.

And in the spring men and women spread the ashes on the marshes drained and plowed for the first time and fertilize the soil with human phosphate.

They have bags tied to their bellies and they stick their hands into the human bone meal which they scatter by the handful over the furrows with the wind blowing the dust back into their faces and in the evening they are all white with lines traced by the sweat that has trickled down over the dust.

*   *   *   *

You who have wept for two thousand years
for one who suffered three days and three nights[1]

what tears will you have
for those who suffered
many more than three hundred nights and many more than
    three hundred days
how much
will you weep
for those who suffered so many agonies
and they were countless

They did not believe in resurrection to eternal life
And they knew that you would not weep.

Translated from the French by John Githens

---

1. The reference is to Jesus.

Death Fugue

Black milk of dawn we drink it at dusk
we drink it at noon and at daybreak we drink it at night
we drink it and drink it
we are digging a grave in the air there's room for us all
A man lives in the house he plays with the serpents he writes
he writes when it darkens to Germany your golden hair Margarete
he writes it and steps outside and the stars all aglisten he whistles
    for his hounds
he whistles for his Jews he has them dig a grave in the earth
he commands us to play for the dance

Black milk of dawn we drink you at night
we drink you at daybreak and noon we drink you at dusk
we drink and we drink
A man lives in the house he plays with the serpents he writes
he writes when it darkens to Germany your golden hair Margarete
Your ashen hair Shulamite[1] we are digging a grave in the air there's
    room for us all

He shouts cut deeper in the earth to some the rest of you sing and
    play
he reaches for the iron in his belt he heaves it his eyes are blue
make your spades cut deeper the rest of you play for the dance

Black milk of dawn we drink you at night
we drink you at noon and at daybreak we drink you at dusk
we drink and we drink
a man lives in the house your golden hair Margarete
your ashen hair Shulamite he plays with the serpents

---

1. Margarete is another name for Gretchen in Goethe's *Faust*. Shulamite is a reference to the beautiful maiden of the Song of Songs (7:1), whose hair is now covered by the ash of the crematorium. The juxtaposition of the two names suggests the paradox of "culture" and "extermination."

He shouts play death more sweetly death is a master from Germany
he shouts play the violins darker you'll rise as smoke in the air
then you'll have a grave in the clouds there's room for you all

Black milk of dawn we drink you at night
we drink you at noon death is a master from Germany
we drink you at dusk and at daybreak we drink and we drink you
death is a master from Germany his eye is blue
he shoots you with bullets of lead his aim is true
a man lives in the house your golden hair Margarete
he sets his hounds on us he gives us a grave in the air
he plays with the serpents and dreams death is a master from
    Germany

your golden hair Margarete
your ashen hair Shulamite

Translated from the German by Joachim Neugroschel

Instructions for Crossing the Border

Imaginary man, go. Here is your passport.
You are not allowed to remember.
You have to match the description:
your eyes are already blue.
Don't escape with the sparks
inside the smokestack:
you are a man, you sit in the train.
Sit comfortably.
You've got a decent coat now,
a repaired body, a new name
ready in your throat.
Go, You are not allowed to forget.

Translated from the Hebrew by Stephen Mitchell

A Woman Said to Her Neighbor

A woman said to her neighbor:
"Since my husband was killed I can't sleep,
when there's shooting I dive under the blanket,
I tremble all night long under the blanket.
I'll go crazy if I have to be alone today,

I have some cigarettes my husband left, please
do drop in tonight."

Translated from the Polish by Magnus J. Krynski
and Robert A. Maguire

Protocols

(Birkenau, Odessa; the children speak alternately.)

We went there on the train. *They had big barges that they towed,*
We stood up, there were so many I was squashed.
There was a smoke-stack, then they made me wash.
It was a factory, I think. *My mother held me up*
And I could see the ship that made the smoke.

When I was tired my mother carried me.
She said, "Don't be afraid." But I was only tired.
Where we went there is no more Odessa.
They had water in a pipe—like rain, but hot;
The water there is deeper than the world

And I was tired and fell in in my sleep
And the water drank me. That is what I think.
And I said to my mother, "Now I'm washed and dried,"
My mother hugged me, and it smelled like hay
And that is how you die. And that is how you die.

Theresienstadt Poem

In your watercolor, Nely Sílvinová
your heart on fire
on the gray cover of a sketchbook
is a dying sun or
a flower
youngest of the summer

the sun itself
the grizzled head of a flower
throbbing
in the cold dusk of your last day
on earth

There are no thorns to be seen
but the color says
thorns

and much else that is not
visible it says also
a burning wound at the horizon
it says Poland and winter
it says painful Terezin
SILVIN VI 25 VI 1944;
and somehow

Theresienstadt was a Nazi concentration camp located at the edge of Terezin, Czechoslovakia. Thousands of Jewish children were confined here before being sent to various death camps. Only a few of these children survived the war. To lift the spirits of the children, the adult prisoners in Theresienstadt organized secret classes in music, drama, and painting. Mezey's poem is a response to an actual watercolor painting by a girl named Nely Silvinova, of whom we know only her age and barracks number and that she died in 1944. The watercolor that inspired the poem, as well as numerous paintings, drawings, and children's poems created in Theresienstadt, may be found in *I Never Saw Another Butterfly*, edited by Hana Volakova (New York: McGraw-Hill, 1964).

above the light body on its bed of coals
it says spring
from the crest of the street it says
you can see the fields
brown and green
and beyond them the dark blue line of woods
and beyond that smoke
is that the smoke of Prague
and it says blood
every kind of blood
blood of Jews
German blood
blood of Bohemia and Moravia
running in the gutters
blood of children
it says free at last
the mouth of the womb it says
SILVIN VI 25 VI 1944;
the penis of the commandant
the enraged color
the whip stock the gun butt
it says it says it says

Petrified god
god that gave up the ghost at Terezin
what does it say but itself
thirteen years of life
and your heart on fire

                              Nely Sílvinová!

Still, Still

Still, still, let us be still.
Graves grow here.
Planted by the enemy,
they blossom to the sky.
All the roads lead to Ponar,[1]
and none returns.
Somewhere father disappeared,
disappeared with all our joy.
Be still, my child, don't cry, my treasure;
tears are of no avail.
No matter the fury of your tears,
the enemy will not notice.
Rivers open into oceans,
prison cells are not a world,
but to our sorrow,
there is no end,
there is no light.

Spring has blossomed in the countryside,
and all about our lives is fall.
Today the day is full of flowers,
but the night alone holds us.
Somewhere a mother is orphaned.

One of the most famous of ghetto songs, "Still, Still" was written in the Vilna
Ghetto in the spring of 1943. In April, the Literary Artistic Circle held a musical
competition in which Alec Volkoviski, age eleven, won first prize for his original
composition. The poet Shmerke Kaczerginski later wrote words to this musical
piece.

1. *Ponary* in Polish. A wooded area outside of Vilna used by the Nazis as an
execution and burial site for victims of the roundups and night raids. Ponar was
to the Vilna Ghetto what Babi Yar was to the Kiev Jews. Thirty-three thousand
Vilna Jews were murdered here in the six months following the German occupation of Vilna on June 24, 1941. Close to eighty thousand people were massa-
cred in the pits of Ponar between 1941 and 1944.

Her child goes to Ponar.
The river Viliye, chained,
convulses in our pain.
Ice floes race through Lithuania
Into the ocean now.
Somewhere there is no darkness.
Somewhere, out of darkness,
suns are burning.
Rider come at once.
Your child calls you.
Your child calls you.

Still, still, wellsprings flow
deep without our hearts.
Until the gates come falling down
we must guard our tongues.
Don't rejoice, child, your very smile
is treachery now.
Let the enemy see the spring
as a leaf in autumn.
Let the wellspring flow its course
and you be still and hope. . . .
Father will return with freedom.
Sleep, my child, be still.
Like the Viliye freed of its chains
and like the trees renewed in green,
freedom's light will glow
upon your face,
upon your face.

Vilna Ghetto, April 1943
Translated from the Yiddish by
Hillel Schwartz and David G. Roskies

Here Too as in Jerusalem

Here too as in Jerusalem
There is the somber Wailing Wall.
Those who stood near it
Will see it no more.

Empty night, empty building, deaf edifice.
From here they were dragged.
Darkness and terror remained,
And the interior—the womb of death.

Buildings in a stony procession,
Under an unappeased sky,
As if thousands of families
Following a funeral.

Christians, thrown to the wolves,
Knew why they were perishing,
But you?—Here is your empty house,
Fire, a blind proprietor, occupies it.

No one cast the good earth
Onto that mass grave—
Greeted by silence,
Free of treacherous words.

When with mouths like wounds,
Parched, you called for water,
No one brought water
To the sealed trains.

Jastrun draws a parallel between the Wailing Wall in Jerusalem—symbol of grief at the destruction of the Temple and the dispersion of the Jews, but also symbol of hope—and the wall of the Warsaw Ghetto, symbol of an evil that leaves no room for hope or affirmation.

The earth fled under the condemned,
Warsaw fell in the smoke of the trains
And in the windows of the buildings
The sun announced dawn.

Translated from the Polish
by Frieda Aaron

Lamentation

They caught flakes in the air
Riding on the roundabout,
The girls' dresses billowed out
In that wind from the burning houses,
Oh they were fun-days,
Those lovely Warsaw Sundays.

Czeslaw Milosz,
"Campo di Fiori"

There was also weeping
the blackmailers wept
the gendarme wiped his eyes on his sleeve
the stormtrooper buried his head in his hands
and the police dog with hair
in mourning from the soot whined

Smoke rose
the enormous shadow of fire
the stinging smoke of krochmalna
gęsia nalewki zamenhof streets[1]
smoke with a red beard a caftan

the wind blew it all the way
here
straight into the eyes

Translated from the Polish by Keith Bosley
with Krystyna Wandycz

1. Streets in the Warsaw Ghetto set afire by the Nazis, the smoke being carried to the "Aryan" side of Warsaw.

Say This City Has Ten Million Souls

Say this city has ten million souls,
Some are living in mansions, some are living in holes:
Yet there's no place for us, my dear, yet there's no place for us.

Once we had a country and we thought it fair,
Look in the atlas and you'll find it there:
We cannot go there now, my dear, we cannot go there now.

In the village churchyard there grows an old yew,
Every spring it blossoms anew:
Old passports can't do that, my dear, old passports can't do that.

The consul banged the table and said;
"If you've got no passport you're officially dead":
But we are still alive, my dear, but we are still alive.

Went to a committee; they offered me a chair;
Asked me politely to return next year:
But where shall we go today, my dear, but where shall
    we go today?

Came to a public meeting; the speaker got up and said:
"If we let them in, they will steal our daily bread";
He was talking of you and me, my dear, he was talking of
    you and me.

Thought I heard the thunder rumbling in the sky;
It was Hitler over Europe, saying: "They must die";
O we were in his mind, my dear, O we were in his mind.

Saw a poodle in a jacket fastened with a pin,
Saw a door opened and a cat let in:
But they weren't German Jews, my dear, but they weren't
    German Jews.

Went down the harbour and stood upon the quay,
Saw the fish swimming as if they were free:
Only ten feet away, my dear, only ten feet away.

Walked through a wood, saw the birds in the trees;
They had no politicians and sang at their ease:
They weren't the human race, my dear, they weren't the
    human race.

Dreamed I saw a building with a thousand floors,
A thousand windows and a thousand doors;
Not one of them was ours, my dear, not one of them was ours.

Stood on a great plain in the falling snow;
Ten thousand soldiers marched to and fro:
Looking for you and me, my dear, looking for you and me.

The housing project at Drancy

Trains without signs flee through Paris.
Wrong trains. The wrong station.
The world as microwave oven, burning from within.
We arrive. Drancy looks like Inkster,
Gary, the farther reaches of Newark.

In the station they won't give directions.
C'est pas notre affaire. We don't deal with that.
Outside five buses limp in five directions
into the hot plain drugged with exhaust.
Nobody ever heard of the camp. They turn away.

Out on the bridge, over marshaling yards:
Here Jews were stuffed into cars nailed shut.
Here children too young to know their names
were counted like so many shoes
as they begged the French police hemming them in

Take me to the bathroom, please, please,
before I wet myself. Mother, I have been so good,
and it is so very dark. Dear concierge,
I am writing to you as everyone else
is dead now and they are taking me away.

Yes, to the land children named Pitchepois,
giant's skull land grimmer than Hansel came to.
On the bridge I saw an old bald workman
staring down and I told myself desperately,
He is a communist and will answer me.

The largest assembly center for deportation from France was located in an unfinished housing project near the Paris suburb of Drancy. About sixty-one thousand Jews left Drancy between July 1942 and August 1944. Most of them
perished in Auschwitz.

I asked him where the camp was, now a housing
project. He asked, Why do you want to know?
I had that one ready. No talk of novels, research.
My aunt was there. Oh, in that case,
he pointed to distant towers. You want that bus.

Where we descended the bus, Never heard of it.
Eyes that won't look. Then a woman asked that
same question, Why do you want to know?
A housing project crammed with mothers.
The guard towers are torn down and lindens grow.

In flats now with heat and plumbing, not eighty
but one family lives. Pain still rises,
the groaning of machinery deep underfoot.
Crimes ignored sink into the soil like PCBs
and enter the bones of children.

Riddle

From Belsen a crate of gold teeth,
from Dachau a mountain of shoes,
from Auschwitz a skin lampshade.
Who killed the Jews?

Not I, cries the typist,
not I, cries the engineer,
not I, cries Adolf Eichmann,[1]
not I, cries Albert Speer.[2]

My friend Fritz Nova lost his father—
a petty official had to choose.
My friend Lou Abrahms lost his brother.
Who killed the Jews?

David Nova swallowed gas.
Hyman Abrahms was beaten and starved.
Some men signed their papers,
and some stood guard,

and some herded them in,
and some dropped the pellets,
and some spread the ashes,
and some hosed the walls,

1. Adolf Eichmann (1906–62), S.S. lieutenant colonel who was instrumental in implementing the "Final Solution," organizing transports of Jews from all over Europe to the death camps. He was arrested at the end of World War II in the American zone of Germany but escaped and disappeared. In 1960, members of the Israeli Secret Service found him in Argentina and brought him to Israel for trial. He was tried in Jerusalem (April–December 1961), convicted, sentenced to death, and executed.
2. Albert Speer (1905–81), Hitler's architect and later German Minister of Armaments from 1942 to 1945.

and some planted the wheat,
and some poured the steel,
and some cleared the rails,
and some raised the cattle.

Some smelled the smoke,
some just heard the news.
Were they Germans? Were they Nazis?
Were they human? Who killed the Jews?

The stars will remember the gold,
the sun will remember the shoes,
the moon will remember the skin.
But who killed the Jews?

from "The Invocation to Kali"

The Concentration Camps

Have we managed to fade them out like God?
Simply eclipse the unpurged images?
Eclipse the children with a mountain of shoes?
Let the bones fester like animal bones,
False teeth, bits of hair, spilled liquid eyes,
Disgusting, not to be looked at, like a blight?

Ages ago we closed our hearts to blight.
Who believes now? Who cries, "merciful God"?
We gassed God in the ovens, great piteous eyes,
Burned God in a trash-heap of images,
Refused to make a compact with dead bones,
And threw away the children with their shoes—

Millions of sandals, sneakers, small worn shoes—
Thrust them aside as a disgusting blight.
Not ours, this death, to take into our bones,
Not ours a dying mutilated God.
We freed our minds from gruesome images,
Pretended we had closed their open eyes

That never could be closed, dark puzzled eyes,
The ghosts of children who went without shoes
Naked toward the ovens' bestial images,
Strangling for breath, clawing the blight,
Piled up like pigs beyond the help of God. . . .
With food in our stomachs, flesh on our bones,

Sarton's five-part poem is headed by an epigraph taken from Joseph Campbell
which identifies Kali as the "Black Goddess . . . the terrible one of many
names." Kali is the dark side of the Indian goddess Devi, who uses violence and
destruction to overthrow evil.

We turned away from the stench of bones,
Slept with the living, drank in sexy eyes,
Hurried for shelter from a murdered God.
New factories turned out millions of shoes.
We hardly noticed the faint smell of blight,
Stuffed with new cars, ice cream, rich images.

But no grass grew on the raw images.
Corruption mushroomed from decaying bones.
Joy disappeared. The creature of the blight
Rose in the cities, dark smothered eyes.
Our children danced with rage in their shoes,
Grew up to question who had murdered God,

While we evaded their too attentive eyes,
Walked the pavane of death in our new shoes,
Sweated with anguish and remembered God.

The Silent Generation

When Hitler was the Devil
He did as he had sworn
With such enthusiasm
That even, *donnerwetter,* [1]
The Germans say, "Far better
Had he been never born!"

It was my generation
That put the Devil down
With great enthusiasm.
But now our occupation
Is gone. Our education
Is wasted on the town.

We lack enthusiasm.
Life seems a mystery;
It's like the play a lady
Told me about: "It's not . . .
It doesn't *have* a plot,"
She said, "it's history."

1. Literally "thunder-weather," but here approximating "damn it."

1980

And when I go up as a pilgrim in winter, to recover
the place I was born, and the twin to self I am in my mind,
then I'll go in black snow as a pilgrim to find
the grave of my savior, Yanova.[1]

She'll hear what I whisper, under my breath:
Thank you. You saved my tears from the flame.
Thank you. Children and grandchildren you rescued from death.
I planted a sapling (it doesn't suffice) in your name.

Time in its gyre spins back down the flue
faster than nightmares of nooses can ride,
quicker than nails. And you, my savior, in your cellar you'll hide
me, ascending in dreams as a pilgrim to you.

You'll come from the yard in your slippers, crunching the snow
so I'll know. Again I'm there in the cellar, degraded and low,
you're bringing me milk and bread sliced thick at the edge.
You're making the sign of the cross. I'm making my pencil its
    pledge.

Translated from the Yiddish by Cynthia Ozick

1. Yanova Bartoszewicz was a Polish woman who hid Sutzkever in her cellar in
the Vilna Ghetto during a period of mass killings in October 1941. Sutzkever
paid tribute to her by planting a tree in her memory in the Avenue of the Righteous Gentiles at the Yad Vashem Memorial in Jerusalem.

Both your mothers

for Bieta

Under a futile Torah
under an imprisoned star
your mother gave birth to you

you have proof of her
beyond doubt and death
the scar of the navel
the sign of parting for ever
which had no time to hurt you

this you know

Later you slept in a bundle
carried out of the ghetto
someone said in a chest
knocked together somewhere in Nowolipie Street[1]
with a hole to let in air
but not fear
hidden in a cartload of bricks

You slipped out in this little coffin
redeemed by stealth
from that world to this world
all the way to the Aryan side
and fire took over
the corner you left vacant

So you did not cry
crying could have meant death
luminal hummed you

1. A street in the Warsaw Ghetto.

its lullaby
And you nearly were not
so that you could be

But the mother
who was saved in you
could now step into crowded death
happily incomplete
could instead of memory give you
for a parting gift
her own likeness
and a date and a name

so much

And at once a chance
someone hastily
bustled about your sleep
and then stayed for a long always
and washed you of orphanhood
and swaddled you in love
and become the answer
to your first word

That was how
both your mothers taught you
not to be surprised at all
when you say
I am

Translated from the Polish
by Keith Bosley
with Krystyna Wandycz

A Poem for Anton Schmidt

*A German army sergeant, executed in
March 1942 for supplying the Jewish
underground with forged credentials
and military vehicles.*

I have properly spoken
hymns for the dead, have planted
white roses in the high air.

And because my pen is a leech
to suck out blood's poison
I had a need to write

of death's clerks and doctors;
but my pen dissolved
in an inkwell of acid

and my paper, litmus of shame,
crumbled to ashes.
Anton Schmidt, I thank you

for breaking the spell that numbed
the singing mouth. I need not write
of the mad and the murderous.

That a vile camaraderie
caused streets and meadows to weep
no longer surprises us;

but a lone soldier's
shining treason
is a cause for holy attention.

Anton Schmidt, whose valor
lessened the vats of human fat
and looms of human hair

I thank you that no poison
is burning my veins
but a wine of praise

for a living man
among clockwork robots
and malevolent puppets.

Silence, and a Starry Night

Silence, and a starry night
Frost crackling, fine as sand.
Remember how I taught you
To hold a gun in your hand?

In fur jacket and beret,
Clutching a hand grenade,
A girl whose skin is velvet
Ambushes a cavalcade.

Aim, fire, shoot—and hit!
She, with her pistol small,
Halts an autoful,
Arms and all!

Morning, emerging from the wood,
In her hair a snow carnation.
Proud of her small victory
For the new, free generation!

Vilna Ghetto, Summer 1942
Translated from the Yiddish
by Jacob Sloan

In the summer of 1942, Itzik Matzkevitch and Vitke Kempner launched the first attack of the Jewish partisans of Vilna against the German Army, blowing up an ammunition column on the outskirts of the city. Hirsh Glik commemorated their deed—and, in particular, the heroism of the female resistance fighter—in this song, also known as "Partisanerlid."

Never Say

Never say you've come to the end of the way,
Though leaden skies blot out the light of the day.
The hour we all long for will surely appear—
Our steps will thunder with the words: We are here!

From lands of palm trees to far-off lands of snow,
We come with anguish, we come with grief,
   with pain and woe;
And where our blood flowed right before our eyes,
There our power'll bloom, our courage will arise.

The glow of morning sun will gild a bright today,
Night's darkness vanish, like the enemy cast away.
But if we perish before this dawn's begun—
This song's a message passed to daughter and to son.

In blood this song was written, and not with pen
   or quill,
Not from a songbird freely flying as he will.
Sung by a people crushed by falling walls—
Sung with guns in hand, by those whom
   freedom calls!

Vilna Ghetto, 1943
Translated from the Yiddish by Shoshana Kalisch
with Barbara Meister

In April 1943, when news of the Warsaw Ghetto uprising reached the Vilna Ghetto, the young poet and partisan Hirsh Glik was inspired to write this song. It had an immense impact and spread from Vilna to other ghettos and then to concentration camps. It very soon became the official hymn of the Jewish underground partisan brigades. Glik wrote many of his poems to well-known Jewish melodies of Russia and Poland.

On the Anniversary of the Ghetto Theater

I

. . . We walled ourselves in
And live apart.
From your freedom outside, do not smile at us,
Do not pity—
For us, even death can blossom into wonder.

How can we sit together
With you in one place?
Your hatred for us will poison you like mice,
Our wounds—love will heal.

As long as the outside is yours—
Ours is the ghetto, here we will lie
And from God's heart, we will knead a redeemer
And polish a melody . . .

II

Perform, Jewish actors, in tatters and in walls,
Where life shrivels like hair that caught fire,
When red drops of your loved ones are seething on stones,
And the alleys convulse like half-slaughtered hens
And cannot arise, fly away, flee . . .
Perform, friends! Let us think: it's a shtetl of yore,
They celebrate a wedding at an autumn graveyard
With Jewish singing and dancing light,
In a joyous circle around the bride and groom!
Perform! From your mouth, let Yiddish sound,

Wherever possible, victims of the Nazi ghettos organized various cultural and theatrical events. These events constituted a form of spiritual resistance.

Pure and clean as the ghost of a slaughtered child,
Harsh and hoarse as the voice of our rifle and gunpowder,
Performing tomorrow
Over the rooftops . . .

And you, melancholy fiddlers,
Who stole out at night
Into the lurking outside,
Shuffling past houses,
Evading patrols,
Creeping to your ruined old home
And digging up your fiddles
Planted before your march into the ghetto—
You play too!
Pluck out the deepest tones!
Let them carry above your bones
And stray far, where a Jew still shimmers . . .
Where a heart still trembles, waiting for good tidings.
Let them carry over fields, over front lines,
Pure and clean as the ghost of a slaughtered child,
Harsh and hoarse as the voice of our rifle and gunpowder,
Performing tomorrow
Over the rooftops . . .

Vilna Ghetto, December 31, 1942
Translated from the Yiddish
by Barbara and Benjamin Harshav

Counterattack

They plodded calmly to the cars
As though disgusted with it all—
Gazed like dogs at the guards' eyes . . .
Cattle! ! !

Dapper officers smirked to see
That nothing got under their skin,
That hordes moved with torpid step
   . . . and only for sport
Lashed their snouts
With whips . . .
Counting-off in the square
Some dropped where they stood
Even before they could sob in the cars
Soaking the sandy ground with tears and blood
And the gentlemen . . .
On the corpses . . .
   let fall in a casual way . . .
      cigarette boxes that said
"Why Junos
are round."[1]

From July through September 1942, about 265,000 Jews were deported from the Warsaw Ghetto to the gas chambers of Treblinka. When, in January 1943, the Nazis attempted to remove some of the seventy thousand survivors of the ghetto, the Nazis were met by organized armed resistance in streets and apartment houses and in the German slave labor factories run by Schultz and Toebbens. This four-day revolt, the basis for Wladyslaw Szlengel's poem, was the first in the history of the ghetto and resulted in a German retreat. In April 1943, the Germans attacked in force, and the Battle of the Warsaw Ghetto raged until June 1943, when the ghetto was reduced to rubble. "Counterattack," written in January 1943, was copied and distributed in various versions throughout the ghetto in the three months before the final uprising in which Szlengel, too, was killed.

1. "Junos are round" was a line of a German cigarette advertisement.

Until the day when at dawn
On the town they'd lulled to sleep
Like hyenas they rushed out of morning fog,
Then the cattle woke up
And . . .
Bared its FANGS.

On Mila Street the first bullet fell—
Gendarme wobbled in a doorway—
Looked astonished . . . stopped a moment . . .
—incredible———
—something isn't right . . .
It had all been so simple, so easy—
Because of special pull
He'd been transferred away from the Eastern Front
(A few days R & R)
To rest a bit in Warsaw
Herding this cattle in the "action"
Cleaning out this sty
And here . . .
On Mila Street BLOOD? ? ?
He backed away from the doorway
And swore: "I'm bleeding for real. . . ."

And meanwhile Brownings barked
On Niska
    On Dzika
        On Pawia———

On twisting stairs where a mother
Was dragged down by the hair
Lies SS-man Hantke . . .
Strangely tensed, as though

He found death indigestible—
This revolt like a bone in his throat—
Choked in bloody drool—
And a box: Junos are round . . .
Round . . .
    round . . .

Golden epaulets trampled in dust!
Everything spins around:
Sky-blue gendarme's uniform lies
On spit-flecked stairs
Of Jewish Pawia Street . . .
    And doesn't know
      That at Schultz's and Toebbens'
Bullets ring in joyous song
Revolt of the Meat!
    Revolt of the meat! ! !
Meat spits grenades out the window
Meat bites with scarlet flames
    And life hangs on from the beams—
Hey! What joy to shoot at their eyes
HERE IS THE FRONT gentlemen!
THE FRONT DEAR SUNSHINE SOLDIERS!
    HIER
TRINKT MAN MEHR KEIN BIER!
    HIER
HAT MAN MEHR KEIN MUT . . .
BLUT . . .
    BLUT—
      BLUT! ! ![2]

2. "Here one drinks no more beer / Here one has no more courage / Blood / Blood / Blood."

Take off the light smooth leather gloves,
Put away the whips—helmets on your heads
   Tomorrow inform the press:
   Toebbens' entry forced with a wedge
   Revolt of the meat . . .
      REVOLT OF THE MEAT! ! ! SONG OF THE MEAT! ! !

   Do you hear, German god,
   How Jews pray in wildcat houses[3]
Crowbars and clubs in their hands:
—We ask of you, God, a bloody battle,
We implore you, a violent death—
May our eyes before they flicker
Not see the tracks stretch out
But give our palms true aim, Lord,
To bloody the coats of blue.
Allow us to see before
Dumb groaning chokes our throats . . .
In those haughty hands—in those paws with whips
Our everyday human FEAR!

   Like purple blossoms of blood
From Niska and Mila and Muranowa
Flames from our gunbarrels flower—
This is our spring, our counterattack—
This wine of battle pounds in our heads. . . .
These our partisan woods
Alleys of Dzika and Ostrowska—

---

3. Tenements emptied of their inhabitants during German military or police operations (Aktions), but which served as temporary illegal hiding places for Jews unable to secure work permits. These persons were not allowed to be in the ghetto, and hence not allowed to live.

Block-numbers flutter on breasts
Our medals in the Jewish War
The shriek of six letters flashes with red
Like a battering-ram it beats REVOLT

And on the street a package
Crushed and sticky with blood!
JUNOS ARE ROUND. . .

Translated from the Polish
by Michael Steinlauf

Black Mountain

On Montagne Noire creeping everywhere under the beech
    trees
were immense black slugs the size and pattern
of blown truck tires exploded by the superhighway.
Diamonds patterned their glossy and glittering backs.

As we watched, leaves, whole flowers disappeared in three
    bites.
Such avidity rebuked our stomachs skittish with alien
water and strange food. In patches of sunlight filtered
down, the slugs shone like wet black glass.

Battlefields are like any other fields; a forest
where men and women fought tanks with sten guns
houses as many owl and rabbit and deer as the next hill
where nothing's happened since the Romans passed by.

Yet I have come without hesitation through the maze
of lumbering roads to this spot where the small marker
tells us we have reached a destination. To die here
under hemlock's dark drooping boughs, better I think

than shoved into the showers of gas to croak like roaches
too packed in to flail in the intense slow pain
as the minutes like lava cooling petrified the jammed
bodies into living rock, basalt pillars whose fingers

gouged grooves in cement. Yes, better to drop in the high
clean air and let your blood soak into the rich leaf mold.

The poem pays tribute to Jews in the French resistance, fighting the Germans in
the mountainous region south of Lacaune. A little monument stands at Montagne
Noire, where Jewish fighters were killed and others were captured.

Better to get off one good shot. Better to remember trains
derailed, turntables wrecked with plastique, raids

on the munitions dump. Better to die with a gun
in your hand you chose to pick up and had time to shoot.
Dying you pass out of choice. The others come, put up
a monument decorated with crosses, no mogen davids.[1]

I come avid and omnivorous as the shining slugs.
I have eaten your history and made it myth;
among the tall trees of your pain my characters walk.
A saw whines in the valley. I say kaddish[2] for you.

Blessed only is the act. The act of defiance,
the act of justice that fills the mouth with blood.
Blessed is the act of survival that saves the blood.
Blessed is the act of art that paints the blood

redder than real and quicker, that restores
the fallen tree to its height and birds. Memory
is the simplest form of prayer. Today you glow
like warm precious lumps of amber in my mind.

1. Hebrew for "shields of David"; the reference is to the six-pointed Jewish star.
2. The Hebrew for the prayer for the dead.

Building the Barricade

We were afraid as we built the barricade
under fire.
The tavern-keeper, the jeweler's mistress, the barber, all of us
cowards.
The servant girl fell to the ground
as she lugged a paving stone, we were terribly afraid
all of us cowards—
the janitor, the market woman, the pensioner.

The pharmacist fell to the ground
as he dragged the door of a toilet,
we were even more afraid, the smuggler-woman,
the dress-maker, the streetcar driver,
all of us cowards.

A kid from reform school fell
as he dragged a sandbag,
you see, we were really
afraid.

Though no one forced us
we did build the barricade
under fire.

Translated from the Polish by
Magnus J. Krynski and Robert A. Maguire

The site of the resistance described in the poem is the Warsaw Ghetto.

And There You Were

in memory of Zivia Lubetkin

And there you were next to
the TV in a tightly packed circle,
everyone watching, following
a small research submarine
sunk at the bottom of the sea.
Tense the way you are.

It was a well-done documentary
about people in distress.
On the small screen
two experienced sailors
were trapped in the depths,
their radio out of order.

We saw the ships. Summoned from Scotland.
And over a vast expanse of sea
fast ships, huge planes rushed
from Canada with the latest rescue equipment,
the whole great effort
for the sake of two young men
on the verge of despair.

You held your breath. I saw you were moved
    like us
by the courage of those boys
in a terrible test of endurance.
Until they were saved.
And I nearly made a fool of myself
saying: Hey! What's the matter—

Lubetkin (1914–78) was a leader of the Warsaw Ghetto uprising who escaped
from the ghetto at the last moment through the sewers. With Abba Kovner, she
was one of the founders of Kibbutz Lohamei ha-Getta'ot in Israel.

why all the fuss? I knew someone,
a frail girl, who was deep
in an ocean—not pacific at all, not the
    Atlantic,
sunk for seven years without
a wireless. Without any radio without a single
connection to the air
outside.

Ships moved above her without
stopping
huge planes travelled without the slightest
change of course.
She called from the depths.
They heard her wrestling with the elements
black
red
blue
struggling for oxygen. For a last breath. Until
the boy came. We know him,
that boy who came from the end of the shaft

to lead her hand in hand blinded by gas
to the exit from Warsaw's sewer.
Luckily it was only half streaming
with excrement. And on to some refuge.

Now Kazik is also glued to the TV
in Baka, Jerusalem, watching astonished
how in a superb performance (the English, those
    English!)
they play back minute by minute the hours of
    distress

of people whose distress can be played back.
His old dog scratches itself at his feet
and he sits after a long day managing the
    supermarket,
dislocated in the soft armchair, his eyes closed.
Boy of the sewers. Looking towards
where you pass now like an atmospheric
    disturbance
between the communications satellite and the
    North Star.

Translated from the Hebrew
by Shirley Kaufman

from "Bashert"

Poland, 1944: My mother is walking down a road.

My mother is walking down a road. Somewhere in Poland. Walking towards an unnamed town for some kind of permit. She is carrying her Aryan identity papers. She has left me with an old peasant who is willing to say she is my grandmother.

She is walking down a road. Her terror in leaving me behind, in risking the separation is swallowed now, like all other feelings. But as she walks, she pictures me waving from the dusty yard, imagines herself suddenly picked up, the identity papers challenged. And even if she were to survive that, would she ever find me later? She tastes the terror in her mouth again. She swallows.

I am over three years old, corn silk blond and blue eyed like any Polish child. There is terrible suffering among the peasants. Starvation. And like so many others, I am ill. Perhaps dying. I have bad lungs. Fever. An ugly ear infection that oozes pus. None of these symptoms are disappearing.

The night before, my mother feeds me watery soup and then sits and listens while I say my prayers to the Holy Mother, Mother of God. I ask her, just as the nuns taught me, to help us all: me, my mother, the old woman. And then catching myself, learning to use memory, I ask the Mother of God to help my father. The Polish words slip easily from my lips. My mother is satisfied. The peasant has perhaps heard and is reassured. My mother has found her to be kind, but knows that she is suspicious of strangers.

My mother is sick. Goiter. Malnutrition. Vitamin deficiencies. She has skin sores which she cannot cure. For months now she has been living in complete isolation, with no point of reference outside of herself. She has been her own sole advisor, companion, comforter. Almost everyone of her world is dead: three sisters, nephews and nieces, her mother, her husband, her in-laws. All gone. Even the remnants of the resistance, those few left after the uprising, have dispersed into the Polish countryside. She is more alone than she could have ever imagined. Only she knows her real name and she is perhaps dying. She is thirty years old.

I am over three years old. I have no consciousness of our danger, our separateness from the others. I have no awareness that we are playing a part. I only know that I have a special name, that I have been named for the Goddess of Peace. And each night, I sleep secure in that knowledge. And when I wet my bed, my mother places me on her belly and lies on the stain. She fears the old woman and hopes her body's warmth will dry the sheet before dawn.

My mother is walking down a road. Another woman joins her. My mother sees through the deception, but she has promised herself that never, under any circumstances, will she take that risk. So she swallows her hunger for contact and trust and instead talks about the sick child left behind and lies about the husband in the labor camp.

Someone is walking towards them. A large, strange woman with wild red hair. They try not to look at her too closely, to seem overly curious. But as they pass her, my mother feels something move inside her. The movement grows and grows till it is an explosion of yearning that she cannot contain. She stops, orders her companion to continue without her. And then she turns.

The woman with the red hair has also stopped and turned. She is grotesque, bloated with hunger, almost savage in her rags. She and my mother move towards each other. Cautiously, deliberately, they probe past the hunger, the swollen flesh, the infected skin, the rags. Slowly, they begin to pierce five years of encrusted history. And slowly, there is perception and recognition.

In this wilderness of occupied Poland, in this vast emptiness where no one can be trusted, my mother has suddenly, bizarrely, met one of my father's teachers. A family friend. Another Jew.

They do not cry, but weep as they chronicle the dead and count the living. Then they rush to me. To the woman I am a familiar sight. She calculates that I will not live out the week, but comments only on my striking resemblance to my father. She says she has contacts. She leaves. One night a package of food is delivered anonymously. We eat. We begin to bridge the gap towards life. We survive.

from *The Testing of Hanna Senesh*
Budapest: June 1944

After the first shock
it's like letting a wave of flame singe your hand:
first a sharp sensation, then no feeling.
I watch myself like a person in a dream
while they invent devices to break me down.

But I never scream.
Screaming means it's happening to me.
I step back and watch it happen around me.

Anger helps. Anger makes a barrier between the whip and me.
They tie me up
and beat my soles, my palms, my back:

                                                  I say

no   no   to myself
don't let them have a sign that I feel it:

think of the blue-green sea that I saw every night
from my tent under the old stars,
the cool winds of evening:

think of that hill in Jerusalem,
the little lights shining in the villages,

Hanna Senesh, born in Budapest in 1921, became a Zionist and emigrated to Palestine at the age of eighteen. Her mother and brother remained in Hungary. In 1943, she joined an expedition of Jews, trained by the British, who parachuted behind Nazi lines in Europe to connect with the partisan underground and to rescue Jews in Hungary, Romania, and Czechoslovakia. She was arrested by the Nazis, imprisoned, tortured, and executed in November 1944. See *Hannah Senesh: Her Life and Diary*, translated by Marta Cohn (New York: Schocken Books, 1972). Several poems by Senesh are included in this volume.

breathe the aromatic Judaean air,
watch the sun set over the Old City,
the shadows creeping up the towers,
pulling the bruised light behind them:

you see: I feel nothing.

It is only my body flopping like a fish.

It is only my body that bleeds.

II. Yugoslavia, 1944
from "Letters in the Family"

Dear Chana,

        where are you now?
Am sending this pocket-to-pocket
(though we both know pockets we'd hate to lie in).
They showed me that poem you gave Reuven,
about the match:[1]
Chana, you know, I never was
for martyrdom. I thought we'd try our best,
ragtag mission that we were,
then clear out if the signals looked too bad.
Something in you drives things ahead for me
but if I can I mean to stay alive.
We're none of us giants, you know,
just small, frail, inexperienced romantic people.
But there are things we learn.
You know the sudden suck of empty space
between the jump and the ripcord pull?
I hate it. I hate it so,
I've hated you for your dropping
ecstatically in free-fall, in the training,
your look, dragged on the ground, of knowing
precisely why you were there.

                My mother's
still in Palestine. And yours
still there in Hungary. Well, there we are.
When this is over—

        I'm
your earthbound friend to the end, still yours—

                      Esther.[2]

This poem is written in the form of a letter to Hanna Senesh ("Channa").
1. "Blessed is the Match" by Hanna Senesh; see note, p. 266.
2. An imagined person.

The Bird

"Ich wünscht', ich wäre ein Vöglein,"[1]
Sang Heinrich, "I would fly
Across the sea . . ." so sadly
It made his mother cry.

At night he played his zither,
By day worked in the mine.
His friend was Hans; together
The boys walked by the Rhine.

"Each day we're growing older,"
Hans said, "This is no life.
I wish I were a soldier!"
And snapped his pocketknife.

War came, and Hans was taken,
But Heinrich did not fight.
"Ich wünscht', ich wäre ein Vöglein,"
Sang Heinrich every night.

"Dear Heinrich," said the letter,
"I hope this finds you fine.
The war could not be better,
It's women, song, and wine."

A letter came for Heinrich,
The same that he'd sent East
To Hans, his own handwriting
Returned, and marked *Deceased.*

---

1. "I wish I were a little bird," a line taken, according to the author, from a German romantic poem.

*

"You'll never be a beauty,"
The doctor said, "You scamp!
We'll give you special duty—
A concentration camp."

And now the truck was nearing
The place. They passed a house;
A radio was blaring
The *Wiener Blut*[2] of Strauss.

The banks were bright with flowers,
The birds sang in the wood;
There was a fence with towers
On which armed sentries stood.

They stopped. The men dismounted;
Heinrich got down—at last!
"That chimney," said the sergeant,
"That's where the Jews are gassed."

*

Each day he sorted clothing,
Skirt, trousers, boot, and shoe,
Till he was filled with loathing
For every size of Jew.

"Come in! What is it, Private?"
"Please Sir, that vacancy . . .
I wonder, could I have it?"
"Your papers! Let me see . . .

2. German for "Vienna Blood," a famous Strauss waltz.

"You're steady and you're sober . . .
But have you learned to kill?"
Said Heinrich, "No, *Herr Ober-
Leutnant*,[3] but I will!"

"The Reich can use your spirit.
Report to Unit Four.
Here is an armband—wear it!
Dismissed! Don't slam the door."

*

"Ich wünscht', ich wäre ein Vöglein,"
Sang Heinrich, "I would fly . . ."
They knew that when they heard him
The next day they would die.

They stood in silence praying
At midnight when they heard
The zither softly playing,
The singing of the Bird.

He stared into the fire,
He sipped a glass of wine.
"Ich wünscht'," his voice rose higher,
"Ich wäre ein Vöglein . . ."

A dog howled in its kennel,
He thought of Hans and cried.
The stars looked down from heaven.
That day the children died.

3. German for Lieutenant, Sir.

*

"The Russian tanks are coming!"
The wind bore from the East
A cannonade, a drumming
Of small arms that increased.

Heinrich went to Headquarters.
He found the Colonel dead
With pictures of his daughters,
A pistol by his head.

He thought, his courage sinking,
"There's always the SS . . ."
He found the Major drinking
In a woman's party dress.

The prisoners were shaking
Their barracks. Heinrich heard
A sound of timber breaking,
A shout, "Where is the Bird?"

*

The Russian was completing
A seven-page report.
He wrote: "We still are beating
The woods . . ." then he stopped short.

A little bird was flitting
Outside, from tree to tree.
He turned where he was sitting
And watched it thoughtfully.

He pulled himself together,
And wrote: "We've left no stone
Unturned—but not a feather!
It seems the Bird has flown.

"Description? Half a dozen
Group snapshots, badly blurred;
And which is Emma's cousin
God knows, and which the Bird!

"He could be in the Western
Or in the Eastern Zone.
I'd welcome a suggestion
If anything is known."

*

"*Ich wünscht', ich wäre ein Vöglein,*"
Sings Heinrich, "I would fly
Across the sea," so sadly
It makes his children cry.

Research

I

We are the civilized—
Aryans:
and do not always kill those condemned to death
merely because they are Jews
as the less civilized might:
we use them to benefit science
like rats or mice:
to find out the limits of human endurance
at the highest altitudes
for the good of the German air force;
force them to stay in tanks of ice water
or naked outdoors for hours and hours
at temperatures below freezing;
yes, study the effects of going without food
and drinking only sea water
for days and days
for the good of the German navy;
or wound them and force wooden shavings or ground glass
into the wounds,
or take out bones, muscles and nerves,
or burn their flesh—
to study the burns caused by bombs—
or put poison in their food
or infect them with malaria, typhus, or other fevers—
all for the good of the German army.
Heil Hitler!

2

A number of Jews had to drink sea water only
to find out how long they could stand it.
In their torment
they threw themselves on the mops and rags
used by the hospital attendants
and sucked the dirty water out of them
to quench the thirst
driving them mad.

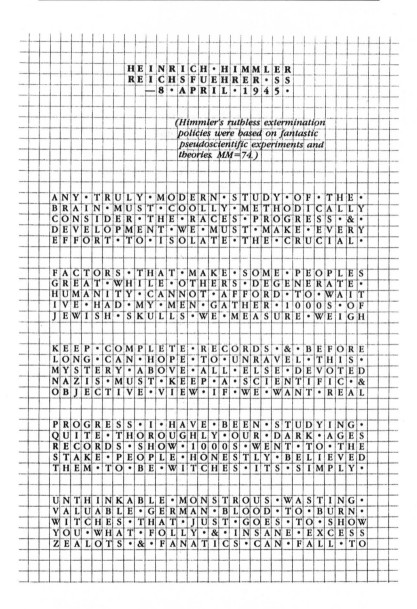

HEINRICH·HIMMLER
REICHSFUEHRER·SS
—8·APRIL·1945·

(Himmler's ruthless extermination policies were based on fantastic pseudoscientific experiments and theories. MM=74.)

ANY·TRULY·MODERN·STUDY·OF·THE·
BRAIN·MUST·COOLLY·METHODICALLY
CONSIDER·THE·RACES·PROGRESS·&·
DEVELOPMENT·WE·MUST·MAKE·EVERY
EFFORT·TO·ISOLATE·THE·CRUCIAL·

FACTORS·THAT·MAKE·SOME·PEOPLES
GREAT·WHILE·OTHERS·DEGENERATE·
HUMANITY·CANNOT·AFFORD·TO·WAIT
IVE·HAD·MY·MEN·GATHER·1000S·OF
JEWISH·SKULLS·WE·MEASURE·WEIGH

KEEP·COMPLETE·RECORDS·&·BEFORE
LONG·CAN·HOPE·TO·UNRAVEL·THIS·
MYSTERY·ABOVE·ALL·ELSE·DEVOTED
NAZIS·MUST·KEEP·A·SCIENTIFIC·&
OBJECTIVE·VIEW·IF·WE·WANT·REAL

PROGRESS·I·HAVE·BEEN·STUDYING·
QUITE·THOROUGHLY·OUR·DARK·AGES
RECORDS·SHOW·1000S·WENT·TO·THE
STAKE·PEOPLE·HONESTLY·BELIEVED
THEM·TO·BE·WITCHES·ITS·SIMPLY·

UNTHINKABLE·MONSTROUS·WASTING·
VALUABLE·GERMAN·BLOOD·TO·BURN·
WITCHES·THAT·JUST·GOES·TO·SHOW
YOU·WHAT·FOLLY·&·INSANE·EXCESS
ZEALOTS·&·FANATICS·CAN·FALL·TO

Heinrich Himmler was the senior leader of the S.S., which he developed, from 1929 on, into the elite paramilitary units of the Nazi party. He was responsible for carrying out the "Final Solution."

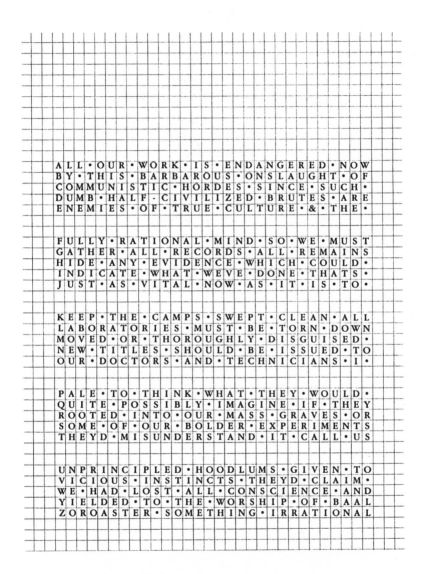

```
ALL·OUR·WORK·IS·ENDANGERED·NOW
BY·THIS·BARBAROUS·ONSLAUGHT·OF
COMMUNISTIC·HORDES·SINCE·SUCH·
DUMB·HALF-CIVILIZED·BRUTES·ARE
ENEMIES·OF·TRUE·CULTURE·&·THE·

FULLY·RATIONAL·MIND·SO·WE·MUST
GATHER·ALL·RECORDS·ALL·REMAINS
HIDE·ANY·EVIDENCE·WHICH·COULD·
INDICATE·WHAT·WEVE·DONE·THATS·
JUST·AS·VITAL·NOW·AS·IT·IS·TO·

KEEP·THE·CAMPS·SWEPT·CLEAN·ALL
LABORATORIES·MUST·BE·TORN·DOWN
MOVED·OR·THOROUGHLY·DISGUISED·
NEW·TITLES·SHOULD·BE·ISSUED·TO
OUR·DOCTORS·AND·TECHNICIANS·I·

PALE·TO·THINK·WHAT·THEY·WOULD·
QUITE·POSSIBLY·IMAGINE·IF·THEY
ROOTED·INTO·OUR·MASS·GRAVES·OR
SOME·OF·OUR·BOLDER·EXPERIMENTS
THEYD·MISUNDERSTAND·IT·CALL·US

UNPRINCIPLED·HOODLUMS·GIVEN·TO
VICIOUS·INSTINCTS·THEYD·CLAIM·
WE·HAD·LOST·ALL·CONSCIENCE·AND
YIELDED·TO·THE·WORSHIP·OF·BAAL
ZOROASTER·SOMETHING·IRRATIONAL
```

1. Baal refers to any of the numerous local deities of the Canaanites or Phoenicians. Zoroaster (circa 628–circa 551 B.C.) was founder of the Persian religion Zoroastrianism, characterized by worship of a supreme god, Ahura Mazda, who requires humanity's good deeds in the cosmic struggle against the evil spirit Ahriman.

How?

How will you fill your goblet
On the day of liberation? And with what?
Are you prepared, in your joy, to endure
The dark keening you have heard
Where skulls of days glitter
In a bottomless pit?

You will search for a key to fit
Your jammed locks. You will bite
The sidewalks like bread,
Thinking: It used to be better.
And time will gnaw at you like a cricket
Caught in a fist.

Then your memory will resemble
An ancient buried town.
And your estranged eyes will burrow down
Like a mole, a mole. . . .

Vilna Ghetto,
February 14, 1943
Translated from the Yiddish by Chana Bloch

Chorus of the Rescued

We, the rescued,
From whose hollow bones death had begun to whittle his
    flutes,
And on whose sinews he had already stroked his bow—
Our bodies continue to lament
With their mutilated music.
We, the rescued,
The nooses wound for our necks still dangle
before us in the blue air—
Hourglasses still fill with our dripping blood.
We, the rescued,
The worms of fear still feed on us.
Our constellation is buried in dust.
We, the rescued,
Beg you:
Show us your sun, but gradually.
Lead us from star to star, step by step.
Be gentle when you teach us to live again.
Lest the song of a bird,
Or a pail being filled at the well,
Let our badly sealed pain burst forth again
and carry us away—
We beg you:
Do not show us an angry dog, not yet—
It could be, it could be
That we will dissolve into dust—
Dissolve into dust before your eyes.
For what binds our fabric together?
We whose breath vacated us,
Whose soul fled to Him out of that midnight
Long before our bodies were rescued
Into the ark of the moment.
We, the rescued,

We press your hand
We look into your eye—
But all that binds us together now is leave-taking,
The leave-taking in the dust
Binds us together with you.

Translated from the German by Michael Roloff

The Silent Partner

Three meters wide
six meters deep
and fifteen meters long—
these are the measurements of one of the pits
in Poland
to which the Germans drove Jews
shot them there
and buried them.
Three meters wide
six meters deep
and fifteen meters long—
the three dimensions.
And the fourth dimension,
the one in which all the slaughtered Jews
cannot die
and cannot live—
is now the silent partner
through all the days of my life.

Translated from the Yiddish
by Aaron Kramer

Words for Primo Levi

"To hit bottom—
four flights down, done
with prostate dam-up, anti-depressant.
Three generations—
born in the room I write.
The mussulmans'[1] opaque intimate
solitude—their depositions never taken.
Saved in
'44. Couched next door
now, struck from speech at ninety-four,
rigid, out of control—Mother
stares. Round-the-clock care.

Hallway . . . my son's door . . . stairwell . . .
not to witness, only fall."

1. See note for Muslims, p. 68.

"More Light! More Light!"

Composed in the Tower[1] before his execution
These moving verses, and being brought at that time
Painfully to the stake, submitted, declaring thus:
"I implore my God to witness that I have made no crime."

Nor was he forsaken of courage, but the death was horrible,
The sack of gunpowder failing to ignite.
His legs were blistered sticks on which the black sap
Bubbled and burst as he howled for the Kindly Light.[2]

And that was but one, and by no means one of the worst;
Permitted at least his pitiful dignity;
And such as were by made prayers in the name of Christ,
That shall judge all men, for his soul's tranquillity.

We move now to outside a German wood.[3]
Three men are there commanded to dig a hole
In which the two Jews are ordered to lie down
And be buried alive by the third, who is a Pole.

The title reflects the reputed last words of poet, scientist, and critic Johann Wolfgang von Goethe (1749–1832), "the sage of Weimar" and Germany's most celebrated author.
1. The Tower of London, a fortress and sometimes a prison. What follows is not a specific execution but a condensed description of the deaths of several Protestant martyrs in England in the sixteenth century.
2. An allusion to the hymn "Lead, Kindly Light," a petition for God's mercy in time of trouble.
3. Such as Buchenwald, the notorious Nazi death camp. The event described is a matter of record and may be found in *The Theory and Practice of Hell* by Eugene Kogon, translated by Heinz Noden (New York: Farrar, Straus, 1950).

Not light from the shrine at Weimar[4] beyond the hill
Nor light from heaven appeared. But he did refuse.
A Lüger settled back deeply in its glove.
He was ordered to change places with the Jews.

Much casual death had drained away their souls.
The thick dirt mounted toward the quivering chin.
When only the head was exposed the order came
To dig him out again and to get back in.

No light, no light in the blue Polish eye.
When he finished a riding boot packed down the earth.
The Lüger hovered lightly in its glove.
He was shot in the belly and in three hours bled to death.

No prayers or incense rose up in those hours
Which grew to be years, and every day came mute
Ghosts from the ovens, sifting through crisp air,
And settled upon his eyes in a black soot.

---

4. Goethe's home place. The Nazis built Buchenwald only a few miles from
Weimar. Prisoners were unloaded at the Weimar station and marched to
the camp.

A Camp in the Prussian Forest

I walk beside the prisoners to the road.
Load on puffed load,
Their corpses, stacked like sodden wood,
Lie barred or galled with blood

By the charred warehouse. No one comes today
In the old way
To knock the fillings from their teeth;
The dark, coned, common wreath

Is plaited for their grave—a kind of grief.
The living leaf
Clings to the planted profitable
Pine if it is able;

The boughs sigh, mile on green, calm, breathing mile,
From this dead file
The planners ruled for them. . . . One year
They sent a million here:

Here men were drunk like water, burnt like wood.
The fat of good
And evil, the breast's star of hope
Were rendered into soap.

I paint the star I sawed from yellow pine—
And plant the sign
In soil that does not yet refuse
Its usual Jews

Their first asylum. But the white, dwarfed star—
This dead white star—
Hides nothing, pays for nothing; smoke
Fouls it, a yellow joke,

The needles of the wreath are chalked with ash,
A filmy trash
Litters the black woods with the death
Of men; and one last breath

Curls from the monstrous chimney. . . . I laugh aloud
Again and again;
The star laughs from its rotting shroud
Of flesh. O star of men!

Simple Truths

When a man has grown a body,
a body to carry with him
through nature for as long as he can,
when this body is taken from him
by other men and women who happen to be,
this time, in uniform,
then it is clear he has experienced
an act of barbarism,

and when a man has a wife,
a wife to love for as long as he lives,
when this wife is marked with a yellow star
and driven into a chamber she will never leave alive,
then this is murder,
so much is clear,

and when a woman has hair,
when her hair is shorn and her scalp bleeds,
when a woman has children,
children to love for as long as she lives,
when the children are taken from her,
when a man and his wife and their children
are put to death in a chamber of gas,
or with pistols at close range, or are starved,
or beaten, or injected by the thousands,
or ripped apart, by the thousands, by the millions,

it is clear that where we are
is Europe, in our century, during the years
from nineteen-hundred and thirty-five
to nineteen-hundred and forty-five
after the death of Jesus, who spoke of a different order,
but whose father, who is our father,

if he is our father,
if we must speak of him as father,
watched, and witnessed, and knew,

and when we remember,
when we touch the skin of our own bodies,
when we open our eyes into dream
or within the morning shine of sunlight
and remember what was taken
from these men, from these women,
from these children gassed and starved
and beaten and thrown against walls
and made to walk the valley
of knives and icepicks and otherwise
exterminated in ways appearing to us almost
beyond even the maniacal human imagination,
then it is clear that this is the German Reich,
during approximately ten years of our lord's time,

and when we read a book of these things,
when we hear the names of the camps,
when we see the films of the bulldozed dead
or the film of one boy struck on the head
with a club in the hands
of a German doctor who will wait
some days for the boy's skull to knit, and will enter
the time in his ledger, and then
take up the club to strike the boy again,
and wait some weeks for the boy's skull to knit,
and enter the time in his ledger again,
and strike the boy again,
and so on, until the boy, who,
at the end of the film of his life

can hardly stagger forward toward the doctor,
does die, and the doctor
enters exactly the time of the boy's death in his ledger,

when we read these things or see them,
then it is clear to us that this
happened, and within the lord's allowance, this
work of his minions, his poor
vicious dumb German victims twisted
into the swastika shapes of trees struck by lightning,
on this his earth, if he is our father,
if we must speak of him in this way,
this presence above us, within us, this
mover, this first cause, this spirit, this
curse, this bloodstream and brain-current, this
unfathomable oceanic ignorance of ourselves, this
automatic electric Aryan swerve, this

fortune that you and I were not the victims, this
luck that you and I were not the murderers, this
sense that you and I are clean and understand, this
stupidity that gives him breath, gives him life
as we kill them all, as we killed them all.

Spit

> . . . then the son of the "superior race" began to spit into the Rabbi's
> mouth so that the Rabbi could continue to spit on the Torah . . .
>
> —THE BLACK BOOK[1]

After this much time, it's still impossible. The SS man with his stiff hair
and his uniform;
the Rabbi, probably in a torn overcoat, probably with a stained beard the
other would be clutching;
the Torah, God's word, on the altar, the letters blurring under the blended
phlegm;
the Rabbi's parched mouth, the SS man perfectly absorbed, obsessed with
perfect humiliation.
So many years and what is there to say still about the soldiers waiting
impatiently in the snow,
about the one stamping his feet, thinking, Kill him! Get it over with!
while back there the lips of the Rabbi and the other would have brushed
and if time had stopped you would have thought they were lovers,
so lightly kissing, the sharp, luger hand under the dear chin,
the eyes furled slightly and then when it started again the eyelashes of both
of them
shyly fluttering as wonderfully as the pulse of a baby.
Maybe we don't have to speak of it at all, it's still the same.
War, that happens and stops happening but is always somehow right there,
twisting and hardening us;
then what we make of God—words, spit, degradation, murder, shame;
every conceivable torment.
All these ways to live that have something to do with how we live
and that we're almost ashamed to use as metaphors for what goes on in us
but that we do anyway, so that love is battle and we watch ourselves in
love

1. *The Black Book: The Nazi Crime against the Jewish People* (New York: Jewish
Black Book Committee, 1946), an early work on the Holocaust, is a record of
Nazi atrocities presented through case histories and testimonies.

become maddened with pride and incompletion, and God is what it is when we're alone
wrestling with solitude and everything speaking in our souls turns against us like His fury
and just facing another person, there is so much terror and hatred that yes,
spitting in someone's mouth, trying to make him defile his own meaning,
would signify the struggle to survive each other and what we'll enact to accomplish it.

There's another legend.
It's about Moses, that when they first brought him as a child before Pharaoh,
the king tested him by putting a diamond and a live coal in front of him
and Moses picked up the red ember and popped it into his mouth
so for the rest of his life he was tongue-tied and Aaron had to speak for him.
What must his scarred tongue have felt like in his mouth?
It must have been like always carrying something there that weighed too much,
something leathery and dead whose greatest gravity was to loll out like an ox's,
and when it moved, it must have been like a thick embryo slowly coming alive,
butting itself against the inner sides of his teeth and cheeks.
And when God burned in the bush, how could he not cleave to him?
How could he not know that all of us were on fire and that every word we said would burn forever,
in pain, unquenchably, and that God knew it, too, and would say nothing Himself ever again beyond this,
ever, but would only live in the flesh that we use like firewood,
in all the caves of the body, the gut cave, the speech cave:
He would slobber and howl like something just barely a man that beats itself again and again onto the dark,

moist walls away from the light, away from whatever would be light for this last eternity.

"Now therefore go," He said, "and I will be with thy mouth."

During the Eichmann Trial

i   When We Look Up

When we look up
each from his being
Robert Duncan

He had not looked,
pitiful man whom none

pity, whom all
must pity if they look

into their own face (given
only by glass, steel, water

barely known) all
who look up

to see—how many
faces? How many

seen in a lifetime? (Not those
that flash by, but those

into which the gaze wanders
and is lost

and returns to tell
Here is a mystery,

a person, an
other, an I?

Count them.
Who are five million?)

'I was used from the nursery
to obedience

all my life . . .
Corpselike

obedience.' Yellow
calmed him later—

'a charming picture'
yellow of autumn leaves in

Wienerwald, a little
railroad station
nineteen-o-eight, Lemburg,

yellow sun
on the stepmother's teatable

Franz Joseph's beard
blessing his little ones.

It was the yellow
of the stars too,

stars that marked
those in whose faces

you had not
looked. "They were cast out

as if they were
some animals, some beasts."

"And what would disobedience
have brought me? And

whom would it have served?"
"I did not let my thoughts

dwell on this—I had
seen it and that was

enough." (The words
"slur into a harsh babble")

"A spring of blood
gushed from the earth."
Miracle

unsung. I see
a spring of blood gush from the earth—

Earth cannot swallow
so much at once

a fountain
rushes towards the sky

unrecognized
a sign—.

Pity this man who saw it
whose obedience continued—

he, you, I, which shall I say?
He stands

isolate in a bulletproof
witness-stand of glass,

a cage, where we may view
ourselves, an apparition

telling us something he
does not know: we are members

one of another.

ii   The Peach tree

The Danube orchards
are full of fruit
but in the city one tree
haunts a boy's dreams

a tree in a villa garden
the Devil's garden
a peach tree

and of its fruit one peach
calls to him

This poem is based on the earliest mention, during the trial, of this incident. In
a later statement it was said that the fruit was cherries, that the boy was already
in the garden, doing forced labor, when he was accused of taking the fruit, and
that Eichmann killed him in a tool shed, not beneath the tree. The poem therefore is not to be taken as a report of what happened but of what I envisioned.—
Author's note.

he sees it yellow and ripe
the vivid blood
bright in its round cheek

Next day he knows
he cannot withstand desire
it is no common fruit

it holds some secret
it speaks to the yellow star within him

he scales the wall
enters the garden of death
takes the peach
and death pounces

mister death who rushes out
from his villa
mister death who loves yellow

who wanted that yellow peach
for himself
mister death who signs papers
then eats

telegraphs simply: **Shoot them**
then eats
mister death who orders
more transports
then eats

he would have enjoyed
the sweetest of all the peaches on his tree

with sour-cream
with brandy

Son of David
's blood, vivid red
and trampled juice
yellow and sweet
flow together beneath the tree

there is more blood than
sweet juice
always more blood—mister
death goes indoors
exhausted

iii Crystal Night

From blacked-out streets
    (wide avenues swept by curfew,
    alleyways, veins
    of dark within dark)

from houses whose walls
    had for a long time known
the tense stretch of skin over bone
as their brick or stone listened—

Kristallnacht is the German name for the pogroms that began on November 9–10, 1938 and took place throughout Germany. Synagogues and Jewish institutions were burned and plundered. The name derives from the glass fragments of broken windows that littered the streets of German towns. These pogroms were prompted by Hershl Grynszpan's assassination of Ernst Von Roth, third secretary in the German embassy in Paris. Grynszpan was a seventeen-year-old Polish student whose parents were expelled from Germany.

The scream!
The awaited scream rises,
the shattering
of glass and the cracking
of bone

a polar tumult as when
black ice booms, knives
of ice and glass
splitting and splintering the silence into
innumerable screaming needles of
yes, now it is upon us, the jackboots
are running in spurts of
sudden blood-light through the
broken temples

the veils
are rent in twain
terror has a white sound
every scream
of fear is a white needle freezing the eyes
the floodlights of their trucks throw
jets of white, their shouts
cleave the wholeness of darkness into
sectors of transparent white-clouded pantomime
where all that was awaited
is happening, it is Crystal Night

it is Crystal Night
these spikes which are not
pitched in the range of common hearing
whistle through time

smashing the windows of sleep and dream
smashing the windows of history
a whiteness scattering
in hailstones
each a mirror
for man's eyes.

A Visitation

Just as you carried out a policy of not wanting to share the earth with
the Jewish people . . . (as though you and your superiors had any
right to determine who should and who should not inhabit the world),
we find that no member of the human race can be expected to want to
share the earth with you.

—Hannah Arendt on Eichmann[1]

At my window, I pull the curtains wide
On the Detroit night. So; it's you, again,
Old ghost? Not left once since the day you died?

    I am faithful, shivering still and pale,
    Streaked yet by traffic lights, waiting outside
    Like the poor dead soldier in some folktale

The Jews, your jailers, couldn't bear to face
Your dutiful Jewish face, in their jail,
On TV, postered, every public place,

    Come to his true love's window, wanting in
    To ask, now their love's final, love's embrace.
    I am true to you; I have always been.

Each usual nightmare. Taking that excuse
You gave to wipe out their (and your own) kin,
They hanged you. So; they've turned you loose.

    My truth enraged them. *You,* perhaps, don't need
    Someone to outcast, loathe, some way to lose
    Track of man's deceit, man's violence, greed—

1. Hannah Arendt (1906–75) was a philosopher and a notable refugee from Nazi
Germany who wrote and lectured extensively on totalitarianism. Her famous
work is *Eichmann in Jerusalem: A Report on the Banality of Evil* (1965).

When were you half so slippery, so alive
As now you're dead? You prowl the world's face, freed
To trace your own types, threaten them, connive . . .

    Take me in. Secure me. Once, your own hand
    Held a nightstick, .45 and sheath knife;
    You've chained men to a steel beam on command.

This last, I admit. I can scarcely claim
To be my brother's keeper on so grand
A scale as yours. In a full lifetime's shame

    Luck, friend, no character. We took the parts
    Our time and place allowed. You played the game;
    There's something beats the same in opposed hearts.

Philosophy's still your crime: the abstract
Gray lie, the sweet cliché that still imparts
Its drugged glow through the brain. The unsung fact

    Who called his weakness, love? His long rage, lust?
    Who called his worst lusts, honesty? Our days exact
    From you, as from me, the deep faults they must.

Proves all the more cause I should keep you there—
How subtle all that chokes us with disgust
Moves in implacably to rule us, unaware.

    My own love, you're all I could wish to be.
    Close your eyes—I'll just wander off somewhere.
    Or watch the way your world moves—you can look through me.

Campo di Fiori

In Rome, on the Campo di Fiori
baskets with olives and lemons
the pavement spluttered with wine
and broken fragments of flowers.
The hawkers pour on the counters
the pink fruits of the sea,
and heavy armfuls of grapes
fall on the down of peaches.

Here, on this very square
Giordano Bruno[1] was burned;
the hangman kindled the flame of the pyre
in the ring of the gaping crowd,
and hardly the flame extinguished
the taverns were full again
and hawkers carried on heads
baskets with olives and lemons.

I recalled Campo di Fiori
in Warsaw, on a merry-go-round,
on a fair night in the spring
by the sound of vivacious music.
The salvoes behind the ghetto walls
were drowned in lively tunes,
and vapors freely rose
into the tranquil sky.

This poem was written in Warsaw in April 1943 and was first published in 1944
in the underground anthology *Z Otchlani* (From the abyss). The volume was dedicated to the Jewish victims of Warsaw by poets living on the "Aryan" side. There
are various versions of the ending of the poem.
1. Italian philosopher (1548–1600) accused of heresy, tried before the Inquisition, and burned at the stake.

Sometimes the wind from burning houses
would bring black kites along,
and people on the merry-go-round
caught the flying charred bits.
This wind from the burning houses
blew open the girls' skirts,
and the happy throngs laughed
on a beautiful Warsaw Sunday.

Perhaps one will guess the moral,
that the people of Warsaw and Rome
trade and play and love
passing by the martyrs' pyres.
Another, perhaps, will read
of the passing of human things,
of the oblivion growing
before the flame expired.

But I that day reflected
on the loneliness of dying men,
on the fate of lone Giordano;
that when he climbed the scaffold
he found no word in human tongue
with which to bid farewell
to those of mankind who remain.

Already they were on the run,
to peddle starfish, gulp their wine;
they carried olives and lemons
in the gay hum of the city.
And he was already remote
as though ages had passed,

and they waited a while
for his flight into the fire.

And those dying alone,
forgotten by the world,
their tongue grew strange to us,
like the tongue of an ancient planet.
And all will become a legend—
and then after many years
the poet's word shall stir revolt,
on the new Campo di Fiori.

Translated from the Polish
by Adam Gillon

A Poor Christian Looks at the Ghetto

Bees build around red liver,
Ants build around black bone.
It has begun: the tearing, the trampling on silks,
It has begun: the breaking of glass, wood, copper, nickel, silver,
    foam
Of gypsum, iron sheets, violin strings, trumpets, leaves, balls,
    crystals.
Poof! Phosphorescent fire from yellow walls
Engulfs animal and human hair.

Bees build around the honeycomb of lungs,
Ants build around white bone.
Torn is paper, rubber, linen, leather, flax,
Fiber, fabrics, cellulose, snakeskin, wire.
The roof and the wall collapse in flame and heat seizes the
    foundations.
Now there is only the earth, sandy, trodden down,
With one leafless tree.

Slowly, boring a tunnel, a guardian mole makes his way,
With a small red lamp fastened to his forehead.
He touches buried bodies, counts them, pushes on,
He distinguishes human ashes by their luminous vapor,
The ashes of each man by a different part of the spectrum.
Bees build around a red trace.
Ants build around the place left by my body.

I am afraid, so afraid of the guardian mole.[1]
He has swollen eyelids, like a Patriarch

1. The mole is Milosz's image for a Jewish victim making his way in the subterranean world of the Warsaw Ghetto's bunkers and sewers.

Who has sat much in the light of candles
Reading the great book of the species.

What will I tell him, I, a Jew of the New Testament,
Waiting two thousand years for the second coming of Jesus?
My broken body will deliver me to his sight
And he will count me among the helpers of death:
The uncircumcised.

Warsaw, 1943
Translated from the Polish by the Author

After Auschwitz

Anger,
as black as a hook,
overtakes me.
Each day,
each Nazi
took, at 8:00 A.M., a baby
and sautéed him for breakfast
in his frying pan.

And death looks on with a casual eye
and picks at the dirt under his fingernail.

Man is evil,
I say aloud.
Man is a flower
that should be burnt,
I say aloud.
Man
is a bird full of mud,
I say aloud.

And death looks on with a casual eye
and scratches his anus.

Man with his small pink toes,
with his miraculous fingers
is not a temple
but an outhouse,
I say aloud.
Let man never again raise his teacup.
Let man never again write a book.
Let man never again put on his shoe.
Let man never again raise his eyes,

on a soft July night.
Never. Never. Never. Never. Never.
I say these things aloud.

I beg the Lord not to hear.

PART II

Lamentation

A Scrap of Time

I want to talk about a certain time not measured in months and years. For so long I have wanted to talk about this time, and not in the way I will talk about it now, not just about this one scrap of time. I wanted to, but I couldn't, I didn't know how. I was afraid, too, that this second time, which is measured in months and years, had buried the other time under a layer of years, that this second time had crushed the first and destroyed it within me. But no. Today, digging around in the ruins of memory, I found it fresh and untouched by forgetfulness. This time was measured not in months but in a word—we no longer said "in the beautiful month of May," but "after the first 'action,' or the second, or right before the third." We had different measures of time, we different ones, always different, always with that mark of difference that moved some of us to pride and others to humility. We, who because of our difference were condemned once again, as we had been before in our history, we were condemned once again during this time measured not in months nor by the rising and setting of the sun, but by a word—"action," a word signifying movement, a word you would use about a novel or a play.

I don't know who used the word first, those who acted or those who were the victims of their action; I don't know who created this technical term, who substituted it for the first term, "round-up"—a word that became devalued (or dignified?) as time passed, as new methods were developed, and "round-up" was distinguished from "action" by the borderline of race. Round-ups were for forced labor.

We called the first action—that scrap of time that I want to talk about—a round-up, although no was rounding anyone up; on that beautiful, clear morning, each of us made our way, not willingly, to be sure, but under orders, to the marketplace in our little town, a rectangle enclosed by high, crooked buildings—a pharmacy, clothing stores, an ironmonger's shop—and framed by a sidewalk made of big square slabs that time had fractured and broken. I have never again seen such huge slabs. In the middle of the marketplace stood the town hall, and it was right there, in front of the town hall, that we were ordered to form ranks.

I should not have written "we," for I was not standing in the ranks, although, obeying the order that had been posted the previous evening, I had left my house after eating a perfectly normal breakfast, at a table that was set in a normal way, in a room whose doors opened onto a garden veiled in morning mists, dry and golden in the rising sun.

Our transformation was not yet complete; we were still living out of habit in that old time that was measured in months and years, and on that lovely peaceful morning, filled with dry, golden mists, we took the words "conscription of labor" literally, and as mature people tend to read between the lines, our imaginations replaced the word "labor" with "labor camp," one of which, people said, was being built nearby. Apparently those who gave the order were perfectly aware of the poverty of our imaginations; that is why they saved themselves work by issuing a written order. This is how accurately they predicted our responses: after finishing a normal breakfast, at a normally set table, the older members of the family decided to disobey the order because they were afraid of the heavy physical labor, but they did not advise the young to do likewise—the young, who, if their disobedience were discovered, would not be able to plead old age. We were like infants.

This beautiful, clear morning that I am digging out of the ruins of my memory is still fresh; its colors and aromas have not faded: a grainy golden mist with red spheres of apples hanging in it, and the shadows above the river damp with the sharp odor of burdock, and the bright blue dress that I was wearing when I left the house and when I turned around at the gate. It was then, probably at that very moment, that I suddenly progressed, instinctively, from an infantile state to a still naive caution—instinctively, because I wasn't thinking about why I avoided the gate that led to the street and instead set off on a roundabout route, across the orchard, along the riverbank, down a road we called "the back way" because it wound through the outskirts of town. Instinctively, because at that moment I still did not know that I wouldn't stand in the marketplace in front of the town hall. Perhaps I wanted to delay that moment, or perhaps I simply liked the river.

Along the way, I stopped and carefully picked out flat stones, and skipped them across the water; I sat down for a while on the little bridge, beyond which one could see the town, and dangled my legs, looking at my reflection in the water and at the willows that grew on the bank. I was not yet afraid then, nor was my sister. (I forgot to say that my younger sister was with me, and she, too, skipped stones across the water and dangled her legs over the river, which is called the Gniezna—a pitiful little stream, some eight meters wide.) My sister, too, was not yet afraid; it was only when we went further along the street, beyond the bridge, and the view of the marketplace leapt out at us from behind the building on the corner, that we suddenly stopped in our tracks.

There was the square, thick with people as on a market day, only different, because a market-day crowd is colorful and loud, with chickens clucking, geese honking, and people talking and bargaining. This crowd was silent. In a way it resembled a rally—but it was different from that, too. I don't know what it was exactly. I only know that we suddenly stopped and my sister began to tremble, and then I caught the trembling, and she said, "Let's run away," and although no one was chasing us and the morning was still clear and peaceful, we ran back to the little bridge, but we no longer noticed the willows or the reflections of our running figures in the water; we ran for a long time until we were high up the steep slope known as Castle Hill—the ruins of an old castle stood on top of it—and on this hillside, the jewel of our town, we sat down in the bushes, out of breath and still shaking.

From this spot we could see our house and garden—it was just as it always was, nothing had changed—and we could see our neighbor's house, from which our neighbor had emerged, ready to beat her carpets. We could hear the slap slap of her carpet beater.

We sat there for an hour, maybe two, I don't know, because it was then that time measured in the ordinary way stopped. Then we climbed down the steep slope to the river and returned to our house, where we heard what had happened in the marketplace, and that our cousin David had been taken, and how they took him, and what message he had left for his mother. After they were taken away, he wrote down again what he asked people to tell her; he threw a note out of the truck and a peasant brought it to her that evening— but that happened later. First we learned that the women had been told to go home, that only the men were ordered to remain standing there, and that the path chosen by our cousin had been the opposite of ours. We had been horrified by the sight of the crowd in the marketplace, while he was drawn towards it by an enormous force, a force as strong as his nerves were weak, so that somehow or other he did violence to his own fate, he himself, himself, himself, and that was what he asked people to tell his mother, and then he wrote it down: "I myself am to blame, forgive me."

We would never have guessed that he belonged to the race of the Impatient Ones, doomed to destruction by their anxiety and their inability to remain still, never—because he was round-faced and chubby, not at all energetic, the sort of person who can't be pulled away from his book, who smiles timidly, girlishly. Only the end of the war brought us the truth about his last hours. The peasant who delivered the note did not dare to tell us what he saw, and although other people, too, muttered something about what they had seen, no one dared to believe it, especially since the Germans offered proof of another truth that each of us grasped at greedily; they measured out doses of it sparingly, with restraint—a perfect cover-up. They went to such trouble, created so many phantoms, that only time, time measured not in months and years, opened our eyes and convinced us.

Our cousin David had left the house later than we did, and when he reached the marketplace it was already known—not by everyone, to be sure, but by the so-called Council, which in time became the *Judenrat*—that the words "conscription for labor" had nothing to do with a labor camp. One friend, a far-sighted older man, ordered the boy to hide just in case, and since it was too late to return home because the streets were blocked off, he led him to his own apartment in one of the houses facing the marketplace. Like us, not comprehending that the boy belonged to the race of the Impatient Ones, who find it difficult to cope with isolation and who act on impulse, he left David in a room that locked from inside. What our cousin experienced, locked up in that room, will remain forever a mystery. Much can be explained by the fact that the room had a view of the marketplace, of that silent crowd, of the faces of friends and relatives, and it may be that finally the isolation of his hiding place seemed to him more unbearable that the great and threatening unknown outside the window—an unknown shared by all who were gathered in the marketplace.

It was probably a thought that came in a flash: not to be alone, to be together with everyone. All that was needed was one movement of his hand.

I think it incorrect to assume that he left the hiding place because he was afraid that they would search the houses. That impatience of the heart, that trembling of the nerves, the burden of isolation, condemned him to extermination together with the first victims of our town.

He stood between a lawyer's apprentice and a student of architecture and to the question, "Profession?" he replied, "Teacher," although he had been a teacher for only a short time and quite by chance. His neighbor on the right also told the truth, but the architecture student lied, declaring himself a carpenter, and this lie saved his life—or, to be more precise, postponed the sentence of death for two years.

Seventy people were loaded into trucks; at the last moment the rabbi was dragged out of his house—he was the seventy-first. On the way to the trucks they marched past the ranks of those who had not yet managed to inform the interrogators about the work they did. It was then that our cousin said out loud, "Tell my mother that it's my own fault and that I beg her forgiveness." Presumably, he had already stopped believing what all of us still believed later: that they were going to a camp. He had that horrifying clarity of vision that comes just before death.

The peasant who that evening brought us the note that said, "I myself am to blame, forgive me," was somber and didn't look us in the eye. He said he had found the note on the road to Lubianki and that he didn't know anything else about it; we knew that he knew, but we did not want to admit it. He left, but he came back after the war to tell us what he had seen.

A postcard from the rabbi arrived two days later, convincing everyone that those who had been taken away were in a labor camp. A month later, when the lack of any further news began to make us doubt the camp, another postcard arrived, this one written by someone else who had been deported—an accountant, I think. After the postcard scheme came the payment of contributions: the authorities let it be understood that kilos of coffee or tea—or gold—would provide a family with news of their dear ones. As a gesture of compassion they also allowed people to send food parcels to the prisoners, who, it was said, were working in a camp in the Reich. Once again, after the second action, a postcard turned up. It was written in pencil, and almost indecipherable. After this postcard, we said, "They're done for." But rumors told a different story altogether—of soggy earth in the woods by the village of Lubianki, and of a bloodstained handkerchief that had been found. These rumors came from nowhere; no eyewitnesses stepped forward.

The peasant who had not dared to speak at the time came back after the war and told us everything. It happened just as rumor had it, in a dense, overgrown forest, eight kilometers outside of town, one hour after the trucks left the marketplace. The execution itself did not take long; more time was spent on the preparatory digging of the grave.

At the first shots, our chubby, round-faced cousin David, who was always clumsy at gymnastics and sports, climbed a tree and wrapped his arms around the trunk like a child hugging his mother, and that was the way he died.

Translated from the Polish by Madeline Levine and Francine Prose

A Ghetto Dog

Anna Nikolaievna, widow of Jacob Simon Temkin, the fur dealer, had only time enough to snatch up a small framed photograph of her husband, for the German was already standing in the open doorway shouting, *"R-raus-s!"*[1]

There were no more Jews in the house by now, and if she had failed to hear the noise they made as they fled it was because with age she had grown hard of hearing and because that very morning, before the light had seeped through the heavy portieres, a desire had come over her to open her piano—a grand piano, black—and let her old parchment-like fingers glide over its yellowed keys. One could scarcely call what she was playing music, since her fingers, which were as gnarled as old fallen bark, had been tremulous with age for years. The echoes of several tunes had been sounding in her deaf ears the whole morning, so that she had failed to hear the German when he appeared shouting on the threshold.

All the while Nicky, the widow's dog, had been lying near one of the heavy portieres, dozing and dreaming an old dog's dream, his pointed muzzle resting on his outstretched paws. He was well along in years; his coat was shedding and light patches showed in its sandy hue. His legs were weak, but his big eyes—brownish with a blue glint—reminded one that he too had once been a puppy.

The widow and her dog led a lonely life. Nicky wandered through the rooms on his weak stumpy legs, his head drooping, and swayed mournfully, his whining quieted by weary thoughts. The Temkins had got him from a farm a long time ago. After his master's death the widow used to listen all day to Nicky moving through the stillness of the house. Whenever she sat by the table and Nicky was in the bedroom opposite (he had refused for several days to leave the bed where his master had died), it seemed to her as though her late husband were again walking through the bedroom in his house slippers. She used to listen to the least noise from the bedroom, pricking up her deaf

Isaiah Spiegel's "A Ghetto Dog" is a revised version of a story he wrote in the Lodz Ghetto some time before the deportations of January–May 1942. The original is more documentary in character, making reference to the Judenrat chairman Rumkowski, the Jewish Ghetto Police, and Germans in charge of the ghetto administration. The later version, written after the liberation and which appears in this volume, is more elegiac in tone and more ennobling of the Jewish victims.

1. German for "Get out!"

ears, and as a sudden pallor spread over her wrinkled forehead she seemed actually to hear Jacob Simon's soft slow tread. Any moment now he would appear on the threshold of the bedroom, seat himself in the plush *fauteuil*,[2] reach out for a plaid rug, and throw it over his knees, which had been rheumatic for so many years.

Between the widow and her dog there had formed a mesh of other-worldly thoughts and dreams. She saw in his drooping old head, in his worn-out fur and his pupils with their blue glints, a shadow of her husband. Perhaps this was because Nicky had been close to his master for so many years and had been ready to lay down his life for him, or perhaps because with time he had taken on his master's soft tread over the rugs, his master's lax mouth and watery eyes—whichever it was, the widow had never clasped the dog's head without feeling some inner disquiet. Between them there was that bond which sometimes springs up between two lonely creatures, one human and the other brute.

While the German was still in the open doorway, and before the widow had time to snatch up the photograph, Nicky had already taken his stand at the threshold. He raised his old head against the German, opened his mouth wide to reveal his few remaining teeth, let out three wild howls, and was set to leap straight for the German's throat. One could see Nicky's hackles rise and hear his old paws scrape as he dashed about, ready to leap at the stranger in the outlandish green uniform. Suddenly the dog had shed his years; his legs straightened and hot saliva drooled from his muzzle as if he would say, "I know you're our enemy, I know! But you just wait—wait!"

The German at the door became confused for a moment. Taken aback by the fire glinting in the old dog's eyes, he clutched at his pistol holster.

"Have pity!" the old woman quavered. "It's only a poor animal—"

With her old body she shielded Nicky from the German and at the same time began patting the dog. In a moment he lay quiet and trembling in the old woman's arms. At last the widow tugged at his leash, and the two of them made their way through the dark hallway and into the street. As she hurried through the hallway she seized a small black cane with a silver knob; without this cane, a memento of her husband, she could hardly take a step.

She found herself in the street, leaning on the black cane with the silver knob, the rescued photograph safe in her bosom, and tugging the dog on his leash. Her eyes could scarcely be said to perceive what was going on around her. The day was frosty, blue; a blue silvery web of mist, spun by the early Polish winter, was spreading over the houses, the street, the sidewalks. The

2. French for armchair.

faces of the fleeing Jews were yellow, pallid. Nicky was still restless and was drawing back all the time; he did not know where his mistress was leading him. From time to time he fixed his eyes on the widow's face, while she, as she trudged along, felt a sudden icy fear grip her heart. From the dog's eyes raised to hers there peered the watery, lifeless gaze of her late husband. And here were the two of them, linked together in the web of frosty mist that was swirling under a lowering dark sky. The two of them were now plodding close to each other, their heads downcast. Cold, angry thoughts kindled in her drowsy old mind. She actually felt a chill breath swishing about her ears and she caught words—far-off words, cold and dead.

The widow who had for so long lived a life apart from Jews and Jewishness had suddenly come to herself, as if awaking from a state of unconsciousness. She had been driven out of her house, of course, as a Jew like any other, although for many years her house had been like any Christian's. Her only son had become an apostate, had married a Christian girl and gone off to Galicia, long before the war, where he was living on his father-in-law's estate. During the Christian holidays various gifts would arrive from him. She knew beforehand what he would send: a big, well-fattened turkey and half a dozen dyed Easter eggs. The turkey she could use, but when it came to the colored eggs the old woman had a strange oppressive feeling. They would lie around for months, gathering dust on their shells, until some evening she peeled them in the bright light of the girandole and then left them on the window sill for the hungry sparrows.

She herself had been estranged from Jewishness since her very childhood. For years on end no Jewish face appeared at her threshold. The war, which had come so suddenly to the town, had during the first few days failed to reach her comfortable home. The catastrophe that had befallen the Jews had not touched her, and the angry prophecy of the storm that was raging in the streets had not beaten upon her door.

When the German had opened it that morning, he had aroused the little old woman from her torpor and had reminded her that she was a Jew and that heavy days had come for her and all other Jews. And though the old woman had during so many years been cut off from Jewishness and Jews, she had accepted the sudden misfortune with courage and resignation, as if an invisible thread had connected her to her people all through the years.

Now she was trudging through the streets with so many others whose faces were strange and distracted. She recognized these faces from her remote youth, faces framed in black unkempt Jewish beards and surmounted by small round skullcaps, which Jacob Simon used to ridicule so in his lifetime. Jews in gaberdines, Jewish women wearing headkerchiefs and marriage wigs, were dragging their children by the hand. Anna's heart was filled with a friendly feeling as, leaning on her black, silver-knobbed cane, she led Nicky with her left hand. The fleeing Jews cast surly sidelong looks at her and the dog. Nicky plodded on without once lifting up his head; the light had gone out of his eyes. A small spotted dog suddenly emerged from the crowd, ran up to Nicky, and placed a paw on the old dog's neck as if seeking consolation; thereafter both dogs walked side by side.

Nicky sensed the strange atmosphere as they turned into the next street. It was poorly paved, with gaping pits; the press was greater here. He could hardly make his way among the thousands of unfriendly feet. They kept stepping on his paws, and once his mistress almost fell. Anna held her head higher and was pulled along by the crowd of Jews. She drew the leash closer to her, every so often saving Nicky from being trampled. By now he kept closer to her, mournful, and with his head still lower.

Fine, wet snowflakes swirled in the air, unwilling to fall to the ground, and settled on Nicky's grizzled, closely curled coat.

The widow found herself in a narrow squalid street in the Balut district of Lodz, where all the hack drivers, porters, and emaciated Jewish streetwalkers lived. She had come here with a host of strangers who quickly made themselves at home in a huge empty barn. The Jewish streetwalkers brought them all sorts of good things baked of white flour. The widow sat in the barn, her gray disheveled head propped on the silver knob of her cane, while Nicky sprawled at her feet and took in the angry din made by the strange people.

It was late at night before everyone in the barn was assigned quarters in the district. The widow found herself in the room of a tart known as Big Rose—a very much disgruntled tart, who did not want a dog in the house.

"It's enough that I have to take in a female apostate!" she kept yelling. "What do I need a sick old hound for?"

Anna stood on the threshold before the tart, the dog close to her on his unsteady legs; his body emanated a forlornness that was both animal and human.

"Quiet, quiet!" The widow's hand fell shakily on Nicky's drooping head and patted it.

The room where Big Rose lived lay under a gabled roof. It held a small shabby sofa, strewn with yellow and red cushions. A low ceiling made the place dreary and depressing. Outside the window was the hostile night, spattered with the silver of the first frost. This night-silver interlaced with the reflections of light from the room and fell on the windowpanes like dancing stars.

The nook that sheltered the widow and her dog was very dark; the warmth lingered there as if in a closed warm cellar. Throughout the room there hovered a sour odor of sin and lust. The old woman did not realize where she had come to; nothing mattered any longer. She and her dog huddled in their nook and for a long while squatted there like two huge rigid shadows. From time to time Nicky put his head in her lap, and a soft, long-drawn-out whine issued from the dark nook, like the moan of a hopelessly sick man.

Later that night, when the old woman and the dog had stretched out in their nook on some rags, Big Rose closed the red hangings which screened the shabby sofa from the rest of the room. The little red flame of the small night-lamp hanging on the wall wavered slowly and angrily, licking at the musty darkness around it.

Only now, when everything had become utterly quiet, did certain shadows appear in the darkness of the threshold. The shadows entered one by one; each hovered for a moment on the threshold, looked about, then disappeared within the hangings. In the dark little hallway on the other side of the door other shadows gathered and waited for the door to open. They did not have to wait long: each shadow, after darting out from behind the hangings, rushed through the door and disappeared down the stairs.

The widow was dozing by now. From time to time she awoke and put her arms around Nicky's warm neck. The dog continued snoring with a low, canine snore. Each time the door opened and a shadow darted within the hangings, from which there immediately issued Big Rose's witchlike snicker, Nicky would emit a low growl.

This suddenly angered Big Rose. She sprang up naked by the drawn-back hangings and, brandishing her arms, shouted at the widow in the nook, "My grand madam! May a curse light on you! Maybe madam would like to step out for a little while on the balcony with the hound? He's driving everybody away, may the devil overtake him! I'll poison that hound!"

The widow, startled from her sleep, was frightened by Big Rose's stark nakedness and its pungent reek.

"Sh, sh, sh!" she at last managed to whisper to the dog.

She stood up in her nook, took Nicky's head, and started for the door. Through the small dark hallway the two of them, the widow and the dog, reached the deserted balcony. Below them lay a tangle of dark Balut streets. The wind drove nearer and scattered the grayish, tenuous whiteness of the still swirling night snow. From the south side of the city the dusty glow of electric lights was borne through the night. The widow watched these lights blinking on and off, like inflamed eyes.

"See there, Nicky? Over there—there. That's our house, our street—"

The dog lifted up his head, stood up on his hind legs, and peered into the darkness. For a while he stood thus, with the widow's arms around him, then suddenly let out a howl. It rent the sky like lightning, beat against the clouds, and then died away in the cold darkness of the earth.

In the morning, when the chilled widow awoke in her nook, the dog was no longer by her side. Nobody had any idea where he had vanished to. Big Rose kept saying that this was no dog but a werewolf and that she hadn't even heard the dog leaving the house.

He was gone the whole day, and only toward evening did they hear him scraping at the door. He fell into the nook in great excitement, with foam on his hanging tongue, and threw himself on the frightened widow's lap.

Nicky lay on her knees, quivering with an ardent, old-dog sob. The widow took his shivering head and for some time gazed into his watery pupils, as if into the small opening of two wells. She could not understand what had happened to the dog. He barked in a subdued way, as if some words were struggling to escape him, as if he were straining to tell everything to the old woman bending over him. His whole body quivered, and his narrow face seemed to wear the twisted grimace of a dog in lament. Yet this was not whining; rather a noisy outburst of joy and consolation. He kept lifting his paws and putting them on the old woman's knees. The widow took the paws and brought them to her aged, withered lips, bent over, and for a long, long time, with her eyes closed, rested her head on them.

For a long time the widow sat in the darkness embracing the dog, while the night-lamp, which had been turned low and had been burning all day near the red hangings, now cast a mysterious reddish reflection on the wall. The sharp silhouette of the dog's pointed head and the widow's arms swayed on the ceiling in a network of dancing shadows.

The next morning Nicky again disappeared and did not come back until nightfall. This was repeated day after day.

These disappearances coincided with the time the Germans built a wall around the ghetto, barbed wires dividing the Balut from the rest of the city. Nobody was allowed to leave or enter the Jewish district. But just the same Nicky used to disappear every day and come back only at night.

Once, when Nicky returned as excited as always, the old woman put her hands on his head and drew them back: they were sticky with blood. His fur was split and torn with open wounds. He was holding his paws on her knees, as always, but this time his pupils were reddish, glowing, and little green fires kept dancing across his watery eyes.

The widow applied rag after rag soaked in cold water to the dog's open wounds. Only now did she realize that Nicky had been crawling through the barbed wire, that each morning he had run off to the city and each evening he had come running home. The widow kept on washing the warm blood and applying the cold wet rags, while Big Rose ran to fetch basins of water. The bitterness she had felt in her heart for the dog had quickly vanished. She took a white blouse from her closet and tore in into narrow bandages; she also procured from somewhere a salve that was good even for human wounds. She smeared torn strips with the salve and then, kneeling by the door, started to bind the dog's wounds.

A sudden fright came over Big Rose; an other-worldly expression appeared on her face, as if she felt a cold breath upon her. She could have sworn by all that was holy that, as she had been binding the dog's wounds, he had given her a mournful human look.

From the day Big Rose had bound the open wounds the dog had got by crawling through the barbed wire strung around the ghetto—from that day her attitude toward the widow had undergone a complete change. She took down the red hangings that had divided the room in two and asked the old woman to leave her dark nook and share the room with her. All three of them, the two women and the dog, now used the sofa. Nicky lay propped up by the colored cushions, lost in an old dog's dream.

This happened just about the time when the Germans issued an order that all animals—horses, cows, goats, and dogs—must be turned over to them. Only two broken-down horses were allowed to remain in the whole ghetto. For generations the old Jewish residents of the Balut had made their meager living as animal-breeders. The hack-drivers and cabbies, the milk dealers, small middlemen, organ-grinders, and inn-keepers had to give up the horses and cows they had tended in the crowded dark stables and stalls. They unharnessed their horses for the last time and embraced the warm necks of their cows; they led out the mournful Jewish cows and the frightened Jewish goats. The draymen led their beautiful, glossy chestnut draft horses through the streets, the whole family marching in step with them, wringing their hands as if they were following the dead to a yawning grave. The women dragged the cows and goats along—the animals became stubborn and refused to budge. At the tail end of the procession, on ropes and leashes, other Jews were leading watchdogs, Dalmatians, poodles with mournful eyes, and common household pets with bobbed tails. The Jews hoped that their dumb creatures would be better fed than they had been in the ghetto. The horses and cows were taken into the city, but the dogs were immediately shot in a field close to the market place.

At daybreak Big Rose had thrown a torn black shawl with long fringes over her, and the widow, without uttering a word, had taken Nicky on his leash with one hand and her small silver-knobbed cane in the other. Both women were going to take the dog to the market place. Big Rose kept mauling her cheeks and softly weeping. The widow's disheveled hair, gray and lifeless, hung over her ashen face.

The compulsory surrender of her dog had come as such a shock to the widow that at first, when Big Rose had shouted the news into her face, she had clutched her head with her withered fingers and had remained still for several minutes. Big Rose thought the old woman had died, standing with her fingers in her hair, and her eyes not even blinking. She just stood there, stunned and stone-cold.

The dog let them do with him whatever they liked. He dropped at their feet and held his pointed head up to them, then yawned and let his muzzle sink to the cold floor.

The two women started out through the small courtyard, Nicky on his long leash between them. The snow was coming down in flakes as slender and chill as needles and stabbed their hands, their faces, and the dog's fur. It was bitter cold. Although dawn had broken a comparatively short while ago, the ghetto seemed already to be in twilight—night can fall abruptly in that region.

Big Rose bit her lips as she walked along. She peered out from the black shawl in which she was wrapped and could see nothing but the widow's half-dead face. Nicky still had his back bound in rags.

As they neared the market place they saw Jewish children emerging from the surrounding little streets, leading gaunt, emaciated dogs on ropes and leashes. There was a pound in the market place where the Germans collected the dogs. The horses and cows had already been transferred to German civilians to bring into the city proper. The dogs within the pound were looking out on the ghetto through barbed wire, their eyes watering. A shadowy terror was frozen upon their frightened, pointed muzzles.

A German stationed near the wicket leading into the pound, relieved each owner of his or her dog, pushed the wicket open, kicked the dog with the point of his boot—and the animal found itself in the pound. Rarely or ever did any dog snarl at the German. Sudden shock paralyzed the dogs, depriving them of their strength and numbing their rage. Perhaps this was due to the reek that now came to them from the field where the dogs were being killed.

By the time the widow and Big Rose approached the pound with Nicky it was full of Jewish dogs. They were jammed together, huddled in twos and threes, their heads resting on one another's shoulders. Perhaps they did this because of the cold, which beat down upon them from the sky. A few of them were close to the barbed wire, prodding it with their paws in an attempt to get free. But they had to fall back with a childlike whimper when they felt their paws become sticky with blood. The barbs of the wire were sharp and rusty and stuck out like little knife points.

The widow and Big Rose halted before the German. He was waiting for the old woman to let go of the leash. But, instead of letting go, she wound the leash still tighter about her wrist and even her forearm. She did this with her eyes closed, the way a Jew winds the straps of a phylactery on his forearm. The German snatched at the leash. The widow staggered on her old legs, since Nicky was by now pulling her into the pound. She let herself be dragged along. In the meantime the German kicked the wicket shut. His loud, tinny laughter ran along the barbed wire.

Big Rose saw the widow standing inside the enclosure ringed by a pack of dogs and still holding Nicky on the leash. In her left hand she had the small cane with the silver knob and was keeping it high over the heads of the dogs. She stood there with her cane raised, her hair disheveled, the dogs circling at her feet. Some of the dogs lifted up their mournful heads and looked into the old woman's face. Nicky alone remained unperturbed. His back was still bound up in the white rags torn from Big Rose's blouse. From time to time he lifted his head toward the wicket where Big Rose was standing, petrified.

Exhausted, the widow sank to her knees in the snow. By now one could barely make out her body. The snow was falling more heavily, in bright shimmering stars. The widow's head stood out in the whiteness like a dazzling aureole.

Big Rose saw another wicket fly open on the other side and someone begin driving the dogs out into an open field. The widow stood up, leaned on her small silver-knobbed cane, and, with Nicky leading, started toward the field. . . .

Big Rose wrapped the small black shawl more tightly about her head. She did not want to hear the dull, tinny sounds that came from the sharp-edged shovels scooping up the frozen ground of the Balut. It was only the wind, playing upon the shovels that delved the narrow black pits—only the wind, chanting its chill night song.

Translated from the Yiddish by Bernard Guilbert Guerney

The Name

Grandfather Zisskind lived in a little house in a southern suburb of the town. About once a month, on a Saturday afternoon, his granddaughter Raya and her young husband Yehuda would go and pay him a visit.

Raya would give three cautious knocks on the door (an agreed signal between herself and her grandfather ever since her childhood, when he had lived in their house together with the whole family) and they would wait for the door to be opened. "Now he's getting up," Raya would whisper to Yehuda, her face glowing, when the sound of her grandfather's slippers was heard from within, shuffling across the room. Another moment, and the key would be turned and the door opened.

"Come in," he would say somewhat absently, still buttoning up his trousers, with the rheum of sleep in his eyes. Although it was very hot he wore a yellow winter vest with long sleeves, from which his wrists stuck out—white, thin, delicate as a girl's, as was his bare neck with its taut skin.

After Raya and Yehuda had sat down at the table, which was covered with a white cloth showing signs of the meal he had eaten alone—crumbs from the Sabbath loaf, a plate with meat leavings, a glass containing some grape pips, a number of jars and so on—he would smooth the crumpled pillows, spread a cover over the narrow bed and tidy up. It was a small room, and its obvious disorder aroused pity for the old man's helplessness in running his home. In the corner was a shelf with two sooty kerosene burners, a kettle and two or three saucepans, and next to it a basin containing plates, knives and forks. In another corner was a stand holding books with thick leather bindings, leaning and lying on each other. Some of his clothes hung over the backs of the chairs. An ancient walnut cupboard with an empty buffet stood exactly opposite the door. On the wall hung a clock which had long since stopped.

"We ought to make Grandfather a present of a clock," Raya would say to Yehuda as she surveyed the room and her glance lighted on the clock; but every time the matter slipped her memory. She loved her grandfather, with his pointed white silky beard, his tranquil face from which a kind of holy radiance emanated, his quiet, soft voice which seemed to have been made only for uttering words of sublime wisdom. She also respected him for his pride, which had led him to move out of her mother's house and live by himself, accepting the hardship and trouble and the affliction of loneliness in his old age. There had been a bitter quarrel between him and his daughter. After

Raya's father had died, the house had lost its grandeur and shed the trappings of wealth. Some of the antique furniture which they had retained—along with some crystalware and jewels, the dim lustre of memories from the days of plenty in their native city—had been sold, and Rachel, Raya's mother, had been compelled to support the home by working as a dentist's nurse. Grandfather Zisskind, who had been supported by the family ever since he came to the country, wished to hand over to his daughter his small capital, which was deposited in a bank. She was not willing to accept it. She was stubborn and proud like him. Then, after a prolonged quarrel and several weeks of not speaking to each other, he took some of the things in his room and the broken clock and went to live alone. That had been about four years ago. Now Rachel would come to him once or twice a week, bringing with her a bag full of provisions, to clean the room and cook some meals for him. He was no longer interested in expenses and did not even ask about them, as though they were of no more concern to him.

"And now . . . what can I offer you?" Grandfather Zisskind would ask when he considered the room ready to receive guests. "There's no need to offer us anything, Grandfather; we didn't come for that," Raya would answer crossly.

But protests were of no avail. Her grandfather would take out a jar of fermenting preserves and put it on the table, then grapes and plums, biscuits and two glasses of strong tea, forcing them to eat. Raya would taste a little of this and that just to please the old man, while Yehuda, for whom all these visits were unavoidable torment, the very sight of the dishes arousing his disgust, would secretly indicate to her by pulling a sour face that he just couldn't touch the preserves. She would smile at him placatingly, stroking his knee. But Grandfather insisted, so he would have to taste at least a teaspoonful of the sweet and nauseating stuff.

Afterwards Grandfather would ask about all kinds of things. Raya did her best to make the conversation pleasant, in order to relieve Yehuda's boredom. Finally would come what Yehuda dreaded most of all and on account of which he had resolved more than once to refrain from these visits. Grandfather Zisskind would rise, take his chair and place it next to the wall, get up on it carefully, holding on to the back so as not to fall, open the clock and take out a cloth bag with a black cord tied around it. Then he would shut the clock, get off the chair, put it back in its place, sit down on it, undo the cord, take out of the cloth wrapping a bundle of sheets of paper, lay them in front of Yehuda and say:

"I would like you to read this."

"Grandfather," Raya would rush to Yehuda's rescue, "but he's already read it at least ten times. . . ."

But Grandfather Zisskind would pretend not to hear and would not reply, so Yehuda was compelled each time to read there and then that same essay, spread over eight, long sheets in a large, somewhat shaky handwriting, which he almost knew by heart. It was a lament for Grandfather's native town in the Ukraine which had been destroyed by the Germans, and all its Jews slaughtered. When he had finished, Grandfather would take the sheets out of his hand, fold them, sigh and say:

"And nothing of all this is left. Dust and ashes. Not even a tombstone to bear witness. Imagine, of a community of twenty thousand Jews not even one survived to tell how it happened. . . . Not a trace."

Then out of the same cloth bag, which contained various letters and envelopes, he would draw a photograph of his grandson Mendele, who had been twelve years old when he was killed; the only son of his son Ossip, chief engineer in a large chemical factory. He would show it to Yehuda and say:

"He was a genius. Just imagine, when he was only eleven he had already finished his studies at the Conservatory, won a scholarship from the Government and was considered an outstanding violinist. A genius! Look at that forehead. . . ." And after he had put the photograph back he would sigh and repeat "Not a trace."

A strained silence of commiseration would descend on Raya and Yehuda, who had already heard these same things many times over and no longer felt anything when they were repeated. And as he wound the cord round the bag the old man would muse: "And Ossip was also a prodigy. As a boy he knew Hebrew well, and could recite Bialik's poems[1] by heart. He studied by himself. He read endlessly, Gnessin, Frug, Bershadsky. . . . You didn't know Bershadsky; he was a good writer[2]. . . . He had a warm heart, Ossip had. He didn't mix in politics, he wasn't even a Zionist, but even when they promoted him there he didn't forget that he was a Jew. . . . He called his son

1. Bialik (1873–1934) was a Ukrainian poet and novelist who wrote mainly in Hebrew. See note for "City of Slaughter," p. 416.

2. Uri Nissan Gnessin (1881–1913), Hebrew author born in the Ukraine, was the first to introduce psychologically oriented prose style into Hebrew literature. His works probe the problems of alienation and uprootedness, particularly as they affected the Jew in the modern age. Shimon Shuel Frug (1860–1916), Yiddish poet born in Kherson province, Russia, was the first poet to treat Jewish themes in Russian verse. His poem "The Goblet," written under the impact of the pogroms of 1881, was translated into Yiddish by I. L. Peretz and sung by Jews around the world. After 1896, Frug himself wrote in Yiddish. Isaiah Bershadsky (1871–1908), Hebrew novelist born in Belorussia, is the author of *Be-Ein Mattarah* (To no purpose), 1899, which became a landmark in Hebrew literature because of the character of Admovitz, the Jewish social misfit. Admovitz became the prototype for the antihero of Hebrew fiction in the first quarter of the twentieth century.

Mendele, of all names, after his dead brother, even though it was surely not easy to have a name like that among the Russians. . . . Yes, he had a warm Jewish heart. . . ."

He would turn to Yehuda as he spoke, since in Raya he always saw the child who used to sit on his knee listening to his stories, and for him she had never grown up, while he regarded Yehuda as an educated man who could understand someone else, especially inasmuch as Yehuda held a government job.

Raya remembered how the change had come about in her grandfather. When the war was over he was still sustained by uncertainty and hoped for some news of his son, for it was known that very many had succeeded in escaping eastwards. Wearily he would visit all those who had once lived in his town, but none of them had received any sign of life from relatives. Nevertheless he continued to hope, for Ossip's important position might have helped to save him. Then Raya came home one evening and saw him sitting on the floor with a rent in his jacket. In the house they spoke in whispers, and her mother's eyes were red with weeping. She, too, had wept at Grandfather's sorrow, at the sight of his stricken face, at the oppressive quiet in the rooms. For many weeks afterwards it was as if he had imposed silence on himself. He would sit at his table from morning to night, reading and re-reading old letters, studying family photographs by the hour as he brought them close to his shortsighted eyes, or leaning backwards on his chair, motionless, his hand touching the edge of the table and his eyes staring through the window in front of him, into the distance, as if he had turned to stone. He was no longer the same talkative, wise and humorous grandfather who interested himself in the house, asked what his granddaughter was doing, instructed her, tested her knowledge, proving boastfully like a child that he knew more than her teachers. Now he seemed to cut himself off from the world and entrench himself in his thoughts and his memories, which none of the household could penetrate. Later, a strange perversity had taken hold of him which it was hard to tolerate. He would insist that his meals be served at his table, apart, that no one should enter his room without knocking at the door, or close the shutters of his window against the sun. When any one disobeyed these prohibitions he would flare up and quarrel violently with his daughter. At times it seemed that he hated her.

When Raya's father died, Grandfather Zisskind did not show any signs of grief, and did not even console his daughter. But when the days of mourning were past it was as if he had been restored to new life, and he emerged from his silence. Yet he did not speak of his son-in-law, nor of his son Ossip, but only of his grandson Mendele. Often during the day he would mention the boy by name as if he were alive, and speak of him familiarly, although he had seen him only in photographs—as though deliberating aloud and turning the matter over, he would talk of how Mendele ought to be brought up. It was hardest of all when he started criticizing his son and his son's wife for not having foreseen the impending disaster, for not having rushed the boy away to a safe place, not having hidden him with non-Jews, not having tried to get him to the Land of Israel in good time. There was no logic in what he said; this would so infuriate Rachel that she would burst out with, "Oh, do stop! Stop it! I'll go out of my mind with your foolish nonsense!" She would rise from her seat in anger, withdraw to her room, and afterwards, when she had calmed down, would say to Raya, "Sclerosis, apparently. Loss of memory. He no longer knows what he's talking about."

One day—Raya would never forget this—she and her mother saw that Grandfather was wearing his best suit, the black one, and under it a gleaming white shirt; his shoes were polished, and he had a hat on. He had not worn these clothes for many months, and the family was dismayed to see him. They thought that he had lost his mind. "What holiday is it today?" her mother asked. "Really, don't you know?" asked her grandfather. "Today is Mendele's birthday!" Her mother burst out crying. She too began to cry and ran out of the house.

After that, Grandfather Zisskind went to live alone. His mind, apparently, had become settled, except that he would frequently forget things which had occurred a day or two before, though he clearly remembered, down to the smallest detail, things which had happened in his town and to his family more than thirty years ago. Raya would go and visit him, at first with her mother and, after her marriage, with Yehuda. What bothered them was that they were compelled to listen to his talk about Mendele his grandson, and to read that same lament for his native town which had been destroyed.

Whenever Rachel happened to come there during their visit, she would scold Grandfather rudely. "Stop bothering them with your masterpiece," she would say, and herself remove the papers from the table and put them back in their bag. "If you want them to keep on visiting you, don't talk to them about the dead. Talk about the living. They're young people and they have no mind for such things." And as they left his room together she would say, turning to Yehuda in order to placate him, "Don't be surprised at him. Grandfather's already old. Over seventy. Loss of memory."

When Raya was seven months pregnant, Grandfather Zisskind had in his absent-mindedness not yet noticed it. But Rachel could no longer refrain from letting him share her joy and hope, and told him that a great-grandchild would soon be born to him. One evening the door of Raya and Yehuda's flat opened, and Grandfather himself stood on the threshold in his holiday clothes, just as on the day of Mendele's birthday. This was the first time he had visited them at home, and Raya was so surprised that she hugged and kissed him as she had not done since she was a child. His face shone, his eyes sparkled with the same intelligent and mischievous light they had in those far-off days before the calamity. When he entered he walked briskly through the rooms, giving his opinion on the furniture and its arrangement, and joking about everything around him. He was so pleasant that Raya and Yehuda could not stop laughing all the time he was speaking. He gave no indication that he knew what was about to take place, and for the first time in many months he did not mention Mendele.

"Ah, you naughty children," he said, "is this how you treat Grandfather? Why didn't you tell me you had such a nice place?"

"How many times have I invited you here, Grandfather?" asked Raya.

"Invited me? You ought to have *brought* me here, dragged me by force!"

"I wanted to do that too, but you refused."

"Well, I thought that you lived in some dark den, and I have a den of my own. Never mind, I forgive you."

And when he took leave of them he said:

"Don't bother to come to me. Now that I know where you're to be found and what a palace you have, I'll come to you . . . if you don't throw me out, that is."

Some days later, when Rachel came to their home and they told her about Grandfather's amazing visit, she was not surprised:

"Ah, you don't know what he's been contemplating during all these days, ever since I told him that you're about to have a child. . . . He has one wish—that if it's a son, it should be named . . . after his grandson."

"Mendele?" exclaimed Raya, and involuntarily burst into laughter. Yehuda smiled as one smiles at the fond fancies of the old.

"Of course, I told him to put that out of his head," said Rachel, "but you know how obstinate he is. It's some obsession and he won't think of giving it up. Not only that, but he's sure that you'll willingly agree to it, and especially you, Yehuda."

Yehuda shrugged his shoulders. "Crazy. The child would be unhappy all his life."

"But he's not capable of understanding that," said Rachel, and a note of apprehension crept into her voice.

Raya's face grew solemn. "We have already decided on the name," she said. "If it's a girl she'll be called Osnath, and if it's a boy—Ehud."

Rachel did not like either.

The matter of the name became almost the sole topic of conversation between Rachel and the young couple when she visited them, and it infused gloom into the air of expectancy which filled the house.

Rachel, midway between the generations, was of two minds about the matter. When she spoke to her father she would scold and contradict him, flinging at him all the arguments she had heard from Raya and Yehuda as though they were her own, but when she spoke to the children she sought to induce them to meet his wishes, and would bring down their anger on herself. As time went on, the question of a name, to which in the beginning she had attached little importance, became a kind of mystery, concealing something preordained, fearful, and pregnant with life and death. The fate of the child itself seemed in doubt. In her innermost heart she prayed that Raya would give birth to a daughter.

"Actually, what's so bad about the name Mendele?" she asked her daughter. "It's a Jewish name like any other."

"What are you talking about, Mother"—Raya rebelled against the thought—"a Ghetto name, ugly, horrible! I wouldn't even be capable of letting it cross my lips. Do you want me to hate my child?"

"Oh, you won't hate your child. At any rate, not because of the name. . . ."

"I should hate him. It's as if you'd told me that my child would be born with a hump! And anyway—why should I? What for?"

"You have to do it for Grandfather's sake," Rachel said quietly, although she knew that she was not speaking the whole truth.

"You know, Mother, that I am ready to do anything for Grandfather," said Raya. "I love him, but I am not ready to sacrifice my child's happiness on account of some superstition of his. What sense is there in it?"

Rachel could not explain the "sense in it" rationally, but in her heart she rebelled against her daughter's logic which had always been hers too and now seemed very superficial, a symptom of the frivolity afflicting the younger generation. Her old father now appeared to her like an ancient tree whose deep roots suck up the mysterious essence of existence, of which neither her daughter nor she herself knew anything. Had it not been for this argument about the name, she would certainly never have got to meditating on the transmigration of souls and the eternity of life. At night she would wake up covered in cold sweat. Hazily, she recalled frightful scenes of bodies of naked children, beaten and trampled under the jackboots of soldiers, and an awful sense of guilt oppressed her spirit.

Then Rachel came with a proposal for a compromise: that the child should be named Menachem. A Hebrew name, she said; an Israeli one, by all standards. Many children bore it, and it occurred to nobody to make fun of them. Even Grandfather had agreed to it after much urging.

Raya refused to listen.

"We have chosen a name, Mother," she said, "which we both like, and we won't change it for another. Menachem is a name which reeks of old age, a name which for me is connected with sad memories and people I don't like. Menachem you could call only a boy who is short, weak and not good-looking. Let's not talk about it any more, Mother."

Rachel was silent. She almost despaired of convincing them. At last she said:

"And are you ready to take the responsibility of going against Grandfather's wishes?"

Raya's eyes opened wide, and fear was reflected in them:

"Why do you make such a fateful thing of it? You frighten me!" she said, and burst into tears. She began to fear for her offspring as one fears the evil eye.

"And perhaps there *is* something fateful in it. . . ." whispered Rachel without raising her eyes. She flinched at her own words.

"What is it?" insisted Raya, with a frightened look at her mother.

"I don't know. . ." she said. "Perhaps all the same we are bound to retain the names of the dead . . . in order to leave a remembrance of them. . . ." She was not sure herself whether there was any truth in what she said or whether it was merely a stupid belief, but her father's faith was before her, stronger than her own doubts and her daughter's simple and understandable opposition.

"But I don't always want to remember all those dreadful things, Mother. It's impossible that this memory should always hang about this house and that the poor child should bear it!"

Rachel understood. She, too, heard such a cry within her as she listened to her father talking, sunk in memories of the past. As if to herself, she said in a whisper:

"I don't know . . . at times it seems to me that it's not Grandfather who's suffering from loss of memory, but ourselves. All of us."

About two weeks before the birth was due, Grandfather Zisskind appeared in Raya and Yehuda's home for the second time. His face was yellow, angry, and the light had faded from his eyes. He greeted them, but did not favor Raya with so much as a glance, as if he had pronounced a ban upon the sinner. Turning to Yehuda he said, "I wish to speak to you."

They went into the inner room. Grandfather sat down on the chair and placed the palm of his hand on the edge of the table, as was his wont, and Yehuda sat, lower than he, on the bed.

"Rachel has told me that you don't want to call the child by my grandchild's name," he said.

"Yes. . . ." said Yehuda diffidently.

"Perhaps you'll explain to me why?" he asked.

"We. . . ." stammered Yehuda, who found it difficult to face the piercing gaze of the old man. "The name simply doesn't appeal to us."

Grandfather was silent. Then he said, "I understand that Mendele doesn't appeal to you. Not a Hebrew name. Granted! But Menachem—what's wrong with Menachem?" It was obvious that he was controlling his feelings with difficulty.

"It's not. . . ." Yehuda knew that there was no use explaining; they were two generations apart in their ideas. "It's not an Israeli name . . . it's from the *Golah*."[3]

"*Golah*," repeated Grandfather. He shook with rage, but somehow he maintained his self-control. Quietly he added, "We all come from the *Golah*. I, and Raya's father and mother. Your father and mother. All of us."

"Yes. . . ." said Yehuda. He resented the fact that he was being dragged into an argument which was distasteful to him, particularly with this old man whose mind was already not quite clear. Only out of respect did he restrain himself from shouting: That's that, and it's done with! . . . "Yes, but we were born in this country," he said aloud; "that's different."

Grandfather Zisskind looked at him contemptuously. Before him he saw a wretched boor, an empty vessel.

"You, that is to say, think that there's something new here," he said, "that everything that was there is past and gone. Dead, without sequel. That you are starting everything anew."

"I didn't say that. I only said that we were born in this country. . . ."

"You were born here. Very nice. . ." said Grandfather Zisskind with rising emotion. "So what of it? What's so remarkable about that? In what way are you superior to those who were born *there*? Are you cleverer than they? More cultured? Are you greater than they in Torah or good deeds? Is your blood redder than theirs?" Grandfather Zisskind looked as if he could wring Yehuda's neck.

"I didn't say that either. I said that *here* it's different. . . ."

Grandfather Zisskind's patience with idle words was exhausted.

"You good-for-nothing!" he burst out in his rage. "What do you know about what was there? What do you know of the *people* that were there? The communities? The cities? What do you know of the *life* they had there?"

"Yes," said Yehuda, his spirit crushed, "but we no longer have any ties with it."

3. Diaspora: The whole body of Jews living dispersed among the Gentiles.—Trans.

"You have no ties with it?" Grandfather Zisskind bent towards him. His lips quivered in fury. "With what . . . with what *do* you have ties?"

"We have . . . with this country," said Yehuda and gave an involuntary smile.

"Fool!" Grandfather Zisskind shot at him. "Do you think that people come to a desert and make themselves a nation, eh? That you are the first of some new race? That you're not the son of your father? Not the grandson of your grandfather? Do you want to forget them? Are you ashamed of them for having had a hundred times more culture and education than you have? Why . . . why, everything here"—he included everything around him in the sweep of his arm—"is no more than a puddle of tapwater against the big sea that was there! What have you here? A mixed multitude! Seventy languages! Seventy distinct groups! Customs? A way of life? Why, every home here is a nation in itself, with its own customs and its own names! And with this you have ties, you say. . . ."

Yehuda lowered his eyes and was silent.

"I'll tell you what ties are," said Grandfather Zisskind calmly. "Ties are remembrance! Do you understand? The Russian is linked to his people because he remembers his ancestors. He is called Ivan, his father was called Ivan and his grandfather was called Ivan, back to the first generation. And no Russian has said: From today onwards I shall not be called Ivan because my fathers and my fathers' fathers were called that; I am the first of a new Russian nation which has nothing at all to do with the Ivans. Do you understand?"

"But what has that got to do with it?" Yehuda protested impatiently. Grandfather Zisskind shook his head at him.

"And you—you're ashamed to give your son the name Mendele lest it remind you that there were Jews who were called by that name. You believe that his name should be wiped off the face of the earth. That not a trace of it should remain. . . ."

He paused, heaved a deep sigh and said:

"O children, children, you don't know what you're doing. . . . You're finishing off the work which the enemies of Israel began. They took the bodies away from the world, and you—the name and the memory. . . . No continuation, no evidence, no memorial and no name. Not a trace. . . ."

And with that he rose, took his stick and with long strides went towards the door and left.

The new-born child was a boy and he was named Ehud, and when he was about a month old, Raya and Yehuda took him in the carriage to Grandfather's house.

Raya gave three cautious knocks on the door, and when she heard a rustle inside she could also hear the beating of her anxious heart. Since the birth of the child Grandfather had not visited them even once. "I'm terribly excited," she whispered to Yehuda with tears in her eyes. Yehuda rocked the carriage and did not reply. He was now indifferent to what the old man might say or do.

The door opened, and on the threshold stood Grandfather Zisskind, his face weary and wrinkled. He seemed to have aged. His eyes were sticky with sleep, and for a moment it seemed as if he did not see the callers.

"Good Sabbath, Grandfather," said Raya with great feeling. It seemed to her now that she loved him more than ever.

Grandfather looked at them as if surprised, and then said absently, "Come in, come in."

"We've brought the baby with us!" said Raya, her face shining, and her glance traveled from Grandfather to the infant sleeping in the carriage.

"Come in, come in," repeated Grandfather Zisskind in a tired voice. "Sit down," he said as he removed his clothes from the chair and turned to tidy the disordered bedclothes.

Yehuda stood the carriage by the wall and whispered to Raya, "It's stifling for him here." Raya opened the window wide.

"You haven't seen our baby yet, Grandfather!" she said with a sad smile.

"Sit down, sit down," said Grandfather, shuffling over to the shelf, from which he took the jar of preserves and the biscuit tin, putting them on the table.

"There's no need, Grandfather, really there's no need for it. We didn't come for that," said Raya.

"Only a little something. I have nothing to offer you today. . . ." said Grandfather in a dull, broken voice. He took the kettle off the kerosene burner and poured out two glasses of tea which he placed before them. Then he too sat down, said "Drink, drink," and softly tapped his fingers on the table.

"I haven't seen Mother for several days now," he said at last.

"She's busy. . ." said Raya in a low voice, without raising her eyes to him. "She helps me a lot with the baby. . . ."

Grandfather Zisskind looked at his pale, knotted and veined hands lying helplessly on the table; then he stretched out one of them and said to Raya, "Why don't you drink? The tea will get cold."

Raya drew up to the table and sipped the tea.

"And you—what are you doing now?" he asked Yehuda.

"Working as usual," said Yehuda, and added with a laugh, "I play with the baby when there's time."

Grandfather again looked down at his hands, the long thin fingers of which shook with the palsy of old age.

"Take some of the preserves," he said to Yehuda, indicating the jar with a shaking finger. "It's very good." Yehuda dipped the spoon in the jar and put it to his mouth.

There was a deep silence. It seemed to last a very long time. Grandfather Zisskind's fingers gave little quivers on the white tablecloth. It was hot in the room, and the buzzing of a fly could be heard.

Suddenly the baby burst out crying, and Raya started from her seat and hastened to quiet him. She rocked the carriage and crooned, "Quiet, child, quiet, quiet. . . ." Even after he had quieted down she went on rocking the carriage back and forth.

Grandfather Zisskind raised his head and said to Yehuda in a whisper:

"You think it was impossible to save him . . . it was possible. They had many friends. Ossip himself wrote to me about it. The manager of the factory had a high opinion of him. The whole town knew them and loved them. . . . How is it they didn't think of it . . . ?" he said, touching his forehead with the palm of his hand. "After all, they knew that the Germans were approaching. . . . It was still possible to do something. . . ." He stopped a moment and then added, "Imagine that a boy of eleven had already finished his studies at the Conservatory—wild beasts!" He suddenly opened eyes filled with terror. "Wild beasts! To take little children and put them into wagons and deport them. . . ."

When Raya returned and sat down at the table, he stopped and became silent, and only a heavy sigh escaped from deep within him.

Again there was a prolonged silence, and as it grew heavier Raya felt the oppressive weight on her bosom increasing till it could no longer be contained. Grandfather sat at the table tapping his thin fingers, and alongside the wall the infant lay in his carriage; it was as if a chasm gaped between a world which was passing and a world that was born. It was no longer a single line to the fourth generation. The aged father did not recognize the great-grandchild whose life would be no memorial.

Grandfather Zisskind got up, took his chair and pulled it up to the clock. He climbed on to it to take out his documents.

Raya could no longer stand the oppressive atmosphere.

"Let's go," she said to Yehuda in a choked voice.

"Yes, we must go," said Yehuda, and rose from his seat. "We have to go," he said loudly as he turned to the old man.

Grandfather Zisskind held the key of the clock for a moment more, then he let his hand fall, grasped the back of the chair and got down.

"You have to go. . . ." he said with a tortured grimace. He spread his arms out helplessly and accompanied them to the doorway.

When the door had closed behind them the tears flowed from Raya's eyes. She bent over the carriage and pressed her lips to the baby's chest. At that moment it seemed to her that he was in need of pity and of great love, as though he were alone, an orphan in the world.

Translated from the Hebrew by Minna Givton

The Night

When night fell I went home; that is, I went to the hotel room I had taken for my wife and myself. I was hurrying, as I knew that my wife was tired out by all the travel and wanted to sleep, and I had no intention of disturbing her.

There was a multitude of people in the streets, mainly new immigrants, who were arriving here from all over the world. For many years they had wasted away in the death camps, or wandered aimlessly over hill and valley, and through forests, all this time without seeing so much as the flicker of a candle, and now that they'd stepped from the dark into this sudden brightness, they seemed puzzled and somewhat suspicious, not being able to grasp whether all the lights had been left burning by an oversight, or whether it was part of some scheme of the authorities.

An old man came toward me, wearing a greenish coat that came down to his knees, exactly like the coat Mr. Halbfried, the bookseller in our town, used to wear for as long as I remember. The coat had lost most of its color, but had kept its original shape. Short coats are better at keeping their shape than long ones, because long coats sweep the ground and get frayed, whereas short coats flutter in the air, and the ground cannot harm them in any way. Even though their appearance might have changed, their hems remain as the tailor finished them and seem to have retained their perfection.

While I was wondering whether this was really Mr. Halbfried, he ran his weary eyes over me and said: "From the day that I arrived here I've been looking for you, and now that we've met I'm happy twice over, once because I've found someone from my home town, and twice because that someone happens to be you." The old man was so excited that he forgot to greet me properly, instead of which he straightway reeled off a string of names, people he'd asked about me, and after each name he'd express his amazement that So-and-so didn't know me, and had he himself failed to recognize me the moment he saw me, he could have passed me as if we were not fellow townsmen. Having come around to mentioning our town, he began talking about the past, the time when we were neighbors, and his bookstore was filled with books that united all the learned people of the town, who were passing in and out of the shop all day, and having heated discussions about what was going on in the world, and about the future, and coming to the conclusion that the world was evolving into a better place, and there was I, a small boy, fingering the books,

climbing the ladder, standing at the top reading, not realizing that I was en-
dangering myself; for had someone blundered into the ladder by mistake, I
could very easily have fallen off. But as if the large stock of books which he
kept were not sufficient for me, I had asked him to get me *The Poem of Jerusalem Liberated*. However, he couldn't remember any more whether he'd
placed the order before I emigrated to the Land of Israel, or whether I did so
before he'd placed the order.

Another thing he was reminded of, said Mr. Halbfried, was the time they
showed my first poems to that old mystic who had written two interpretations
of the prayerbook, and the old man had looked at them and murmured, *"Ke-
hadin kamtza dilevushe mine uve"* ["like the snail whose garb is a part of it"],
and the learned listeners tried hard to understand the meaning of these
words, and did not succeed. He, Mr. Halbfried continued, was still puzzled
that they never took the trouble to look them up in a dictionary, and that he
himself did not do so, although he had a number of dictionaries in stock, and
could have done so quite easily, yet somehow never did.

He broke off his story and asked me was I angry with his brother?—Why?
His brother had just passed us and greeted me, and I made as if I didn't
see him.

Mr. Halbfried's last words shocked and saddened me. I had not noticed
anyone greeting me; as for the man who had passed us, I was under the impression that it was Mr. Halbfried himself. As I didn't wish him to think that
I would turn my eyes away from people who greet me, I said to him: "I swear
I didn't notice your brother; had I noticed him, I would have been the first to
greet him." So Mr. Halbfried began talking once more of the good old days,
of his bookshop and the people who came to it. Every time Mr. Halbfried
mentioned a name, he did so with great warmth, the way we used to talk
about good friends in those long-lost days before the war.

After a while, Mr. Halbfried stopped and said: "I shall leave you now, as
I do not want you to keep a man waiting who wishes to see you." With that
he shook my hand and went away.

The man Mr. Halbfried had mentioned was not known to me, nor did he
seem to be waiting for me; however, Mr. Halbfried's mistake came in handy,
as it enabled me to shake the old man off politely, and so avoid disturbing my
wife's sleep.

But Mr. Halbfried had not been mistaken; after I'd gotten rid of him, this
man barred my way, then poked his stick into the ground and leaned on it
with both hands, while looking at me. Then he lifted his hand in greeting,
lifted it to his cap, a round cap of sheepskin leather, and while he was doing
so, he said: "Don't you know me?" I said to myself: Why tell him I don't
know him? So I gave him a warm look and said: "Certainly I know you,

you're none other than—" He interrupted me and said: "I was sure you'd know me, if not for my own sake, then for the sake of my son. What do you think of his poems?" From this I realized that he was the father of someone or other who had sent me his book of poems. I said to myself: Why tell him that I haven't looked at them yet? So I gave him a warm look and said whatever it is one says on these occasions. Yet he didn't seem satisfied with it. So I said to myself: Why not add a few nice words? So I added a few compliments; but he was still unsatisfied, and began singing his son's praises himself, and I kept nodding my head in agreement, so that an onlooker would have thought that the praise came from my mouth.

Having done, he said: "No doubt you wish to make my son's acquaintance, so go to the concert hall, that's where you'll find him. My son is a well-loved man, all the doors are open to him, not only the doors of music but the doors of all the important houses in town. Why, if my son desired, let's say, to ride on a mouse, why, the animal would rush up to him with its tail between its legs and beg him to take a ride. Truly, I myself would love to go to that concert, all the best members of our intelligentsia will be there, the trouble is they won't let you in if you haven't got a ticket." Saying this, he rubbed two fingers together and made a noise with his lips, as if to say, you need real coins for that.

I kept quiet and did not say a word. It was some years now that I hadn't gone to a concert. I could never understand how a crowd of people could assemble at a fixed date and hour, in a special hall, just to hear some singing. Nor could I understand how it was that the singers were ready to lift up their voices in song at the exact hour the ticket holders were filling the hall, ready to listen.

I'm just a small-town boy; I can grasp that someone is singing because his heart is full; but this singing in front of an audience rich enough to buy tickets, because some impresario organized it all, was beyond me. So when I saw how much this man wanted to go to the concert, I asked myself whether I should help him, and decided to buy him a ticket. He saw what I was thinking, and said, "I won't go without you." I asked myself whether to go with him, and then I said, "All right, I'll buy two tickets, and we'll go together." He started feeling the air, as if it were full of tickets. Again he rubbed two fingers together, and made a popping noise, like a cork coming out of a bottle.

So we walked together, and he kept praising the concert hall, where there was so much music one could almost drown in it. Then he told me about this violinist whose violin was so precious that even the case he carried it in was worth more than the instruments of other violinists. Then he returned to his son, to whom poetical rhymes came for the sole purpose of the matching of words. Then he returned to the subject of the tickets, out of respect for which the doors used to open themselves. Suddenly he began worrying, as it occurred to him that he could be wasting his time, for, although I seemed willing enough to buy him a ticket, what if every seat was sold out, or supposing there was only one single ticket left—wouldn't I buy it for myself, and leave him standing outside. Thus we came to my hotel.

I said to him: "Wait here, I'm going in to change, and then we're off to the concert." He poked his stick into the ground, leaned on it with both hands, and stood there.

I left him outside and told the doorman I wanted two tickets for the concert. The doorman said: "I have two good tickets, which were ordered by the Duke of Ilivio, but he left them with me, as he cannot come since he has been called to the Emperor." Here the doorman whispered to me that the Emperor had arrived secretly in town, with most of his retinue, dukes, lords, and officers, and that some of them were actually staying at our hotel.

I took the tickets and went up to my room, leaving the door open so that I could change by the light in the corridor, and not have to turn on the light in the room, which would have awakened my wife. I walked in on tiptoe, noiselessly, and to my surprise and distress I found a strange man in the room. Who was that who dared to enter my room in the dark of the night? Should the earth refuse to open at his feet and swallow him, then I would be forced to throw him out myself, and not too politely, either.

As I approached him, I saw that it was Moshele, a relative of mine. This Moshele and I had grown up together, and we went through difficult times together, until one day he was called up into the army, where he stayed until he was wounded and dismissed. We thought that he had been burned in the gas chambers of Auschwitz, but here he stood, alive, in my room.

I said, "What brought you here?" He said, "My troubles brought me here. I have been shuffling from one mound of refuse to another without a roof over my head, and when I heard you were here I came running, for I was sure that you would put me up."

I said to him: "Do I have a home that you should ask to sleep here? As you can see, I'm myself but a guest for the night."

He said: "All I'm asking is a place on the floor."

I began laughing. A hotel where dukes and lords live, and he wants to sleep on the floor.

I don't know if his brain succeeded in grasping what I meant and if his heart accepted my words. In any case, he got up and left.

I went to the window to watch him go, and I saw him in the street, cowering as he was hit by the whips of the coachmen who drove the coaches of the nobility. I called to him, but he didn't answer me; I called to him again and he didn't answer, probably being too busy trying to evade the whips to hear my voice. I decided to call louder, but then I remembered that my wife was sleeping, so I didn't. And it is probably just as well, for, had I shouted, all the other coachmen would have seen him too, and joined in beating him.

I looked after Moshele until he disappeared from view. Then I went to the wardrobe to change.

Two small children came in and started walking around me in circles. As I opened the door of the wardrobe to take some clothes, one of them jumped in, and his brother jumped after him, and they shut the wardrobe door behind them. I was somewhat perplexed; as they were probably the sons of a duke or a lord, I couldn't very well be rude to them. On the other hand, I couldn't let them go on playing, as they were liable to wake my wife.

Their governess came and helped me out of this trouble. She said to them: "If I may be so bold as to say, it behooves not the princes to enter the room of a strange person."

I apologized to the governess for having left the door of my room open and caused the two king's sons to enter my room. I added that I was going to the concert and had only come to dress.

The governess examined my clothes with her eyes and said: "You can't show yourself in that collar you're wearing." I said to her: "Yes, you're quite right." She said: "Surely, you can find another collar." "Probably," I said. She said: "Go on, put it on." I said to her: "I am afraid that when the king's son did me the honor of jumping into my wardrobe, he trampled on my collars, and they got soiled." She said: "In that case, I'll tie your tie. Your gracious highnesses, would you be so kind as to leave the room until I finish tying the tie of this gentleman, who is the brother of your teacher." The little boys stood there and looked very surprised that this creature, which had been created to serve them, should now wish to serve a simple mortal.

The graciousness of the young lady and the envy of the king's sons put me into a much better mood. I stuttered somewhat and said: "It is not my custom to go to concerts, but what is a custom worth if you're not ready to disregard it for the sake of another person." The young lady didn't pay much attention to my words; she was too busy tying and then untying every knot she tied, saying, "It wasn't such a knot I meant to tie, now I shall tie one that is much handsomer." Finally, she stroked my arm and said: "Look in the mirror and see how beautifully tied your tie is." I said to her: "I cannot look in the mirror." "Why?" "Because the mirror is screwed onto the inside of the wardrobe door, and if I opened it wide it would squeak and wake my wife." "Your wife?" screamed the young lady in a rage. "And here you were talking to me as if we were alone in the room. If your wife is here, then go and be happy with her." With that the young lady went away.

"Who were you talking to," asked my wife. I said to her: "No one." She said: "I must have been dreaming." I said to her: "Dream or not, I'm going out for a walk, and won't be back till after midnight."

I went looking for the man who was waiting for me in front of the hotel, but he was nowhere to be seen. I asked the doorman about him; he answered: "Some time ago I did see a person loitering in front of the hotel. Had I known he was a friend of yours, sir, I would have looked at him more carefully." I said to the doorman: "Where could he be now?" "Where? I really don't know." "Which way did he go?" "Well," said the doorman, "I seem to remember that he turned right, or maybe it was left, people like these have round shoulders and one never knows quite which way they turn." I gave him a tip. He bowed low and said: "If your excellency would care to listen to my advice, he would visit the servants' quarters in the hotel, as the serfs of the nobles have brought a Jewish clown with them, and it is quite possible that the man your excellency is looking for has gone there to see the fun."

I went to the servants' quarters of the hotel, and saw the serfs sitting like masters, their bellies shaking with laughter, and a small man, shrunken and beautiful, standing on the big stage doing tricks, and talking all the while. When the tricks were funny, his voice was sad, and when they were sad, his voice was funny. I wondered whether he did it on purpose. It seemed to me to be great art, being funny in a sad voice, and being sad in a funny voice. I looked around and found the man I was searching for. I waved the two tickets at him, but he pretended not to see me, and left. It seemed as if his leaving were only temporary, because of me, that is, and he was likely to return as soon as I had gone.

Another man came up to me; he had a long face and a cheerful beard. He stroked his beard and said: "Who are you looking for?" I told him. He said: "I could manage to go with you to the concert." I threw a look at him and shouted in amazement: "What! You?" He shook his beard and said: "Why not?" I repeated what I had said before, only with a great deal of sarcasm: "What! You?" He disappeared, and so did his beard. "What do we do now?" I thought to myself. I waved the tickets in the air, but nothing happened. The man I was waving at didn't show up. So I said to myself: Not only can't I give him the pleasure of a concert, I'm even preventing him from the pleasure of seeing the clown, as he won't show his face in the audience as long as I'm here. I got up and left.

As this man didn't wish to come, I gave up the idea of going to the concert; but, having told my wife that I wouldn't be in before midnight, not until the singer had finished his recital, I had time to take a walk. I began thinking about what had happened, about these incidents which seemed to grow each out of the other, and yet there was no connection between them. I started from the beginning, from the ladder in the bookstore, *The Poem of Jerusalem Liberated,* and that small creature whose garb is a part of him.

After skipping over some matters, I got to thinking of Moshele, my own flesh and blood, who had escaped the fires of cremation and now was shuffling from one mound of refuse to another. As the concert had not yet come to an end and it was not yet time for me to return to my room, I was able to think a great many thoughts. As I strolled along I thought: If only I could find Moshele now that I am just strolling and have nothing else to do, I would talk to him and let him tell me all his troubles; I would appease him and bring him to the inn, give him food and drink and order a soft, warm bed, and we would part from each other with a hearty goodnight. As I was strolling and thinking such thoughts, it suddenly dawned on me that there could be nothing finer. But favors do not come at all times, or to anyone. Moshele had been saved from cremation, and as an added favor it had been given him to find his own flesh and blood. Whereas I, who was his flesh and blood—no favors at all were granted to me, and I couldn't find Moshele again.

Finally, the singer ended his song and the audience went home. I too returned to the room at the hotel and closed the door behind me carefully, as an open door calls to uninvited guests. But there are guests who come no matter how tightly one's door is shut, as they are the thoughts surrounding our actions. So many guests came that the air in the room got fouler and fouler, and I was afraid I was going to choke. I then untied the knot which the young lady had made in my tie, and that helped a little. Now there was more air to breathe, and the guests brought some more guests, and very soon I was choking again.

Translated from the Hebrew by Yoram Matmor

Hanka

This trip made little sense from the start. First, it didn't pay financially to leave New York and my work for two and a half months to go to Argentina for a lecture tour; second, I should have taken an airplane instead of wasting my time on a ship for eighteen days. But I had signed the contract and accepted a first-class round-trip ticket on *La Plata* from my impresario, Chazkel Poliva. That summer, the heat lasted into October. On the day I embarked, the thermometer registered ninety degrees. I was always assailed by premonitions and phobias before a trip: I would get sick; the ship would sink; some other calamity would occur. An inner voice warned me, Don't go! However, if I had made a practice of acting on these premonitions, I would not have come to America but would have perished in Nazi-occupied Poland.

As it happened, I was provided with all possible comforts. My cabin looked like a salon, with two square windows, a sofa, a desk, and pictures on the walls. The bathroom had both a tub and a shower stall. The number of passengers was small, mostly Latin Americans, and the service staff was large. In the dining room I had a special wine steward who promptly filled my glass each time I took a sip of wine. A band of five musicians played at lunch and dinner. Every second day the captain gave a cocktail party. But for some reason I could not make any acquaintances on this ship. The few passengers who spoke English kept to themselves. The men, all young six-foot giants, played shuffleboard and cavorted in the swimming pool. The women were too tall and too athletic for my taste. In the evening, they all danced or sat at the bar, drinking and smoking. I made up my mind that I would remain isolated, and it seemed that others sensed my decision. No one spoke a word to me. I began to wonder if by some magic I had become one who sees and is not seen. After a while I stopped attending the cocktail parties and I asked that my meals be served in my cabin. In Trinidad and in Brazil, where the ship stopped for a day, I walked around alone. I had taken little to read with me, because I was sure that the ship would have a library. But it consisted of a single glass-doored bookcase with some fifty or so volumes in Spanish and perhaps a dozen in English—all moldy travel books printed a hundred years ago. This book-case was kept locked, and each time I wanted to exchange a book there was a commotion about who had the key; I would be sent from one member of the staff to the other. Eventually an officer with epaulets would write down my name, the number of my stateroom, the titles and authors of my books. This took him at least fifteen minutes.

When the ship approached the Equator, I stopped going out on deck in the daytime. The sun burned like a flame. The days had shortened and night came swiftly. One moment it was light, the next it was dark. The sun did not set but fell into the water like a meteor. Late in the evening, when I went out briefly, a hot wind slapped my face. From the ocean came a roar of passions that seemed to have broken through all barriers: "We must procreate and multiply! We must exhaust all the powers of lust!" The waves glowed like lava, and I imagined I could see multitudes of living beings—algae, whales, sea monsters—reveling in an orgy, from the surface to the bottom of the sea. Immortality was the law here. The whole planet raged with animation. At times, I heard my name in the clamor: the spirit of the abyss calling me to join them in their nocturnal dance.

In Buenos Aires I was met by Chazkel Poliva—a short, round person— and a young woman who introduced herself as my relative. Her name was Hanka and she was, she said, a great-granddaughter of my Aunt Yentel from her first husband. Actually, Hanka was not my relative, because my Uncle Aaron was Yentel's third husband. Hanka was petite, lean, and had a head of pitch-black hair, full lips, and eyes as black as onyx. She wore a dark dress and a black, broad-brimmed hat. She could have been thirty or thirty-five. Hanka immediately told me that in Warsaw someone had hidden her on the Aryan side—the way she was saved from the Nazis. She was a dancer, she said, but even before she told me I saw it in the muscles of her calves. I asked her where she danced and she replied, "At Jewish affairs and at my own troubles."

Chazkel Poliva took us in his car to the Hotel Cosmopolitan on Junín Street, which was once famous as the main street of the red-light district. Poliva said that the neighborhood had been cleaned up and all the literati now stayed in this hotel. The three of us ate supper in a restaurant on Corrientes Avenue, and Chazkel Poliva handed me a schedule covering my four weeks in Argentina. I was to lecture in Buenos Aires at the Théâtre Soleil and at the Jewish Community Center, and also I was to go to Rosario, Mar del Plata, and to the Jewish colonies in Moisés Ville and in Entre Ríos. The Warsaw Society, the Yiddish section of the P.E.N. Club, the journalists of the newspaper that published my articles, and a number of Yiddish schools were all preparing receptions.

When Poliva was alone with me for a moment, he asked, "Who is this woman? She says that she dances at Jewish affairs, but I've never seen her anywhere. While we were waiting for you, I suggested that she give me her address and telephone number in case I needed to get in touch with her, but she refused. Who is she?"

"I really don't know."

Chazkel Poliva had another engagement that evening and left us after dinner. I wanted to pay the bill—why should he pay for a woman who was supposed to be my relative?—but he would not permit it. I noticed that Hanka ate nothing—she had only a glass of wine. She accompanied me back to the hotel. It was not long after Perón had been ousted, and Argentina was in the midst of a political and perhaps economic crisis. Buenos Aires, it seemed, was short of electricity. The streets were dimly lit. Here and there a gendarme patrolled, carrying a machine gun. Hanka took my arm and we walked through Corrientes Avenue. I couldn't see any physical resemblance in her to my Aunt Yentel, but she had her style of talking: she jumped from one subject to another, confused names, places, dates. She asked me, "Is this your first visit to Argentina? Here the climate is crazy and so are the people. In Warsaw there was spring fever; here one fevers all year round. When it's hot, you melt from the heat. When the rains begin, the cold eats into your bones. It is actually one big jungle. The cities are oases in the pampas. For years, the pimps and whores controlled the Jewish immigrants. Later, they were excommunicated and had to build a synagogue and acquire a cemetery of their own. The Jews who came here after the Holocaust are lost creatures. How is it that they don't translate you into Spanish? When did you last see my great-grandmother Yentel? I didn't know her, but she left me as an inheritance a chain with a locket that was perhaps two hundred years old. I sold it for bread. Here is your hotel. If you're not tired, I'll go up with you for a while."

We took the elevator to the sixth floor. From childhood I have had a liking for balconies; there was one outside my room and we went there directly. There were few high constructions in Buenos Aires, so we could see a part of the city. I brought out two chairs and we sat down. Hanka was saying, "You must wonder why I came to meet you. As long as I had near relatives—a father, a mother, a brother, a sister—I did not appreciate them. Now that they are all ashes, I am yearning for relatives, no matter how distant. I read the Yiddish press. You often mention your Aunt Yentel in your stories. Did she really tell you all those weird tales? You probably make them up. In my own life, things happened that cannot possibly be told. I am alone, completely alone."

"A young woman does not have to be alone."

"Just words. There are circumstances when you are torn away like a leaf from a tree and no power can attach you again. The wind carries you from your roots. There's a name for it in Hebrew, but I've forgotten."

"Na-v'nad —a fugitive and a wanderer."

"That's it."

I expected that I would have a short affair with Hanka. But when I tried to embrace her she seemed to shrink in my arms. I kissed her and her lips were cold. She said, "I can understand you—you are a man. You will find plenty of women here if you look for them. You will find them even if you don't look. But you are a normal person, not a necrophile. I belong to an exterminated tribe and we are not material for sex."

My lecture at the Théâtre Soleil having been postponed for some days, Hanka promised to return the next evening. I asked for her telephone number and she said that her telephone was out of order. In Buenos Aires, when something is broken, you can wait months until it is repaired. Before she left, Hanka told me almost casually that while she was looking for relatives in Buenos Aires she had found a second cousin of mine—Jechiel, who had changed his name to Julio. Jechiel was the son of my granduncle Avigdor. I had met Jechiel twice—once in the village of Tishewitz, and the second time in Warsaw, where he came for medical treatment. Jechiel was about ten years older than I—tall, darkish, and emaciated. I remembered that he suffered from tuberculosis and that Uncle Avigdor had brought him to Warsaw to see a lung specialist. I had felt sure that Jechiel did not survive the Holocaust, and now I heard that he was alive and in Argentina. Hanka gave me some details. He came to Argentina with a wife and a daughter, but he divorced his wife and married a Frampol girl whom he met in a concentration camp. He became a peddler—a knocker, as they were called in Buenos Aires. His new wife was illiterate and was afraid to go out of the house by herself. She hadn't learned a word of Spanish. When she needed to go to the grocery for a loaf of bread or for potatoes, Jechiel had to accompany her. Lately, Jechiel had been suffering from asthma and had to give up his peddling. He was living on a pension—what kind of a pension Hanka did not know: perhaps from the city or from some charitable society.

I was tired after the long day, and the moment Hanka left I fell onto the bed in my clothes and slept. After a few hours, I awoke and went out onto the balcony. It was strange to be in a country thousands of miles from my present home. In America fall was approaching; in Argentina it was spring. It had rained while I slept and Junín Street glistened. Old houses lined the street; its stalls were shuttered with iron bars. I could see the rooftops and parts of the brick walls of buildings in adjoining streets. Here and there a reddish light glimmered in a window. Was someone sick? Had someone died? In Warsaw, when I was a boy, I often heard gruesome tales about Buenos Aires: a pimp would carry a poor girl, an orphan, away to this wicked city and try to seduce her with baubles and promises, and, if she did not give in, with blows, tearing her hair and sticking pins into her fingers. Our neighbor Basha used to talk about this with my sister Hinda. Basha would say, "What could the girl do? They took her away on a ship and kept her in chains. She had already lost her innocence. She was sold into a brothel and she had to do what she was told. Sooner or later she got a little worm in her blood, and with this she could not live long. After seven years of disgrace, her hair and teeth fell out, her nose rotted away, and the play was over. Since she was defiled, they buried her behind the fence." I remember my sister's asking, "Alive?"

Now Warsaw was destroyed and I found myself in Buenos Aires, in the neighborhood where misfortunes like this were supposed to have taken place. Basha and my sister Hinda were both dead, and I was not a small boy but a middle-aged writer who had come to Argentina to spread culture.

It rained all the next day. Perhaps for the same reason that there was a shortage of electricity, the telephones didn't work properly—a man would be speaking to me in Yiddish when suddenly I was listening to a female laughing and screaming in Spanish. In the evening Hanka came. We could not go out into the street, so I ordered supper from room service. I asked Hanka what she wanted to eat and she said, "Nothing."

"What do you mean by nothing?"

"A glass of tea."

I didn't listen to her and I ordered a meat supper for her and a vegetarian platter for myself. I ate everything; Hanka barely touched the food on her plate. Like Aunt Yentel, she spewed forth stories.

"They knew in the whole house that he was hiding a Jewish girl. The tenants certainly knew. The Aryan side teemed with *szmalcownicy*[1]—this is what they were called—who extorted the last penny from Jews to protect them and then denounced them to the Nazis. My Gentile—Andrzej was his name—had no money. Any minute someone could have notified the Gestapo[2] and we would have all been shot—I, Andrzej, Stasiek, his son, and Maria, his wife. What am I saying? Shooting was considered light punishment. We would have been tortured. All the tenants would have paid with their lives for that crime. I often told him, 'Andrzej, my dear, you have done enough. I don't want to bring disaster on all of you.' But he said, 'Don't go, don't go. I cannot send you away to your death. Perhaps there is a God after all.' I was hidden in an alcove without a window, and they put a clothes closet at the door to conceal the entrance. They removed a board from the back of the closet and through it they passed my food and, forgive me, they took out the chamber pot. When I extinguished the little lamp I had, it became dark like in a

1. Term of disparagement: greasers; those who got "fat" on or took advantage of the victimization of Jews.

2. Gestapo: (*Geheime Staatspolizei* or Secret State Police). Together with the *Kriminalpolizei*, the Gestapo constituted the Security Police (*Sicherheitspolizei*).

grave. He came to me, and both of them knew about it—his wife and their son. Maria had a female sickness. Their son was sick, too. When he was a child he developed scrofula or some glandular illness and he did not need a woman. I don't think he even grew a beard. He had one passion—reading newspapers. He read all the Warsaw papers, including the advertisements. Did Andrzej satisfy me? I did not look for satisfaction. I was glad that he was relieved. From too much reading, my eyesight dimmed. I became so constipated that only castor oil would help me. Yes, I lay in my grave. But if you lie in a grave long enough, you get accustomed to it and you don't want to part from it. He had given me a pill of cyanide. He and his wife and their son also carried such pills. We all lived with death, and I want you to know that one can fall in love with death. Whoever has loved death cannot love anything else any more. When the liberation came and they told me to leave, I didn't want to go. I clung to the threshold like an ox being dragged to the slaughter.

"How I came to Argentina and what happened between me and José is a story for another time. I did not deceive him. I told him, 'José, if your wife is not lively enough, what do you need a corpse for?' But men do not believe me. When they see a woman who is young, not ugly, and can dance besides, how can she be dead? Also, I had no strength to go to work in a factory with the Spanish women. He bought me a house and this became my second grave—a fancy grave, with flowerpots, bric-a-brac, a piano. He told me to dance and I danced. In what way is it worse than to knit sweaters or to sew on buttons? All day long I sat alone and waited for him. In the evening he came, drunk and angry. One day he spoke to me and told me stories; the next day he would be mute. I knew that sooner or later he would stop talking to me altogether. When it happened I was not surprised, and I didn't try to make him talk, because I knew it was fated. He maintained his silence for over a year. Finally I told him, 'José, go.' He kissed my forehead and he left. I never saw him again."

The plans for my lecture tour began to go awry. The engagement in Rosario was called off because the president of the organization suffered a heart attack. The board of directors of the Jewish Community Center in Buenos Aires had a falling out over political differences, and the subsidy that they were to give to the colonies for my lectures there was withheld. In Mar del Plata, the hall I was to speak in suddenly became unavailable. In addition to the problems of the tour, the weather in Buenos Aires worsened from day to day. There was lightning, thunder, and from the provinces came news of windstorms and floods. The mail system didn't seem to be functioning. Proofs of a new book were supposed to come by airmail from New York, but they did not arrive and I worried that the book might be published without my final corrections. Once I was stuck in an elevator between the fourth and fifth floors and it took almost two hours before I got free. In New York I had been assured that I would not have hay fever in Buenos Aires, because it was spring there. But I suffered from attacks of sneezing, my eyes watered, my throat constricted—and I didn't even have my antihistamines with me. Chazkel Poliva stopped calling, and I suspected that he was about to cancel the whole tour. I was ready to return to New York—but how could I get information about a ship when the telephone did not work and I didn't know a word of Spanish?

Hanka came to my room every evening, always at the same time—I even imagined at the same minute. She entered noiselessly. I looked up and there she was, standing in the dusk—an image surrounded by shadows. I ordered dinner and Hanka would begin her soliloquy in the quiet monotone that reminded me of my Aunt Yentel. One night Hanka spoke about her childhood in Warsaw. They lived on Hoźa Street in a Gentile neighborhood. Her father, a manufacturer, was always in debt—on the edge of bankruptcy. Her mother bought her dresses in Paris. In the summer they vacationed in Zoppot, in the winter in Zakopane. Hanka's brother Zdzislaw studied in a private high school. Her older sister, Edzia, loved to dance, but their mother insisted it was Hanka who must become another Pavlova or Isadora Duncan. The dance teacher was a sadist. Even though she was ugly and a cripple herself, she demanded perfection from her pupils. She had the eyes of a hawk, she hissed like a snake. She taunted Hanka about her Jewishness. Hanka was saying, "My parents had one remedy for all our troubles—assimilation. We had to be one-hundred-per-cent Poles. But what kind of Poles could we be when my grandfather Asher, your Aunt Yentel's son, could not even speak Polish? Whenever he visited us, we almost died from shame. My maternal grandfather, Yudel, spoke a broken Polish. He once told me that we were descended from Spanish Jews. They had been driven from Spain in the fifteenth century, and our ancestors wandered first to Germany and then, in the Hundred Years' War, to Poland. I felt the Jewishness in my blood. Edzia and Zdzislaw were both blond and had blue eyes, but I was dark. I began at an early age to ponder the eternal questions: Why is one born? Why must one die? What does God want? Why so much suffering? My mother insisted that I read the Polish and French popular novels, but I stealthily looked into the Bible. In the Book of Proverbs I read the words 'Charm is deceitful, and beauty is vain,' and I fell in love with that book. Perhaps because I was forced to make an idol of my body, I developed a hatred for the flesh. My mother and my sister were fascinated by the beauty of movie actresses. In the dancing school the talk was always of hips, thighs, legs, breasts. When a girl gained as much as a quarter of a pound, the teacher created a scene. All this seemed petty and vulgar to me. From too much dancing, we developed bunions and bulging muscles. I was often complimented for my dancing, but I was possessed by the dybbuk[3] of an old Talmudist, one of those whitebeards who used to come to us to ask for alms and were chased away by our maid. My dybbuk would ask, 'For whom are you going to dance—for the Nazis?' Shortly before the war, when Polish students chased the Jews through the Saxony Gardens and my brother Zdzislaw had to stand up at the lectures in the university because he refused to sit on the ghetto benches, he became a Zionist. But I realized that the worldly Jews in Palestine were also eager to imitate the Gentiles. My brother played football. He belonged to the Maccabee sports club. He lifted weights to develop his muscles. How tragic that all my family who loved life so much had to die in the concentration camps, while fate brought me to Argentina.

"I learned Spanish quickly—the words seemed to flow back into me. I tried to dance at Jewish affairs, but everything here is rootless. Here they believe that the Jewish State will end our misfortunes once and forever. This is sheer optimism. We are surrounded there by hordes of enemies whose aim is the same as Hitler's—to exterminate us. Ten times they may not succeed—but the eleventh, catastrophe. I see the Jews being driven into the sea. I hear the wailing of the women and the children. Why is suicide considered such a sin? My own feeling is that the greatest virtue would be to abandon the body and all its iniquities."

That night, when Hanka left, I did not ask her when she would return. My lecture in the Théâtre Soleil had been advertised for the next day, and I expected her to attend. I had slept little the night before, and I went to bed and fell asleep immediately. I wakened with a feeling that someone was whispering in my ear. I tried to light the lamp by my bed, but it did not go on. I groped for the wall switch, but I could not locate it. I had hung my jacket containing my passport and traveler's checks on a chair; the chair was gone. Had I been robbed? I felt my way around the room like a blind man, tripping and bruising my knee. After a while, I stumbled into the chair. No one had taken my passport or my traveler's checks. But my gloom did not lessen. I knew that I'd had a bad dream, and I stood in the dark trying to recollect it. The second I closed my eyes, I was with the dead. They did things words cannot express. They spoke madness. "I will not let her into my room again," I murmured. "This Hanka is my angel of death."

I sat down on the edge of the bed, draped the covers over my shoulders, and took calculation of my soul. This trip had stirred up all my anxieties. I had not prepared any notes for my lecture, "Literature and the Supernatural,"

3. A condemned soul that attempts to inhabit the body of a living person and control that person's actions.

and I was apprehensive that I might suddenly become speechless; I foresaw a bloody revolution in Argentina, an atomic war between the United States and Russia; I would become desperately sick. Wild absurdities invaded my mind: What would happen if I got into bed and found a crocodile there? What would happen if the earth were to split into two parts and my part were to fly off to another constellation? What if my going to Argentina had actually been a departure into the next world? I had an uncanny feeling of Hanka's presence. In the left corner of the room I saw a silhouette, a dense whorl that stood apart from the surrounding darkness and took on the shadowy form of a body—shoulders, head, hair. Though I could not make out its face, I sensed in the lurking phantom the mocking of my cowardices. God in heaven, this trip was waking all the fears of my cheder days,[4] when I dared not sleep alone because monsters slithered around my bed, tore at my sidelocks, screeching at me with terrifying voices. In my fright, I began to pray to God to keep me from falling into the hands of the Evil Ones. It seems that my prayer was heard, for suddenly the lamp went on. I saw my face in the mirror—white as after a sickness. I went to the door to make sure it was locked. Then I limped back to the bed.

The next day I spoke in the Théâtre Soleil. The hall was filled with people in spite of the heavy rain outside. I saw so many familiar faces in the audience that I could scarcely believe my eyes. True, I did not remember their names, but they reminded me of friends and acquaintances from Bilgoray, Lublin, Warsaw. Was it possible that so many had been saved from the Nazis and come to my lecture? As a rule, when I spoke about the supernatural, there were interruptions from the audience—even protest. But here, when I concluded, there was ominous silence. I wanted to go down into the audience and greet these resurrected images of my past; instead, Chazkel Poliva led me behind the stage, and by the time I made my way to the auditorium the overhead lights were extinguished and the seats empty. I said, "Shall I speak now to the spirits?"

As if he were reading my mind, Poliva asked, "Where is your so-called cousin? I didn't see her in the hall."

"No, she did not come."

"I don't want to mix into your private affairs, but do me a favor and get rid of her. It's not good for you that she should trail after you."

"No. But why do you say this?"

Chazkel Poliva hesitated. "She frightens me. She will bring you bad luck."

4. Days spent at an old-fashioned Hebrew elementary school. *Cheder* is Hebrew for *room*. Hebrew classes in Eastern Europe were originally held in the room where the teacher and his family resided.

"Do you believe in such things?"

"When you have been an impresario for thirty years, you have to believe in them."

I had dozed off and evening had fallen. Was it the day after my lecture or a few days later? I opened my eyes and Hanka stood at my bedside. I saw embarrassment in her eyes, as if she knew my plight and felt guilty. She said, "We are supposed to go to your cousin Julio this evening."

I had prepared myself to say to her, "I cannot see you again," but I asked, "Where does Julio live?"

"It's not too far. You said that you like to walk."

Ordinarily I would have invited her to dinner, but I had no intention of dallying with her late into the night. Perhaps Julio would offer us something to eat. Half asleep, I got up and we walked out onto Corrientes. Only an occasional street light was lit, and armed soldiers were patrolling the streets. All the stores were closed. There was an air of curfew and Black Sabbath.[5] We walked in silence, like a pair who have quarreled yet must still go visiting together. Corrientes is one of the longest boulevards in the world. We walked for an hour. Each time I asked if we were nearing our destination Hanka replied that we had some distance to go yet. After a while we turned off Corrientes. It seemed that Julio lived in a suburb. We passed factories with smokeless chimneys and barred windows, dark garages, warehouses with their windows sealed, empty lots overgrown with weeds. The few private homes we saw looked old, their patios enclosed by fences. I was tense and glanced sideways at Hanka. I could not distinguish her face—just two dark eyes. Unseen dogs were barking; unseen cats mewed and yowled. I was not hungry but unsavory fluids filled my mouth. Suspicions fell on me like locusts: Is this my final walk? Is she leading me into a cave of murderers? Perhaps she is a shedevil and will soon reveal her goose feet and pig's snout?

As if Hanka grasped that her silence made me uneasy, she became talkative. We were passing a sprawling house, with no windows, the remnants of a fence, and a lone cactus tree in front. Hanka began, "This is where the old Spanish Gentiles live. There is no heat in these houses—the ovens are for cooking, not for heating. When the rains come, they freeze. They have a drink that they call maté. They cover themselves with ragged clothes, sip maté, and lay out cards. They are Catholics, but the churches here are half empty even on Sunday. The men don't go, only the women. They are witches who pray to the devil, not to God. Time has stopped for them—they are a

---

5. Any sabbath chosen by the Nazis as a time to commit an atrocity.

throwback to the era of Queen Isabella and Torquemada.[6] José left me many books, and since I stopped dancing and have no friends I keep reading. I know Argentina. Sometimes I think I have lived here in a former incarnation. The men still dream of inquisitions and autos-da-fé. The women mutter incantations and cast spells on their enemies. At forty they are wrinkled and wilted. The husbands find mistresses, who immediately begin to spawn children, and after a few years they are as jealous, bitter, and shabby as the wives. They may not know it, but many of them descend from the Marranos.[7] Somewhere in the faraway provinces there are sects that light candles Friday evening and keep a few other Jewish customs. Here we are."

We entered an alley that was under construction. There was no pavement, no sidewalk. We made our way between piles of boards and heaps of bricks and cement. A few unfinished houses stood without roofs, without panes in the windows. The house where Julio lived was narrow and low. Hanka knocked, but no one answered. She pushed the door open, and we went through a tiny foyer into a dimly lit room furnished only with two chairs and a chest. On one chair sat Jechiel. I recognized him only because I knew that it was he. He looked ancient, but from behind his aged face, as if from behind a mask, the Jechiel of former times showed. His skull was bald, with a few wisps of side hair that were neither gray nor black but colorless. He had sunken cheeks, a pointed chin, the throat of a plucked rooster, and the pimpled nose of an alcoholic. Half of his forehead and one cheek were stained with a red rash. Jechiel did not lift his eyelids when we entered. I never saw his eyes that evening. On the other chair sat a squat, wide-girthed woman with ash-colored, disheveled hair; she was wearing a shabby housecoat. Her face was round and pasty, her eyes blank and watery, like the eyes one sees in asylums for the mentally sick. It was hard to determine whether she was forty or sixty. She did not budge. She reminded me of a stuffed doll.

From the way Hanka had spoken, I presumed that she was well acquainted with them and that she had told them of me. But she seemed to be meeting them for the first time.

I said, "Jechiel, I am your cousin Isaac, the son of Bathsheba. We met once in Tishewitz and later in Warsaw."

"*Sí.*"

---

6. Queen Isabella of Spain (1451–1504) placed the Inquisition under royal control and was a prime mover in the expulsion of the Jews (1492). Tomas de Torquemada was inquisitor general during the Spanish Inquisition.

7. Spanish term applied to those Jews in Spain who, after the 1391 persecutions, were compelled to adopt Christianity yet in many cases secretly practiced Judaism and remained faithful to it.

"Do you recognize me?"

"*Sí.*"

"You have forgotten Yiddish?" I asked.

"No."

No, he had not forgotten Yiddish, but it seemed that he had forgotten how to speak. He dozed and yawned. I had to drag conversation from him. To all my questions he answered either "*Sí,*" "*No,*" or "*Bueno.*" Neither he nor his wife made an effort to bring something for us to sit on or a glass of tea. Even though I am not tall, my head almost touched the ceiling. Hanka leaned against the wall in silence. Her face had lost all expression. I walked over to Jechiel's wife and asked, "Do you have someone left in Frampol?"

For what seemed a very long time there came no answer; then she said, "Nobody."

"What was your father's name?"

She pondered as if she had to remind herself. "Avram Itcha."

"What did he do?"

Again a long pause. "A shoemaker."

After a half hour, I wearied of drawing answers from this numb couple. There was an air of fatigue about them that baffled me. Each time I addressed Jechiel, he started as if I had wakened him.

"If you have an interest in me, you can call the Hotel Cosmopolitan," I said at last.

"*Sí.*"

Jechiel's wife did not utter a sound when I said good night to her. Jechiel mumbled something I could not understand and collapsed into his chair. I thought I heard him snore. Outside, I said to Hanka, "If this is possible, anything is possible."

"We shouldn't have visited them at night," Hanka said. "They're both sick. He suffers from asthma and she has a bad heart. I told you, they became acquainted in Auschwitz. Didn't you notice the numbers on their arms?"

"No."

"Those who stood at the threshold of death remain dead."

I had heard these words from Hanka and from other refugees before, but in this dark alley they made me shudder. I said, "Whatever you are, be so good as to get me a taxi."

"*Sí.*"

Hanka embraced me. She leaned against me and clung to me. I did not stir. We stood silent in the alley, and a needlelike rain began to fall on us. Someone extinguished the light in Julio's house and it became as dark around us as in Tishewitz.

The sun was shining, the sky had cleared, it shone blue and summery. The air smelled of the sea, of mango and orange trees. Blossoms fell from their branches. The breezes reminded me of the Vistula and of Warsaw. Like the weather, my lecture tour had also cleared up. All kinds of institutions invited me to speak and gave banquets for me. Schoolchildren honored me with dancing and songs. It was bewildering that such a fuss should be made about a writer, but Argentina is isolated and when they get a guest they receive him with exaggerated friendliness.

Chazkel Poliva said, "It's all because you freed yourself of Hanka."

I had not freed myself. I was searching for her. Since the night we visited Julio, Hanka had not come to see me. And there was no way I could get in touch with her. I did not know where she lived; I didn't even know her surname. I had asked for her address more than once, but she had always avoided answering. Neither did I hear from Julio. No matter how I tried to describe his little alley, no one could identify it for me. I looked in the telephone book—Julio's name was not listed.

I went up to my room late. Going onto the balcony at night had become a habit with me. A cool wind was blowing, bringing me greetings from the Antarctic and South Pole. I raised my eyes and saw different stars, different constellations. Some groups of stars reminded me of consonants, vowels, and the musical notations I had studied in cheder—an *aleph,* a *hai,* a *shuruk,* a *segul,* a *tsairai,* a *chain.* The sickle of the moon seemed to hang reversed, ready to harvest the heavenly fields backward. Over the roofs of Junín Street, the southern sky stretched, strangely near aud divinely distant, a cosmic illumination of a volume without a beginning and without an end—to be read and judged by the Author himself. I was calling to Hanka, "Why did you run away? Wherever you are, come back. There can be no world without you. You are an eternal letter in God's scroll."

In Mar del Plata, the hall had become available, and I went there with Chazkel Poliva. On the train he said to me, "You may think it crazy, but here in Argentina Communism is a game for the rich. A poor man cannot become a member of the Communist Party. Don't ask me any questions. So it is. The rich Jews who have villas in Mar del Plata and will come tonight to your lecture are all leftists. Do me a favor and don't speak about mysticism to them. They don't believe in it. They babble constantly about the social revolution, although when the revolution comes they will be its first victims."

"This in itself is a mystery."

"Yes. But we want your lecture to be a success."

I did what Poliva told me to do. I didn't mention the hidden powers. After the lecture, I read a humorous sketch. When I finished and the question-

and-answer period began, an old man rose and asked me about my inclination toward the supernatural. Soon questions on this subject came from all sides. That night the rich Jews in Mar del Plata showed great interest in telepathy, clairvoyance, dybbuks, premonitions, reincarnation: "If there is life after death, why don't the slaughtered Jews take revenge on the Nazis?" "If there is telepathy, why do we need the telephone?" "If it is possible that thought influences inanimate objects, how does it come that the bank in the casino makes high profits just because it has one chance more than its clients?" I answered that if the existence of God, the soul, the hereafter, special providence, and everything that has to do with metaphysics were scientifically proven, man would lose the highest gift bestowed upon him—free choice.

The chairman announced that the next question would be the last one, and a young man got up and asked, "Have you had personal experience of that sort? Have you ever seen a spirit?"

I answered, "All my experiences have been ambiguous. None of them could serve for evidence. Just the same, my belief in spirits becomes even stronger."

There was applause. As I bowed and thanked them, I saw Hanka. She was sitting in the audience, clapping her hands. She wore the same black hat and black dress she had worn at all our meetings. She smiled at me and winked. I was stunned. Had she traveled after me to Mar del Plata? I looked again and she had vanished. No, it had been a hallucination. It lasted only one instant. But I will brood about this instant for the rest of my life.

Translated from the Yiddish by the author and Blanche and Joseph Nevel

The Day My Sister Married

On the day my sister married I got up early, even before the sound of my alarm, which I had set for seven o'clock. I walked to the window, which stood halfway open, pushed it open further and leaned out.

A woman came out of her kitchen door barefoot and in a pink bathrobe. Carefully, as though she were testing the first ice, she took a few steps over the flagstones to the garden path, after which she quickly went back, pulling her legs up high. It was still chilly, but the grayish white sky had already started to lighten and it looked as though it would be a sunny spring day. A few gardens away someone let a bucket roll down a step. A red tomcat was balanced on top of the fence. Perhaps he was the one who in the middle of the night had given the intense scream that had awakened me with a start. I had remained still, listening, but heard nothing else. Everyone had seemed to be sleeping quietly. For a moment I had the sensation that I was in my room in our old house. Lately that had happened more often. I had to look intently at the door and the window, which were located differently with respect to my bed, to confirm that it had been a dream. As I closed my eyes and turned over on my other side, I heard it again. It came from outside. It was the piercing screech of a tomcat, and I didn't understand that I had mistaken this sound for a human scream. I shivered from the morning cold coming in and closed the window.

"May is a lovely month to get married," the grocer had said yesterday as he placed a big box of food on the kitchen table. "People are marrying anyway. All that continues as usual." It was early in May '42 and we had been wearing the stars for a few days. It was not our intention to give a real wedding party, but my mother thought that we couldn't just let it go by and that we should invite some family members. "Who knows," she said, "how long it will be before we have the opportunity to be all together again." Not much family could come, a few uncles and aunts. It was no longer as before in our larger house in Breda where every occasion was seized upon to invite as many people as possible. If it had been up to my sister, they would have just gone to the synagogue for the wedding service, nothing more. I believe she found it a relief that without any of us present, they had had the civil service in Amsterdam. One week before the wedding day she'd called me to ask if I would take care of the bridal bouquet. "That's much easier for us," she'd said. "Then we don't have to bring it along from here." I promised that I would go to the florist that very day. "What should it be?" I asked. "Just choose something you find appropriate," she said, as though it went without saying that I was experienced in such things.

I went downstairs and found my mother already quite busy in the kitchen. "You're early too," she said. "That's very convenient, there is still a lot to do."

"It won't be that busy." I looked into the box with the rented glassware. "How many people are you counting on anyway?"

"Oh, you never know. It's always possible that more people will come than we had thought. And perhaps they'll be bringing friends along from Amsterdam."

"She didn't say anything about it."

"That isn't necessary. She knows that everyone is welcome here."

"I wouldn't know who would be coming with them."

"Oh, we'll see." My mother gave me a tea towel. "Will you please polish these glasses?"

She left the kitchen. I had a strong feeling that she wanted to pretend that nothing had changed, that she was going to have a house full of guests. She would walk through the rooms again and picture the way it had always been: furniture pushed aside, long rows of chairs, tables pushed together, everywhere vases with flowers. And my father seemed to subscribe to that view, for I heard him say: "I'll leave the front door ajar, then they can push it open with one knee." It was a standard joke of his.

The bridal bouquet was delivered early. It was in a long box with a ribbon around it. I took the box to my room and placed it on my bed, without opening it. What had made me choose just those Japanese blossoms? It has always bothered me. I am rather superstitious. I seldom walk under a ladder. I attach special significance to things that happen on the thirteenth, especially when that day also falls on a Friday; when I deal with numbers I add them to see whether the result can be divided by eleven or thirteen. I check myself when performing certain actions at home to convince myself that I have done them well, not out of a feeling of duty, but because I think that something unpleasant will happen to me otherwise. I leave the bathroom and look back to see if I have turned off the faucet, although I'm almost sure that I have done it. I open a window halfway, get into bed and get up again to make sure I have fastened it. But in choosing that bouquet I had no premonition at all. Before I entered the flower shop I had hesitated in front of the window for a while. I'd had no idea what I would get and once I was inside and saw all those pots with spring flowers, I no longer knew at all what I should choose. The florist, a ruddy-faced man in a light brown smock, had asked if the bride would be in white.

"She won't be in white," I'd said. I wasn't wearing a star yet. The regulation would go into effect a few days later. Therefore he could not know that we had our reasons to keep the wedding party simple. While he was putting some sprigs of green in a bunch of freesias, he asked how the bride would be dressed, and because I didn't answer that immediately, he turned towards me, making it look as if he were taking a small bow.

"Is she wearing a long gown?"

"I don't think so."

"Do you perhaps know the color of her gown?" he'd pressed. "Then I can take that into consideration in creating the bouquet."

I'd shrugged my shoulders. I couldn't enlighten him about that either. I hadn't asked her. The time when we had always gone dressed alike because we were one year apart was already long past. My mother did try to keep it up as long as possible. She'd knitted the same dresses and sweaters for us, we'd worn the same coats, even our shoes were alike. It wasn't until we left elementary school that we no longer had to walk around like twins.

The florist had advised me to take orchids. He made bridal bouquets from them regularly and they were also suitable as corsages for the wedding guests.

"I don't think that corsages will be worn."

The heavy scent of flowers in the shop had begun to oppress me. I got the feeling that if I hesitated any longer, he would push something on me that I didn't want at all. He had already pulled forward a big vase with orchids, and he squatted down and held a few together to show the effect.

"Very lovely." Then in the back of the store I'd spotted, on a small platform, a stone pot with branches on which were small star-shaped pink blossoms. I asked him what it was. He stood up. "That is Japanese blossom."

"Can you make a bouquet from that?"

"I can create bridal bouquets from everything that is here. That is not the point," he said. He looked doubtful. My choice had probably struck him as unusual and I quite understood that he preferred using orchids. But I thought that the Japanese blossom suited my sister exactly. He acknowledged that people never asked for such bridal bouquets. The bride must have a very distinctive taste. He'd promised that it would become something special.

Although I was curious to see it, I waited before opening the box until the arrival of my sister. As soon as she arrived with Hans I wanted to take her upstairs. But my mother held us back. First we had to go in where an uncle was waiting for her with a present. It was my uncle Herman from Assen, a short, effusive man who had taken the first train to be at our house in time. He had with him a black hatbox from which he took his top hat. He held it with the inside towards himself, made a few quick hand motions and started pulling something out of it. It was a piece of blue silk, which, as in a magic act, seemed to be endless. He let it flutter in the air a moment and then draped it over two chairs while he looked at us triumphantly.

"She'll certainly be able to get two dresses out of that," said my mother. She stroked the material, right in the middle, which created a hollow.

"Or an evening gown with a small train," I said.

"She doesn't need an evening gown now, I think."

My mother carefully folded the cloth.

"Perhaps for after the war," said Hans.

"Of course," said my uncle, "it is pure silk. You can always keep that. And the Germans won't hold out that long anymore. Mark my words."

He took a small flat brush from his pocket, rubbed the hat, put it on and sat down at the table across from my mother. To indicate how many bolts of wool and silk he still had in the warehouse of his textile business, he made imaginary stacks with his hands and looked up. Even if the war were still to last a few years, he could get on with his fabrics.

I pulled my sister out of the room. She had kissed my uncle on his cheeks, but had not said a word. Upstairs I pointed to the box on the bed.

"Your bridal bouquet is in there."

"What is it like?"

"I haven't looked yet."

"Why not?" She took off her coat and laid it on the bed.

"I wanted to wait for you."

She loosened the ribbon and took the lid off the box. A gentle fragrance rose from it. Carefully she unwrapped the tissue paper. The florist had tied the bouquet together with pink ribbons and had worked sprigs of different shades of green into it. My sister immediately walked to the mirror with it.

"What do you think, should I hold it like this?"

"I think so."

"What is the name of these flowers?"

"It's Japanese blossom. I didn't know what you'd be wearing."

"Just this. The color goes very well with it. Wait, I'll do it all for real." From her purse she pulled a small veil, which is required for the wedding service in a synagogue, put it on and again went to stand in front of the mirror with the bouquet.

"How do you like it?"

She was wearing a soft green dress with long sleeves and tight at the waist, which made her seem even slimmer. Her chestnut-brown hair curled out from under the small cap of the veil. She had always been much better looking than I, which in the past had often made me jealous. I used to envy her because she had many more boyfriends than I; they came to pick her up from school, waited for her everywhere, jostled each other at school parties to dance with her.

The doorbell rang. I heard voices in the hall, the banging of the doors, my father greeting someone, and through it all the whistling of a teakettle. I sat down on the bed and pushed her coat aside, which caused the star to become visible. I turned it over. "You look very good," I said.

She walked back and forth in front of the mirror a few times, taking long steps, the way we used to in the attic with an old curtain around our heads and a feather duster in our hands as a bridal bouquet. I wondered whether she now also remembered how as teenagers we had imagined a wedding. We had derived that image from the films we'd seen: Lillian Harvey and Willy Fritsch, who waltzed into marriage under enormous chandeliers, and Ginger Rogers and Fred Astaire, who promised each other eternal fidelity while tap-dancing on a shiny floor. It wasn't even that long ago; it seemed that way only because the war had come between things. My sister laid the bouquet on a cabinet, took off the veil and folded it.

"What are you doing now?"

"You don't think I'm going to keep it on?"

"Oh no."

"I'm not going out in the street with it. I'll put it on right at the door of the synagogue."

"Yes, I understand that."

"How long is the walk?"

"About ten minutes. A carriage would perhaps not take as long."

"A carriage?"

"I just mean. . . ."

She looked at me slightly surprised, the veil folded small in her hand.

"Do you think that under normal circumstances we would really be getting married with such a fuss? Not like us." She laughed and put the veil next to her coat on the bed. Someone was coming upstairs. It was Hans. He wore a black suit and was holding a prayer book, with which I had seen him arrive, still clasped under his arm.

"Do you always carry that with you?" I asked.

"I'm afraid that I'll forget it otherwise."

"It looks like a beautiful edition."

"It was my father's." He handed it to me. It was gilt-edged, bound in heavy leather. I opened it, turned it around, and opened it again. On the first page a name was written in Gothic letters above the Hebrew title, and under it *Berlin 1910*. Hans came from Berlin, where he had studied law. He had not been able to complete his studies and in '33 had fled with his mother to our country. His father, a well-known heart specialist, had donated his private clinic to the city of Berlin at the end of the twenties. Shortly before the Nazi takeover he had died. Hans was a Zionist and apprenticed in factories and on farms because he wanted to go to Palestine already trained.

After my sister had become engaged to him, she had given up painting and gone into nursing in Amsterdam. In her attic studio she had left everything behind, her paint box, her paints and brushes, stretcher bars, panels, an easel covered with colorful crusts. On a stand, portfolios full of drawings, her canvases turned to the wall. "I'll come and get that stuff one of these days," she'd said. "Maybe I'll have time in Palestine to do it again."

None of us at home was a Zionist. Once I went with my sister to such a meeting in the small hall above the synagogue in Breda, where girls in blue-and-white dresses danced the hora and sang lively songs. We didn't much feel like participating in the movement, but later, under the influence of Hans, my sister started to be more interested in it.

"How do you like the bridal bouquet, Hans?"

"Nice flowers. Just like little stars."

"Except that they are pink."

"There is something else in the box," said my sister. "A corsage."

"He added that after all. I had said it wasn't necessary."

"Who wants it?" She held up the spray with the stem wrapped in silver foil.

"Just give it to me," said Hans. "That must be the idea." He fastened the corsage with a safety pin to his lapel. "Come downstairs, they're asking for you."

"Don't forget your book."

Laughing a little, they walked down the stairs.

While everyone was in the hall putting on coats, another uncle and aunt arrived from Zeist. This caused some crowding because my uncle held the company back at the front door. He first had to tell them something. The fact that his wife was non-Jewish had confused him when he was filling out forms at the population register. Inadvertently he had written that he had only *two* Jewish grandparents. "But I went back to correct it a few days later," he said as he pointed, grinning, at the star on his chest.

"You could have tried," said another uncle.

"I prefer not to let myself in for unnecessary difficulties."

"That's what I said too," said Aunt Mien. "It is better this way." She had a thin, somewhat crooked mouth that drew in even more when she brushed invisible bits of fluff from her spotless, starless coat. One by one they went outside. As the last one, I wanted to pull the door shut behind me, but I changed my mind and went inside again. In the hall I stood for a moment under the almost empty coatrack. I opened the door to the room. A smell of cigar smoke and coffee hung there.

The piece of blue silk lay neatly folded on the buffet, next to Uncle Herman's hat box. I went to the table, on which there was a full ashtray. A cigar stub was still smoldering in it. Half a cigarette had been folded and crushed out. Slowly I walked back to the door, turned to lean back against the jamb, and looked around. The silence in the room gave me a feeling of oppression, as though I were in a house to which no one would return. The irregular rows of chairs gave the impression of having been pushed back suddenly.

In the hall I picked up my gloves, which I had left on the small table, and hurried outside. The others were almost at the end of the street. In front walked my father and my uncles, wearing their black top hats, the way they went to the synagogue every Saturday. Behind them, my mother with the aunts in their dark coats, my brother, taller than the others, a black hat slightly tilted on his head, and on his arm his wife in a light beige suit, her blue-black hair in a knot against her neck. The bridal couple slowly walked behind. On the other side of the street, some people stopped. A man tipped his hat, some children turned around, a curtain was pushed aside. While I started walking faster to catch up with them, I had the same sensation as in an often recurring dream: I'm running after someone in just such a sunny street and cannot reach him because the distance becomes ever greater, although the other doesn't quicken his pace.

"They also do this in Amsterdam," said my sister when I came up next to her. "Yesterday there were even people who for no reason shook my hand on the street."

"How annoying. I think I'll hold my purse in front of it from now on."

"You shouldn't do that," said Hans. "That could get you into bad trouble."

We were now greeted repeatedly by passersby and I saw that my mother nodded back cheerfully as if she knew all those people. In the narrow street in front of the synagogue door, some more friends were waiting and went inside with us. We didn't have to go upstairs to the women's gallery. The wedding service is the only one during which the women may remain downstairs.

The place was not half-filled and that gave the ceremony a private quality. We stood closely gathered around the canopy, under which the bridal couple was sitting on special chairs. It was as though, by the circle we made, we wanted to protect them from the outside world. I thought of the game we played as children: "In Holland stands a house." The man chooses a wife, naturally my sister. Together they stand inside the circle and we chant the rest of the lines, of the child and the maid and the manservant and all the things which are still chosen after that, until finally the house is burned or torn down. My sister's face was hidden under the veil; I could not observe her reactions. I didn't ask her later what she had felt. The rest of the day she remained looking very beautiful but also slightly unapproachable. And afterwards I had no opportunity to talk with her about it. Three weeks later, during the first Nazi raid in Amsterdam-Zuid, she was taken out of her house with Hans and put on a transport.

During the whole service my mother was very moved. Her handkerchief was constantly in use. I knew that so well about her. She was always easily touched, not only at family occasions. Even seeing the queen stirred a strong emotion within her. I remember that when I was young Queen Wilhelmina once made a drive through Breda. As soon as the carriage with the queen and Queen-mother Emma came in sight, tears streamed over my mother's cheeks. On the wedding day she repeatedly had the chance for tears. As soon as we came out of the synagogue my brother took photos: of the bride and groom in the open door, for which my sister had to keep her veil on for a moment; of the bride and groom with the parents; and a picture of the whole family. I had the impression that the big white handkerchief had not left my mother's face for a moment, but when I later saw the prints, she seemed to be smiling in all of them.

"You're next," my uncle Herman said to me.

"That would cost you another piece of cloth."

"I'd be glad to sacrifice it for that. I still have a whole bolt of white silk, of the best quality."

"I'll warn you in time. I've always wanted to get married in white."

"She still has time," said my mother. We were sitting at the table. I was next to my uncle from Delft, my mother's brother, a tall, thin man with a pince-nez. He was a teacher of French, German and English, languages of which he also knew several dialects. In addition to cockney and a Berlin dialect, he preferred potatoes. We called him the "potato-eater" and when he came to stay with us my mother served him only the best kinds, which he could identify by name after just a few bites. He remained as thin as a rail and we assumed that he didn't get enough to eat at home. Aunt Hilda, his wife, of German origin, was not only extremely frugal but also had her husband firmly under her thumb. She looked very German; her skirts fell amply over her broad hips, her hair in tightly rolled braids like headphones on her ears. Their two children, a boy and a girl with their father's intelligence, were already knowledgeable about the political happenings in Germany when very young and could take part in the conversation like adults. The family did not radiate much happiness. The few times that they made an outing to Scheveningen, my aunt and the children went by tram and my uncle, to save buying a ticket, had to ride behind on his bike. He told us that he could keep up pretty well with the tram because there were many long stops. Those gave him the chance to make up the lost distance and his children, who stood on the platform of the second car, could then wave to him each time. He did a lot of bicycling in his life. During school vacations he sometimes came to Breda with two saddlebags full of books. All day long he would be reading, his long legs on a chair on which he had first spread a newspaper, while in the kitchen my mother was busy peeling kilos of potatoes. He conducted his correspondence with us on postcards which always had the same opening words: "We sincerely hope that everything is going well for all of you." Even his last card, which he wrote a few days before he and his family were taken away and which reached only me, because the others had been deported in the meantime, began with that sentence.

My father tapped against his glass and stood up. Already at the first few words of his speech I saw my mother reach for her handkerchief. My father was a skilled after-dinner speaker and it cost him no difficulty to give a picture of my sister as she had been in her youth. He compared her special qualities and character traits to those of Hans and, quoting many Hebrew texts pertaining to marriage, he came to the conclusion that it was an ideal union. He concluded by proposing a toast to their future in Palestine. After we had all drained our glasses, it became quiet for a moment. He had not said a word about the war circumstances. I looked around the table where we sat slightly crowded in the small room, the chairs pushed close together, so that during dinner we continually bumped elbows. After the war I continued to see that full room before me. For a long time I had difficulty entering a room where many people were together.

The silence was broken by Uncle Maurits with a speech full of French and English sayings, which he translated for our convenience. He predicted that we would never be able to say "married in haste, repent in leisure" about the newlyweds, a pronouncement which the family took up eagerly.

After dinner the bride and groom went back to Amsterdam. My sister took the bridal bouquet, which had lain on the table in front of her. An aunt advised her never to throw it away.

"You should dry it," she said.

"I'll save it carefully," my sister promised.

"Just lay it down in your linen closet."

"No, you should hang it above your bed."

"I wouldn't like to be in Amsterdam right now," said another aunt.

"You are better off in the country."

"It doesn't make much difference where you are."

"You shouldn't say that. There are more Germans around in such a city."

"They are everywhere," said my father.

"Just let these children go to Amsterdam," called out my uncle Herman. "What is going to happen anyway?"

My sister and Hans had left and everyone had gone to drink coffee in the other room. I remained sitting at the table. No one had noticed it as far as I could tell—at any rate I hadn't shown how upset I was when my sister picked up the bouquet. It is a bad sign, I thought, while I looked at the pink flowers that remained on the table. A bridal bouquet should not fall apart.

My aunts came to clear off the table. It became increasingly empty, the last glasses were carried to the kitchen, the last serving dish, the napkins, the knife holders, until on the tablecloth smeared with crumbs, wine and food stains, there were only the star-shaped flowers. They already looked wilted. I kept looking at them, sniffed them briefly and noticed that they had also lost their scent.

"Lift your arm a moment," I heard. Someone took the tablecloth by the corners and carried it away like a bag to shake it out above the garbage can. When I stood up I also saw a few flowers on the floor next to her chair. I stepped over them and went to my room. The box was still on my bed, with the lid on it. I took it off and held the box up to my face. The fragrance had lingered in it.

Translated from the Dutch by Jeannette K. Ringold

The Cheek of the Trout

"Enjoy the city for me," he kept saying, as if he *counted* on the difference between them. He had lived there and she had not, he was European and she American, he steeped in politics and she in art history, on the lookout for the interesting and beautiful. They were the same age, but on this trip she felt younger than her husband. He kept trying to explain something and then stopping, as if he thought it was hopeless, she could never understand. She almost agreed. His explanations seemed to be falling into some part of her that was missing.

This didn't happen so much when they were going around the official part of the city: he had not lived his boyhood there. But when they walked into the old, outer districts, he would now and then stop in his tracks. She found herself stopping too, and when he stared at a house or a corner of a street on which there was nothing, she also stared, and her heart began to pound.

Once, stopping, he said, "My uncle's store was there, someone must have stepped right in, right away, afterward. Look, it's still going strong, which neighbor could it have been?" And he stood trying to imagine which one, but making no move toward the place.

As they walked away she said—like a fool, but it was out of tenderness for what he had said, and tact, a certain kind of tact that knew he required her not to speak directly or with pity for any of this—that she loved the old-fashioned wood dividers of the front windows. He nodded, he acknowledged what she said, but had no reply to it then. Later, in another place, he said, "Here's a carved door for you!" pleased to have found it for her.

In the formal part of the city things were easier. "Be a tourist," he said. "Look at everything and enjoy it, otherwise it's not fair to yourself."

Sometimes she complained, "You think I don't know anything about life because, compared to this, I've only been happy." It was her happiness grumbling. She accepted her role. The beauty of the city was making her drunk, in spite of what she knew—of course she knew it! And to be there with her husband, who had at his fingertips history and politics and languages and art, too, though he lingered least on that, felt to her like the supremest security.

"The Cheek of the Trout" is the second of a two-part piece (the first is an essay commenting on the use of Holocaust material). Both parts originally appeared in *Testimony*, edited by David Rosenberg (Random House, 1989) under the title "Notes Toward a Holocaust Fiction."

He relied on her too, of course, to see the beauty of the place where he had been born, leaving him free to be as blind to it as he needed to be on this first return after four decades. Had she expected to see bridges sag? Facades pockmarked by corruption as if they were paintings by the Albrecht twins? As if a place could be punished like the picture of Dorian Gray? She reported to him, as if he were blind: Now there is beauty, wholeness, prosperity, repair. Buildings bore fine stone sculpture, even the ones without special plaques. On rooftops, life-sized stone figures offered books, instruments of music and science, to the populace below. She turned her gaze up to them, drinking in their gifts. Doing her job, she described them, she snapped their pictures with her camera.

When they needed directions, he did the asking, caught for a moment with strangers in the intimacy of mother tongue. His manner with people seemed perfect—his dignity, his self-control. He was stocky, handsome, gray-haired. She would watch him approach each one, guessing at whether they guessed why he was a stranger now, though in command of their dialect. Nothing was betrayed on either side—polite, polite.

When people in the street seemed about the right age she asked, "Can any of these possibly be the same as the ones who were here then?" And to show how much she knew—of course she knew!—"I mean the neighbors who put on their swastika buttons right after Hitler marched in—you told me they did that—as if they'd already worn them hidden under their coats?" Then, her voice rising in a kind of anxious demand that he acknowledge that she knew: "The ones who attacked your father? Who slapped you in the street one day, a child on your way to school?" Her voice broke on that, ample warning, if she needed it, that this was the wrong tone. She stopped at once.

In silence they stood before the doorway of the house where he had lived; in silence followed his path to school through the tree-shaded alleys of the *Augarten,* a park so clean and neatly planted she might never have believed in its existence; in silence sat on a bench beside the broad road called the *Hauptallee,* where his parents rested in the open air on Sundays and his little-boy self, untouched by sadness then, played with friends. When the bench sent forth too many emanations, he got up and walked rapidly away. She shot after him, catching at his hand. He fumbled with the other across both their chests, not looking, to give the side of her hair a quick caress—he reassuring *her*!

From the beginning they knew the trip would be too painful. From the beginning it was too full of silences between them. She filled them in for herself. She imagined they were not who they were, a couple approaching this pain from their own chronology, one of them having had the worst experience it is possible to have, and now for the first time going back. She invented: We are a young man and young woman, his name is Joshua, hers is—whatever—Joan, it's better to be young here, we're intimate with each other but in a different way, we have empathy for the past, but with veils of distance, we'd each have parents, but it's Joshua's father who's the Holocaust survivor, his pain wouldn't so immediately be ours. She imagined this as much for her husband as herself, wanting him to have some refuge.

She'd read of people, there are case histories about them, who under the assault of pain split off into other personalities. But she was fearful of what she was doing. How could she dare attempt such an alleviating gesture? After a while she developed little ironies about it. "Really? You're not just yanking away a few years? Not just preening yourself on giving comfort where there's none to be given?"

It came anyway—little waves of Joshua and Joan, invention making its own complications.

Joshua telephones his father and Joan hears him too in the echoing booth warning Joshua to keep this, keep that, afraid of more losses.

"Keep your dignity," his father says. "If you accidentally bump into someone, keep your head high. Keep your distance, you're an American, you're looking them over. Right now I'd like to pull you out of there but all right, you're another generation, you can keep separate, it's not the same for you."

Then Joan calls her mother and Joshua has to hear her tell Joan to give everything away. "You're holding back for Joshua's sake, and that's not right. There's not a thing in the world wrong with that city, it's the cleanest and safest of any in Europe, your father and I had a wonderful time when we were there, but you're not giving yourself to it. It's not Joshua, it's his father I blame, someone who can't allow people to give themselves to the present now where they're completely safe and well. . . ."

Joshua is small-boned, with curly brown hair, unbelievably watchful eyes, and now a new reddish mustache, started for their trip. Joan thinks: *their* trip, but it's Joshua's, it's Joshua's father's with Joshua making it for him. The complications of the invention grow. How, for example, did Joan meet Joshua? In an art history lecture at a university, the same as themselves? Yes, Joan made a beeline toward the vacant seat beside Joshua, toward the two expressions in his face, sadness and the wish to be happy. "Oh, I'll see you're happy," Joan is always thinking.

On the second day they went to the Jewish cemetery, they themselves, not Joshua and Joan. They searched for a gravestone arranged for from America. Her husband held a slip of paper with location, row and number, and a lone laborer encountered in the otherwise empty vastness, a Yugoslav worker, helped with hand signs. At last they found the place, swelling in the earth, neglected stones pushed crooked like teeth in an infected gum, but it was not from his parents, they were not buried anywhere, though her husband for this moment wanted to believe his father's ashes were here. Would they be? Would the bureaucrats of Buchenwald where his father died of typhus have ordered the ashes of individuals to be carefully scooped and labeled and sent home because it was still in the early years of killings, or had they shoveled and dumped the bushel-loads and picked names to call them? Did it matter whose ashes these were? Yes, for now, to her husband, it mattered, and mattered that his mother's could never be reclaimed. Where is Antigone in a world of human ashpits?

Late afternoon summer sun spilled over the ground and honeyed the leaves on the trees. In this prodigality of light, who would believe in darkness? She stood apart. Her husband began to speak a prayer before the writing on the stone. Mother and Father, names on a gravestone. When his voice broke into tight, fought-off sobs, she thought, Where are Joshua and Joan? But it was no use, it was themselves standing there. A little door opened in her husband's broad chest and a twelve-year-old tumbled out weeping. She opened her arms to catch him.

Leaving, they lost their way. The gravestones on this path were bigger, they had elaborate gothic lettering, titles. *Vize-burgermeister* and *Obermedizinalrat* and *Kaiserlicher Rat* and *Reichsratsabgeordneter.* "What's this, what's that?" she asked. "Heads of things," he answered. "Medical organizations, city councils." "Why are these so bare?" She meant the names beneath the ornamented ancestors. Then she noticed the dates, 1937 to 1945. There was luck even among the dead.

She could sound out these words herself. *Vergast Belsec, Gestorben in Theresienstadt.* Jews of the world, you know more German than you think. *Verschleppt nach Auschwitz. Umgekommen in Dachau. Ermordet in Belsen.*[1] She copied words into her notebook, but not fast enough, and turned to snapping the camera. Sun glinted on granite, obliterating names, but she went on snapping till she couldn't anymore, and ran down the path, he after her.

Then they were back at the beginning, and entered a low room, cryptlike, filled with filing cabinets. Her husband spoke to a man reading behind a desk who rose, a long cotton coat of rusty black uncreasing itself down to his shoetops.

At first her husband translated for her. "This gentleman is the keeper of records here. He spent the Hitler years in Argentina." Then the man spoke to

---

1. "Gassed in Belsec, died in Theresienstadt. . . . deported to Auschwitz, perished at Dachau. Murdered in Belsen."

her in good English. "Enjoy this beautiful city." The man's smile was sweet. Not a melancholy smile, only slow. "It is your first time here, enjoy it."

She flinched a little at that, as usual. "And also go to the mountains," said the record-keeper, the cemetery man, like a sybil, like a good elf, "my mother's favorite place, ah, the wonderful air. In the mountains was always my mother's cure, you should go, enjoy everything."

An encouraging breath expanded inside her. She blurted, God knew why, knowing it was idiocy the moment she spoke, "Is she there now?" The record-keeper's smile slowly faded. He gave her a prolonged look, as if assessing how it might be possible to infuse intelligence into her at last.

On the trolley ride back to the hotel, silent again, she imagined the life of the cemetery man in Argentina. What was it? He had to learn Spanish. All right, that was no problem, she quickly arranged for him to do so. He had to learn to live. How? She pictured the little man in rusty black duster (take that off him, for God's sake, he's not wearing it in Argentina!) blundering with a prayer book under his arm among the gauchos and tango dancers. At first the fantasy diverted her. Then in winding streets it turned grim. Searching out a fellow Jew to speak German with, he encountered instead a fled Nazi prospering there. Mengele, who delighted in medical experiments, would ask if he had a twin, would fancy the special shape of those ironically slanted eyes, those drooping earlobes.

No—no, have him meet Borges, the great Argentinian writer![2] "You yourself, dear man"—it's Borges speaking so kindly—"even without your old texts and Talmud-study companions, may dream commentaries. You yourself can write *A Guide to the Perplexed* by Maimonides."[3] When the little fantasy was over she still saw the cemetery record-keeper in his long black coat, standing at the low window of his cryptlike room. Her husband stared through the window of the swaying trolley. A recorded voice announced street destinations in guttural German: *"Karl Lueger Strasse. . . ."*

For days after that they quieted themselves in the gilt-and-marble vaults of the Kunsthistorische Museum. Rembrandt, Brueghel, Bosch. . . . They followed a guide through the royal red-brocaded rooms of the Hofburg castle, stepping backward through history to the safe rococo Hapsburg monarchy. Hoop-la! The empress installed handrings in her apartment so she could turn somersaults.

Her husband said, "I feel the city's about to explode." But it was in themselves that the explosion came. One evening in a restaurant they encountered

2. Jorge Luis Borges (b. 1899), Argentine poet, critic, and short-story writer.
3. Moses ben Maimon (1135–1204), Jewish rabbi, physician, and philosopher born in Spain. One of the greatest Hebrew scholars.

a couple from the States eating dinner at an adjacent table, the woman a small, neat body quietly consulting her guidebook, the man enormously fat and talky, his belly a Humpty Dumpty belted barrel. They had been, the man informed them from his table, on a whirlwind tour of highspots in the Slavic countries—Budapest, Prague, Dubrovnik, Warsaw.

"And what did I come for?" the man asked rhetorically, though they hadn't inquired. "I came to see a concentration camp." His little round eyes filled with tears, his voice choked off, he was unable to speak another word.

In their room that night she asked indignantly, "What right has he to cry like that? Why hasn't grief taken off a few pounds, why didn't he first lose weight if he was going to be a public mourner?" Her husband turned on her with a violence like the swing in a weather vane, like the stiff sudden movement of the medieval figures in the Hoher Markt Anker Clock.

"He has a right to his feelings no matter what he looks like!" Aesthetics had perverted her, he said in a fury, the city had done its work and seduced her with its beauty. "It's all you care about!"

"Then stop telling me to enjoy myself," she shouted back. "I'm not a tourist! How could I know you and not think of what went on here? I would think of it even if I didn't know you!"

What was horrible to them was that in this place he had fled as a child, had to be rescued from it before it hacked him to bits, they now hacked at one another. This was happening in their hotel room, itself a work of beauty, stuffed with darkly polished Biedermeier furniture, or at least with good enough imitations of it, its balcony overlooking the stone figures giving counsel to the populace below.

She had backed away from his outburst into the brass lock of the gleaming armoire and had hurt her elbow. He was pacing up and down the room in a rigid line while he circled his hand over his chest, like someone practicing a complicated coordination. She rubbed her arm, he circled with his palm what gripped in his chest. It was as if they were solving the riddle of where to locate pain. That was when they remembered the advice of the cemetery man, and wondered if it could save them.

"This reminds me—yes, the contrasts!—something like a Bosch"—in the mountains it was easier to recover the enthusiasm they both required of her—"or one of the Brueghels we saw, was that Salon Twelve or Thirteen?—never mind!" She would look it up later, but he knew what she meant. "At one side someone's painted a multitude climbing up, at the other side, what? All those people treading the downward path to the boiling lake?"

She had succeeded in making him laugh. He was relaxed now and wryly commenting. "So it's a level of hell after all?"

Enthusiasm always made her exaggerate, but there surely was this duality in the little mountain resort. The two important places were several miles apart. At one end of the village was the entrance to the mountain-climbing trails, at the other, a little beyond the center of the village, were the thermal pools. The place divided itself between the healthy and the sick.

"Everything's in twos!" she announced. "The city and the spa, the monument and the mountain, this generation, that generation. . . ." She let him know what she had been thinking about Joshua and Joan, too. He brushed his lips back and forth on her cheek—"Thanks for the mustache"—so they could both imagine the feel of it, bushy and red.

The dining room of their hotel was vast, but with only five tables set for breakfast. In the morning, among the scattered guests, they heard Italian, German, French. The waitress, a robust young woman, greeted them in a cheery voice: *"Kaffee zweimal?"* After she brought the two coffees and rolls she ran to the window to watch her husband drive the crane that was dismantling the hotel next door.

The proprietress was on crutches. Not, she assured them, from a skiing accident, but only a stupid slip in her bathroom. Dressed in sweater and skirt of matching loden green, she hung genteelly between her props. "The young people nowadays prefer beaches in the south of France. They have forgotten the mountains of their parents." Not her voice, but the striking of her crutches on the flagstones of the lobby, made the bitter sound.

The parents were out in full force. Handsome, hearty couples in their silver-haired age strolled the streets. They wore sweaters beautifully embroidered with edelweiss, knickers of moss-green suede, knee socks of double-woven wool patterned in lozenge. Their shoes were stout-soled brown leather, their alpine staffs armored with medallions: mountain goats and silver jugs and green garlands edging the curved silver shields, emblems of Bad Gastein and Salzburg and Bad-am-See.

One day her husband said, "An attendant gave me some information about this place. There are special baths here that contain a form of radon. The sick ones come for the radon cure."

The absurdity seemed to fit in perfectly—soaring beauty above, deadly emanations from below. Radon treatment was offered in the special baths as well as in the various inhalings and absorptions from the gold mines deep underground. The brochures showed men and women lying on cots in full nakedness, with lifted relaxed knees exposing the shadowed entrance between the thighs, or the winesac of the scrotum and its soft spout.

The proprietress, confronted on her crutches, said forthrightly, "Sure, before this, people came and sat for hours in the baths or baked in the mines, then they went home and got sick! Now they know better. They must consult a doctor here, who will regulate everything."

One afternoon they sat at a table of an open-air restaurant at the foot of the mountain, sipping coffee and breathing in the thin, delicious air. They watched the climbers in their suedes and lodens, as frozen in time as if the hands of the clock had never moved. She saw from her husband's face what was the matter, and didn't need to ask. They were all about the right age.

They decided then to consort with the sick. It was there, among those wanting to be healed in the warm bubbly water, that they began to encounter other Jews. Before they left home, she had bought a tiny gold Shield of David[4] on a chain to wear around her neck. All sorts of Jews swam up to them because of her star, she believed. All of them expressed preference for people of a different part of the world.

A Rumanian couple, widely traveled, said they could stomach all nationalities except Poles: "Terrible, terrible anti-Semites." "Personally we were made to feel comfortable when we visited Poland," said another couple from Europe. There were those who would not "set foot in Germany" and those who made a point of it. No matter which country was mentioned, someone was sure to say, "Others were as bad or worse." "And where we are this minute, Austria, do you want to start on that? We have to show that we are again a part of the universe."

These Jews, some younger, some older, seemed to be struggling to regain a kind of global poise. What attitude should they take toward the world? "This generation," they said, "is not that generation; this decade is not the one of forty years ago."

An Israeli couple swam over. They were leaving soon for Munich. They reported that Germans, Austrians, and Poles had been personally very nice to them when they visited there. "Israel is a small country, you have to travel."

Outside the pool they met a bearded Belgian Jew of about fifty who walked with a hip-hiking limp. He was married to a German woman in her twenties with piercing blue eyes, buck teeth, and a frank manner. The Belgian had a way of not speaking until he had taken one or both of them by the arm and moved a little ways off from where they had been standing: he could only be understood on fresh ground. He spoke in a confidential manner, even his jokes imparted directly into the ear like state secrets. He had one about the countries of Europe where Jews lived before Hitler: "They only killed you there"—he smiled and whispered—"you could live with it."

4. Six-pointed Jewish star.

One day he drew both of them to one side, though not so far that his wife couldn't hear. "She is a better Jew than I am," he said, dipping his head toward his wife. She approached, laughing. "What he means is that when we married, I tried to wake him early so he could attend Saturday services, but always he went back to sleep."

At night in their room they compared notes about the people they met. She wanted to say that the Belgian was too intimate about trivialities, too public about what should be private. But she remembered how they had quarreled over the fat man's tears and kept it to herself.

One day she sat on the edge of the pool, waiting for her husband to finish his swim, when a female voice beside her said, "Too much illness and bad legs, how will I stand it here!" She turned to see an attractive young woman in a red bikini, beating up small waves in the water with her feet. "Still, if it helps Heinrich, I will certainly stay."

At that moment her husband emerged from the pool in the company of a man. "There he is," the young woman said, "there's Heinrich!" "And that's my husband." "So we have all become acquainted at the same time." The woman stuck out her hand with a smile. "Elsa. From Germany."

Elsa and Heinrich were both in their early thirties, an attractive couple. Heinrich looked struck by sunlight—even his eyebrows and lashes were blond. But he was melancholy. "I am supposed to be young, but this knee doesn't know it. After one little skiing accident, it refuses to heal properly and becomes arthritic."

"Heinrich is bored," Elsa announced.

"This literary conversation in the pool with your husband," Heinrich said, "is the first interest that has penetrated my life here."

"Heinrich is depressed. And we will have two more weeks of this." Elsa was laughing.

"Shall we meet for dinner tonight?" Heinrich asked in his drawling yet somehow excited English, "if we are not too boring and depressing for you? There is a restaurant called The Trout that serves fresh fish. A rarity in the mountains, yes?"

"What do you think of the young couple?" she called through the bathroom door while her husband showered. After glancing briefly at her, he had agreed to dinner in the most matter-of-fact way. His answer came muffled, but when he emerged, his naked body ruddy from its toweling, he looked directly at her and asked, "Did you feel we shouldn't go?"

In the shower, water drumming on her head, she'd heard an echo of *Heinrich's* father this time, telephoning his son with homilies from Hamburg: "If you meet any Jews, don't hang your head. It's true your grandfather joined the Nazi party for business reasons, and I became an S.S. officer when I was young, but whatever we did you're another generation, you had nothing to do with it, you don't owe an apology. If you meet a Jew, you can be friendly, offer a glass of wine if you can stand to be with them, but on no account are you required to apologize."

Her head was becoming like the thermal pool—there were traces in it of everything. "Oh, no!" she had answered, "of course we should go!"

In the restaurant, still another pool, this time a long narrow one built into the length of the floor, where the dark shapes of the trout twisted slowly back and forth. Everyone made a quip. "Look, they're in their own thermal bath." "Rheumatic trouts, poor things." "Perhaps they need a little radon bath?" She hadn't made her quip yet, so she said, "Now we'll have to choose our victims," and was horrified, but no one seemed to notice.

At the table, Heinrich satirized his own obsession with his cure. In a mock-elderly voice, he gave a little lecture about the healthfulness of eating trout prepared "blue."

"Plain boiled," he said, lifting a finger, "what more can anyone want than that?"

When the waiter came they all humored Heinrich, an agreeable moment, everyone smiling indulgently. Then they sipped wine.

"Heinrich's digestion is unreliable," Elsa said. "His nerves are in a state." Her voice was quick and light. "He works in a publishing house his family owns. Sometimes he writes poetry. It's very good!" Heinrich's melancholy was being visibly broken up, pierced everywhere by bright, deft arrows. "Heinrich and I have been living together in Munich for three years. And"—Elsa never faltered for a minute over this—"Heinrich could not make up his mind to marry. I waited and waited, now there is a child coming."

"So that, of course"—Heinrich's voice, pleasant and open and unembarrassed, broke in—"was the help to deciding."

In the telephone booth of her head a voice said, "It's the right way. You do that too, be more open and that will help." Her husband could sit with this couple and eat a meal and speak of books with them because he thought they were innocent and because they were in the world together, and he was a man who felt responsible to what was in the world, but the rest she must do.

"Sometimes," she said, "my husband and I have trouble looking at Germans or Austrians of a certain age. We think of what they were doing during the Hitler years."

After only the slightest pause, holding their wine midair as if wand-struck, Heinrich and Elsa cried out together, "Yes, yes, that is natural, understandable!" They were dressed in the softest of colors, Heinrich in a pale blue wool sweater and beige slacks, Elsa in a peach knit dress that showed not the least bulge of baby. Her husband was wearing his navy blue jacket with a checked blue shirt open at the throat. The convex metal buttons on his sleeves caught light, and light-formed shapes at the edge of the buttons gave off twisting gleams. She felt his eyes on her.

The dinner arrived. Each fish was covered with a skin that had turned to blue velvet, each was propped, seallike, on the plate, fins like hands supporting the body's upper part, head raised above the curving breast, a mythological creature about to speak: "Consume me and be cured."

For a moment she was afraid she might blurt: "I can't eat this, it's like a character in a children's book!" But she said no such thing. She worked open a snap at the neck of her blouse and waited.

Elsa at once contributed something special to enjoy. "The cheek of the trout is the best part. Not easy to find, though!" Wielding knife and fork precisely, her blond head bent to the task, she folded back a flap of blue velvet in the head of the fish, searched carefully, then put something into her mouth with her fork and looked satisfied. Heinrich also lifted a velvet flap on the head of the fish, poked with his fork and knife, and brought something to his mouth. "Aha."

It was hopeless to try for Elsa's prize; she was not adept with fish, but her husband had the European knack. He began to press a bit of trout against the back of his fork in case of bones. Had he found the small delicacy? She had been staring around the table and might have missed it. She felt certain, somehow, that he hadn't even tried. Why should so silly a thing become an emblem of happiness? Her heart flooded with sorrow for her husband, for what had been stolen from him. If he were Joshua, if she were Joan, she would call out to him, "Find it, oh, please, find it!" Her husband lifted his gaze as if she had spoken, smiling as if to encourage her to find it.

What was it like? The nugget of meat in the little spoonshaped pelvic bone of the roast chicken? The heart of a boiled artichoke, when you finally got to it, dipped in spicy vinaigrette sauce? The eye of a tiny, butter-soft, baby broiled lambchop, her favorite meal that her mother had cooked for her again and again all the while she was growing up? Her mouth filled with remembered tastes of things that were rare and delicious, gone in a minute.

My Quarrel with Hersh Rasseyner

In 1937 I returned to Bialystok, several years after I had been a student in the Novaredok Yeshiva of the Mussarists, a movement which gives special importance to the ethical and ascetic elements in Judaism. When I came back I found many of my old schoolmates still there. A few even came to my lecture one evening. Others visited me secretly, to keep the head of the Yeshiva from finding out. I could see that their poverty had brought them suffering and that the fire of their youthful zeal had slowly burned itself out. They continued to observe all the laws and usages meticulously, but the weariness of spiritual wrestlings lay upon them. For years they had tried to tear out of their hearts the desire for the pleasures of life, and at last they realized they had lost the war with themselves. They had not overcome the evil urge.

There was one I kept looking for all the time and could not find, my former schoolmate Hersh Rasseyner. He was a dark young man with bright, downcast eyes. I did not meet him, but heard that he kept to his garret in solitude and did not even come to the Yeshiva.

Once we met unexpectedly in the street. He was walking with his eyes lowered, as is the custom with the Novaredok Mussarists; they do not wish to be "eye to eye" with the world. But he saw me anyway. He put his arms behind him, thrusting his hands into his sleeves, so that he would not have to shake hands with me. The closer he came, the higher rose his head. When we finally stood face to face, he looked at me intently. He was so moved his nostrils seemed to quiver—but he kept silent.

Among the Mussarists when you ask, How are you? the question means, What is the state of your religious life? Have you risen in spirituality? But I had forgotten and asked quite simply, "Hersh Rasseyner, how are you?"

Hersh moved back a little, looked me over from head to toe, saw that I was modishly dressed, and shrugged. "And how are you, Chaim Vilner? My question, you see, is more important."

My lips trembled and I answered hotly, "Your question, Hersh Rasseyner, is no question at all. I do what I have to."

Right there, in the middle of the street, he cried out. "Do you think, Chaim Vilner, that by running away from the Yeshiva you have saved yourself? You know the saying among us: Whoever has learned Mussar can have no enjoyment in his life. You will always be deformed, Chaim Vilner. You will remain a cripple the rest of your life. You write godless verses and they reward you by patting you on the cheek. Now they're stuffing you with applause as they would stuff a goose with grain. They make a fuss about you, you're treated like a child born in his parents' old age. But later you'll see, when you've begun to go to their school, oh won't the worldly ones beat you! Which of you isn't hurt by criticism? Is there one of you really so self-confident that he doesn't go around begging for some authority's approval? Is there one of you who's prepared to publish his book anonymously? The big thing with you people is that your name should be seen and known. You have given up our tranquility of spirit for what? For passions you will never be able to satisfy and for doubts you will never be able to answer, no matter how much you suffer."

When he had spoken his fill, Hersh Rasseyner began to walk away with a quick, energetic stride. But I had once been a Mussarist too, so I ran after him.

"Hersh, listen to me now. No one knows better than I how torn you are. You're proud of yourself because you don't care if the whole street laughs at your for wearing your *tzitzit*[1] down to your ankles. You've talked yourself into believing that the cloth with the woolen fringes is a partition between you and the world. You despise yourself because you're afraid you may find favor in the eyes of the world, that Potiphar's wife. You fear you won't have the strength to tear yourself away like the righteous Joseph. So you flee from temptation and think the world will run after you. But when you see that the world doesn't run after you, you become angry and cry out: Nobody enjoys life. You want to console yourself with that idea. When you live in solitude in your garret, that's because you would rather have nothing at all than take the crumb that life throws you. Your modesty is pride, not self-denial.

"And who told you that I seek pleasure? I seek a truth you don't have. For that matter, I didn't run away, I simply returned to my own street—to Yat-kev Street in Vilna. I love the porters with their backs broken from carrying their burdens; the artisans pouring sweat at their workbenches; the market women who would cut off a finger to give a poor man a crust of bread. But you scold the hungry for being sinners, and all you can tell them is to repent. You laugh at people who work because you say they don't trust in god. But you live on what others have made. Women exhausted with work bring you something to eat, and in return you promise them the world to come. Hersh Rasseyner, you have long since sold your share of the world to come to those poor women."

1. The fringes on the four corners of the linen or woolen cloth worn under the upper garment by Orthodox Jews. The fringes serve as a reminder of the obligation to keep God's
commandments.

Hersh Rasseyner gave a start and disappeared. I returned to Vilna with a burden removed from my conscience. In the disputation with the Mussarist I myself began to understand why I had left them. If at the time, I said to myself, I didn't know why and where I was going, someone else thought it for me, someone stronger than I. That someone else stronger than I was—my generation and my environment.

2

Two years passed. War broke out between Germany and Poland. The western Ukraine and western White Russia were taken over by the Red Army. After they had been in Vilna a few weeks, the Russians announced that they were giving the city back to the Lithuanians. To Vilna there began to come refugees who did not want to remain under Soviet rule. The Novaredok Yeshiva came also. Meanwhile, the Soviets remained. Hunger raged in the city. Every face was clouded with fear because of the arrests carried out at night by NKVD[2] agents. My heart was heavy. Once I was standing in line for a ration of bread. Suddenly I saw Hersh Rasseyner.

I had heard that in the meanwhile he had married. His face was framed with a little black beard, his gait more restrained, his clothing more presentable. I was so glad to see him that I left my place in the line, pushed through the crowd, and came up to him.

He spoke little and was very cautious. I understood why. He did not trust me and was afraid of trouble. I could see that he was trying to make up his mind whether to speak to me. But when he saw how despondent I was, he hid his mouth with his hand, as though to conceal his twisted smile, and a gleam of derision came into his eye. With his head he motioned toward the bridge, on which were parked a few tanks with Red Army soldiers.

"Well, Chaim," Hersh said to me quietly, "are you satisfied now? Is this what you wanted?"

I tried to smile and answered just as quietly, "Hersh, I bear no more responsibility for all that than you do for me."

He shook himself and pronounced a few sharp, cutting words, seeming to forget his fear: "You're wrong, Chaim, I do bear responsibility for you." He retreated a few steps and motioned with his eyes to the Red Army soldiers, as though to say: And you bear responsibility for them.

2. Acronym for Narodnyi Komissariat Vnutrennikh Del, People's Commissariat of Internal Affairs, or the Russian secret police.

3

Nine more years passed, years of war and destruction, during which I wandered across Russia, Poland, and Western Europe. In 1948, on a summer afternoon, I was riding in the Paris Métro. Couples stood close together. Short Frenchwomen, as though fainting, hung by the side of their black-haired lovers.

I saw a familiar face. Until then it had been concealed by someone's shoulder, and only when the couples had had to move a little did that corner of the car open up. My heart began to pound. Could he really be alive? Hadn't he been in Vilna under the German occupation? When I returned to the ruins of my home in 1945 I did not see him or hear of him. Still, those were the same eyes, the same obstinately upturned nose; only the broad black beard had begun to turn gray. It was astonishing to me that he could look at the couples so calmly, and that a good-natured smile lit up his melancholy glance. That was not like him. But after a moment I noticed that there was a faraway look in his eyes. He really did not see the people on the train. He was dressed neatly, in a long cloak and a clean white shirt buttoned at the throat, without a necktie. I thought to myself: He never wore ties. This more than anything else convinced me it was he.

I pushed my way to him through the passengers and blurted out, "Excuse me, aren't you Reb Hersh Rasseyner?"

He looked at me, wrinkled his forehead and smiled. "Ah, Chaim, Chaim, is that you? *Sholom aleichem!* How are you?"

I could tell that this time when Hersh Rasseyner asked, "How are you?" he did not mean what he had meant eleven years before. Then his question was angry and derisive. Now he asked the question quietly, simply. It came from his heart and it showed concern, as for an old friend.

We got into a corner and he told me briefly that he had been in a camp in Latvia. Now he was in Germany, at the head of a Yeshiva in Salzheim.

"The head of a Yeshiva in a camp in Germany? And who are your students, Reb Hersh?"

He smiled. "Do you think that the Holy One is so to speak an orphan? We still have lads, praise be to the Almighty, who study Torah."

He told me that he had been in the camp with about ten pupils. He had drawn them close to him and taught them Jewishness. Because they were still only children and very weak he helped them in their work. At night they used to gather about his cot and all would recite Psalms together. There was a doctor in the camp who used to say that he would give half his life to be able to recite Psalms too. But he couldn't. He lacked faith, poor man.

I was happy to meet him and I preferred to avoid a debate, so I merely asked, "And what brings you here so often? Are you in business?"

"Of course we're in business." He stroked his beard with satisfaction. "Big business. We bring Yeshiva people here and and send them off to Israel and America. We take books back from here. With the help of the Almighty, I have even flown twice to Morocco."

"Morocco? What did you do there, Reb Hersh?"

"Brought back students from the Moroccan Jews, spoke in their synagogue."

"And how did you talk to them? You don't know Arabic or French."

"The Almighty helps. What difference does it make how you speak? The main thing is *what* you speak."

Unexpectedly he began to talk about me. "How will it be with you, Chaim? It's time for you to start thinking about repentance. We're nearer rather than farther."

"What do you mean?"

"I mean," he said, drawing out his words in a chant, "that we have both lived out more than half our lives. What will become of Reb Chaim?" He strongly accented the word Reb. "Where are you voyaging? Together with them, perhaps?" His eyes laughed at the young couples. "Will you get off where they do? Or do you still believe in this merciless world?"

"And you, Reb Hersh," I asked in sudden irritation, "do you still believe in particular providence? You say that the Holy One is not as it were an orphan. But we are orphans. A miracle happened to you, Reb Hersh, and you were saved. But how about the rest? Can you still believe?"

"Of course I believe," said Hersh Rasseyner, separating his hands in innocent wonder. "You can touch particular providence, it's so palpable. But perhaps you're thinking of the kind of man who has faith that the Almighty is to be found only in the pleasant places of this world but is not to be found, God forbid, in the desert and wastelands? You know the rule: just as a man must make a blessing over the good so must he make a blessing over evil. We must fall before the greatness—"

"What do you want, Reb Hersh?" I interrupted. "Shall I see the greatness of God in the thought that only He could cause such destruction, not flesh and blood? You're out-doing the Psalms you used to recite on your bed in the concentration camp. The Psalmist sees the greatness of God in the fact that the sun rises every day, but you see miracles even in catastrophes."

"Without any doubt," Hersh Rasseyner answered calmly, "I see everywhere, in everything, at every moment, particular providence. I couldn't remain on earth for one minute without the thought of God. How could I stand it without Him in this murderous world?"

"But I won't say that His judgment is right. I can't!"

"You can," said Hersh Rasseyner, putting a friendly hand on my shoulder, "you can—gradually. First the penitent understands that the world can't be without a Guide. Then he understands that the Guide is the God of Israel and that there is no other power besides Him to help Him lead the world. At last he recognizes that the world is in Him, as we read: 'There is no place void of Him.' And if you understood that, Chaim, you would also understand how the Almighty reveals himself in misfortune as well as in salvation."

Hersh Rasseyner spoke in a warm voice. He did not once take his hand off my shoulder. I felt a great love for him and saw that he had become more pious than ever.

4

We left the Métro near the Jewish quarter, at the rue de Rivoli, and we passed the old city hall, the Hotel de Ville. In the niches of the walls of the Hotel de Ville, between the windows, in three rows, stand stone figures, some with a sword, some with a book, some with brush and palette, and some with geometers' instruments.

Reb Rasseyner saw me looking at the monuments.

He glanced at them out of the corner of his eye and asked, "Who are those idols?"

I explained to him that they were famous Frenchmen: statesmen, heroes, scholars, and artists.

"Reb Hersh," I pleaded with him, "look at those statues. Come closer and see the light streaming from their marble eyes. See how much goodness lies hidden in their stone faces. You call it idolatry, but I tell you that quite literally, I could weep when I walk about Paris and see those sculptures. It's a miracle, after all. How could a human being breathe the breath of life into stone? When you see a living man, you see only one man. But when you see a man poured out in bronze, you see mankind itself. Do you understand me? That one there, for instance, is a poet famous all over the world. The great writer broadens our understanding and stirs our pity for our fellow men. He shows us the nature of the man who can't overcome his desires. He doesn't punish even the wicked man, but sees him according to his afflictions in the war he wages with himself and the rest of the world. You don't say he's right, but you understand that he can't help it. Why are you pulling at your beard with such anger, Reb Hersh?"

He stared at me with burning eyes and cried out, "For shame! How can you say such foolish things? So you could weep when you look at those painted lumps of matter? Why don't you weep about the charred walls which alone remain of the Gaon of Vilna's synagogue? Those *artistes* of yours, those monument-choppers; those poets who sang about their emperors; those tumblers who danced and played before the rulers—did those masters of yours even bother to think that their patron would massacre a whole city and steal all it had, only to buy them, your masters, with gold? Did the prophets flatter kings? Did they take gifts of harlots' wages? And how merciful you are! The writer shows how the wicked man is the victim of his own evil inclinations. I think that's what you said. It's really a pity about the arrogant rebel! He destroys others, and of course he's destroyed too. What a pity! Do you think it's easier to be a good man than an adulterer? But you particularly like to describe the lustful man. You know him better, there's something of him in you artists. If you make excuses for the man who exults in his wickedness, then as far as I'm concerned all your scribbling is unclean and unfit. Condemn the wicked man! Condemn the glutton and drunkard! Do you say he can't help it? He has to help it! You've sung a fine song of praise to the putrid idols, Chaim Vilner."

Hersh Rasseyner looked into my eyes with the sharp, threatening expression I had seen eleven years earlier, when we met in that Bialystok street. His voice had become hard and resounding. Passers-by stopped and stared at the bearded Jew who shook his finger at the sculptures of the Hotel de Ville. Hersh did not so much as notice the passers-by. I felt embarrassed in the face of these Frenchmen, smiling and looking at us curiously.

"Don't shout so," I told him irritably. "You really think you have a monopoly on mercy and truth. You're starting where we left off eleven years ago. In Novaredok you always kept the windows closed, but it was still too light for you in the House of Study, so you ran off to your garret. From the garret you went down into a cellar. And from the cellar you burrowed down into a hole under the earth. That's where you could keep your commandment of solitude and that's where you persuaded yourself that a man's thoughts and feelings are like his hair; if he wants to, he can trim his hair and leave nothing but a beard and earlocks—holy thought and pious conduct. You think the world is what you imagine it, and you won't have anything to do with it. You think men are what you imagine them, but you tell them to be the opposite. But even the concentration camps couldn't make men different from what they are. Those who were evil became worse in the camps. Otherwise they might have lived out their lives and not known themselves for what they were, but in the crisis men saw themselves and others undisguised. And when we were all freed, even the better ones among us weren't freed of the poison we'd had to drink behind the barbed wire. Now, if the concentration camp couldn't change men from top to bottom, how can you expect to change them?"

Reb Rasseyner looked at me with astonishment. The anger that had flared in his eyes died down, though a last flicker of it seemed to remain.

"You don't know what you're talking about, Chaim," he said quietly and reluctantly. "Whoever told you that afflictions as such make people better? It's quite clear that external causes can't drag people back to a Jewish life. A man's heart and mind have to be ready.

"If a man didn't come there with a thirst for a higher life, he certainly didn't elevate himself in the concentration camp. But the spiritual man knows that always and everywhere he must keep mounting higher or else he will fall lower. And as for the claim that a man can't change—that is a complete lie. 'In my flesh shall I see God!' The case of Hersh Rasseyner proves that a man can change. I won't tell you a long story about how many lusts I suffered from; how often the very veins in my head almost burst from the boiling of the blood; how many obstinacies I had to tear out of myself. But I knew that whoever denies himself affirms the Master of the World. I knew that the worst sentence that can be passed on a man is that he shall not be able to renounce his old nature. And because I truly wanted to conquer myself, the Almighty helped me."

"You are severe in your judgments," I answered. "You always were, Reb Hersh, if you'll pardon my saying so. You call these wise men putrid idols, but you refuse to see that they lifted mankind out of its bestial state. They weren't butchers of the soul and they didn't talk themselves into believing that human beings can tear their lower urges out of themselves and lop them off. They were very well aware of the hidden root of the human race. They wanted to illuminate men's minds with wisdom, so that men would be able to grow away from their untamed desires. You can't banish shadows with a broom, only with a lighted lamp. These great men—"

Hersh began to laugh so loud that I had to interrupt myself. He immediately stopped laughing and sighed. "I am very tired," he said. "I have been traveling the whole night. But somehow I don't want to leave you. After all, you were once a student at Novaredok; perhaps there is still a spark of the spirit left in you somewhere."

We walked to a bench in silence. On first meeting him I had thought that he had become milder. Now I realized regretfully that his demands upon me and his negation of the whole world had grown greater. I hoped, though, that the pause would ease the tension that had arisen between us and I was in no hurry to be the first to talk again. Hersh, however, wrinkled his forehead as though he were collecting his thoughts, and when we were seated he returned to my last words.

"Did you say there were great men? The Germans insist they produced all the great men. I don't know whether they produced the very greatest, but I don't suppose that you worldly people would deny that they did produce learned men. Well, did those philosophers influence their own nation to become better? And the real question is, were the philosophers themselves good men? I don't want you to think that I underestimate their knowledge. During my years in the concentration camp I heard a good deal. There were exceptionally learned men among us, because the German mixed us all together, and in our moments of leisure we used to talk. Later, when with the help of the Almighty I was saved, I myself looked into the books of you worldly people, because I was no longer afraid that they would hurt me. And I was really very much impressed by their ideas. Occasionally I found in their writings as much talent and depth as in our own holy books, if the two may be mentioned in the same breath. But they are satisfied with talk! And I want you to believe me when I say that I concede that their poets and scientists wanted to be good. Only—only they weren't able to. And if some *did* have good qualities, they were exceptions. The masses and even their wise men didn't go any farther than fine talk. As far as talking is concerned, they talk more beautifully than we do.

"Do you know why they weren't able to become better? Because they are consumed with a passion to enjoy life. And since pleasure is not something that can be had by itself, murder arose among them—the pleasure of murder. And that's why they talk such fine talk, because they want to use it for fooling themselves into doing fine deeds. Only it doesn't help. They're satisfied with rhetoric, and the reason is that they care most of all for systems. The nations of the world inherited from the Greeks the desire for order and for pretty systems.

"First of all, they do what they do in public. They have no pleasure from their lusts if they can't sin openly, publicly, so that the whole world will know. They say of us that we're only hypocrites, whereas they do what they want to do publicly. But they like to wage war, not only with others, but with themselves as well, argue with themselves (of course, not too vigorously), even suffer and repent. And when they come to do repentance, the whole world knows about that too. Theirs is the kind of repentance that gives them an intense pleasure; their self-love is so extreme it borders on sickness. They even like their victims, because their victims afford them the pleasure of sinning and the sweet afflictions of regret."

The Rasseyner had moved away from me to the other end of the bench and had begun to look at me as though it had occurred to him that by mistake he might be talking to a stranger. Then he lowered his head and muttered as though to himself: "Do you remember, that time in Bialystok?" He was silent for a moment and pulled a hair out of his beard as though he were pulling his memories out with it. "Do you remember, Chaim, how you told me on that Bialystok street that we were running away from the world because we were afraid we wouldn't be able to resist temptation? A Mussarist can labor for a lifetime on improving his qualities, yet a single word of criticism will stick in him like a knife. Yes, it's true! All the days of my youth I kept my eyes on the earth, without looking at the world. Then came the German. He took me by my Jewish beard, yanked my head up, and told me to look him straight in the eye. So I had to look into his evil eyes, and into the eyes of the whole world as well. And I saw, Chaim, I saw—you know what I saw. Now I can look at all the idols, and read all the forbidden impurities and contemplate all the pleasures of life, and it won't tempt me any more because now I know the true face of the world. Oh, Reb Chaim, turn and repent! It's not too late. Remember what the prophet Jeremiah said: 'For my people have committed two evils; they have forsaken Me, the fountain of living waters, and hewed them out cisterns, broken cisterns, that can hold no water.'"[3]

Hersh had spoken like a broken man. Tears were dropping on his beard. He rubbed his eyes to hold the tears back, but they continued to flow down his cheeks. I took his hand and said to him with emotion:

"Reb Hersh, you say that I have forsaken a fountain of living waters for a broken cistern. I must tell you that you're wrong. I draw water from the same fountain as you, only with a different vessel. But calm yourself, Reb Hersh.

"You yourself said that you believe that the nations of the world had men of wisdom and men of action who wanted to be good, but couldn't. I think I'm quoting you accurately. What I don't understand is this. It's a basic principle of Judaism that man has free will. The Novaredok people actually maintain that it's possible to attain such a state of perfection that we can do good deeds without the intervention of our physical bodies. Well then, if a man can actually peel the evil husks from himself, as he would peel an onion, how do you answer this question: Since the wise men among the Gentiles wanted to be good, why couldn't they?"

I wasn't able to keep a mocking note of triumph out of my question. It stirred the Rasseyner out of his mournful abstraction. With deliberation he straightened himself and answered gently.

"Chaim, you seem to have forgotten what you learned at Novaredok, so I'll remind you. In this great love for mankind, the Almighty has endowed us

3. From Jeremiah 2:13.

with reason. If our sages, of blessed memory, tell us that we can learn from the animals, surely we can learn from reason as well. And we know that the elders of Athens erected systems of morality according to pure reason. They had many disciples, each with his own school.

"But the question hasn't changed. Did they really live as they taught, or did their systems remain only systems? You must understand once and for all that when his reason is calm and pure, a man doesn't know what he's likely to do when his dark desire overtakes him. A man admires his own wisdom and is proud of his knowledge, but as soon as a little desire begins to stir in him he forgets everything else. Reason is like a dog on a leash who follows sedately in his master's footsteps—until he sees a bitch. With us it's a basic principle that false ideas come from bad qualities. Any man can rationalize whatever he wants to do. Is it true that only a little while ago he was saying the opposite of what he is now saying? He'll tell you he was wrong then. And if he lets you prove to him that he wasn't wrong then, he'll shrug and say: When I want to do something, I can't be an Aristotle. As soon as his desire is sated, his reason revives and he's sorry for what he did. As soon as he feels desire beginning to stir once more, he forgets his reason again. It's as though he were in a swamp; when he pulls one foot out, the other sinks in. There is delicacy in his character, he has a feeling for beauty, he expresses his exalted thoughts in measured words, and there is no flaw in him; then he sees a female ankle and his reason is swallowed up. If a man has no God, why should he listen to the philosopher who tells him to be good? The philosopher himself is cold and gloomy and empty. He is like a man who wants to celebrate a marriage with himself.

"The one way out is this. A man should choose between good and evil only as the Torah chooses for him. The Torah wants him to be happy. The Torah is the only reality in life. Everything else is a dream. Just as the Master of the World showed Moses in the wilderness a fiery tabernacle and said to him: Such a tabernacle shalt thou make for Me, so should a man do in every particular what is done by the fiery Complete Man, who is constructed of the letters in which the Torah is written. Even when a man understands rationally what he should do, he must never forget that before all else he should do it because the Torah tells him to do it. That is how he can guard against the time when his reason will have no power to command him.

"Wait a moment, I'm not through yet. A man may tell himself: I don't live according to reason but according to the Torah. And he may feel certain that when temptation comes, he'll look into the appropriate book to see what he should do, and he'll do it. He tells himself that he is free. Actually, the freedom of his choice goes no farther than his wish. Even a man who has a Torah won't be able to withstand his temptation if he doesn't watch over himself day and night. He Who knows all secrets knew that our father Abraham would stand ready to sacrifice Isaac; but only after the Binding did the angel say to Abraham: Now I know. Hence we learn that until a man has accomplished what he should, the Torah does not trust him. A child has the capacity to grow, but we don't know how tall he'll grow. His father and mother may be as high as the trees, but he may favor a dwarf grandfather. Only by good deeds can we drive out bad deeds. Therefore the Jews cried out at Sinai: 'We will do'—only do, always do; 'and we will obey'—and now we want to know what the Torah tells us to do. Without deeds all inquiry is vain.

"That is the outlook and the moral way of 'the old one,' Reb Joseph Yoyzl, may his merit be a shield for us, and thousands of students at Novaredok steeped themselves in it day and night. We labored to make ourselves better, each of us polished and filed his own soul, with examiners gathering evidences of improvement like pearls. But you laughed at us. Then came the German, may his name be blotted out, and murdered our sainted students. And now we're both face to face with the destruction of the Community of Israel. But you are faced with another destruction as well—the destruction of your faith in the world. That's what hurts you and torments you, so you ask me: Why weren't the wise men of the Gentiles able to be good, if they wanted to be good? And you find contradictions in what I said. But the real contradiction you find is not in what I said but in yourself. You thought the world was striving to become better, and you discovered it was striving for our blood.

"Even if they wanted to, the wise men of the Gentiles couldn't become good to the very roots of their being because they don't have a Torah and because they didn't labor to perfect their qualities all their life long. Their ethics were worked out by human minds. They trusted their reasoned assumptions as men trust the ice of a frozen river in winter. Then came Hitler and put his weight on the wisdom of the wise men of the nations. The ice of their slippery reasoning burst, and all their goodness was drowned.

"And together with their goodness to others their own self-respect was drowned. Think of it! For a word they didn't like they used to fight with swords or shoot each other. To keep public opinion from sneering or a fool from calling them coward, though they trembled at the thought of dying, they went to their death. For generation after generation their arrogance grew like a cancer, until it ended by eating their flesh and sucking their marrow. For centuries they speculated, they, talked and they wrote. Does duty to nation and family come first, or does the freedom of the individual come before his obligations to parents, wife, and children—or even to one's self? They considered the matter solemnly and concluded that there are no bonds that a nation is not free to break; that truth and reason are like the sun, which must rise; can the sun be covered by throwing clods of earth at it? So there came in the West a booted ruler with a little mustache and in the East a booted ruler with a big mustache, and both of them together struck the wise man to the ground, so that he sank into the mud. I suppose you'll say that the wise men wanted to save their lives. I can understand that. But hadn't they insisted that freedom, truth and reason are more precious to the philosopher than his life? Take that wise man whose statue is standing there, with his instruments for measuring the stars and planets. When everyone else argued: 'The sun revolves about the earth,' he said: 'Not so; do what you will to me, break me, draw and quarter me, the earth revolves around the sun!' What would he have said to his grandchildren today? If the spirit of life could return to him, he would crawl down from his niche in the wall, strike his stone head against the stone bridge and recite Lamentations."

6

The Rasseyner had begun by speaking slowly, like the head of a Yeshiva trying to explain a difficult passage to his pupil for the hundredth time, pausing briefly every now and then so that I could follow what he was saying. Gradually his animation grew; I was reminded of the discussions we used to have at Novaredok during the evenings after the Sabbath in the weeks before the Days of Awe.[4] He began to speak more quickly, there was more excitement in his voice, and he ended his sentences like a man hammering nails into a wall. He shouted at me as though I were a dark cellar and he was calling to someone hiding in me.

The square and the neighboring streets had grown quieter and the flow of people had thinned out. On the benches in the little park passers-by sat mutely, exhausted by the intense heat of the day and trying to get some relief from the cool evening breeze that had begun to blow in the blue twilight of Paris.

"Hear me out, Chaim," Hersh resumed, "I'll tell you a secret. I have to talk to you. I talked to you during all those years when I was in the ghetto and later in the camps. Don't wonder at it, because you were always dear to me, from the time you were a student in Bialystok. Even then I had the feeling that you stood with one foot outside our camp. I prayed for you. I prayed that you would remain Jewish. But my prayers didn't help. You yourself didn't want to be pious. You left us, but I never forgot you. They used to talk about you in the Yeshiva, your reputation reached us even there. And I suppose you remember the time we met in Bialystok. Later our Yeshiva was

4. Jewish High Holy Days

in Vilna, under the Bolsheviks, and we met again, only then you were very downhearted. In the ghetto they said you had been killed while trying to escape. Afterward we heard from partisans in the forest that you were living in Russia. I used to imagine that if we were both saved, a miracle might happen. We would meet and I could talk to you. That's why you mustn't be surprised if I talk to you as fluently as though I were reciting the daily prayers. Believe me, I have had so many imaginary debates with you that I know my arguments as well as the first prayer of the morning."

"Reb Hersh," I said, "it's getting late. The time for afternoon prayers will be over soon."

"Don't worry about my afternoon prayers, Chaim," he laughed, "I said them just after twelve o'clock. In the camp it became a habit with me not to delay carrying out any commandment. I reasoned that if any hour was to be my last, I didn't want to come to heaven naked.

"Do you have time and strength to go on listening to me? You do? Good. So far I've talked to you about the Gentile wise men. But first we ought to be clear in our own minds about our relation to them and to the whole world. And one thing more: if anything I say strikes you as being too harsh, don't take it amiss. Even though I'm talking to you, I don't mean you personally; I really mean secular Jews in general. So don't be angry.

7

"Your Enlighteners used to sing this tune: 'Be a Jew at home and a man in public.' So you took off our traditional coat and shaved your beard and earlocks. Still when you went out into the street, the Jew pursued you in your language, in your gestures, in every part of you. So you tried to get rid of the incubus. And the result was that the Jew left you, like an old father whose children don't treat him with respect; first he goes to the synagogue and then, because he has no choice, to the home for the aged. Now that you've seen— woe, what has happened to us!—you've turned your slogan around. Now it's be a man at home and a Jew in public. You can't be pious at home because you're lacking in faith. Out of anger against the Gentile and nostalgia for the father you abandoned, you want to parade your Jewishness in public. Only the man you try to be at home, as you call it, follows you out of your house. The parable of the Prince and the Nazirite applies to you. A dog was invited to two weddings, one near and one far. He thought: I won't be too late for the nearer one. So he ran first to the farther wedding—and missed it. Out of breath he ran to the one nearer home, and came after the feast. When he tried to push through the door, all he got was the stick. The upshot was that he missed both. The moral may be coarse, but you remember from your No-

varedok days that it was applied to those who wanted to have both the pleasures of this world and the Torah.

"You cried in the public square: 'The nations of the world dislike us because we're different; let us be like them!' And you were like them. Not only
that, but you stood at the head of their civilization. Where there was a famous
scientist, thinker, writer—there you found a Jew. And it was precisely for
that reason that they hated us all the more. They won't tolerate the idea of our
being like them.

"During the Middle Ages the priests wanted to baptize us. They used to
delight in the torments of a Jew who tried to separate himself from the Community of Israel—with his family mourning him as though he were dead and
the entire congregation lamenting as though it were the fast of the Ninth of
Ab.[5] In our day, though, when they saw how easy it became for a Jew to leap
over into their camp, they stationed themselves at the outposts with axes in
their hands, as though to fend off wild beasts. But you were hungry and
blind, so you leaped—onto their axes.

"When you ran away from being Jewish, you disguised your flight with
high-sounding names. An enlightened man would talk in the most elevated
rhetoric about Enlightenment; but what he really had in mind was to become
a druggist. He yearned for the fleshpots of Egypt. His ambition was to dig
his hands into the pot with no one to look him in the eye, like the miser who
doesn't like anyone to be near him when he's eating. With the nations of the
earth the great thing is the individual—his sovereignty, his pleasure and his
repose. But they understand that if they acted on the principle that might is
right, one man would devour the other; so they have a government of individuals, and the rule is: Let me alone and I'll let you alone. With us Jews the
individual doesn't exist, it's the community that counts. What's good for all
must be good each. Till your rebellion Jews lived as one—in prayer and in
study, in joy and in sorrow. But you incited the tribes: 'Every man to your
tents, O Israel!' Let each of us follow his own law, like the nations of the
world. What's more, not only did you want to live as individuals, you wanted
to die as individuals too. To avoid being confused with the other dead on
the day of your death, you spend your lives erecting monuments for your-
selves—one by great deeds; another by imposing his dominion; a third by a
great business enterprise; and you by writing books. You didn't violate the
commandment against idolatry. Of course not! You were your own gods. You
prophesied: 'Man will be a god.' So naturally he became a devil.

5. A day known as Tish'ah b'Av, which commemorates national calamities throughout
Jewish history, such as the destruction of both the First and Second Temples, the fall of Bar
Kokhba's fortress Bethar, and the expulsion from Spain in 1492.

"Why are you uneasy, Reb Chaim? Didn't we agree you wouldn't be angry? I don't mean you personally; I'm only speaking figuratively. But if you really feel I mean you, then I do! The wicked are as the unquiet sea. Every wave thinks it will leap over the shore, though it sees millions of others shattered before its eyes. Every man who lives for this world alone thinks that he will succeed in doing what no one else has ever been able to do. Well, you know now how far you got! But instead of looking for solace in the Master of the World and in the Community of Israel, you're still looking for the glass splinters of your shattered dreams. And little as you'll have the world to come, you have this world even less.

"Still, not all of you secularists wanted to overthrow the yoke of the Law altogether. Some grumbled that Judaism kept on getting heavier all the time: Mishna on Bible; Gemara on Mishna; commentaries on Gemara; codes; commentaries on the codes; commentaries on the commentaries, and commentaries on them. Lighten the weight a little, they said, so what is left can be borne more easily. But the more they lightened the burden, the heavier the remainder seemed to them. I fast twice a week without difficulty, and they can hardly do it once a year. Furthermore, what the father rejected in part, the son rejected in its entirety. And the son was right! Rather nothing than so little. A half-truth is no truth at all. Every man, and particularly every young man, needs a faith that will command all of his intellect and ardor. The devout cover a boy's head with a cap when he's a year old, to accustom him to commandments; but when a worldly father suddenly asks his grown son to cover his head with a paper cap and say the blessing over the wine on a Friday evening, the young man rightly thinks the whole thing is absurd. If he doesn't believe in creation, and if the exodus from Egypt is not much of a miracle as far as he's concerned, and if the Song of Songs is to him only the song of a shepherd and a shepherdess—God forbid!—and not the song of love between the Assembly of Israel and the Holy One, blessed be He, or between the supernal soul and the Almighty, why should he bless the Sabbath wine? Anyone who thinks he can hold on to basic principles and give up what he considers secondary is like a man who chops down the trunk of a tree and expects the roots not to rot.

"I've already told you, Chaim, that we of the Mussar school are very mindful of criticism. Do you remember telling me, on a street in Bialystok, that we try to escape by withdrawal because we would rather have nothing in this world than only a little? That's true. We want a more onerous code, more commandments, more laws, more prohibitions. We know that all the pleasures of life are like salt water: the more a man drinks of it, the thirstier he becomes. That's why we want a Torah that will leave no room in us for anything else.

"Suppose the Master of the World were to come to me and say: 'Hersh, you're only flesh and blood. Six hundred and thirteen commandments are too many for you, I will lighten your burden. You don't need to observe all of them. Don't be afraid, you won't be deprived of the resurrection of the dead!' Do you understand, Chaim, what it means to be at the resurrection of the dead and see life given again to all the Jews who fell before my eyes? If the Father of Mercy should ask less self-sacrifice of me, it would be very bitter for me. I would pray: 'Father of Mercy, I don't want my burden to be lightened, I want it to be made heavier.' As things are now, my burden is still too light. What point is there to the life of a fugitive of a Jew saved from the crematorium, if he isn't always ready to sacrifice his bit of a rescued life for the Torah? But you, Chaim, are you as daring in your demands upon the world as I am in my demands upon the Master of the World? When you were studying with us, you were so strong and proud that you could be satisfied only by getting to the very bottom of the truth. And now do you think it right to crawl under the table of life, hoping for a bone from the feast of unclean pleasures, or a dry crumb of the joys of this world? Is that what's left to you of your pride and confidence in the warfare of life? I look at you and think: I'm still very far from what I ought to be. If I had reached a higher stage, my heart would be torn for you.

"The rebellious seducer rejected everything, while the one who halts between two opinions left something; but both of them, when they wanted to show their unfaltering good sense, first denounced the Community of Israel for allowing itself to be bound in the cobwebs of a profitless dialectic, living in a cemetery and listening to ghost stories; concerning itself with unrealities and thinking that the world ends at the ruined mill on the hilltop. The clever writer described it with great artistry and the vulgar laughed. And the secularist reformers with their enlightened little beards justified themselves with a verse: 'Whom the Lord loveth He correcteth.' In other words, only because they really loved us Jews did they attack us. But they groveled before everything they saw elsewhere. They called us sycophants—but with their own souls, as with rags, they wiped the gentry's boots. The overt rebel and the man who prayed secretly and sinned secretly—why antagonize either side?— were at one in this, that the thing they mocked us for most enthusiastically was our belief in being chosen. What's so special about us? they laughed. And I say, you may not feel very special—but you have to be! You may not want it, but the Almighty does! Thousands of years ago the God of Israel said through Ezekiel His prophet: 'And that which cometh into your mind shall not be at all; in that ye say: We will be as the nations, as the families of the countries, to serve wood and stone. As I live, saith the Lord God'—Do you hear, Chaim? The Almighty swears by His own life!—'As I live, saith the

Lord God, surely with a mighty hand, and with an outstretched arm, and with fury poured out, will I be king over you."[6] You're a writer; write it on your forehead. You don't seem very impressed. You don't consider a verse to be proof. But the German is a proof, isn't he? Today, because so many Jews have been cut down, you don't want to remember how you used to laugh at them. But tomorrow, when the destruction will be forgotten, you'll laugh again at the notion that God has chosen us. That's why I want to tell you something.

"You know I was in a camp. I lay on the earth and was trampled by the German in his hobnailed boots. Well, suppose that an angel of God had come to me then, that he bent down and whispered into my ear: 'Hersh, in the twinkling of an eye I will turn you into the German. I will put his coat on you and give you his murderous face; and he will be you. Say the word and the miracle will come to pass.' If the angel had asked—do you hear, Chaim?—I would not have agreed at all. Not for one minute would I have consented to be the other, the German, my torturer. I want the justice of law! I want vengeance, not robbery! But I want it as a Jew. With the Almighty's help I could stand the German's boots on my throat, but if I had had to put on his mask, his murderous face, I would have been smothered as though I had been gassed. And when the German shouted at me: "You are a slave of slaves,' I answered through my wounded lips: 'Thou hast chosen me.'

"I want to ask you only one question, no more. What happened is known to all Jews. 'Let the whole House of Israel bewail the burning which the Lord hath kindled.' All Jews mourn the third of our people that died a martyr's death. But anyone with true feeling knows that it was not a third of the House of Israel that was destroyed, but a third of himself, of his body, his soul. And so we must make a reckoning—you as well as I. Anyone who doesn't make the reckoning must be as bestial as the beasts of the wood. Let's make the reckoning together. In justice and in mercy, may we forgive the murderers? No, we may not! To the end of all generations we may not forgive them.

"Neither you nor I have the right to close our eyes at night. We have no right to flee the laments, the eyes, and the out-stretched arms of the murdered; though we break under the anguish and afflictions, we have no right to flee their outcry. What then? I know that the reckoning is not yet over; far from it. And I have never thought for one moment that anyone in the world besides the jealous and vengeful God would avenge the helpless little ones

6. From Ezekiel 20:32–33.

that the Gestapo stuffed into the trains for Treblinka, treading on their delicate little bodies to get as many children as possible into the cars. That is why I don't have the slightest shadow of a doubt that the great and terrible day, behold it comes! When I hear people quibbling about politics, and calculating the position of the powers, I know that there is another set of books, kept in fire and blood. There's no use asking me whether I want it that way or not, that's the way it has to be!

"But you, Chaim, how can you eat and sleep and laugh and dress so elegantly? Don't you have to make your reckoning too? How can you thrust yourself into the world when you know it consorts with the murderers of the members of your own house? And you thought the world was becoming better! Your world has fallen! I have greater faith than ever. If I had only as much faith as in the past, that would be an offense against the martyred saints. My answer is, more and more self-sacrifice for the Master of the World; to cry out until the spirit is exhausted: 'For Thy sake are we killed all the day'; to go about, until the soul departs, with a shattered heart and hands raised to heaven: 'Father, Father, only You are left to us!' But what has changed with you, Chaim? What is your answer?"

8

The Rasseyner's speech was like a dry flame, progressively taking fire from itself. I realized he was unburdening himself of much accumulated anger. Finally he grew quiet. His lips were pinched with the effort he had to make to obey himself and speak no more.

The blue of the evening sky was growing darker. The stone figures around the Hotel de Ville had shrunk, as though frightened by what the Rasseyner had said, and quietly burrowed deeper into the walls. The old building was now half in darkness. The street lamps brought out the flat green color of our surroundings. Black shining autos slid quietly over the asphalt. A thin little rain began to come down. Windows were lighting up. The people walking along on the other side of the street seemed to be moving with a silent, secret pace behind a thick silken curtain, woven of the summer rain.

From our little empty corner in the shade I looked across the street. In the light of the electric lamps the raindrops looked like millions of fireflies hastening down from the sky in hurried joy. I had an impulse to merge myself with the human stream flowing down the surrounding lighted streets. I stirred, and I felt the little pricks of pain in my stiffened limbs. The light rain came to an end. Hersh sat near me, motionless and as though deaf, his shoulders sharp and angular and his head bowed and sunk in darkness. He was waiting for me to answer.

"Reb Hersh," I finally said, "as I sat here listening to you, I sometimes thought I was listening to myself. And since it's harder to lie to yourself than to someone else, I will answer you as though you were my own conscience, with no thought either of merely being polite or of trying to win a debate. I am under no greater obligation than you to know everything. I don't consider it a special virtue not to have doubts. I must tell you that just as the greatness of the faithful consists in their innocence and wholeness, so the heroism of thinkers consists in their being able to tolerate doubt and make their peace with it. You didn't discover your truth; you received it ready-made. If anyone should ask you about something in your practice of which you yourself don't know the meaning, you answer: 'The work of my fathers is in my hands.' As a rule, a man is a rebel in his youth; in age he seeks tranquility. You had tranquility in your youth, while I don't have it even now; you once predicted it would be so with me. But is your tranquility of soul a proof that the truth is with you? For all your readiness to suffer and make sacrifices, there is an element of self-satisfaction in you. You say of yourself that you were born in a coat of many colors—with the truth.

"They used to call 'the old one,' the founder of Novaredok, the master of the holes. It was said that Reb Joseph Yoyzl lived apart for many years in the woods in a hut that had two holes in the wall; through one they would hand him milk foods and through the other meat foods. When he put his withdrawal behind him and came back into the world, his philosophy was either milk or meat, one extreme or the other, but nothing in between. His disciples, including you, took this teaching from him. His disciples want what they call wholeness too, and they have no use for compromises. What you said about our wanting a small Torah so that it would be easier for us was simply idle words. On the contrary, we make it harder for ourselves, because we acknowledge a double responsibility—toward Jewish tradition and toward secular culture.

"You said that among Jews the important thing was always the community and not the individual, until we came along and spoiled it; we wanted to be like the Gentiles, for whom the I is more important than anything else. And in order to hurt me, you tried to persuade me that what I want to do is to climb up the Hotel de Ville and put myself there as a living monument to myself. You allow yourself to mock, because after all, what you do is for the sake of heaven, isn't that so? I won't start now to tell you historical facts about leaders and rulers who made the community their footstool. As for what you say, that the principle among Jews was always the community until we came, I agree. We secularists want to free the individual. You say a man should tear his individual desires out of himself. But for hundreds of years men have gone to torture and death so that the commonwealth shall consist of free and happy individuals. I could read you an all but endless list of our own boys and girls whose youth was spent in black dungeons because they would not be deterred from trying to make the world better. You yourself know about Jewish workers in our own day and in former days who fought against all oppressors and tyrants. The only thing is that you won't concede that free-thinkers can sacrifice themselves too, so you complain that they left Jewish tradition only to enjoy forbidden pleasures. That is untrue. In my own quarter I knew as many 'seekers' as in Novaredok—and more. Because you denied the world, Reb Hersh, you withdrew into an attic. But these young people dearly loved the world, and they sacrificed themselves—to better it.

"What right then do you have to complain to us about the world? You yourself said that we dreamed about another, a better world—which nullifies your accusation. We carried into the world our own vision of what the world should be, as the Jews in the wilderness carried the Ark with the tablets of the Covenant, so that they could enter the land of Canaan with their own Law. You laugh; you said that we deceived ourselves. I'll ask you: Do you renounce Judaism because the Samaritans and the Karaites[7] distorted the Law of Moses?

"But I don't have to apologize to you. You lump me together with the murderers and demand an accounting of me for the world. I can be as harsh an accuser as you. I can cry out against you and demand an accounting of you. If we have abandoned Jewish tradition, it's your fault! You barricaded yourself, shut the gates, and let no one out into the open. If anyone put his head out, you tried to pull him back by his feet; and if you couldn't, you threw him out bodily and shut the doors behind him with a curse. Because he had no place to go back to he had to go farther away then he himself would have wished. From generation to generation you became more fanatical. Your hearts are cold and your ears deaf to all the sciences of the world. You laugh at them and say they are futile things. If you could, you would put people in the pillory again, as the Gaon of Vilna[8] did to a follower of the Enlightenment who dared say that the old exegetes did not know Hebrew grammar too well. Even today, for the smallest transgression you would impose the gravest punishment, if you could. But because you can't, you shorten your memories. You pretend not to remember how you used to persecute anyone who was bold

7. The Samaritans follow a form of Judaism based on the Torah alone, rejecting the oral tradition and the prophetical writings. The Karaites represent another sect within Judaism that rejects Talmudic authority and rabbinic Judaism in favor of individual interpretation of biblical teachings.

8. Head rabbi of Vilna who issued a ban against the Hasidim in 1772.

enough to say anything different from you without basing himself on the authority of the ancient sages, of blessed memory, or even with their authority. All your life your studied *The Path of the Upright.* Do you know how much its author was suspected and persecuted, how much anguish they caused him, how they hunted for heresy in his writings? Do you know that, at least? And you yourself, didn't you examine the contents of your students' trunks, looking for forbidden books? Even now doesn't your voice have in it something of the voice of the trumpet of excommunication? Doesn't your eye burn like the black candle of excommunication? And do you really think that with all your protestations, you love Jews more than the writers for whom it was so painful to write critically of the Jewish community? Didn't you bury them outside the wall, when you could, with no stone to mark their grave? Incidentally, Reb Hersh, I want you to know that this neighborhood we're in is old Paris. Here by the Hotel de Ville, where we're sitting, is the Place de Grève—that is, Execution Square, where they used to torture and execute those who were condemned to death. It was right here, more than seven hundred years ago, that Maimonides' *Guide to the Perplexed*[9] was burned, on a denunciation by eminent and zealous rabbis. Rabbi Jonah Gerondi had a hand in it. Later, when the priests began to burn the Talmud too, Rabbi Jonah felt that it was a punishment from Heaven for his warfare against Maimonides, and he repented. That was when he wrote his *Gates of Repentance.* In Novaredok they used to read the *Gates of Repentance* with such outcries that their lungs were almost torn to shreds; but they never thought to learn its moral, which is not to be fanatical.

How estranged you feel from all secular Jews can be seen in your constant repetition of 'we' and 'you.' You laugh at us poor secularists. You say that our suffering is pointless; we don't want to be Jews, but we can't help it. It would follow that the German made a mistake in taking us for Jews. But it's you who make that mistake. The enemies of Israel know very well that we're the same; they say it openly. And we're the same not only for the enemies of Israel, but for the Master of the World as well! In the other world your soul won't be wearing a cap or a beard or sidecurls. Your soul will come there as naked as mine. You would have it that the real Community of Israel is a handful of Hersh Rasseyners. The others are quarter-Jews, tenth-Jews—or not even that. You say that being Jewish is indivisible, all or nothing. So you make us Jews a thousand times fewer than we already are.

"You were right when you said that it was not a third of our people that was murdered, but rather a third was cut out of the flesh and soul of every Jew

9. One of the greatest philosophical works of the Middle Ages, the *Guide* was written by Maimonides in order to reconcile reason with faith and to harmonize Judaism with philosophy.

who survived. As far as you're concerned, though, Reb Hersh, was it really a third of our people that perished? The gist of what you say—again the same thing—is that anyone who isn't your kind of Jew is not a Jew at all. Doesn't that mean that there were more bodies burned than Jews who were murdered? You see to what cruelty your religious fanaticism must lead.

"I want you to consider this and settle it with yourself. Those Jews who didn't worry night and day about the high destiny of man, who weren't among the thirty-six hidden righteous men who sustain the world, but who lived a life of poverty for themselves, their wives, and their children; those Jews who got up in the morning without saying the proper morning prayers and ate their black bread without saying the blessing over bread; those Jews who labored on the Sabbath and didn't observe the last detail of the Law on Holy Days; those Jews who waited submissively and patiently at the table of this world for a crumb to fall their way (that's what you, Reb Hersh, the hermit of Novaredok, the man who lives apart, taunted them with), those Jews who lived together in neighborliness, in small quarrels and small reconciliations, and perished together in the same way—do you admit them to your paradise or not? And where will they sit? At the east wall, together with the Mussarists, or at the door, with their feet outside? You will tell me that the simple man is saintly and pure, because he perished as a Jew. But if he survived, is he wicked and evil, because he doesn't follow in your way? Is that your mercy and love for the Community of Israel? And you dare to speak in their name and say you're the spokesman of the sainted dead! Why are you getting up? Do you want to run away? But you assured me you used to dream of meeting me and talking it out with me. Can you only talk and not listen? Novaredok Mussarist, sit down and hear me out!

"If secular Jews are so alien to you, why should I be surprised at the blackness of your hatred aaginst the whole non-Jewish world? But let's not quarrel any more, Reb Hersh; let's reckon our accounts quietly. May we hate the whole non-Jewish world? You know as well as I do that there were some who saved the lives of Jews. I won't enter into a discussion with you about the exact number of such people. It's enough for me that you know there were some.

"In 1946, in Poland, I once attended a small gathering in honor of a Pole, a Christian who had hidden ten Jews. At that little party we all sat around a table. We didn't praise the doctor, we didn't talk about noble and exalted things, about humanity and heroism, or even about Jews and Poles. We simply asked him how it was that he wasn't afraid to hide ten Jews behind the wall of his office. The doctor was a small, gray-haired man. He kept on smiling, almost childishly, and he thanked us in embarrassment for the honor—a great honor!—that we were doing him. He answered our question in a low voice, almost tongue-tied: when he hid the Jews he felt sure that since it was a good deed, nothing bad would happen to him.

"Here in Paris there's an old lady, a Lithuanian. I know her well. Everybody knows that in the Vilna ghetto she saved the lives of Jews, and also hid books. The Germans sentenced her to death, but she was spared by a miracle. They sent her to a camp in France. Since she was liberated she has been associating with Jewish refugees. She's an old revolutionist, an atheist; that is to say, she doesn't believe in God.

"Imagine that both of them, the old lady and the old man, the Lithuanian and the Pole, the revolutionist and the Christian, were sitting here listening to us! They don't say anything, they only listen. They are frightened by your accusations, but not angry, because they understand that your hatred grows out of sorrow. Neither do they regret having saved the lives of Jews; they only feel an ache in their hearts, a great pain. Why do you think they saved the lives of Jews? The devout Christian didn't try to convert anyone. The old revolutionist didn't try to make anyone an atheist; on the contrary, she hid our sacred books. They saved the lives of Jews not from pity alone, but for their own sakes as well. They wanted to prove to themselves—no one else could possibly have known—that the whole world does not consist only of criminals and those who are indifferent to the misfortune of others. They wanted to have their own faith in human beings, together with the lives of Jews. Now you come along and repudiate everything in the world that isn't piously Jewish. I ask you: is there room in your world for these two old people? Don't you see that you would drive them out into the night? Will you take them, the righteous of the nations of the world, out of the category of Gentile and put them in a special category? They didn't risk their lives so that Reb Hersh Rasseyner, who hates everyone, everyone, could make an exception of them.

"But you ask me what was changed for me since the destruction. And what has changed for you, Reb Hersh? You answer that your faith has been strengthened. I tell you openly that your answer is a paltry, whining answer. I don't accept it at all. You must ask God the old question about the righteous man who fares ill and the evil man who fares well—only multiplied for a million murdered children. The fact that you know in advance that there will be no explanation from Heaven doesn't relieve you of the responsibility of asking, Reb Hersh! If your faith is as strong as Job's, then you must have his courage to cry to Heaven: 'Though He slay me, yet will I trust in Him; but I will argue my ways before Him!'[10] If a man hasn't sinned, he isn't allowed

10. From Job 13:15.

to declare himself guilty. As for us, even if we were devils, we couldn't have sinned enough for our just punishment to be a million murdered children. That's why your answer that your faith has been strengthened is no answer at all, as long as you don't demand an accounting of Heaven.

"Reb Hersh, we're both tired and burned out from a whole day of arguing. You ask what has changed for me. The change is that I want to make peace with you, because I love you deeply. I never hated you and I never searched for flaws in your character, but what I did see I didn't leave unsaid. When you became angry with me before I left, I became angry with you, but now I'm filled with love for you. I say to you as the Almighty said to the Jews assembled in Jerusalem on the feast days: I want to be with you one day more, it is hard for me to part from you. That's what has changed for me and for all Jewish writers. Our love for Jews has become deeper and more sensitive. I don't renounce the world, but in all honesty I must tell you we want to incorporate into ourselves the hidden inheritance of our people's strengths, so that we can continue to live. I plead with you, do not deny us a share in the inheritance. However loudly we call to Heaven and demand an accounting, our outcry conceals a quiet prayer for the Divine Presence, or for the countenance of those destroyed in the flames, to rest on the alienated Jews. The Jewish countenance of the burned still hangs in clouds of gas in the void. And our cry of impotent anger against Heaven has a deeper meaning as well: because we absolutely refuse our assent to the infamous and enormous evil that has been visited on us, because we categorically deny its justice, no slavish or perverse acquiescence can take root in our hearts, no despairing belief that the world has no sense or meaning.

"Reb Hersh, we have been friends since the old days in the Yeshiva. I remember that I once lost the little velvet bag in which I kept my phylacteries. You didn't eat breakfast and you spent half a day looking for it, but you couldn't find it. I got another bag to hold my phylacteries, but you're still looking for the old one.

"Remember, Reb Hersh, that the texts inscribed in my phylacteries are about the Community of Israel. Don't think that it's easy for us Jewish writers. It's hard, very hard. The same misfortune befell us all, but you have a ready answer, while we have not silenced all our doubts, and perhaps we never will be able to silence them. The only joy that's left to us is the joy of creation, and in all the travail of creation we try to draw near to our people.

"Reb Hersh, it's late, let us take leave of each other. Our paths are different, spiritually and practically. We are the remnant of those who were driven out. The wind that uprooted us is dispersing us to all the corners of the earth. Who knows whether we shall ever meet again? May we both have the merit of meeting again in the future and seeing how it is with us. And may I then be as Jewish as I am now. Reb Hersh, let us embrace each other. . . ."

Translated from the Yiddish by Milton Himmelfarb

from "Lekh-lekho"

And now, Blimele, dear child,
Look outside, how the second group
Is already wandering into Exile.[1]
Soon we'll have to set out, too.

And although, child, you're a little girl
And he who teaches his daughter Torah
It is as if he taught her
To commit an unworthy sin—

Yet the evil day has come,
The evil hour has come,
When I must teach you, a little girl,
The terrible chapter *"Lekh-lekho."*

But how can one compare it
To the bloody *"Lekh-lekho"* of today?
"And God said to Abram:
Go forth from your land

And from the place of your birth
And from your father's house
To a land that I will show you
And there make of you a great people."

This poem was the response of Shayevitsh to the first deportation of ten thousand
Jews from the Lodz Ghetto from January 16 to 29, 1942. The destination of the
transports were unknown to the victims. The author was powerfully moved by the
plight of the victims and by knowledge of what lay in store for him and his family. In the poem, the ten thousand are emblemed in three: a father (the speaker),
a mother, and a child (Blimele). The title of the poem refers ironically to God's
words to Abraham in Genesis 12:1, "Go forth from your native land and from
your father's house to the land that I will show you."
1. The mass deportations of January 1942 resumed on February 22 of the same
year.

And now the great people must go
To the unknown distant road—
Sick and weary—broken ships
That do not reach a shore.

One of them, faint with hunger
Will sit down in the snow
And quietly, in pain,
Die like a hurt puppy.

Another's eyes will fail
For terror on the road,
His heartstring will suddenly snap
And he'll fall heavy as a stone.

And someone's shivering child
Will freeze to death in the frost-fire,
And its mother will long carry it
Thinking it's still moving.

And fathers will call to their children
And children demand things from their mothers—
Families will get lost
And never find themselves.

And for a long way they'll carry
The great heavy pack on their shoulders
And throw it away at last, and often
Have no pillow under their head.

And the sick man, strengthless,
Will come to a halt in deep snows.

Birds will fly past
And be frightened, as by a scarecrow.

....

And from every shrub
And every twig, hands will lift
And from every little tree
Eyes, as of wolves and lions, will peer.

Someone in the forest waste
Who lies in ambush for your step—
Your vaporous breath will ring
Like the flow of your own warm blood.

So greetings to you, grandfather Abraham!
We go on your hard journey
But won't you be ashamed
Of your grandchildren's bloody tears?

And now, Blimele, dear child,
Put on your little coat, let's go.
The third group sways in readiness
And we must join them now.

But let us not weep.
Let us not lament, but in spite of all foes
Smile, only smile, so those
Who know the Jews will wonder

And not understand that in our blood
Flows the power of our grandfathers
Who in all generations
Climbed atop so many Moriahs;

That although our step is unsteady
Like a blind man's at a strange door,
There rings in it the echo
Of our uncle's stride on Siberian roads,

That although, as in a fallen beast,
Terror in our eyelash trembles,
Pride burns in flaming lightning-bolts
As in our father on the gallows.

And although at any minute
We can be tortured and shot,
Well—it is nothing new:
Our sister was whipped naked.

So let us not weep,
Let us not lament, but in spite of all foes
Smile, only smile, so those
Who know the Jews will wonder

And not know that today
The same angels go with us as before:
On the right Michael, on the left Gabriel,
Uriel in front and Raphael in the rear.

And although beneath our feet is death,
Over our head is God's Presence.
So child, let us go with devotion renewed
And our old proclamation of Oneness.

Lodz Ghetto, February 23, 1942
Translated from the Yiddish
by Elinor Robinson

from "Spring 1942"

2.

And in an hour of good fortune
Spring is here again—
The tree will send another root
Deeper into the earth,
And the birds will build
New cozy nests.
Only my ghetto brothers
Still must leave their homes,
With their gold-spun dreams
In herds—in dozens,
In hundreds—to trudge
Day after day, night after night
Down to the gathering place
To receive the blessing of expulsion.
Tired and sick, their steps
Totter, reel like drunkards.
But they are not drunk from wine
Or whiskey but from anguish and agony,
From despair and bitterness.
Half-numb, their hands—which
Can hardly move—are like sick birds' wings.
Their glances—abysmal, black—
Like those of sheep being led to slaughter.
And in their hearts fear strikes,
Like clumps of earth falling on graves.

"Spring 1942" is comprised of ten sections.
The title refers to the deportations from Lodz Ghetto to death camps in April
1942.

3.

And in an hour of good fortune
Spring—God be praised—is here again.
Night blows on the silvery horn
Of the young moon
And learns a new tune
In honor of Spring, which this year
Came as a very late guest.
But like a camel a mother is hunched
With a pack on her back,
Her five children dragging behind her,
One smaller than the next,
Clad in rags
And torn shoes
Tied with string,
With heavy sacks
Like beggars' bags
Hung on them.
They are tired and can walk no further.
The mother spreads her arms like a hen.
The oldest she leaves unattended,
The second she scolds,
The third she pushes ahead,
The fourth she pleads with,
And the fifth she takes in her arms.
But soon she stands still, breathless
Like a dead fish,
With staring eyes
And open mouth,
And the pack on her back and the child in her arms
Rock cumbrously—

On the mother's scale—
Down and up
Back and forth,
Up and down
Back and forth.

7.

And in an hour of good fortune
Ha, ha, ha, Spring is here again.
The grass, the trees will dress
Themselves in dew, as though with pearls,
And the sun will again present the world
With her gold, squandering it extravagantly.
But why do a branch, a bush
Crack and break when you step on it?
And poor cursed heart of mine,
Do you not break from the pain
When your brothers are driven like dogs?!
Whorish, benumbed heart,
Why don't you die?
Why don't you take leave of your mind
And dance in the middle of the street
And do somersaults—with your head upside down.
With your feet to the sky.
With your fists clenched on your breast.
With your fists clenched toward Him above.
And you bang your head on the wall
And sing a holiday song.
And bite off a piece of your hand,
While tears flow from your eyes,
Pailsful, pailsful.

You poor, cursed heart,
Why don't you burst from pain?

8.

And in an hour of good fortune
Life turns over
Like pages of a book
And Spring is here again.
But where is the great ghetto Jew,
Where is Don Isaac Abrabanel,[1]
Who should be a pillar for us
As he once was in Spain?
I do not have the strength for it,
Nor do you, friend,
So what will be?
What will be with the thousands
Of poor ghetto Jews?
Who will comfort them in their terrible tragedy?
Who will ease their agony
On their horrible unknown road?
Who will heal the sick,
Who will bind the wounds,
Who will lift up the fallen,
Who will feed the weak,
Who will quench the thirsty,
Who will bury the dead
And still the crying of the child?
Alas and woe—where is the great ghetto Jew,

1. Statesman, philosopher, and biblical exegete, Abrabanel (1437–1508) was prominent in fifteenth-century Spain just before the expulsion of the Jews in 1492.

Where can we get Isaac Abrabanel?!
But how could such a one help us today?
In the ghetto he himself would walk
With a bent, aching back
And would consider the whole Spanish expulsion
And all the bitter edicts that followed
Child's play, when compared to today.

9.

And in an hour of good fortune
May no Evil Eye befall us, Spring is here again.
Even graves will be covered in green.
So rise up, great poet,
Master of the "City of Slaughter,"[2]
From your green-laureled grave.
I invite you to walk with me.
In our ghetto you will be quickly satisfied.
Although we are exposed here to ridicule and shame,
No wife's husband—even the most pious—will run to the rabbi
To ask if he may continue living together with his wife.
In our ghetto you will be satisfied.
Not like there in the other "City,"
Where they decreed a fast
And gathered together in the synagogues
"With wild horrible cries
With a burning sea of tears."
I doubt, great poet, if today you will find

2. "The City of Slaughter" is a well-known poem by Hayyim Nahman Bialik
(1873–1934) concerning the Kishinev pogroms. Bialik's often-quoted line "The
sun shines, the acacia blossoms and the slaughterer slaughters" suggests the in-
debtedness of Shayevitsh to Bialik.

Anywhere in a ghetto synagogue a *minyan*[3] to recite the *Kaddish*.
One trudges quietly on the desolate march
And even more quietly one expires
And the bridegroom leaves his weeping bride
And the lover does not know of his bride's remains
And the child is torn in rage from her mother's arms
And the gun pursues her further
With cries: "Shoot—shoot—."
But forgive them, great and wrathful poet.
Although we still have no fist
And the great thunder still does not echo
Vengeance for all "generations"
And although you mocked and ridiculed
Such innocent victims and martyrs,
You will bow your head three times to the ghetto Jew
And murmur with ecstasy, "Holy, Holy, Holy."
God with a mild hand
Also presented us with twins,
A death expulsion and a Spring.
The garden blooms, the sun shines
and the slaughterer . . . slaughters.
And yet we do not demand acknowledgment,
For when a man is slaughtered
They also slaughter his God.
But do you know, poet of wrath and vengeance,
What I require of you?
I ask that you wake from their sleep
Our mother Rachel,
And the Saint of Berdichev[4]

3. Hebrew for a prayer group requiring ten or more men.
4. The Hasidic leader Levi Yitzchak of Berdichev (1740–1810), well known for arguing the case of the Jewish people before the heavenly court.

And that the three of you go together before God.
You will thunder and demand.
Rachel will weep and plead,
And Levi Yitzhak will argue his lawsuit, proclaiming:
—If, Lord of the Universe, You will not be the Savior
Of Living Jews,
You will, God forbid, be the Savior of Corpses.

10.

And in an hour of good fortune
The circling wheel turns
Round and around
And Erev Pesach,[5]
Blessed be His name, is here again.
So let us sit down
To the poor holy *seder.*[6]
Matzoh is here.
There will be four goblets of wine:
Of our tears
And *Morer* and the *Charoyses*[7]
Are also here—
Our dismal anguish
And the dark, sad, wrinkled faces.
Now, Blimele, my child,
Ask the question:
"*Ma*"—Why is this night
No different from every other night:
Every night people leave their homes—

5. Hebrew for Passover eve.
6. Hebrew for the Passover service in the home, including the ceremonial meal.
7. *Morer* is Hebrew for bitter herbs; *charoyses* is Hebrew for a mixture of fruit, wine, and nuts.

"Halaylo haze"—And this night of Passover—also.
"Ma"—Why did miracles occur each time
And today we are so wretched?
And, my lovely child, you should know
That I do not have an answer for you.
Just this once—
Let Mother—
Our dear and beloved friend—
Open the door
And with my father's holy melody
Translating it, as was his custom,
Into plain Yiddish:
—*Shfoykh hamoskho al hagoyim*—
Pour out Your wrath on the nations
—*Asher lo yedsukho*—
Who do not wish to know You
—*Ki akhol as Yaakov*—
Because they devour Jacob
—*Veos navehu heshamu*—
And destroy his home.
Tirdof beaf
Vetashmidem mitakhas shmay adonoy
Chase them in anger
And destroy them from the heaven of God . . .

Erev Pesach [Passover Eve] 1942
Translated from the Yiddish by Chana Mlotek

from *The Song of the Murdered Jewish People*

VI   The First Ones

1

And it continued. Ten a day, ten thousand Jews a day.
That did not last very long. Soon they took fifteen thousand.
Warsaw! The city of Jews—the fenced-in, walled-in city,
Dwindled, expired, melted like snow before my eyes.

2

Warsaw, packed with Jews like a *shul* on Yom Kippur,[1] like a bustling
    marketplace—
Jews trading and worshipping, both happy and sad—
Seeking their bread, praying to their God.
They crowded the walled-in, locked-in city.

3

You are deserted now. Warsaw, like a gloomy wasteland.
You are a cemetery now, more desolate than a graveyard.
Your streets are empty—not even a corpse can be found there.
Your houses are open, yet no one enters, no one leaves.

4

The first to perish were the children, abandoned orphans,
The world's best, the bleak earth's brightest.[2]
These children from the orphanages might have been our comfort.
From these sad, mute, bleak faces our new dawn might have risen.

1. A synagogue on the Day of Atonement
2. The stanza alludes to Hayyim Nahman Bialik's "Upon the Slaughter," written
in May 1903 in response to the pogrom in Kishinev, Russia, in which forty-nine
Jews were murdered.

5

At the end of the winter of forty-two I was in such a place.
I saw children just brought in from the street. I hid in a corner—
And saw a two-year-old girl in the lap of a teacher—
Thin, deathly pale and with such grave eyes.

6

I watched the two-year-old grandmother,
The tiny Jewish girl, a hundred years old in her seriousness and grief.
What her grandmother could not dream she had seen in reality.
I wept and said to myself: Don't cry, grief disappears, seriousness
   remains.

7

Seriousness remains, seeps into the world, into life and affects it deeply.
Jewish seriousness sobers, awakens and opens blind eyes.
It is like a Torah, a prophecy, a holy writ for the world.
Don't cry, don't . . . Eighty-million criminals for one Jewish child's
   seriousness.

8

Don't cry . . . I saw a five-year-old girl in that "home."
She fed her younger, crying brother . . .
She dipped hard bread crumbs in watery marmalade
And got them cleverly into his mouth . . . I was lucky

9

To see it, to see the five-year-old mother feeding him,
And to hear her words. My mother, though exceptional, was not that
   inventive.
She wiped his tear with her laughter and talked him into joy.

O little Jewish girl. Sholem Aleichem[3] could not have done any better.
I saw it.

10

I saw the misery in that children's home.
I entered another room—there, too, it was fearfully cold.
From afar a tin stove cast a glow on a group of children,
Half-naked children gathered around the glowing coal.

11

The coal glowed. One stretched out a little foot, another a frozen hand,
A naked back. A pale young boy with dark eyes
Told a story. No, not a story! He was stirred and excited—
Isaiah! you were not as fervent, not as eloquent a Jew.

12

He spoke a mix of Yiddish and holy tongue. No, it was all the holy
    tongue.
Listen! Listen! See his Jewish eyes, his forehead,
How he raises his head . . . Isaiah! you were not as small, not as great,
Not as good, not as true, not as faithful as he.

13

And not only the little boy who spoke in that children's home,
But his little sisters and brothers who listened to him with open mouths—
O no, you countries, you old and rebuilt European cities,
The world never saw such children before; they never existed on earth.

14

They, the Jewish children, were the first to perish, all of them,
Almost all without father or mother, eaten by cold, hunger and vermin,

3. Pen name of the noted Yiddish writer Sholem Rabinowitz (1859–1916).

Saintly messiahs, sanctified by pain . . . O why such punishment?
Why were they first to pay so high a price to evil in the days of
  slaughter?

15

They were the first taken to die, the first in the wagon.
They were flung into the big wagons like heaps of dung—
And were carried off, killed, exterminated,
Not a trace remained of my previous ones! Woe unto me, woe.

November 2–4, 1943
Translated from the Yiddish by Noah H. Rosenbloom

IX   To the Heavens

1

And thus it came to pass, and this was the beginning . . . Heavens tell
  me, why?[4]
Tell me, why this, O why? What have we done to merit such disgrace?
The earth is dumb and deaf, she closed here eyes. But you, heavens on
  high,
You saw it happen and looked on, from high, and did not turn your
  face.

2

You did not cloud your cheap-blue colors, glittering in their false light.
The sun, a brutal red-faced hangman, rolled across the skies;
The moon, the old and sinful harlot, walked along her beat at night;
And stars sent down their dirty twinkle, with the eyes of mice.

3

Away! I do not want to look at you, to see you any more.
False and cheating heavens, low heavens up on high, O how you hurt!

4. Katzenelson echoes the opening lines of Bialik's "Upon the Slaughter."

Once I believed in you, sharing my joy with you, my smile, my tear—
Who are not different from the ugly earth, that heap of dirt!

4

I did believe in you and sang your praises in each song of mine.
I loved you as one loves a woman, though she left and went.
The flaming sun at dusk, its glowing shine,
I likened to my hopes: "And thus my hope goes down, my dream is
  spent."[5]

5

Away! Away! You have deceived us both, my people and my race.
You cheated us—eternally. My ancestors, my prophets, too, you have
  deceived.
To you, foremost, they lifted up their eyes, and you inspired their faith.
And full of faith they turned to you, when jubilant or grieved.

6

To you they first addressed themselves: *Hearken, O Heavens, you*—[6]
and only afterwards they called the earth, praising your name.
So, Moses. So Isaiah—mine, my own. *Hear, O hear,* cried Jeremiah, too.[7]
O heavens open wide, O heavens full of light, you are as Earth, you are
  the same.

7

Have we so changed that you don't recognize us, as of old?
But why, we are the same—the same Jews that we were, not different.
Not I . . . Not I will to the prophets be compared, lo and behold!

5. An allusion to Katzenelson's own song *"Di zun fargeyt in flamen"* (The sun sets
in flames).
6. Deuteronomy 32:1.
7. Isaiah 1:2; Jeremiah 2:12.

But they, the millions of my murdered ones, those murdered out of
  hand—

8

It's they . . . They suffered more and greater pains, each one.
The little, simple, ordinary Jew from Poland of today—
Compared with him, what are the great men of a past bygone?
A wailing Jeremiah, Job afflicted, Kings despairing, all in one—it's they!

9

You do not recognize us any more as if we hid behind a mask?
But why, we are the same, the same Jews that we were, and to ourselves
  we're true.
We're still resigned to others' happiness. Saving the world we still see as
  our task.
O why are you so beautiful, you skies, while we are being murdered,
  why are you so blue?

10

Like Saul, my king[8] I will go to the goddess Or, bearing my pain.
In dark despair I'll find the way, the dark road to Ein Dor; I shall
From underground awaken all the prophets there—*Look ye again,
Look up to your bright heavens, spit at them and tell them: Go to Hell!*

11

You heavens, high above, looked on when, day and night,
My people's little children were sent off to death, on foot, by train.
Millions of them raised high their hands to you before they died.
Their noble mothers could not shake your blue-skinned crust—they cried
  in vain.

8. I Samuel 28.

425

12

You saw the little Yomas, the eleven-year-olds, joyous, pure and good;
The little Bennys, young inquiring minds, life's remedy and prize.
You saw the Hannas who had born them and had taught them to serve
God.
And you looked on . . . You have no God above you. Nought and
void—you skies!

13

You have no God in you! Open the doors, you heavens, fling them open
wide,
And let the children of my murdered people enter in a stream.
Open the doors up for the great procession of the crucified,
The children of my people, all of them, each one a God—make room!

14

O heavens, empty and deserted, vast and empty desert, you—
My only God I lost in you, and they have not enough with three:
The Jewish God, the holy ghost, the Jew from Galilee—they killed him,
too.
And then, not satisfied, sent all of us to heaven, these worshippers of
cruelty.

15

Rejoice, you heavens, at your riches, at your fortune great!
Such blessed harvest at one stroke—a people gathered in entire.
Rejoice on high, as here below the Germans do, rejoice and jubilate!
And may a fire rise up to you from earth, and from you strike,
earthwards, devouring fire!

November 23–26, 1943
Translated from the Yiddish by Jacob Sonntag

God of Mercy

O God of Mercy
For the time being
Choose another people.
We are tired of death, tired of corpses,
We have no more prayers.
For the time being
Choose another people.
We have run out of blood
For victims,
Our houses have been turned into desert,
The earth lacks space for tombstones,
There are no more lamentations
Nor songs of woe
In the ancient texts.

God of Mercy
Sanctify another land,
Another Sinai.
We have covered every field and stone
With ashes and holiness.
With our crones
With our young
With our infants
We have paid for each letter in your Commandments.

God of Mercy
Lift up your fiery brow,
Look on the peoples of the world,
Let them have the prophecies and Holy Days
Who mumble your words in every tongue.
Teach them the Deeds
And the ways of temptation.

God of Mercy
To us give rough clothing
Of shepherds who tend sheep
Of blacksmiths at the hammer
Of washerwomen, cattle slaughterers
And lower still.
And O God of Mercy
Grant us one more blessing—
Take back the divine glory of our genius.

1945
Translated from the Yiddish
by Irving Howe

Without Jews

Without Jews there is no Jewish God.
If we leave this world
The light will go out in your tent.
Since Abraham knew you in a cloud,
You have burned in every Jewish face,
You have glowed in every Jewish eye,
And we made you in our image.
In each city, each land,
The Jewish God
Was also a stranger.
A broken Jewish head
Is a fragment of divinity.
We, your radiant vessel,
A palpable sign of your miracle.

Now the lifeless skulls
Add up into millions.
The stars are going out around you.
The memory of you is dimming,
Your kingdom will soon be over.
Jewish seed and flower
Are embers.
The dew cries in the dead grass!

The Jewish dream and reality are ravished,
They die together.
Your witnesses are sleeping:
Infants, women,
Young men, old.
Even the Thirty-six,

Your saints, Pillars of your World,[1]
Have fallen into a dead, an everlasting sleep.

Who will dream you?
Who will remember you?
Who deny you?
Who yearn for you?
Who, on a lonely bridge,
Will leave you—in order to return?

The night is endless when a race is dead.
Earth and heaven are wiped bare.
The light is fading in your shabby tent.
The Jewish hour is guttering.
Jewish God!
You are almost gone.

Translated from the Yiddish
by Nathan Halper

1. A reference to the Jewish legend of the thirty-six saints in each generation
through whose merit the world still stands.

Psalm

No one moulds us again out of earth and clay,
no one conjures our dust.
No one.

Praised be your name, no one.
For your sake
we shall flower.
Towards
you.

A nothing
we were, are, shall
remain, flowering:
the nothing—, the
no one's rose.

With
our pistil soul-bright,
with our stamen heaven-ravaged,
our corolla red
with the crimson word which we sang
over, O over
the thorn.

Translated from the German
by Michael Hamburger

The "Lovers of Israel" at the Belzhets Death Camp

Reb Moyshe Leyb of Sossov points to the heaps of ash
(The storm is but recently weathered).
His beard trembles; his body and life are embittered:
"See, Lord. Ah, take a good look," he says.

"Listen, gentlemen, listen," Reb Volf of Zborosh murmurs;
His voice, like an evening fiddle, is tired—
"The Lord above has not looked well to his vineyard. . . .
Proof: These heaps abandoned on earth."

Trembling and feverish, Reb Meirl of Przemyslan
Waits, leaning on his old stick. "Gentlemen,"
He says, "Let us in unison call

To God, 'Creator of worlds, Thou art mighty and great,
But we Galacian Jews forever erase
Your name from the list of true Lovers of Israel.' "

Translated from the Yiddish by Leonard Wolf

Belzhets was a concentration camp near Lublin, Poland (sometimes referred to as Belzec). A forced labor camp in 1940, it became an annihilation camp after March 1942. The corpses of gassed Jews were cremated on bonfires. By December 1942, some six hundred thousand had been murdered at Belzhets. The poem presents an imagined trial of God by three famous Hasidic rabbis whose kindness and charity had won them the title "Lovers of Israel."

Draft of a Reparations Agreement

All right, gentlemen who cry blue murder as always,
nagging miracle-makers,
quiet!
Everything will be returned to its place,
paragraph after paragraph.
The scream back into the throat.
The gold teeth back to the gums.
The terror.
The smoke back to the tin chimney and further on and inside
back to the hollow of the bones,
and already you will be covered with skin and sinews and you will
    live,
look, you will have your lives back,
sit in the living room, read the evening paper.
Here you are. Nothing is too late.
As to the yellow star:
it will be torn from your chest
immediately
and will emigrate
to the sky.

Translated from the Hebrew by Stephen Mitchell

Isaac

Toward morning the sun strolled in the forest
Together with me and with father,
My right hand was in his left.

Like lightning flash, a knife between the trees
And I fear the terror of my eyes opposite the blood on the
　　leaves.

Father, Father, come quickly and save Isaac
That no one may be missing at the noon meal.

It is I who am slaughtered, my son,
And my blood is already on the leaves.
Father's voice choked.
His face grew pale.

And I wanted to scream, writhing not to believe
And I opened my eyes wide.
And I awoke.

Bloodless was my right hand.

Translated from the Hebrew by Ruth Finer Mintz

The poem reinterprets the biblical episode of the sacrifice of Isaac (Genesis 22:1–19)
in the light of the Holocaust.

Elegy

Named for my father's father, cousin, whose cry
Might have been my cry lost in that dark land—
Where shall I seek you? On what wind shall I
Reach out to touch the ash that was your hand?
The Atlantic gale and the turning of the sky
Unto the cubits of my ambience
Scatter the martyr-motes. Flotsam-of-flame!
God's image made the iotas of God's name!
Oh, through a powder of ghosts I walk; through dust
Seraphical upon the dark winds borne;
Daily I pass among the sieved white hosts,
Through clouds of cousinry transgress,
Maculate with the ashes that I mourn.

Where shall I seek you? There's not anywhere
A tomb, a mound, a sod, a broken stick,
Marking the sepulchres of those sainted ones
The dogfaced hid in tumuli of air.
O cousin, cousin, you are everywhere!
And in your death, in your ubiquity,
Bespeak them all, our sundered cindered kin:
David, whose cinctured bone—
Young branch once wreathed in phylactery!—
Now hafts the peasant's bladed kitchenware;
And the dark Miriam murdered for her hair;
The relicts nameless; and the tattoo'd skin
Fevering from lampshade in a cultured home—
All, all our gaunt skull-shaven family—
The faces are my face! that lie in lime,
You bring them, jot of horror, here to me,
Them, and the slow eternity of despair
That tore them, and did tear them out of time.

Death may be beautiful, when full of years,
Ripe with good works, a man, among his sons,
Says his last word, and turns him to the wall.
But not these deaths! Oh, not these weighted tears!
The flesh of Thy sages, Lord, flung prodigal
To the robed fauna with their tubes and shears;
Thy chosen for a gold tooth chosen; for
The pervert's wetness, flesh beneath the rod—
Death multitudinous as their frustrate spore!—
This has been done to us, Lord, thought-lost God;
And things still hidden, and unspeakable more.

A world is emptied. Marked is that world's map
The forest colour. There where Thy people praised
In angular ecstasy Thy name, Thy Torah[1]
Is less than a whisper of its thunderclap.
Thy synagogues, rubble. They academies,
Bright once with Talmud[2] brow and musical
With song alternative in exegesis,
Are silent, dark. They are laid waste, Thy cities,
Once festive with Thy fruit-full calendar,
And where Thy curled and caftan'd congregations
Danced to the first days and the second star,
Or made the marketplaces loud and green
To welcome in the Sabbath Queen;
Or through the nights sat sweet polemical
With Rav and Shmuail (also of the slain)—
Oh, there where dwelt the thirty-six—world's pillars!—

1. The body of wisdom and law contained in Jewish scripture and other sacred literature.
2. The authoritative body of Jewish tradition comprising the Mishnah and Gemara. The reference is to the brows of students engaged in the study of Talmud.

And tenfold Egypt's generation, there
Is nothing, nothing . . . only the million echoes
Calling Thy name still trembling on the air.

Look down, O Lord, from Thy abstracted throne!
Look down! Find out this Sodom[3] to the sky
Rearing and solid on a world atilt
The architecture by its pillars known.
This circle breathed hundreds; that round, thousands—
And from among the lesser domes descry
The style renascent of Gomorrah built.
See where the pyramids
Preserve our ache between their angled tons:
Pass over, they have been excelled. Look down
On the Greek marble that our torture spurned—
The white forgivable stone.
The arch and triumph of subjection, pass;
The victor, too, has passed; and all these spires
At whose foundations, dungeoned, the screw turned
Inquisitorial, now overlook—
They were delirium and sick desires.
But do not overlook, oh pass not over
The hollow monoliths. The vengeful eye
Fix on these pylons of the sinister sigh,
The well-kept chimneys daring towards the sky!
From them, now innocent, no fumes do rise.
They yawn to heaven. It is their ennui:
Too much the slabs and ovens, and too many
The man-shaped loaves of sacrifice!

3. One of the two cities of ancient Palestine destroyed by God for its wickedness, the other being Gomorrah (Genesis 18:20, 21; 19:24–28).

As Thou didst do to Sodom, do to them!
But not, O Lord, in one destruction. Slow,
Fever by fever, limb by withering limb,
Destroy! Send through the marrow of their bones,
The pale treponeme burrowing. Let there grow
Over their eyes a film that they may see
Always a carbon sky! Feed them on ash!
Condemn them double deuteronomy!
All in one day pustule their speech with groans,
Their bodies with the scripture of a rash,
With boils and buboes their suddenly breaking flesh!
When their dams litter, monsters be their whelp,
Unviable! Themselves, may each one dread,
The touch of his fellow, and the infected help
Of the robed fauna with their tubes and shears!
Fill up their days with funerals and fears!
Let madness shake them—rooted down—like kelp.
And as their land is emptying, and instructed,
The nations cordon the huge lazaret—
The paring of Thy little fingernail
Drop down: the just circuitings of flame,
And as Gomorrah's name, be their cursed name!

Not for the judgment sole, but for a sign
Effect, O Lord, example and decree,
A sign, the final shade and witness joined
To the shadowy witnesses who once made free
With that elected folk Thou didst call Thine.
Before my mind, still unconsoled, there pass
The pharaohs risen from the Red Sea sedge,
Profiled; in alien blood and peonage
Hidalgos lost; shadows of Shushan; and
The Assyrian uncurling into sand;

Most untriumphant frieze! and darkly pass
The shades Seleucid; dark against blank white
The bearded ikon-bearing royalties—
All who did waste us, insubstantial now,
A motion of the mind. Oh, unto these
Let there be added, soon, as on a screen,
The shadowy houndface, barking, never heard,
But for all time a lore and lesson, seen,
And heeded; and thence, of Thy will our peace.

Vengeance is thine, O Lord, and unto us
In a world wandering, amidst raised spears
Between wild waters, and against barred doors,
There are no weapons left. Where now but force
Prevails, and over the once blest lagoons
Mushroom new Sinais, sole defensive is
The face turned east, and the uncompassed prayer.
Not prayer for the murdered myriads who
Themselves white liturgy before Thy throne
Are of my prayer; but for the scattered bone
Stirring in Europe's camps, next kin of death,
My supplication climbs the carboniferous air.
Grant them Ezkiel's prophesying breath!
Isaiah's cry of solacing allow![4]
O Thou who from Mizraim once didst draw
Us free, and from the Babylonian lair;
From bondages, plots, ruins imminent
Preserving, didst keep Covenant and Law,
Creator, King whose banishments are not
Forever—for Thy Law and Covenant,

4. Hebrew prophets who consoled the Babylonian exiles after the destruction of
the First Temple in Jerusalem, 587 B.C.E. (Ezekiel 37:1–28; Isaiah 43:1–28).

Oh, for Thy promise and Thy pity, now
At last, this people to its lowest brought
Preserve! Only in Thee our faith. The word
Of eagle-quartering kings ever intends
Their own bright eyrie; rote of parakeet
The labouring noise among the fabians heard;
Thou only art responseful.

                  Hear me, who stand
Circled and winged in vortex of my kin:
Forgo the complete doom! The winnowed, spare!
Annul the scattering, and end! And end
Our habitats on water and on air!
Gather the flames up to light orient
Over the land; and that funest eclipse,
Diaspora-dark, revolve from off our ways!
Towered Jerusalem and Jacob's tent
Set up again; again renew our days
As when near Carmel's mount we harboured ships,
And went and came, and knew our home; and song
From all the vineyards raised its sweet degrees,
And Thou didst visit us, didst shield from wrong,
And all our sorrows salve with prophecies;
    Again renew them as they were of old,
    And for all time cancel that ashen orbit
    In which our days, and hopes, and kin, are rolled.

from "I Believe"

Thy would-be gods!
They—and those other shadows, ism and ism!
More hollow than ever their claims
After the all-destroying flames.
In whom can I believe if not in Him,
my living God of cataclysm,
God of naked revenge and secret consolation?
One is—what one is.
I am Jew as He is God.
Can I then choose not to believe
in that living God whose purposes
when He destroys, seeming to forsake me,
I cannot conceive;
choose not to believe in Him
Who having turned my body to fine ash
begins once more to wake me?
If I become a storm, or if I blaze
in rebellion against Him,
is He not still the One who bleeding in my wounds,
my cries still praise?
For even my pain confirms Him.
Who would rebel against pale Jesuses?
And who would rage
against a Spinozan god,[1]
a nonbeing being?

> Translated from the Yiddish by Robert Friend

1. The reference is to the pantheistic beliefs of Baruch Spinoza (1632–77), Dutch philosopher excommunicated by the Jewish community in Amsterdam in 1656 for his heretical thought.

Sometimes I Want to Go Up

Sometimes I want to go up
on tiptoe
to a strange house
and feel the walls with my hands—
what kind of clay is baked in the bricks,
what kind of wood is in the door,
and what kind of god has pitched his tent here,
to guard it from misfortune and ruin?

What kind of swallow under the roof
has built its nest from straw and earth
and what kind of angels disguised as men
came here as guests?[1]

What holy men came out to meet them,
bringing them basins of water
to wash the dust from their feet,
the dust of earthly roads?

And what blessing did they leave
the children—from big to small,
that it could protect and guard them
from Belzec, Maidanek, Treblinka?[2]

From just such a house,
fenced in with a painted railing,
in the middle of trees and blooming flowerbeds,
blue, gold, flame,
there came out—

1. See Genesis 18:1–8.
2. Killing centers located in Poland. See also notes pp. 69, 115.

the murderer of my people,
of my mother.

I'll let my sorrow grow
like Samson's hair long ago,
and I'll turn the millstone of days
around this bloody track.

Until one night
when I hear over me
the murderer's drunken laugh,
I'll tear the door from its hinges
and I'll rock the building—
till the night wakes up
from the shaking coming through every pane,
every brick, every nail, every board of the house,
from the very ground to the roof—

Although I know, I know, my God,
that the falling walls
will bury only me
and my sorrow.

    Translated from the Yiddish by Ruth Whitman

For Adolf Eichmann

The wind runs free across our plains,
The live sea beats forever at our beaches.
Man makes earth fecund, earth gives him flowers and fruits:
He lives in toil and joy, he hopes, fears, begets sweet offspring.

And you have come, our precious enemy,
forsaken creature, man ringed by death.
What will you say now, before our assembly?
Will you swear by a god? What god?
Will you leap happily into the grave?
Or will you at the end, like the industrious man
Whose life was too brief for his long art,
Lament your sorry work unfinished,
The thirteen million still alive?

Oh son of death, we do not wish you death.
May you live longer than anyone ever lived:
May you live sleepless five million nights,
And may you be visited each night by the suffering of everyone who
  saw
Shutting behind him, the door that blocked the way back,
Saw it grow dark around him, the air filled with death.[1]

> Translated from the Italian by Ruth Feldman and Brian Swann

1. The reference is to the suffocating gas chambers.

We Were Not Like Dogs

We were not like dogs among the Gentiles . . . they pity a dog,
They pet him, even kiss him with the Gentile mouth.
Like a fat baby, one of their very own,
They pamper him, always laughing and playing;
And when the dog dies, how bitterly the Gentiles mourn him!

We were not brought in the boxcars like lambs to the slaughter,
Rather, like leprous sheep,
Through all the beautiful landscapes of Europe,
They shipped us to Death.
They did not handle their sheep as they handled our bodies;
They did not yank out their teeth before they killed them;
Nor strip the wool from their bodies as they stripped our skin;
Nor shovel them into the fire to make ashes of their life,
And scatter the ashes over streams and sewers.

Where are there other analogies to this,
This monstrous thing we suffered at their hands?
There *are* none—no other analogies! (All words are shadows of
    shadows)—
That is the horror: no other analogies!
No matter how brutal the torture a man may endure in a Christian
    country,
He who comes to compare will compare it thus:
He was tortured like a Jew.
Every fear, every anguish, every loneliness, every agony,
Every scream, every weeping in this world,
He who compares things will say:
This is the Jewish kind.

There is no retribution for what they did to us—
Its circumference is the world:

The culture of Christian kingdoms to its peak
Is covered with our blood,
And all their conscience, with our tears.

Translated from the Hebrew
by Robert Mezey

Under the Tooth of Their Plow

Once more the snows have melted there—and the murderers are farmers now. [1]
They have gone out to plow their fields—fields that are my graveyards.
If the tooth of their plow digs up a skeleton which rolls over the furrow,
The ploughman will neither grieve nor tremble
But will smile—he will note where his instrument left its mark.

Once more a spring landscape—bulbs, lilac, twittering birds.
Herds lie down by the shallow waters of the clear stream.
Only there are no more Jews—no Jews with beards and sidecurls.
They are gone from the inns with their prayershawls and fringes.
Gone from the shops that sold trinkets, or clothing, or food.
Gone from their workplaces, gone from the trains, the markets, the
    synagogues—
All, all under the tooth of the plough of Christians.
With abounding grace has God visited his Gentiles.
But springtime is springtime—and the summer will be fat.
Roadside trees swell like those in the gardens.
Never has fruit been so red now that Jews are no more.

Alas, Jews have no bells for summoning God.
Blessed is Christianity for it has bells ringing from steeples.
Even now, the voice of bells rings across the plain, flowing over a bright
    and fragrant landscape.
The bells are a mighty voice, master of everything.
Once they passed over the roofs of Jews—but no more.
Blessed is Christianity for it has bells in the heights
To honor a God who brings good to Christians and to all. . . .

1. The reference is to Poles who collaborated with the Nazis in the murder
of Jews.

And all the Jews are laid under the tooth of their plow,
Or under pasture grass,
Or in forest graves,
Or on the banks of rivers, or within them,
Or on the roadsides.

Praise be to Yezenyu with solemn bells: Ding-Dong!

Translated from the Yiddish
by Milton Teichman

Song of the Yellow Patch

How does it look, the yellow patch
With a red or black Star-of-David
On the arm of a Jew in Naziland—
Against the white ground of a December snow?
How would it look, a yellow patch
With a red or black Star-of-David
On the arms of my wife and my sons,
On my own arm—
On the white ground of a New York snow?
Truly—
The question gnaws like a gnat in my brain,
The question eats at my heart like a worm.

And why should we escape with mere words?
Why not share in full unity
And wear on our own arms
The destined yellow patch with the Star-of-David
Openly, in New York as in Berlin,
In Paris, in London, in Moscow as in Vienna?
Truly—
The question gnaws like a gnat in my brain,
The question eats at my heart like a worm.

Today the first snow descended.
Children are gliding on sleds in the park,
The air is filled with clamor of joy.—
Like the children, I love the white snow,
And I have a special love for the month of December.
(Somewhere far, somewhere far away
Lies a prisoner, lies alone.)

O dear God, God of Abraham, of Isaac and of Jacob,
Scold me not for this love of mine—

Scold me for something else—
Scold me for not kneading
This wonderful snow of New York into a Moses,
For not building a Mount Sinai of snow.
As I used to in my childhood.—

(Somewhere wanders a man,
Deeply covered in snow.)

Scold me for not really wearing
The six-towered Star-of-David
And the infinite circle of the yellow patch—
To hearten the sons of Israel in Hangman's-Land
And to praise and raise our arm
With the pride of our ancestral emblem
In all the lands of the wide world.
Truly—
The question gnaws like a gnat in my brain,
The question eats at my heart like a worm.

(Somewhere far, somewhere far away,
Lies the land, the forbidden land.)

circa 1940
Translated from the Yiddish
by Benjamin and Barbara Harshav

Already embraced by the arm of heavenly solace

Already embraced by the arm of heavenly solace
The insane mother stands
With the tatters of her torn mind
With the charred tinders of her burnt mind
Burying her dead child,
Burying her lost light,
Twisting her hands into urns,
Filling them with the body of her child from the air,
Filling them with his eyes, his hair from the air,
And with his fluttering heart—

Then she kisses the air-born being
And dies!

Translated from the German by Michael Roloff

If I only knew

If I only knew
On what your last look rested.
Was it a stone that had drunk
So many last looks that they fell
Blindly upon its blindness?

Or was it earth,
Enough to fill a shoe,
And black already
With so much parting
And with so much killing?

Or was it your last road
That brought you a farewell from all the roads
You had walked?

A puddle, a bit of shining metal,
Perhaps the buckle of your enemy's belt,
Or some other small augury
Of heaven?

Or did this earth,
Which lets no one depart unloved,
Send you a bird-sign through the air,
Reminding your soul that it quivered
In the torment of its burnt body?

Translated from the German
by Ruth Mead and Matthew Mead

At Night

Without a door, through the smooth wall,
somewhat blue,
comes my murdered father
who looks silently into my eyes.

Enters my grandfather, also murdered,
and remains standing
not far from my father.
A bit late, and following them both,
my grandmother comes in,
covered with wounds.

My brain then fails
because of my bitter labor
to understand
what it means not to die a natural death,
but to be shot, to be shot.

Three frozen, bloody heads.
Three mournful, glazed pairs of eyes.
The wall has pulled them back
into itself,
and covered them over with blackness.

Translated from the Yiddish
by Gabriel Preil and
Howard Schwartz

Burnt

Burdened with family feelings, I went
To my aunt's place,
                to see my uncle,

To press my girl cousins to my breast,
Who were so carried away,
                as it happened,
By music and the other arts!

I found neither uncle nor aunt,
I did not see my cousins either,
But I remember,
                remember
                        to this day,
How their neighbors,
                looking down at the ground,
Said to me quietly: They were burnt.

Everything's gone up in flames: the vices with the virtues,
And children with their aged parents.
And there am I, standing before these hushed witnesses,
And quietly repeating:
                burnt.

Translated from the Russian by Daniel Weissbort

Boris Slutsky is one of a handful of Soviet writers (among them Kuznetsov, Yevtushenko, and Katayev) who resisted the Soviet ban on the theme of the Jewish
tragedy. The silence concerning the Holocaust in Russian literature is remarkable
when we consider that, next to Poland, the Soviet Union was the second greatest
scene of Jewish devastation.

from "My Little Sister"

My sister sits happy
at her bridegroom's table. She does not cry.
My sister will do no such thing:
what would people say!

My sister sits happy
at her bridegroom's table. Her heart is awake.
The whole world drinks
kosher chicken soup.

The dumplings of unleavened flour
were made by her mother-in-law. The world is amazed
and tastes the mother's dessert.

My sister-bride sits. A small dish
of honey before her. Such a huge crowd!
Father twisted
the braids of the hallah. [1]

Our father took his bread, bless God,
forty years from the same oven. He never imagined
a whole people could rise in the ovens
and the world, with God's help, go on.

My sister sits at the table in her bridal veil
alone. From the mourners' hideout
the voice of a bridegroom comes near.
We will set the table without you;
The marriage contract will be written in stone.

Translated from the Hebrew
by Shirley Kaufman

---

1. The twisted loaf of Sabbath bread, which was part of the festive wedding meal along with chicken soup.

Against Parting

My tailor is against parting.
That's why, he
said, he's not going away;
he doesn't want to part
from his one daughter. He's definitely
against parting.

Once, he parted from his wife, and
she he
saw no more of (Auschwitz).
Parted
from his three sisters and
these he never
saw (Buchenwald).
He once parted from his mother (his father
died of a fine, and ripe age). Now
he's against parting.

In Berlin he
was my father's kith and kin. They passed
a good time in
that Berlin. The time's passed. Now
he'll never leave. He's
most definitely
(my father's died)
against parting.

Translated from the Hebrew
by Jon Silkin

After Thersienstadt

For Vera

It does not matter;
it is only a word:

Maria Theresia's fortress,
a collection of stones.

If you move the letters around
like furniture—thick

and upholstered as great-aunts—
they will not complain.

Here is the word
which you entered in childhood

and here is the word
which took away

your breathing
and here is the word

grown wrinkled and dangerous
which labors to spit you

back into the world again.

Theresienstadt was collection point for the gas chambers.

September Song

born 19.6.32 – deported 24.9.42

Undesirable you may have been, untouchable
you were not. Not forgotten
or passed over at the proper time.

As estimated, you died. Things marched,
sufficient, to that end.
Just so much Zyklon[1] and leather, patented
terror, so many routine cries.

(I have made
an elegy for myself it
is true)

September fattens on vines. Roses
flake from the wall. The smoke
of harmless fires drifts to my eyes.

This is plenty. This is more than enough.

1. Also Zyklon B (Hydrogen cyanide). A pesticide used in the gas chambers of the death camps.

Lament for the European Exile

The thin mask of my sleep
Caught fire.
I woke
With my face seared.
I had seen the flames of the sunset,
But this was a new sun,
A red sun
That lit up the night
With a strange, cruel light,
In which I saw the heavens
Swallowing hell,
And the earth spawning out
Living death.

I knew that this sun
Was the blood of my people
Gathering in the sky,
Ripping the darkness
With a flaring cry.
For on the highways of the world
It poured along,
In the world's fields
It watered,
The blood knew no rest.
It rose
And split the night's calm.

The Angel of Death
Said to me:
"Thou art my son.
Today I watched thy birth."
And a new heart
Beat in me

Weak-voiced,
Jerking in agonies of death.
My flesh
Became dead flesh.
The blood flowed dumb
In my veins.

Can I mourn?
I am an elegy.
Lament?
My mind is lamentation.
Can I rise
With death heavy on my limbs,
Or see
When Nothing hangs at my eyelash?
I will mourn and rise.
Your look will ask in my eyes
Atonement for your blood
At the hands of the world
That shed it.

Translated from the Hebrew
by A. C. Jacobs

To the Six Million

But put forth thine hand now, and
touch his bones and his flesh . . . [1]

I

If there is a god,
he descends from the power.
But who is the god rising from death?
(So, thunder invades the room, and brings with it
a treble, chilly and intimate, of panes rattling
on a cloudy day in winter.
But when I look through the window,
a sudden blaze of sun is in the streets,
which are, however, empty and still. The thunder
repeats.) Thunder here. The emptiness resounds
here on the gods' struggle-ground
where the infinite negative retreats,
annihilating where it runs,
and the god who must possess pursues, pressing
on window panes, passing through.
Nothing's in the room but light
wavering beneath the lamp
like a frosty rose the winter bled.
No one is in the room (I possess nothing),
only power pursuing, trying
corpses where the other god went,
running quickly under the door. In
the chill, the empty room
reverberates. I look from the window.

*

There is someone missing.
Is it I who am missing?

1. Job 2:5.

And many are missing.
And outside, the frozen street extends
from me like a string, divides, circles,
with an emptiness the sun
is burnishing.
        In the street
there is nothing, for many are missing,
or there is the death of many
missing, annulled, dispossessed,
filling the street, pressing their vacancy
against the walls, the sunlight, the thunder.
Is a god
in the street? where nothing is left
to possess, nothing to kill;
and I am standing
dead at the window looking out.

                *

What did you kill? Whom did you save? I ask
myself aloud, clinging to the window
of a winter day.
        Survivor, who are you?
ask the voices that disappeared,
the faces broken and expunged.
I am the one who was not there.
Of such accidents I have made my death.

Should I have been with them
on other winter days in the snow
of the camps and ghettos?
And on the days of their death that was
the acrid Polish air?—

I who lay between the mountain of myrrh
and the hill of frankincense,
dead and surviving, and dared not breathe,
and asked, By what right am I myself?
Who I am I do not know,
but I believe myself to be one
who should have died, and the dead one
who did die.
Here on the struggle-ground, impostor
of a death, I survive reviving,
perpetuating the accident.
And who is at the window pane,
clinging, lifting himself like a child
to the scene of a snowless day?

                    *

"Whatsoever is under the whole heaven
Is mine." Charred, abandoned, all this,
who will call these things his own?

Who died not
to be dying, to survive
my death dead as I am
at the window (possessing nothing),
and died not to know
agony of the absence,
revive on a day
when thunder rattles the panes,
possessed by no one;
bone and flesh of me, because
you died on other days
of actual snow and sun,
under mists and chronic rain,

my death is cut to the bone,
my survival is torn from me.
I would cover my nakedness
in dust and ashes. They burn,
they are hot to the touch. Can my
death live? The chill treble
squeaks for a bone. I was
as a point in a space,
by what right can I be myself?
At the window and in the streets,
among the roots of barbed wire,
and by springs of the sea,
to be dying my death again
and with you,
in the womb of ice, and where
the necessity of our lives is hid.
Bone and flesh of me,
I have not survived,
I would praise the skies,
leap to the treasures of snow.

II

By night on my bed I sought him whom my soul loveth;
I sought him, but I found him not.

I will rise now, and go about the city in the streets,
and in the broad ways I will seek him
whom my soul loveth. . . .[2]

What can I say?

          Dear ones, what can I say?

You died, and emptied the streets

2. Song of Songs 3:1–2.

and my breath, and went from my seeing.
And I awoke, dying at the window
of my wedding day, because
I was nowhere; the morning that revived
was pain, and my life that began again was pain,
I could not see you.
                    What can I say?
My helpless love overwhelmed me,
sometimes I thought I touched your faces,
my blindness sought your brows again,
and your necks that are towers,
your temples that are as pieces
of pomegranate within your locks.
Dead and alive,
your shadows escaped me. I went
into the streets, you were not there,
for you were murdered and befouled.
And I sought you in the city,
which was empty, and I found you not,
for you were bleeding at the dayspring
and in the air. That emptiness
mingled with my heart's emptiness,
and was at home there, my heart
that wished to bear you again, and bore
the agony of its labor, the pain
of no birth. And I sought for you
about the city in the streets, armed
with the love hundreds had borne me.
And before the melancholy in the mazes,
and the emptiness in the streets,
in the instant before our deaths,
I heard the air (that was
to be ashen) and the flesh

(that was to be broken), I heard
cry out, Possess me!
And I found you whom my soul loves;
I held you, and would not let you go
until I had brought you
into my mother's house, and into the chamber
of her that conceived me.

Dear ones, what can I say?
I must possess you no matter how,
father you, befriend you,
and bring you to the lighthearted dance
beside the treasures and the springs,
and be your brother and your son.
Sweetness, my soul's bride,
come to the feast I have made,
my bone and my flesh of me,
broken and touched,
come in your widow's raiment of dust and ashes,
bereaved, newborn, gasping for
the breath that was torn from you,
that is returned to you.
There will I take your hand
and lead you under the awning,
and speak the words it behooves to speak.
My heart is full, only the speech
of the ritual can express it.
And after a little while,
I will rouse you from your dawn sleep
and accompany you in the streets.

At the Rim of the Heavens

Like Abraham and Sarah by the
terebinths of Mamre[1] before the
precious tidings, and like David and
Bathsheba, in the king's palace, in the
tenderness of their first night—my
martyred father and mother rise in the
West over the sea with all the aureoles
of God upon them. Weighed down by
their beauty they sink, slowly. Above
their heads flows the mighty ocean,
beneath it is their deep home.

This home has no walls on any side, it
is built of water within water. The
drowned of Israel come swimming
from all the corners of the sea, each
with a star in his mouth. And what
they speak of there, the poem does not
know; only they know who are in the sea.

And I, their good son, am like a lyre
whose radiant melody has been stopped,
as I stand, towering with Time, on the
seashore.

And at times the evening and the sea
run into my heart, and I run to the sea.
I am summoned, as if to the rim of the
heavens, to behold: on either side of
the sinking globe of the sun, he is seen,

---

1. Where the angels announced to Abraham that Sarah would bear him a son
(Genesis 18.1 ff.).—Trans.

she is seen: my father to the right and
my mother to the left; and beneath
their bare feet flows the burning sea.

Translated from the Hebrew
by T. Carmi

How They Killed My Grandmother

How did they kill my grandmother?
This is how they killed my grandmother:
In the morning a tank
Rolled up to the city bank.

One hundred fifty Jews of the town,
Weightless
        from a whole year's starvation,
Pale,
  with the pangs of death upon them,
Came there, carrying bundles.
Polizei and young German soldiers
Cheerfully herded the old men and old women,
And led them, clanking with pots and pans,
Led them
      far out of town.

But my diminutive grandmother, Lilliputian,
My seventy-year-old grandmother,
Swore at the Germans,
Cursed like a trooper,

Yelled at them where I was.
She cried: "My grandson's at the front.
Just you dare
Lay hands on me.
Those are our guns
        that you hear, Boche!"

Grandmother wept and shouted
And walked.
      And then started
Shouting again.

From every window rose a din.
Ivanovs and Andreyevnas leant down,
Sidorovnas and Petrovnas wept:

"Keep it up, Polina Matveyevna!
You just show them. Give it them straight!"
They clamored:
                    "What's there to be so scared
About this German enemy!"
And so they decided to kill my grandmother,
While they were still passing through the town.

A bullet kicked up her hair.
A gray lock floated down,
And my grandmother fell to the ground.
That's how they did it to her.

Translated from the Russian
by Daniel Weissbort

The Death of an Ox

With burning horns, two twisted wax candles under a radiant yellow halo, an ox lunges from the flaming stable with a hoarse bellow, as if a gilded slaughter-knife had remained stuck in its throat. Purple rings rise like smoke from the dried manure on its backside, and along the forelegs as far up as the jaw the very flesh blazes like kindled wildgrass.

The first snowfall—as if someone had chased a great flock of pearl-white baby doves from their heavencoop, forcing them to sinful earth from out of their warm sleep—the snow cannot quench the fire. When the sparks, flying red needles, wake the falling doves with a thin prick—it lasts less than a sigh—the doves are swallowed up by the greedy fire. With the power of the swallowed snowdoves the fire rages ever wilder, more joyously around the victim, chaining the ox in copper ribs, sitting on its back like a naked satyr and lashing it with pyreal whips.

It ears catch the sound of a distant mooing, a terrible yearning mooo, a thunderclap with severed wings.

It cannot answer. Its mouth is open, but it has truly lost its tongue.

Its momentum drives the ox forward, the fire rising from the ground, from the dark sunken swamps that reach all the way to a lake.

Only then, when it storms into the lake up to its knees, and when its reflected elliptical eyes, like molten glass of many colors, catch sight of a second ox in the water, upside-down, with its burning horns pointing downward, into the sky—a human smile begins to wrinkle its face.

Its copper ribs burst.

The snow falls and falls.

The ox turns its head to the left, in the direction of its home village where only one dark chimney remains, like a dead hand, and remains motionless.

Its horns flicker for a while, like candles beside a dead man, and are extinguished with the day.

Translated from the Yiddish by Ruth R. Wisse

This symbolic narrative is one of fifteen prose poems that Sutzkever wrote in the 1950s about the Vilna Ghetto and the resistance of Jewish partisans in the nearby forests. These poems appeared under the title *Green Aquarium*.

I Hear a Voice

The sun rose over a mound of corpses
And one, who witnessed it, asked:
—Are you not ashamed to rise, sun?
He asked and received no reply,
For in that moment he said to himself:
—Are you not ashamed to live on?
And he sat down opposite the mount,
And looked at the bodies as they lay,
Some face down to the ground
And some face upward to the sun.
And again he asked:
—Are you not ashamed to look at the sun?
And in that moment he said to himself:
—Are you not ashamed to sit while they lie—
And he lay down, like one of the dead,
Face up, and lay this way for hours.
While he lay there, a melody rose within him
That sang of his own shame,
And the melody began to sing out from within,
he stood up
And allowed the melody to spread
And the mount of corpses
Picked up his melody
And answered with an echo
Like a resounding choir.

Translated from the Yiddish
by David G. Roskies

Nightsong

Strangers' eyes don't see
how in my small room I open a door
and begin my nightly stroll among the graves.
(How much earth—if you can call it earth—does it take to
    bury smoke?)
There are valleys and hills
and hidden twisted paths,
enough to last a whole night's journey.
In the dark I see shining towards me
faces of epitaphs
wailing their song.
Graves of the whole
vanished Jewish world
blossom in my one-man tent.
And I pray:
Be a father, a mother to me,
a sister, a brother,
my own children, body-kin,
real as pain,
from my own blood and skin,
be my own dead,
let me grasp and take in
these destroyed millions.

At dawn I shut the door
to my people's house of death.
I sit at the table and doze off,
humming a tune.
The enemy had no dominion over them.
Fathers, mothers, children from their cradles
ringed around death and overcame him.
All the children, astonished,
ran to meet the fear of death

without tears, like little Jewish bedtime stories.
And soon they flickered into flames
like small namesakes of God.

Who else, like me, has
his own nighttime
dead garden?
Who is destined for this, as I am?
Who has so much dead earth waiting for him, as for me?
And when I die
who will inherit my small house of death
and that shining gift, an eternal deathday light
forever flickering?

Translated from the Yiddish by Ruth Whitman

5.8.1942

in memory of Janusz Korczak

What did the Old Doctor do
in the cattle wagon
bound for treblinka on the fifth of august
over the few hours of the bloodstream
over the dirty river of time

I do not know

what did Charon of his own free will
the ferryman without an oar do
did he give out to the children
what remained of gasping breath
and leave for himself
only frost down the spine

I do not know

did he lie to them for instance
in small
numbing doses
groom the sweaty little heads
for the scurrying lice of fear

I do not know

yet for all that yet later yet there
in treblinka

On August 5, 1942, Janusz Korczak, Polish-Jewish doctor, writer and educator, was forced to gather the two hundred orphans under his care in the Warsaw Ghetto and lead them to the train that would take them to their death. Refusing Nazi offers for his own safety, Korczak accompanied his charges to Treblinka, where he perished with them.

all their terror all the tears
were against him

oh it was only now
just so many minutes say a lifetime
whether a little or a lot
I was not there I do not know

suddenly the Old Doctor saw
the children had grown
as old as he was
older and older
that was how fast they had to go grey as ash

so when he was struck
by the guard or the ss man
they saw the Doctor
had become a child like them
smaller and smaller still
until he had not been born.

from now on together with the Old Doctor
they are all nowhere

I know

Translated from the Polish
by Keith Bosley with Krystyna Wandycz

They

There they were many, O God, so many,
Such vital ones and unafraid,
Such noble ones, with beard and braid—
And talking in a marvelous strange way.

And under every roof they would sing—
With Torah chant and scripture cymbals—
Such rare songs, proud and boastful:
Of the golden peacock and Elimelekh the king. [1]

But above their heads only the sun in its stare
Saw the raw fury, the killer's cold blade,
How with wild force it descended,
And what massacres were there.

Now they are but a trace of that fury:
An axed forest, a couple of trees.

Translated from the Yiddish
by David G. Roskies and Hillel Schwartz

1. "Torah chant and scripture cymbals" refer to the musical tradition of the synagogue as well as to the ancient music of the Jews. Songs of the "golden peacock and Elimelekh the king" refer to well-known Yiddish folksongs.

Babi Yar

There are no monuments on Babi Yar,
A steep ravine is all, a rough memorial.
Fear is my ground—
Old as the Jewish people, a Jew myself it seems,
I roam in Egypt in her ancient days,
I perish on the cross, and even now
I bear the red marks of nails.

I am Dreyfus,[1] detested, denounced,
Snared behind prison bars:
Pettiness
Is my betrayer and my judge.
Shrieking ladies in fine ruffled gowns
Brandish their umbrellas in my face.

And now a boy in Bielostok,
I seem to see blood spurt and spread over the floor.
The tavern masters celebrate:
Under the smell of vodka and of onions
And of blood.
Kicked by their heavy boots I lie
Begging in vain for pity.
The rampant pogrom roars
"Murder the Jews! Save Russia!"
A man is beating up my mother.

Babi Yar is a ravine two miles from the outskirts of Kiev, where the Nazis mas-
sacred more than thirty-three thousand Jews on September 29–30, 1941. Over
the next months, the executions of Jews, Gypsies, and Soviet POWs raised the
total murdered at Babi Yar to approximately a hundred thousand.
1. Captain Alfred Dreyfus (1859–1935), a French officer and an Alsatian Jew
convicted of treason by a court-martial in 1894, sentenced to life imprisonment,
and sent to Devil's Island. In 1898 it was learned that much of the evidence
against Dreyfus had been forged; however, it was not until 1906 that he was ex-
onerated and his innocence established.

Anne Frank, I am she,
A translucent twig of April
And I am filled with love that needs no words.
We are forbidden the sky and the green leaves
But in this dark room we can embrace.
Love, do not fear the noise—it is the rushing
Of spring itself.
Come, let us kiss . . .
The sounds of thawing ice change to pounding on the door.

Wild grasses rustle over Babi Yar,
The trees stare down, stern as my judge,
Silent the air howls.
I bare my head, graying now,
And I am myself an endless soundless howl
Over the buried
Thousands and thousands of thousands,
And I am every old man shot down here
And every child.
In no limb of my body can I forget.

O Russian people,
I know your heart
Lives without bounds
But often men
With dirty hands abuse
The body of your clear name.
Shamelessly,
Without the quiver of a nerve
These pompous anti-Semites call themselves
"The union of the Russian people."

Let the Internationale
Be sung

When the last reviler of the Jews is dead.
No Jewish blood is mixed in mine, but let me be a Jew
For all anti-Semites to hate, to spit upon.
Only then can I call myself
Russian.

Adapted from the Russian
by Rose Styron

The Pripet Marshes

Often I think of my Jewish friends and seize them as they are and
transport them in my mind to the *shtetlach*[1] and ghettos,

And set them walking the streets, visiting, praying in *shul*,[2] feasting
and dancing. The men I set to arguing, because I love dialectic and
song—my ears tingle when I hear their voices—and the girls and
women I set to promenading or to cooking in the kitchens, for the
sake of their tiny feet and clever hands.

And put kerchiefs and long dresses on them, and some of the men I
dress in black and reward with beards. And all of them I set
among the mists of the Pripet Marshes, which I have never seen,
among wooden buildings that loom up suddenly one a a time,
because I have only heard of them in stories, and that long ago.

It is the moment before the Germans will arrive.

Maury is there, uncomfortable, and pigeon-toed, his voice is rapid
and slurred, and he is brilliant;
And Frank who is goodhearted and has the hair and yellow skin of a
Tartar and is like a flame turned low;
And blonde Lottie who is coarse and miserable, her full mouth is
turning down with a self-contempt she can never hide, while the
steamroller of her voice flattens every delicacy;
And Marian, her long body, her face pale under her bewildered black
hair and of the purest oval of those Greek signets she loves; her
head tilts now like the heads of the birds she draws;
And Adele who is sullen and an orphan and so like a beaten creature
she trusts no one, and who doesn't know what to do with herself,
lurching with her magnificent body like a despoiled tigress;

The Pripet Marshes are in the northwest Ukraine and South Belorussia.
1. Yiddish plural of shtetl: a village.
2. Yiddish for synagogue.

And Munji, moping melancholy clown, arms too short for his barrel
chest, his penny-whistle nose, and mocking nearsighted eyes that
want to be straightforward and good;
And Abbie who, when I listen closely, is speaking to me, beautiful
with her large nose and witty mouth, her coloring that always
wants lavender, her vitality that body and mind can't quite master;
And my mother whose gray eyes are touched with yellow, and who
is as merry as a young girl;
And my brown-eyed son who is glowing like a messenger impatient
to be gone and who may stand for me.
I cannot breathe when I think of him there.
And my red-haired sisters, and all my family, our embarrassed love
bantering our tenderness away.

Others, others, in crowds filling the town on a day I have made
sunny for them; the streets are warm and they are at their ease.

How clearly I see them all now, how miraculously we are linked!
And sometimes I make them speak Yiddish in timbres whose
unfamiliarity thrills me.

But in a moment the Germans will come.

What, will Maury die? Will Marian die?

Not a one of them who is not transfigured then!

The brilliant in mind have bodies that glimmer with a total dialectic;
The stupid suffer an inward illumination; their stupidity is a subtle
tenderness that glows in and around them;
The sullen are surrounded with great tortured shadows raging with
pain, against whom they struggle like titans;
In Frank's low flame I discover an enormous perspectiveless depth;

The gray of my mother's eyes dazzles me with our love;
No one is more beautiful than my red-haired sisters.
And always I imagine the least among them last, one I did not love,
    who was almost a stranger to me.
I can barely see her blond hair under the kerchief; her cheeks are
    large and faintly pitted, her raucous laugh is tinged with shame as
    it subsides; her bravado forces her into still another lie;
But her vulgarity is touched with a humanity I cannot exhaust, her
    wretched self-hatred is as radiant as the faith of Abraham, or
    indistinguishable from that faith.
I can never believe my eyes when this happens, and I want to kiss
    her hand, to exchange a blessing

In the moment when the Germans are beginning to enter the town.

But there isn't a second to lose, I snatch them all back,
For, when I want to, I can be a God.
No, the Germans won't have one of them!
This is my people, they are mine!

And I flee with them, crowd out with them; I hide myself in a
    pillowcase stuffed with clothing, in a woman's knotted
    handkerchief, in a shoebox.

And one by one I cover them in mist, I take them out.
The German motorcycles zoom through the town,
They break their fists on the hollow doors.
But I can't hold out any longer. My mind clouds over.
I sink down as though drunk or beaten.

Good Night, World

Good night, wide world,
great, stinking world.
Not you, but I slam the gate.
With the long gabardine,
with the yellow patch—burning—
with proud stride
I decide—:
I am going back to the ghetto.[1]
Wipe out, stamp out all traces of apostasy.
I wallow in your filth.
Blessed, blessed, blessed,
hunchbacked Jewish life.
Go to hell, with your polluted cultures, world.
Though all is ravaged,
I am dust of your dust,
sad Jewish life.

Prussian pig and hate-filled Pole;
Jew-killers, land of guzzle and gorge.
Flabby democracies, with your cold
sympathy compresses.
Good night, electro-impudent world.
Back to my kerosene, tallowed shadows,
eternal October, minute stars,
to my warped streets and hunchbacked lanterns,
my worn-out pages of the Prophets,
my Gemaras, to arduous
Talmudic debates, to lucent, exegetic Yiddish,

The poem contrasts the wide world of modern secular culture with traditional
Jewish values and Jewish law, the use of Yiddish, and the study of Jewish texts.
1. Glatstein is not using *ghetto* in the Nazi sense but in the sense of insular Jewish
communities where Jewish values and traditions predominate.

to Rabbinical Law, to deep-deep meaning, to duty, to what is
    right.
World, I walk with joy to the quiet ghetto light.

Good night. It's all yours, world. I disown
my liberation.
Take back your Jesusmarxists, choke on their arrogance.
Croak on a drop of our baptized blood.
And though He tarries, I have hope;
day in, day out, my expectation grows.
Leaves will yet green
on our withered tree.
I don't need any solace.
I return to our cramped space.
From Wagner's pagan-music to chants of sacred humming.
I kiss you, tangled strands of Jewish life.
Within me weeps the joy of coming home.

April 1938
Translated from the Yiddish by Richard Fein

Old Jewish Cemetery in Worms

February 1974

My steps are wet from the cold death
you received in your warm beds;
that of your children was *hot:*
smoke columns signified their end.
Not you, but I, was witness to this.
In the forest of death where you rest
time wears away rhymed phrases
stating regret at being severed
from life in the country you loved
and thought to be your own.
Grandsons of assassins act as guides,
emphasizing what has survived the Reich.
There's no one here to take the blame;
only the innocent returned:
the guilty either died or fled.
Stones placed on graves by the faithful
a century ago, now crack and crumble:
a silent reproach, a stifled scream—
the questions will remain unanswered,
and no new graves will be dug here.

Epilogue
In April 1974, the old Jewish cemetery in Worms was devastated.
Gravestones were pulled out of the ground and smashed. Those left
were desecrated with the swastika.

Translated from the German
by Herbert Kuhner

In the Darkness

If they show me a stone and I say stone
they say stone. If they show me a tree
and I say tree they say tree. But if they
show me blood and I say blood they
say paint. *If they show me blood and I
say blood they say paint.*

Translated from the Hebrew
by T. Carmi

Shema

You who live secure
In your warm houses,
Who, returning at evening, find
Hot food and friendly faces:
    Consider whether this is a man,
    Who labors in the mud
    Who knows no peace
    Who fights for a crust of bread
    Who dies at a yes or a no.
    Consider whether this is a woman,
    Without hair or name
    With no more strength to remember
    Eyes empty and womb cold
    As a frog in winter.
Consider that this has been:
I commend these words to you.
Engrave them on your hearts
When you are in your house, when you walk on your
    way
When you go to bed, when you rise:
Repeat them to your children.
    Or may your house crumble,
    Disease render you powerless,
    Your offspring avert their faces from you.

Translated from the Italian
by Ruth Feldman and Brian Swann

Shema [hear] is the first of six Hebrew words that have been the keynote of Judaism through the ages, the English rendering being "Hear, O Israel, the Lord is our God, the Lord is One" (Deuteronomy 6:4). The entire poem echoes Deuteronomy 6:4–9 and 11:13–21.

A Story About Chicken Soup

In my grandmother's house there was always chicken soup
And talk of the old country—mud and boards,
Poverty,
The snow falling down the necks of lovers.

Now and then, out of her savings
She sent them a dowry. Imagine
The rice-powdered faces!
And the smell of the bride, like chicken soup.

But the Germans killed them.
I know it's in bad taste to say it,
But it's true. The Germans killed them all.

*

In the ruins of Berchtesgaden
A child with yellow hair
Ran out of the doorway.

A German girl-child—
Cuckoo, all skin and bones—
Not even enough to make chicken soup.
She sat by the stream and smiled.

Then as we splashed in the sun
She laughed at us.
We had killed her mechanical brothers,
So we forgave her.

*

The sun is shining.
The shadows of the lovers have disappeared.

They are all eyes; they have some demand on me—
They want me to be more serious than I want to be.

They want me to stick in their mudhole
Where no one is elegant.
They want me to wear old clothes,
They want me to be poor, to sleep in a room
    with many others—

Not to walk in the painted sunshine
To a summer house,
But to live in the tragic world forever.

Written in Pencil in the
Sealed Railway-Car

here in this carload
i am eve
with abel my son
if you see my other son
cain son of man
tell him that i

Translated from the Hebrew
by Stephen Mitchell

In Spite

You say:
"You are a Jew and a poet
And you've written no poems
On the destruction.
How can a Yiddish poet not,
When the destruction is enormous,
So enormous?"

Simple:
In spite of the destroyers,
To spite them I will not cry openly,
I will not write down my sorrow
On paper.
(A degradation to write
"Sorrow" on paper.)
To spite them
I'll walk the world
As if the world were mine.
Of course it's mine!
If they hindered me,
Fenced in my roads,
The world would still be mine.

To spite them I will not wail
Even if (God forbid) my world becomes
As big as where my sole stands—
The world will still be mine!

To spite them
I'll marry off my children
That they shall have children—
To spite the villains who breed

In my world
And make it narrow
For me.

Translated from the Yiddish
by Kathryn Hellerstein

Contributors

SHMUEL YOSEF AGNON was born in 1888 in Galicia (formerly a part of Austria Hungary, now Poland). He settled in Palestine (later Israel) in 1924 and remained there until his death in 1970. A short-story writer and novelist of exceptional originality, he drew upon a vast knowledge of Jewish tradition. His Hebrew prose style is simple but highly allusive. His writings appear in sixteen languages. English translations of his works include *The Bridal Canopy, A Guest for the Night, In the Heart of the Seas, Twenty-one Stories,* and *Shira.* Agnon received the Nobel Prize for Literature in 1966, sharing it with the German-Jewish poet Nelly Sachs.

AHARON APPELFELD, one of the foremost writers on the Holocaust in Hebrew literature, was born in Chernovitz, the Ukraine, in 1932. His boyhood experiences included imprisonment in camps, escape, temporary refuge in monasteries, and years of flight and hiding. He arrived in Palestine in 1946, when he was fourteen. During the 1960s, Appelfeld was a prolific writer of short stories. During the 1970s, he turned his attention to the novella: *Badenheim 1939* and *The Age of Wonders* were the first of his novellas to be published in English translation. The power of his fiction comes, in part, from the discrepancy between overwhelming events and feelings and a highly understated style.

W. H. AUDEN, poet, editor, translator, and critic, was born in York, England, in 1907. He became recognized in the 1930s for a poetry characterized by its witty Marxian and Freudian perspectives. He is now considered one of the major poets of the century. In 1939, Auden emigrated to the United States, becoming a citizen in 1946. His criticism is collected in *The Dyer's Hand* (1962). Auden died in 1973.

GIORGIO BASSANI, son of Italian Jews, was born in Bologna, Italy, in 1916 and reared in the city of Ferrara. Fiction writer, poet, and critic, he is recognized as one of Italy's most accomplished writers. He published his first book, *Una citta di pianura* [A city on the plains] in 1940. The plight of Italian Jews during the Fascist tyranny is reflected in *Le storie ferraresi* [Stories of Ferrara] (1960). With his novel *Il giardino dei Finzi-Contini* (1962) [The garden of the Finzi-Continis, 1965], he gained international reknown. Vittorio De Sica created a film based on the novel. Bassani was active in the Italian resistance during World War II.

RACHEL BOIMWALL was born in Russia in 1913. Daughter of the playwright and director Yehudah Leib Boimwall, she was evacuated to the city of Tashkent during the war. She later emigrated to Israel, where she now lives. Her poetic works include a book of children's poems, *Pioneers* (1934), *Tarah* (1934), *Poems* (1936), and *Love* (1947), all written in Yiddish and all published in Moscow.

TADEUSZ BOROWSKI, a short-story writer, poet, and journalist, was born to Polish parents in the Soviet Ukraine in 1922. As a result of association with activist literary friends in Warsaw, Borowski was imprisoned in Dachau and Auschwitz. Freed by American forces in 1945, he became a Stalinist in 1949 and committed suicide in 1951. During his brief lifetime he achieved recognition as one of Poland's outstanding although controversial literary figures. He is known to English readers primarily for his volume *This Way for the Gas, Ladies and Gentlemen and Other Stories* (1967). Borowski refused to spiritualize the experience of suffering in the death camp. Underneath his cynicism, however, is a profound sadness at what the brutality of the Nazi system did to human beings.

PAUL CELAN (ANCZEL), poet and translator, was born in Romanian Bukovina in 1920. During the Nazi occupation, his parents were taken to an extermination camp, and Celan was sent to a forced labor camp, from which he escaped. After short stays in Vienna and Bucharest, Celan settled in Paris in 1948. He traveled to Germany occasionally to read poetry and receive literary awards. Six volumes of his poems were published during his lifetime, three more posthumously. Celan committed suicide in 1970. Two translations of his work appear in English, *Selected Poems* (1972) and *Speech-Grille and Selected Poems* (1971).

CHARLOTTE DELBO was arrested with her husband in 1942 for being members of the French resistance. Her husband was shot, and Delbo was imprisoned in La Sante and Fort de Romainville. She was deported to Auschwitz in 1943. She is best known for her remarkably imaginative memoir of Auschwitz, *None of Us Will Return* (1965; 1968 English), written as poetry and fiction. In addition, she has published two other books, *Les belles-lettres* (1961) and *Le convoi du 24 janvier* (1965).

RICHARD FEIN, poet, critic, and translator, was born in New York City in 1929. His books include a volume of poems, *Kafka's Ear* (1990); a critical study, *Robert Lowell* (revised edition, 1979); a memoir, *The Dance of Leah* (1986); and translations from the Yiddish, *Selected Poems of Yankev Glatshteyn* (1987). His poetry, articles, and reviews have appeared in numerous journals. Formerly a professor of English at the State University of New York at New Paltz, Fein now devotes himself to writing poetry.

IRVING FELDMAN, poet and professor of English at the State University of New York at Buffalo, was born in New York City in 1928. His books of poetry *The Pripet Marshes and Other Poems* and *Leaping Clear* were nominated for the National

Book Award. His most recent collections are *New and Selected Poems* (1979), *Teach Me, Dear Sister* (1985), and *All of Us Here* (1986).

JERZY FICOWSKI, born in Poland in 1924, has written seven collections of poems in Poland and has translated poems from Romanian, Romany, Spanish, and Yiddish. He has written short stories and essays, including studies of gypsy folklore and of Bruno Schultz, who was murdered in a wartime ghetto. *A Reading of Ashes* (1981) is the first of his books of poetry to be translated into English. In his poetry, he condemns the unparalleled Nazi crimes against the Jews of Poland.

IDA FINK, born in Poland in 1921, is the author of numerous short stories and radio plays. She suffered the ordeals of ghetto life through 1942 and then went into hiding until the end of the war. She emigrated to Israel with her husband and daughter in 1957. She is well known for her radio play "The Table," which has been broadcast in Israel and Europe and dramatized on Israeli and German television. *A Scrap of Time and Other Stories* has been translated from Polish into Hebrew, Dutch, and German. In 1985, the book received the first Anne Frank Prize for Literature. Her most recent work is a novel, *The Journey* (1992).

PIERRE GASCAR (PIERRE FOURNIER) was born in Paris in 1916. He began his writing career as a journalist but went on to become a literary critic and fiction writer. Gascar was taken prisoner by the Nazis during World War II, escaped twice, but was captured and transported to a concentration camp in the Ukraine. *Le temps des mortes* [The season of the dead], like many of his other works, reflects his war experiences. His works in English translation include: *Beasts and Men* (1956), *The Seed* (1956), *Women and the Sun* (1958), *The Coral Barrier* (1961), and *The Fugitive* (1964). For *The Season of the Dead,* he received the Prix Goncourt in 1953.

AMIR GILBOA was born in Razywilow (the Ukraine) in 1917. He emigrated illegally to Palestine in 1937. Before joining the Jewish Brigade in 1942, Gilboa worked at various jobs in kibbutzim, stone quarries, and British army camps. Today, he is considered one of Israel's most original and experimental poets. He has received the Prime Minister's Award for Creative Writing and the Bialik Prize. Gilboa is especially noted for his synthesis of traditional and colloquial forms and personal and national motifs. *The Light of Lost Suns* (1979) is an English translation of his selected works.

JACOB GLATSTEIN, poet, was born in Lublin, Poland, in 1896. He emigrated to the United States in 1914, where he worked as a writer and editor for New York Yiddish newspapers. He helped to found the introspective movement, which promoted the use of experimental forms, the natural rhythms of Yiddish speech, and free verse, thus placing Yiddish poetry in the larger movement of literary modernism. One of the foremost writers of Yiddish in America, Glatstein published thirteen volumes of poetry. He died in 1971. Ruth Whitman and Richard Fein have translated some of his work into English.

HIRSH GLIK, born in Vilna in 1920, was the author of a great number of poems and songs, only a few of which have survived. He wrote originally in Hebrew and later in Yiddish under the influence of the Yunge Vilne movement. Active in the literary-artistic circle of the Vilna Ghetto, he was deported to a concentration camp in Estonia in 1943. He escaped in July of 1944 and died as a partisan fighter that same year. His song "Zog nit keyn mol" [Never say] became the hymn of the Jewish partisans.

LEYB GOLDIN was born in Warsaw in 1906. Raised in poverty, he became active in Warsaw's communist youth organizations. In 1936, he joined the Bund (the Jewish Social Democratic party). Before the war, he published essays and literary criticism in Yiddish and also translated from Russian, French, and German literature. During the war, Goldin published in the Bundist underground press. His story "Chronicle of a Single Day" was found among materials in Emanuel Ringelblum's Warsaw archives and was published for the first time in 1955. Goldin died of hunger in the Warsaw Ghetto in 1942.

CHAIM GRADE was born in Vilna, Poland, in 1910. He first distinguished himself as a poet before turning to fiction. His collections of Yiddish poetry include *Refugees* (1947), *Light of Extinguished Stars* (1950), and *The Man of Fire* (1962). His novel, *The Well*, was translated into English in 1967. He now enjoys a high rank among contemporary Yiddish writers. Losing family and friends in the destruction, Grade began to reconstruct his life first in Paris and then in New York, where he settled in 1948. Thoroughly trained in Talmudic and Rabbinic sources, Grade studied for a time among the Mussarists, the ascetic sect described in his story "My Quarrel with Hersh Rasseyner." This story was the first work to make Grade's reputation in English. David Brandes and Kim Todd produced a film *The Quarrel* (1992), based on this story. Grade died in 1982.

URI ZVI GREENBERG was born in Bialy Kamien, Poland, in 1896. He emigrated to Palestine in 1923 and returned to Poland in the thirties as an editor and writer for Zionist newspapers. He escaped for Palestine two weeks after the Nazis marched into Warsaw in 1939. His parents and sisters stayed behind and perished. In 1951, Schocken Books published *Rehovot hanahar: Sefer ha'iliyot vehakoah* [Streets of the river: The book of dirges and power], which included Greenberg's many poems on the Holocaust. His poetry powerfully links personal experience with Jewish-Messianic destiny and rails against his generation's complacency in the face of the persecution of the Jewish people. Greenberg died in Israel in 1981.

ANTHONY HECHT, considered one of the outstanding poets of his generation, was born in New York City in 1923. He served in World War II, first in Europe and then in Japan. His experience of the war has been a major influence in his poetry. Hecht was awarded the Pulitzer Prize in poetry for *The Hard Hours* (1967). His other books include *Millions of Strange Shadows* (1977), *The Venetian Vespers* (1980), *Obbligati: Essays in Criticism* (1986), and *Transparent Man* (1990). He teaches at Georgetown University in Washington, D.C.

WILLIAM HEYEN, poet and essayist, was born in Brooklyn, New York, in 1940. His volumes of poetry include *Noise in the Trees: Poems and a Memoir* (1974), *The Swastika Poems* (1977), *Long Island Light: Poems and a Memoir* (1979), and *Erika: Poems of the Holocaust* (1991). There is a personal dimension to Heyen's poems on the Holocaust because he and his wife both had German immigrant parents. Heyen is professor of English at the State University of New York at Brockport.

GEOFFREY HILL was born in 1932 at Bromsgrove, Worcestershire, England. He was educated at Keble College, Oxford, and is a university teacher of English. His poems are collected in *Somewhere Is Such a Kingdom: Poems 1952–1971* (1975). Hill's poetry is characterized by subtle use of imagery, controlled irony, and strong sense of form. He is typically represented in anthologies of major British writers.

RANDALL JARRELL, poet and editor, was born in Nashville, Tennessee, in 1914 and served in the air force in World War II. *Losses* (1948) and *The Woman at the Washington Zoo* (1960) are collections of poetry that reflect a sensitive, tragic worldview. In the mid-1940s, he distinguished himself as poetry editor of *The Nation*. He has also written children's books, a novel, and critical essays. The latter were collected in *Poetry and the Age* (1953). His poem "A Camp in the Prussian Forest" is considered one of the most significant Holocaust poems written in America. Jarrell died in 1965.

MIECZYSLAW JASTRUN, Polish-Jewish poet, was born in 1903. An avowed secularist who wrote in Polish, he was influenced primarily by European literary traditions. Hiding on the aryan side of Warsaw during the German occupation, Jastrun produced a body of poetry, *Godzina strzezona* [The defended hour], published in 1944. His biography of the Polish poet Adam Mickiewicz has been translated into many languages. Jasturn is also an essayist and literary critic. Along with Czeslaw Milosz, Jastrun left a significant mark on postwar Polish poetry. He died in Poland in 1983.

SHMERKE KACZERGINSKI, born in Vilna in 1908, was a poet who belonged to the prewar literary Yunge Vilne group. A member of the United Partisan Organization in Vilna, he also helped to save Jewish documents from the Nazis. He settled in Argentina after the war and recorded his experiences in the Vilna Ghetto in various works of Yiddish poetry and prose. With H. Leivick, he edited a volume called *Lider Fun Ghettos un Lagern* [Songs from the ghettos and camps], published in 1948. He died in an airplane crash in Argentina in April 1954.

YITZHAK KATZENELSON, educator, poet, and playwright, was born in Lithuania in 1886. He achieved recognition for his writings in Hebrew and Yiddish before World War II, but his major writings were composed in response to the destruction of Warsaw Jewry and European Jewry in general—among them his *Vittel Diary*, written in Hebrew, and his great threnody "Dos lid fun oysgehargetn yidishn folk" [The song of the murdered Jewish people], written in Yiddish. Katzenelson has been called the "Jeremiah of the Holocaust." He perished in Auschwitz in 1944.

JOSEPH KIRMAN was born in Warsaw in 1896 and raised in poverty. Working as a laborer, he wrote poems and stories in Yiddish in which his main theme was the poor Jewish souls of Warsaw. He was arrested because of his leftist views. During the German occupation of Warsaw, he published poems and stories in the underground press. A great number of his ghetto compositions were lost, but some were found in Ringelblum's archives and published for the first time in 1955. Deported to the labor camp of Poniatow, he died in 1943.

ALFRED KITTNER, poet, translator, and journalist, was born in Czernowitz, Bukovina, in 1906 and studied in Vienna. Imprisoned in concentration camps in Transnistria during World War II, he said in later years that his writing in the camps gave him the strength to survive. His postwar works include *Hungermarsch un Stacheldraht* [Hunger-march and barbed wire], 1956, considered a major work of Holocaust literature; *Flaschenpost* [Bottle-mail], 1970; and *Die schönsten Gedichte* [The most beautiful poems], 1973. Kittner is known also as a translater of Romanian poets into German. He died in Germany in 1991.

A. M. KLEIN was born in Montreal in 1909 and studied law at McGill University and the University of Montreal. His poetry is regarded as a central part of Canada's literary heritage. He published four volumes of poetry: *Hath Not a Jew, Poems, The Hitleriad*, and *The Rocking Chair and Other Poems*. Klein died in 1972. Most of his poems have been included in *The Collected Poems of A. M. Klein* (1974).

IRENA KLEPFISZ was born in Warsaw in 1941. A child survivor, Klepfisz came to the United States in 1949. She is the author of *Keeper of Accounts* (1982); coeditor with Melanie Kaye-Kantrowitz of *The Tribe of Dina: A Jewish Women's Anthology* (1989); and author of *A Few Words in the Mother Tongue: Poems Selected and New* (1990). In 1989, Klepfisz was translator-in-residence at YIVO Institute for Jewish Research. She has been active in the Jewish and lesbian-feminist communities and has taught English, Yiddish, and women's studies.

GERTRUD KOLMAR (GERTRUD CHODZIESNER) was born in Berlin in 1894. During World War I, she worked as a translator in the German Foreign Office. In 1938, when she published the highly original volume of lyric verse *The Woman and the Beast*, she became recognized as a significant figure in the German-Jewish cultural upsurge in the early years of Hitler's regime. Witness to the deportation of German Jews to extermination camps, she was herself a slave laborer in a Berlin munitions factory and was later sent to her death in an extermination camp.

RACHEL KORN was born in 1898 in the village of Podliski in East Galicia. She moved first to Lvov, then to Warsaw, from which she escaped to the Soviet Union in 1941. In 1948, Korn emigrated to Montreal. Before World War II, her poetry, written in Yiddish, contained narrative elements reminiscent of her fiction. After the war, her poetry was more intimately lyrical and reflective. Between 1928 and 1977, Korn published eight volumes of poems, including *Home and Homelessness* (1948), *From the Other Side of a Poem* (1962), *On the Edge of a Moment* (1972), and *Bitter Reality* (1977). She died in 1982.

ABBA KOVNER, Israeli poet, was born in the Ukraine in 1918 and grew up in Vilna. During the Nazi occupation, he was a leader of partisans in the Vilna Ghetto and the last commandant of the United Partisan Organization. After the war, he settled on a kibbutz in Israel and was a member of the Givati Brigade in Israel's War of Independence. The Holocaust and the birth of Israel are two major concerns of his poetry and prose. Most of his books of poetry are lyric-dramatic sequences written in a highly allusive style. He received the Israel Prize in 1970. Kovner died in Israel in 1987.

MANI LEIB, Yiddish poet and translator, was born in the Ukraine in 1883. He emigrated to New York in 1905 and later became a leader in the Di Yunge group of American-Yiddish poets. Simplicity was one of Leib's esthetic goals, which drew him to folk song and folk motif. He published six volumes of poems between 1918 and 1930, including *The Song of Bread* (1918), *Little Flowers, Little Wreaths* (1922), and *Wonder upon Wonder* (1930). Leib translated poems from Russian and Ukrainian that appeared in the *Jewish Daily Forward*. He died in New York in 1953.

H. LEIVICK (LEIVICK HALPERN) was born in Igumen, Byelorussia, in 1886. Sentenced to a lifetime of exile and forced labor in Siberia for belonging to the Bund, he managed to escape in 1913 and emigrate to the United States. Member of the Di Yunge group, he achieved recognition as one of the strongest Yiddish poetic voices of the century. He is best known for his verse drama *The Golem* (1920). Like most American-Yiddish poets, he was deeply affected by the Holocaust. He died in 1962.

DENISE LEVERTOV, poet and critic, was born in Essex, England, in 1923. She served as a nurse in World War II and came to the United States in 1948. Levertov became associated with the Black Mountain poets and was a political activist through the 1960s, 1970s, and 1980s. She has published numerous books of poetry, including *With Eyes at the Back of Our Heads* (1960) and *Jacob's Ladder* (1961). Her critical essays have been collected in *The Poet in the World* (1973) and *Light up the Cave* (1981). She has taught at universities in New York, California, and Massachusetts.

PRIMO LEVI, memoirist, essayist, and poet, was born in Turin, Italy, in 1919 and trained as a chemist. Deported from Italy in 1943 for his part in anti-Fascist resistance, he was interned in Buna-Monowitz, a munitions labor camp at Auschwitz. His two classic memoirs, *Survival in Auschwitz* and *The Reawakening*, recount his experience of the death camp and his later travels through Eastern Europe upon liberation. In 1977 he retired as manager of a Turin chemical factory to devote himself to full-time writing. He committed suicide in Turin in April 1987.

JAKOV LIND, short-story writer and novelist, was born in Vienna in 1927. He survived the war in occupied Holland and later in Germany itself. Constantly threatened by the fear of discovery and deportation, Lind in his fiction reflects the nightmare world he knew firsthand. In *Soul of Wood and Other Stories* (1964), from which "Journey through the Night" is taken, and in his novel *Landscape in Concrete* (1966), Lind recreates the banality and terror that were two prominent features of the German catastrophe. Obsessed with the horrors and ultimate absurdity of human existence, Lind employs a gallows humor reminiscent of works by Franz Kafka and Günter Grass.

ARNOST LUSTIG, short-story writer, novelist, and author of screen plays and radio plays, was born in Prague in 1926. With his parents, he was deported to Auschwitz, where his father perished. He was then transferred to Buchenwald. He came to the United States in 1970 and is now a citizen. His story "The Lemon" was chosen as the best short story of 1962 by the University of Melbourne. His novel *A Prayer for Katerina Horovitzova* was nominated for the National Book Award in 1974. Lustig has lectured on film and literature at universities in Czechoslovakia, Israel, Japan, Canada, and the United States. His fiction has been translated into many languages.

ITSIK MANGER was born in Chernowitz, Romania, in 1901. In Warsaw from 1928 through 1938, he won recognition as a poet, essayist, lecturer, and occasional dramatist. After fleeing the Nazis, he lived in London until 1951 and then in New York. In the early 1960s he settled in Israel. Because of the humor and accessibility of many of his poems and the pleasure he took in folk sources, he is one of the most popular of modern Yiddish poets. In *Medresh Itsik,* the best known of his works, he provided poetic interpretations of important personages and events in the Bible. Manger died in Tel Aviv in 1969.

AHARON MEGGED was born in Poland in 1920 and came to Palestine with his family in 1926. After graduating from high school, he became one of the founding members of S'dot Yam, a fishing kibbutz on the Mediterranean. He began his literary career after the establishment of the state of Israel and has distinguished himself as a short-story writer, novelist, and playwright. Megged's novels, *Fortunes of a Fool* (1962) and *Living on the Dead* (1970) are available in English translation. His characteristic tone is that of gentle satire, although pathos seems to dominate "The Name," the story included in this volume.

ROBERT MEZEY, poet, translator, and teacher, was born in Philadelphia in 1935. His first book of poetry, *The Lovemaker,* won the Lamont Poetry Award in 1960. His other books include *White Blossoms, The Door Standing Open, Selected Translations,* and, most recently, *Evening Wind,* which was awarded the Bassine Citation and a special prize from PEN West. His translation of Cesar Vallejo's 1931 novel *Tungsten* appeared in 1989. Mezey teaches at Pomona College in California.

CZESLAW MILOSZ, Polish poet, essayist, translator, and novelist, was born in Lithuania in 1911 and was a leader in the avant-garde poetry movement in Poland in the 1930s. During World War II, he was a member of the Resistance and active in underground literary publications. Milosz was awarded the Neustadt International Prize for Literature in 1978 and the Nobel Prize for Literature in 1980. Many of his poems on the Holocaust are included in *Selected Poems* (1973). *The Witness of Poetry* (1983) contains critical essays on the impact of the events of the twentieth century on literature. Milosz has taught in the Department of Slavic Languages and Literature at the University of California at Berkeley.

MARGA MINCO is the name Sara Menco assumed when she was in hiding during World War II. Born in Holland in 1920, Minco was twenty-three when her parents were arrested in Amsterdam's Jewish ghetto. She was the only member of her family to survive the war. Her first book, *Bitter Herbs* (1957), addressed her wartime experiences through the perspective of a fifteen-year-old narrator. She has also written three novels that have been translated into English—*An Empty House, The Fall,* and *The Glass Bridge*—and two collections of short stories. Her narrative style is marked by an unusual combination of directness and restraint. Minco is one of Holland's most acclaimed writers.

KADYA MOLODOVSKY, Yiddish poet, novelist, and dramatist, was born in White Russia in 1894. From 1922 to 1935, she lived in Warsaw, where she taught in secular Yiddish schools and wrote verse, ballads, and poetic tales for adults and children. In 1935, she came to the United States and became active in New York literary circles. She wrote several collections of poetry, including *Angels Come to Jerusalem* (1952) and *Light of a Thorn Tree* (1965). Her other works include a drama, *Toward the God of the Desert* (1949), and the novel *At the Gate* (1975). Her themes reflect her interests in Jewish folkways, Jewish life during World War II, the birth of Israel, and women's roles. She died in New York in 1975.

SARA NOMBERG-PRZYTYK, memoirist and journalist, was born in Lublin, Poland, in 1915. In 1939, when Germany invaded Poland, she fled east. From 1941 to 1943, she survived in the Bialystok Ghetto until she was deported to Auschwitz. After the war, she worked as a journalist in Lublin but was forced to leave in 1968, when she emigrated to Israel. Nomberg-Przytyk now lives in Canada. In addition to her fictionalized account of her Auschwitz experience, *Auschwitz: True Tales of a Grotesque Land,* Nomberg-Przytyk has also published *Columny Samsona* [Pillars of Samson] in 1966, a narration of events in the Bialystok Ghetto until the time of its liquidation.

CYNTHIA OZICK, born in New York City in 1928, is an essayist, critic, translator, short-story writer, and novelist. She belongs to the front rank of contemporary American writers. A reflective and introspective storyteller and a stylist of considerable literary richness, Ozick attempts in her fiction to move beyond the conventional modes of realistic narrative. Jewish themes pervade her work, the Holocaust being a recurring concern. "Rosa," a lengthy sequel to "The Shawl," deals with Rosa's later life in Miami and with the mental consequences of the suffering presented in "The Shawl."

DAN PAGIS, Israeli poet and literary scholar, was born in Bukovina in 1930 and grew up in a German-speaking environment. During World War II, he was interned in a Ukrainian concentration camp from which he escaped in 1944. Pagis wrote poems of his European experience in *Transformations* (1970). In 1946, Pagis came to Israel, where he teaches medieval Hebrew literature at the Hebrew University. He has written studies of esthetics and medieval secular poetry and has edited a collection of the poetry of the Israeli poet David Vogel. Pagis's *Selected Poems* appeared in English in 1976.

MARGE PIERCY, novelist and poet, was born in Detroit in 1936. Her novels include *Small Changes* (1973), *Woman on the Edge of Time* (1977), and *Gone to Soldiers* (1988). She has also published a number of collections of poetry, including *Breaking Camp* (1968), *The Moon Is Always Female* (1980), and *Available Light* (1988). Piercy is also the author of a collection of essays, *Parti-Colored Blocks for a Quilt*

(1982), and the editor of an anthology, *Early Ripening: American Women's Poetry Now* (1987). A prolific author, Piercy is strongly concerned with social issues involving gender, race, and class. She is the recipient of numerous honors and awards and has taught at many universities in the United States and abroad.

WILLIAM PILLIN, poet and ceramic craftsman, was born in Alexandrowsk, Russia, in 1910. He attended Lewis Institute of Chicago, Northwestern University, and The University of Chicago. His nine volumes of poetry include *Theory of Silence* (1949), *Dance without Shoes* (1956), *Passage after Midnight* (1958), and *Pavanne for a Fading Memory* (1964). He saw his poetry as related more to European than to Anglo-American currents and acknowledged the influence of Rilke, Lorca, and Neruda. He was especially well known as a potter in Los Angeles, where he and his wife, Polia, created hundreds of pieces of pottery, which they exhibited in numerous galleries. Pillin died in 1985.

MIKLOS RADNOTI, Hungarian poet, novelist, critic, and translator, was born in 1909. Before the war, he published seven books of poetry, an autobiographical novel, four books of translations, and a critical biography of the Hungarian author Margit Kafka. Beginning in 1940, he was a forced laborer in various work camps. In 1946, his wife found his body in a mass grave in Abda, Hungary. In the pocket of his trench coat, she found a notebook containing poems he had written at the Bor copper mine in Yugoslavia, as well as five poems written during his last days. A selection of his poems, *Clouded Sky* (1972), appears in English.

CHARLES REZNIKOFF, poet and dramatist, was born in New York City in 1894. After studying journalism and law, he turned to writing as a career. He began to receive recognition with the publication of *By the Waters of Manhattan: Selected Verse* (1962). In 1963, he won the Jewish Book Council of America's Award, and in 1971 the Morton Dauwen Zabel Award for Poetry. He identified with "objectivist" verse, which he described in 1970: "Images clear but the meaning not stated but suggested by the objective detail and the music of the verse." His themes were chiefly Jewish, American, and urban. Reznikoff died in 1976.

ADRIENNE RICH, born in Baltimore in 1929, is one of America's leading poets and an influential feminist scholar and lecturer. Her poetry includes *Diving into the Wreck* (1973), for which she won the National Book Award for poetry, and *The Dream of a Common Language* (1978). *Of Woman Born* (1976) is a prose investigation of motherhood. Rich's poetry often addresses themes of social justice, women's consciousness, and the need for an authentic human community. She has been active in the civil rights and antiwar movements and in the women's movement as a lesbian. Rich is a professor of English and feminist studies at Stanford University.

NORMA ROSEN was born in New York City. She has published five works of fiction: a novel, *Joy to Levine!* (1962); *Green,* a novella and short stories (1967); the novel *Touching Evil* (1969; reissued in 1990); and the novels *At the Center* (1989) and *John and Anzia: An American Romance* (1989). Her short fiction and essays have appeared in numerous magazines. Her essays are collected in *Accidents of Influence: Writing as a Woman and a Jew in America* (1992) She is also the author of a play, *The Miracle of Dora Wakin.* Rosen has taught writing seminars at Yale and Harvard universities, The University of Pennsylvania, The New School for Social Research, and is currently teaching at the Tisch School at New York University.

NELLY SACHS, born in Berlin in 1891, is one of the most powerful poetic voices dealing with the Holocaust. In 1940, she escaped with her mother to Sweden, partly through the good offices of the Swedish writer Selma Lagerlof (1858–1940). Departing from an earlier romantic style of expression, she began in 1943 to write volume after volume dealing in German with the tragedy that befell her people. Translations of her work appear in *O the Chimneys!* (1967) and *The Seeker and Other Poems* (1970). In 1966, she received the Nobel Prize for Literature, sharing it with Samuel Agnon of Israel. She died in 1970.

MAY SARTON was born in Belgium and came to the United States in 1916. She joined Eva LeGallienne's Repertory Theater in New York and experimented with her own theatrical company. She has published widely in the forms of poetry, fiction, and memoir. One of her most noted novels is *Mrs. Stevens Hears the Mermaids Singing* (1965). *At Seventy: A Journal* (1985) won the American Book Award of the Before Columbus Foundation. She has been a Fellow of the American Academy of Arts and Sciences since 1958. Her work treats the themes of identity, aging and death, and female creativity.

ANNE SEXTON was born in Newton, Massachusetts, in 1928. A distinguished American poet, her many collections include *To Bedlam and Part Way Back* (1960) and *Live or Die* (1966), for which she won the Pulitzer Prize. *The Awful Rowing Toward God* (1975) was published posthumously. Sexton used the details of her life as metaphors for broader social issues and wrote on many subjects that were considered taboo, including incest, adultery, and drug addiction. She was a professor of creative writing at Boston University, where as a young poet she had studied with Robert Lowell. She committed suicide in 1974.

SIMCHA BUNIM SHAYEVITSH, Yiddish poet and storyteller, was born in Lenschitz, Poland, in 1907. Mostly self-educated, he earned a living in Lodz as a textile worker. His poems reflect the influence of the Haskalah movement in that they refer to secular as well as religious learning, modern as well as ancient culture. In the Lodz Ghetto he turned to epic poetry. Only two of his ghetto works,

"Lekh-lekho" and "Spring 1942," were recovered after the war. Shayevitsh was deported to Auschwitz in 1944 and perished shortly before liberation.

LOUIS SIMPSON, distinguished American poet, was born in Jamaica, British West Indies, in 1923. His father was Scotch; his mother came from a family of Polish Jews. Simpson served in the U.S. Army during World War II. The senseless violence of the war and its aftermath are major themes in his poetry. His finely crafted and witty poems appear in *The Arrivistes* (1949); *At the End of the Open Road* (1963), for which he won the Pulitzer Prize; and *In the Room We Share* (1989). He has been a professor of English at the State University of New York at Stony Brook since 1967.

ISAAC BASHEVIS SINGER was born in Radzymin Poland, in 1904 and came to the United States in 1935. Author of numerous novels and hundreds of short stories, Singer also wrote plays, essays, memoirs, and children's books. Writing in Yiddish, he dealt frequently with Jewish folklore and with life in the Polish shtetls, remembering and recreating the lost world of East European Jewry. In later years, he set some of his tales in America and dealt with survivors who have not quite survived. His works have been translated into numerous languages. In 1978, Singer was awarded the Nobel Prize in Literature. He died in 1991.

MYRA SKLAREW, born in Baltimore in 1934, is an important voice among modern Jewish poets who write in English. Her books include *In the Basket of the Blind* (1975), *From the Backyard of the Diaspora* (1976), *The Science of Goodbyes* (1982), *Blessed Art Thou, No-One* (1982), and *Altamira* (1987). Sklarew won the di Castagnola Award from the Poetry Society of America in 1972 and the National Book Council Award in 1978. She has taught in the Department of Literature at American University in Washington, D.C.

BORIS SLUTSKY, Russian poet, was born in the Ukraine in 1919. A graduate of the Gorki Institute of Literature, he served in the Red Army between 1941 and 1945. His numerous publications include *Vremia* [Time] (1959); *Rabota* [Work] (1964); *Dobrota dnia* [Goodness of a day] (1973); and *Prodlennyi polden* [Prolonged noon] (1975). Slutsky is considered one of the most important representatives of the war generation of Russian poets and a crucial figure in the post-Stalin literary revival. His poetry is intimate in tone and deliberately prosaic and conversational.

W. D. SNODGRASS, poet and translator, was born in 1926 in Wilkinsburg, Pennsylvania. His numerous books of poetry include *Heart's Needle* (1959), *After Experience* (1967), *The Fuehrer Bunker* (1977), *The House the Poet Built* (1986), and *The Death of Cock Robin* (1989). Snodgrass has translated troubadour songs, traditional Hungarian songs, and (with Lore Segal) the poetry of Christian Morgenstern. His early poetry is confessional and self-analytical. In later poems, he experiments with multiple voices and musical devices. Snodgrass is considered one of the most versatile and accomplished poets of his generation. He won the Pulitzer Prize for poetry in 1960.

ISAIAH SPIEGEL, born in 1906, grew up in Lodz, where he later taught Yiddish and Yiddish literature in the Yiddish schools of the Bund. He published his first book of poems at the age of twenty-four. He was one of the most prolific and important writers in the Lodz Ghetto, writing many short stories and poems. At the liquidation of the ghetto in August 1944, he was deported to Auschwitz-Birkenau but managed to survive. After the liberation, he returned to Lodz and found the manuscripts he had hidden of sixteen of his stories. These he published with modifications, reducing the documentary detail. Speigel now lives in Israel where he writes stories dealing with Israeli themes.

A. L. STRAUSS, poet, fiction writer, and literary critic, was born in Aachen in 1892. He taught German literature at Aachen University until the Nazi rise to power. In 1935, he fled to Palestine and later taught at Hebrew University. Among Hebrew poets, Strauss is noted for his poetry on the Holocaust. He died in 1953.

ABRAHAM SUTZKEVER was born in Byelorussia in 1913, studied literature and criticism at Vilna University, and at age twenty received the acclaim of the Yunge Vilne writers for his poems in Yiddish. During the German occupation, Sutz-kever wrote poetry in hiding, then in the Vilna Ghetto, and later in the forests as a partisan. He is one of the earliest and most articulate poets of the Holocaust. His later work, beginning with *Di festung* [The fortress] in 1945, is informed by his wartime experiences. Sutzkever settled in Palestine in 1947. He has been the editor of the premier Yiddish journal, *Di Goldene Keyt,* since 1948.

ANNA SWIRSZCZYNSKA, daughter of a painter, was born in Warsaw. Before the war, she wrote a volume of refined prose poems. She served as a military nurse in the Warsaw Ghetto uprising. Although she attempted to write about her wartime experiences, she was dissatisfied with her wordiness and pathetic tone. It was not until 1979 in her volume of short poems *Building the Barricade* that she was able, without meter or rhyme, to convey something of her experience.

WLADYSLAW SZLENGEL, born in Warsaw in 1914, is the most prolific of the ghetto poets who wrote in Polish. During the German occupation, he was founder and central figure of both an underground literary journal, *Zywy Dzien-nik* [Living daily], and the cabaret *Sztuka* [Art]. His forceful poem "Counterat-tack," written during the first armed resistance in the Warsaw Ghetto in January 1943, is a song of tribute to the Jewish fighters and to Jewish heroism. Szlengel died during the Warsaw ghetto uprising of April 1943. His documentary poems on ghetto life were published after the war in *Co czytalem umarlym* [This I read to the dead].

MALKA HEIFETZ TUSSMAN was born in Bolshaya-Chaitcha, Ukraine in 1896 and came to the United States in 1912. Her poems, stories, and essays have appeared in many American and European Yiddish journals and magazines. In addition to several volumes of her own poetry, among them *Poems* (1949) and *Mild My Wild* (1958), she translated works of Dylan Thomas, Akhmatova, and Tagore into Yiddish. Her poetry reflects a highly personal style in which she addresses her audience—sometimes the reader, sometimes God—with dramatic immediacy. Heifetz Tussman died in Los Angeles in 1987.

RUTH WHITMAN, translator, poet, and essayist, was born in 1922. She has published seven volumes of original poetry, translated three volumes of poetry from Yiddish, including the poetry of Abraham Sutzkever and Jacob Glatstein, and published one collection of essays. Her volume of original poetry *The Marriage Wig and Other Poems* (1968) won the Alice Fay di Castagnola Award and the Kovner Award of the Jewish Book Council in America. Whitman teaches poetry at Radcliffe College and the Massachusetts Institute of Technology.

ELIE WIESEL was born in Sighet, Romania, in 1928 and survived Auschwitz and Buchenwald. His memories of the camps are unforgettably recorded in *Night,* which received international acclaim. Wiesel is one of the foremost writers of our time and has made the Holocaust a major theme of his work. His numerous novels, short stories, plays, and nonfiction writings (written chiefly in French) deal less with the physical than with the moral and spiritual aspects of the Holocaust. Wiesel is Andrew Mellon Professor in the Humanities at Boston University and chair of the United States Holocaust Memorial Council. In 1986, he was awarded the Nobel Peace Prize.

C. K. WILLIAMS was born in 1936 in Newark, New Jersey. His numerous books of poetry include *A Day for Anne Frank* (1968), *I Am the Bitter Name* (1972), *Tar* (1983), *The Lark, The Thrush, The Starling* (1983), and *Flesh and Blood* (1988). Williams's poetry has a metaphysical dimension suggested by his preoccupation with ultimate questions. His awards include the National Book Critics Circle Prize (1987) and the Morton Dauwen Zabel Prize (1989). He has been a professor of English at George Mason University, Virginia. He lives in Paris.

YEVGENY ALEKSANDROVICH YEVTUSHENKO was born in Russia in 1933. One of the most famous young poets in Russia during Krushchev's term of office, he played an active role in the early days of de-Stalinization. His major themes are faith in a new Russia, the inhumanity of bureaucracy, and anti-Semitism in Russia. Yevtushenko read his poem "Babi Yar" for the first time in November 1961 in the heart of Moscow, beside the statue of Mayakovsky, a rallying point for protesting, literary-minded youths.

NATAN ZACH was born in Berlin in 1930 and came to Palestine in 1935. Among his volumes of poetry in Hebrew are *First Poems* (1955) and *All the Milk and Honey* (1966). He has translated into Hebrew the plays of Frisch, Brecht, Durrenmatt, and others. In his controversial literary criticism, Zach has attempted a revaluation of the older generation of Hebrew poets. He has lectured on literature at various universities in Israel.

AARON ZEITLIN, Yiddish poet, dramatist, fiction writer, and essayist, was born in Gomel, the Ukraine, in 1898, the son of the Yiddish religious writer Hillel Zeitlin. In addition to his own writing, he edited a number of important literary journals in Warsaw between the world wars. Invited to New York for the production of his play *Esterke* in 1939, he was spared the fate that befell his wife and family in Warsaw. A definitive collection of all his poetry was published between 1967 and 1970: *Songs of Destruction and Songs of Faith* (Vol. 1) and *Songs of Destruction and Faith and Janus Korshak's Last Walk* (Vol. 2). In his writings, Zeitlin drew upon the Jewish religious and mystical tradition. He died in New York in 1973.

JOZEF ZELKOWICZ was born in Konstantynow, near Lodz, in 1897. Although ordained as a rabbi, he chose instead to devote himself to research and writing in the fields of history and ethnography, first writing in Polish and then in Yiddish. During the occupation, he served on the staff of the Lodz Ghetto Archives and the Lodz *Chronicle*. Because his essays on ghetto life often make pronounced use of fictional techniques, they frequently become short stories of a documentary kind. Zelkowicz's major work written in the Lodz Ghetto is entitled *In yene koshmarne teg* [In these nightmarish days], a lengthy monograph on the events of September 1942, including the deportations. Zelkowicz died in Auschwitz in 1944.

RAJZEL ZYCHLINSKY was born in 1910 in Gombin, Poland. She fled Warsaw during the war and took refuge in Soviet Russia. Her family perished at the hands of the Germans. She came to the United States in 1951 and settled in New York. Zychlinsky has published several volumes of poetry in Yiddish, including *Poems* (1936), *The Rain Sings* (1939), *To Fair Shores* (1948), *Silent Doorways* (1968), and *Autumn Squares* (1969). In 1975, she won Israel's prestigious Itzik Manger Prize. A German translation of her selected poems was published in Leipzig in 1981.

Bibliography

The list that follows constitutes a selected bibliography of Holocaust literature along with interpretive materials and relevant works of historical, philosophic, and theological interest. All works listed are in English or in English translation. Many significant works in foreign languages still await translation.

Readers who wish additional bibliographical assistance should consult the second edition of *The Holocaust: An Annotated Bibliography,* edited by Harry James Cargas (Chicago: American Library Association, 1985); the *Bibliography on Holocaust Literature,* edited by Abraham J. Edelheit and Hershel Edelheit (Boulder: Westview Press, 1986, supplement 1990); and *The Holocaust: An Annotated Bibliography and Resource Guide,* edited by David M. Szonyi (New York: Ktav Publishing for the National Jewish Resource Center, 1985).

For a useful reference work containing more than nine hundred articles on almost all aspects of the Holocaust including the creative literature in various languages, see the four-volume *Encyclopedia of the Holocaust,* edited by Yisrael Gutman (New York: Macmillan, 1990).

Anthologies

Adelson Alan, and Robert Lapidus, eds. *Lodz Ghetto: Inside a Community under Siege.* New York: Viking, 1989.

Dobroszycki, Lucjan, ed. *The Chronicle of the Lodz Ghetto, 1941–1944.* New Haven: Yale University Press, 1984.

Eliach, Yaffa. *Hassidic Tales of the Holocaust.* New York: Oxford University Press, 1982.

Fishman, Charles, ed. *Blood to Remember: American Poets on the Holocaust.* Lubbock: Texas Tech University Press, 1991.

Friedlander, Albert H., ed. *Out of the Whirlwind: A Reader of Holocaust Literature.* New York: Union of American Hebrew Congregations, 1968; New York: Schocken Books, 1976.

Fuchs, Elinor. *Plays of the Holocaust: An International Anthology.* New York: Theatre Communications Group, 1987.

Gillon, Adam, ed. *Poems of the Ghetto: A Testament of Lost Men.* New York: Twayne, 1969.

Glatstein, Jacob, Israel Knox, and Samuel Margoshes, eds. *Anthology of Holocaust Literature.* Philadelphia: The Jewish Publication Society, 1969.

Harshav, Benjamin, and Barbara Harshav, eds. *American Yiddish Poetry: A Bilingual Anthology.* Berkeley: University of California Press, 1987.

Howe, Irving, and Eliezer Greenberg, eds. *A Treasury of Yiddish Poetry.* New York: Schocken Books, 1976.

Howe, Irving, Ruth R. Wisse, and Khone Shmeruk, eds. *The Penguin Book of Modern Yiddish Verse.* New York: Viking Penguin, 1987.

Kalisch, Shoshana, with Barbara Meister, eds. *Yes, We Sang! Songs of the Ghettos and Concentration Camps.* New York: Harper and Row, 1985.

Kermish, Joseph, ed. *To Live with Honor and Die with Honor: Selected Documents from the Warsaw Ghetto Underground Archives "O.S."* ["Oneg Shabbath"]. Jerusalem: Yad Vashem, 1986.

Kuncewicz, Maria, ed. *The Modern Polish Mind: An Anthology of Stories and Essays by Writers Living in Poland Today.* New York: Universal Library, 1963.

Mlotek, Eleanor, and Malka Gottlieb, eds. *We Are Here: Songs of the Holocaust.* Translated by Roslyn Resnick-Perry. New York: Education Department of the Workman's Circle, 1983.

Rosenberg, David, ed. *Testimony: Contemporary Writers Make the Holocaust Personal.* New York: Random House, 1989.

Roskies, David G. *The Literature of Destruction: Jewish Responses to Catastrophe.* Philadelphia: The Jewish Publication Society, 1988.

Skloot, Robert, ed. *The Theater of the Holocaust.* Madison: University of Wisconsin Press, 1982.

Diaries, Journals, and Memoirs

Bettelheim, Bruno. *The Informed Heart.* Glencoe: Free Press, 1960.

Czerniakow, Adam. *The Warsaw Diary of Adam Czerniakow.* Edited by Raul Hilberg, Stanislaw Staron, and Josef Kermisz. New York: Stein and Day, 1979.

Delbo, Charlotte. *None of Us Will Return.* Translated by John Githens. New York: Grove, 1968.

Donat, Alexander. *The Holocaust Kingdom: A Memoir.* New York: Holt, Rinehart and Winston, 1965; New York: Holocaust Library, 1978.

Dribben, Judith. *A Girl Called Judith Strick.* New York: Cowles Book Company, 1970.

Fenelon, Fania. *Playing for Time.* Translated by Judith Landry. New York: Atheneum, 1977.

Flinker, Moshe. *The Diary of Young Moshe.* Jerusalem: Yad Vashem, 1971.

Frank, Anne. *The Diary of Anne Frank: The Critical Edition.* Edited by David Barnouw and Gerrold van der Stroom. New York: Doubleday, 1989.

Frankl, Viktor E. *Man's Search for Meaning: An Introduction to Logotherapy.* Translated by Ilse Lasch. New York: Washington Square Press, 1963.

Friedlander, Saul. *When Memory Comes.* New York: Farrar, Straus and Giroux, 1979.

Gray, Martin. *For Those I Loved.* Translated by Anthony White. Boston: Little, Brown, 1972.

Heimler, Eugene. *Night of the Mist.* Translated by Andre Ungar. New York: Vanguard Press, 1959. Reprint. Westport: Greenwood Press, 1978.

Jackson, Livia Bitton. *Elli.* New York: Times Books, 1980.

Kaplan, Chaim A. *The Warsaw Diary of Chaim A. Kaplan.* Translated by Abraham Katsh. New York: Collier Books, 1973.

Katzenelson, Yitzhak. *Vittel Diary.* Translated by Myer Cohen. Tel Aviv: Beit Lohamei Hagettaot and Hakibbutz Hameuchad Publishing House, 1972.

Klein, Gerda. *All But My Life.* New York: Hill and Wang, 1957.

Kogen, Eugen. *The Theory and Practice of Hell.* Translated by Heinz Norden. New York: Farrar, Straus and Company, 1950.

Korczak, Janusz. *Ghetto Diary.* New York: Holocaust Library, 1978.

Lengyel, Olga. *Five Chimneys: The Story of Auschwitz.* Translated by Paul B. Weiss. Chicago: Ziff-Davis, 1947.

Levi, Primo. *Moments of Reprieve: A Memoir of Auschwitz.* Translated by Ruth Feldman. New York: Summit Books, 1986.

———. *The Reawakening.* Translated by Stuart Woolf. New York: Collier Books, 1965.

———. *Survival in Auschwitz: The Nazi Assault on Humanity.* Translated by Stuart Woolf. New York: Collier Books, 1986. Originally published as *If This Is a Man* (New York: Orion Press, 1959).

Mark, Ber. *Uprising in the Warsaw Ghetto.* Translated by Gershon Freidlin. New York: Schocken Books, 1975.

Meed, Vladka. *On Both Sides of the Wall.* Tel Aviv: Beit Lohamei Hagettaot and Hakibbutz Hameuchad Publishing House, 1973.

Minco, Marga. *Bitter Herbs.* Translated by Roy Edwards. London: Oxford University Press, 1960.

Nyiszli, Miklos. *Auschwitz: A Doctor's Eyewitness Account.* Translated by Tibere Kremer and Richard Seaver. Greenwich: Fawcett Crest, 1960.

Rabinowitz, Dorothy. *New Lives: Survivors of the Holocaust Living in America.* New York: Alfred A. Knopf, 1976.

Ringelblum, Emmanuel. *Notes from the Warsaw Ghetto.* Translated by Jacob Sloan. New York: McGraw-Hill, 1958.

Senesh, Hannah. *Hannah Senesh: Her Life and Diary.* Translated by Marta Cohn. New York: Schocken Books, 1972.

Tillion, Germaine. *Ravensbruck*. Garden City: Doubleday, 1975.

Wells, Leon. *The Janowska Road*. New York: Macmillan, 1963. Reprinted as *The Death Brigade* (New York: Holocaust Library, 1978).

Fiction

Aichinger, Ilse. *Herod's Children*. Translated by Cornelia Schaeffer. New York: Atheneum, 1963.

Amichai, Yehuda. *Not of This Time, Not of This Place*. Translated by Shlomo Katz. New York: Harper and Row, 1968.

Anatoli, A. [Kuznetsov]. *Babi Yar*. Translated by David Floyd. London: Jonathan Cape, 1970.

Andersch, Alfred. *Efraim's Book*. New York: Doubleday, 1970.

Appelfeld, Aharon. *Badenheim 1939*. Translated by Dalya Bilu. Boston: D. R. Godine, 1980.

———. *Tzili: The Story of a Life*. Translated by Dalya Bilu. New York: E. P. Dutton, 1983.

Bartov, Hanoch. *The Brigade*. Translated by David Segal. Philadelphia: The Jewish Publication Society, 1967.

Bassani, Giorgio. *Five Stories of Ferrara*. Translated by William Weaver. New York: Harcourt Brace Jovanovich, 1971.

———. *The Garden of the Finzi-Continis*. Translated by William Weaver. New York: Harcourt Brace Jovanovich, 1977.

Becker, Jurek. *Jacob the Liar*. Translated by Melvin Kornfield. New York: Harcourt Brace Jovanovich, 1975.

Bellow, Saul. *The Bellarosa Connection*. New York: Penguin Books, 1989.

———. *Mr. Sammler's Planet*. New York: Viking, 1970.

Berger, Zdena. *Tell Me Another Morning*. New York: Harper, 1961.

Bor, Josef. *The Terezin Requiem*. Translated by Edith Pargeter. New York: Alfred A. Knopf, 1963.

Borges, Jorge Luis. "Deutsches Requiem" and "The Secret Miracle." In *Labyrinths, Selected Stories and Other Writings*. Edited by Donald A. Yates and James E. Irby. New York: New Directions, 1964.

Borowski, Tadeusz. *This Way for the Gas, Ladies and Gentlemen and Other Stories*. Translated by Barbara Vedder. New York: Penguin Books, 1967.

Bryks, Rachmil. *A Cat in the Ghetto*. Translated by S. Morris Engel. New York: Block Publishing Company, 1959.

———. *Kiddush Hashem*. Translated by S. Morris Engel. New York: Behrman House, 1977.

Cohen, Arthur A. *In the Days of Simon Stern*. New York: Random House, 1973.

Dayan, Yael. *Death Had Two Sons*. New York: McGraw Hill, 1968.

Epstein, Leslie. *King of the Jews.* New York: Coward, McCann and Geoghegan, 1979; New York: Summit Books, 1989.

Fink, Ida. *The Journey.* Translated by Joanna Weschler and Francine Prose. New York: Farrar, Straus and Giroux, 1992.

———. *A Scrap of Time and Other Sories.* Translated by Madeline Levine and Francine Prose. New York: Pantheon Books, 1987.

Forsyth, Frederick. *The Odessa File.* New York: Viking, 1972.

Fuks, Ladislaw. *Mr. Theodore Mundstock.* Translated by Iris Unwin. New York: Orion Press, 1968.

Gary, Romain. *The Dance of Ghengis Cohn.* Translated by the author and Camilla Sykes. New York: World Publishing Company, 1968.

Gascar, Pierre. *Beasts and Men.* Translated by Jean Stuart and Merloyd Lawrence. London: Methuen, 1956; New York: Meridian Books, 1960.

Gotfryd, Bernard. *Anton the Dove Fancier and Other Tales of the Holocaust.* New York: Washington Square Press, 1990.

Gouri, Haim. *The Chocolate Deal.* Translated by Seymour Simckes. New York: Holt, Rinehart and Winston, 1968.

Grade, Chaim. *The Seven Little Lanes.* Translated by Curt Leviant. New York: Bergen-Belsen Memorial Press, 1972.

Grossman, David. *See Under—Love.* Translated by Betsy Rosenberg. New York: Farrar, Straus and Giroux, 1989.

Grossman, Ladislav. *The Shop on Main Street.* Translated by Iris Unwin. Garden City: Doubleday, 1970.

Habe, Hans. *The Mission.* Translated by Michael Bullock. New York: Coward-McCann, 1966.

Hersey, John. *The Wall.* New York: Knopf, 1950; New York: Vintage Books, 1988.

Jabes, Edmond. *The Book of Questions.* Translated by Rosemarie Waldrop. Middletown: Wesleyan University Press, 1977.

Kanfer, Stefan. *Fear Itself.* New York: Putnam, 1981.

Kaniuk, Yoram. *Adam Resurrected.* Translated by Seymour Simckes. New York: Atheneum, 1971.

Karmel, Ilona. *An Estate of Memory.* Boston: Houghton Mifflin, 1969.

Ka-Tzetnik 135633 [Yehiel DeNur]. *Atrocity.* New York: Lyle Stuart, 1963.

———. *House of Dolls.* New York: Pyramid Books, 1969.

Klein, A. M. *The Second Scroll.* Montreal: McClelland and Stewart, 1966.

Kosinski, Jerzy. *The Painted Bird.* 2d ed. with introduction by the author. Boston: Houghton Mifflin, 1976; New York: Modern Library, 1983.

Kuznetsov, Anatoli. *Babi Yar.* Translated by Jacob Guralsky. Revised ed. New York: Farrar, Straus and Giroux, 1970; New York: Pocket Books, 1982.

Langfus, Anna. *The Whole Land Brimstone.* Translated by Peter Wiles. New York: Pantheon Books, 1962.

Lind, Jakov. *Landscape in Concrete.* Translated by Ralph Manheim. New York: Grove, 1966.

———. *Soul of Wood and Other Stories.* Translated by Ralph Manheim. New York: Fawcett Crest, 1966; New York: Hill and Wang, 1986.

Lustig, Arnost. *Darkness Casts No Shadows.* Translated by Jeanne Nemcova. Washington, D.C.: Inscape, 1976.

———. *Diamonds of the Night* (short stories). Translated by Jeanne Nemcova. Washington, D.C.: Inscape, 1976.

———. *Dita Saxova.* Translated by George Theiner. London: Hutchinson, 1966; New York: Harper and Row, 1980.

———. *Night and Hope* (short stories). Translated by George Theiner. New York: E. P. Dutton, 1962; New York: Avon, 1978.

Malamud, Bernard. "The German Refugee." In *Idiots First.* New York: Delta, 1963.

———. "The Lady of the Lake." In *The Magic Barrel.* New York: Farrar, Straus and Cudahy, 1953.

Minco, Marga. "The Address." Translated by Jeanette K. Ringold. *Triquarterly,* no. 61 (Fall 1984): 37–40.

———. *The Fall.* Translated by Jeannette K. Ringold. Chester Spring: Peter Owen/Dufour, 1984.

Morante, Elsa. *History: A Novel.* Translated by William Weaver. New York: Alfred Knopf, 1977; New York: Avon, 1979.

Morgenstern, Soma. *The Third Pillar.* Translated by Ludwig Lewisohn. New York: Farrar, 1955.

Nomberg-Przytyk, Sara. *Auschwitz: True Tales from a Grotesque Land.* Translated by Roslyn Hirsch. Chapel Hill: University of North Carolina Press, 1985.

Orlev, Uri. *The Lead Soldiers.* Translated by Hillel Halkin. New York: Taplinger, 1980.

Ozick, Cynthia. *The Cannibal Galaxy.* New York: Alfred A. Knopf, 1983.

———. "Envy; or, Yiddish in America" and "The Suitcase." In *The Pagan Rabbi and Other Stories.* New York: Alfred A. Knopf, 1971.

———. *The Shawl.* New York: Vintage Books, 1990. (Contains the short story "The Shawl" and a novella entitled "Rosa.")

———. *Trust.* New York: New American Library, 1966.

Rawicz, Piotr. *Blood from the Sky.* Translated by Peter Wiles. New York: Harcourt, Brace and World, 1964.

Rosen, Norma. *Touching Evil.* New York: Harcourt Brace and World, 1969.

———. "Fences." *Orim: A Jewish Journal at Yale* 1 (Spring 1986): 75–83.

Rudnicki, Adolf. *Ascent to Heaven* (short stories). Translated by H. C. Stevens. New York: Dennis Dobson, 1951.

Schaeffer, Susan Fromberg. *Anya*. New York: Macmillan, 1974; New York: Avon Books, 1976.

Schwarz-Bart, Andre. *The Last of the Just*. Translated by Stephen Becker. New York: Atheneum, 1960.

Semprun, Jorge. *The Long Voyage*. Translated by Richard Sedaver. New York: Schocken Books, 1990.

Shaw, Robert. *The Man in the Glass Booth*. New York: Harcourt, Brace and World, 1967; New York: Grove, 1969.

Singer, Isaac Bashevis. *Enemies, a Love Story*. New York: Farrar, Straus and Giroux, 1972.

————. "The Mentor." In *A Friend of Kafka and Other Stories*. Translated by Isaac Bashevis Singer and Evelyn Torton Beck. New York: Dell, 1962.

————. *The Slave*. Translated by Cecil Hemley and Isaac Bashevis Singer. New York: Farrar, Straus and Cuddahy, 1962.

————. "A Wedding in Brownsville." In *Short Friday and Other Stories*. Translated by Chana Faerstein and Elizabeth Pollett. Greenwich: Fawcett Books, 1961.

Sperber, Manes. . . . *Than a Tear in the Seas*. Translated by Constantine Fitzgibbon. Introduction by Andre Malraux. New York: Bergen-Belsen Memorial Press, 1967.

Spiegelman, Art. *Maus: A Survivor's Tale*. New York: Pantheon Books, 1986.

————. *Maus: A Survivor's Tale II: And Here My Troubles Began*. New York: Pantheon Books, 1991.

Steiner, George. *The Portage to San Christobal of A. H.* New York: Simon and Schuster, 1982.

Steiner, Jean-Francois. *Treblinka*. Translated by Helen Weaver. New York: Simon and Schuster, 1976; New York: New American Library, 1979.

Styron, William. *Sophie's Choice*. New York: Random House, 1979.

Teichman, Milton. "A Teacher of the Holocaust." *Agada*, no. 9 (Spring–Summer 1986): 16–27.

Uhlman, Fred. *Reunion*. New York: Farrar, Straus and Giroux, 1977; New York: Penguin Books, 1978.

Uris, Leon. *Mila 18*. New York: Doubleday, 1961.

Wallant, Edward. *The Pawnbroker*. New York: Harcourt, Brace and World, 1961.

Wander, Fred. *The Seventh Well* (short stories). New York: International Publishers, 1976.

Weil, Grete. *My Sister, My Antigone*. New York: Avon Books, 1984.

Wiesel. Elie. *The Accident*. Translated by Anne Borchardt. New York: Hill and Wang, 1962.

————. *Dawn*. Translated by Anne Borchardt. New York: Hill and Wang, 1961.

————. *The Gates of the Forest.* Translated by Frances Frenaye. New York: Holt, Rinehart and Winston, 1966.

————. *Legends Of Our Time* (stories, essays, and autobiographical sketches). New York: Holt, Rinehart and Winston, 1968.

————. *Night.* Translated by Stella Rodway. New York: Hill and Wang, 1960.

————. *One Generation After* (stories and essays). New York: Random House, 1970.

Wiesenthal, Simon. *The Sunflower.* Translated by H. A. Piehler. London: W. H. Allen, 1970; New York: Schocken Books, 1976.

Poetry

Brodsky, Louis Daniel. *Gestapo Crows.* St. Louis: Time Being Books, 1992.

Bryks, Rachmil. *Ghetto Factory 76.* Translated by Theodor Primack and Eugen Kullman. New York: Block Publishing Company, 1967.

Celan, Paul. *Poems of Paul Celan.* Translated with an introduction by Michael Hamburger. New York: Persea Books, 1988.

————. *Selected Poems.* Translated by Michael Hamburger and Christopher Middleton. Middlesex, England: Penguin Books, 1972.

————. *Speech-Grille and Selected Poems.* Translated by Joachim Neugroschel. New York: E. P. Dutton, 1971.

Feldman, Irving. *The Pripet Marshes and Other Poems.* New York: Viking Press, 1965.

————. *New and Selected Poems.* New York: Penguin Books, 1979.

Ficowski, Jerzy. *A Reading of Ashes.* Translated by Keith Bosley and Krystyna Wandycz. London: Menard Press, 1981.

Gershon, Karen. *Selected Poems.* New York: Harcourt, Brace and World, 1966.

Gillon, Adam. "Here as in Jerusalem: Selected Poems of the Ghetto." *Polish Review* 10, no. 3 (1965): 22–45.

Glatstein, Jacob. *Poems.* Translated by Etta Blum. Tel Aviv: I. L. Peretz Publishing House, 1970.

————. *Selected Poems of Yankev Glatshteyn.* Translated, edited, and with an introduction by Richard Fein. Philadelphia: The Jewish Publication Society, 1987.

————. *The Selected Poems of Jacob Glatstein.* Translated by Ruth Whitman. New York: October House, 1972.

Greenberg, Uri Zvi. From *Streets of the River.* Translated by Robert Friend and others. In *Anthology of Modern Hebrew Poetry,* edited by S. Y. Penneli and A. Ukhmani. Vol. 2, 259–80. Jerusalem: Israel Universities Press, 1966.

Hecht, Anthony. *The Hard Hours.* New York: Atheneum, 1967.

Heyen, William. *Erika: Poems of the Holocaust.* St. Louis: Time Being Books, 1991.

————. *The Swastika Poems*. New York: Vanguard, 1977.

Hill, Geoffrey. *Somewhere Is Such a Kingdom: Poems 1952–1971*. Boston: Houghton Mifflin, 1975.

Jarrell, Randall. *The Complete Poems*. New York: Farrar, Straus and Giroux, 1969.

Katzenelson, Yitzhak. *The Song of the Murdered Jewish People*. Edited and translated by Noah H. Rosenbloom. Tel Aviv: Ghetto Fighters' House and Kibbutz Hameuchad, 1980.

Kaufman, Walter. *Cain and Other Poems*. New York: Random House, 1971.

Klein, A. M. *Collected Poems*. Toronto: McGraw-Hill Ryerson, 1974.

Kolmar, Gertrud. *Dark Soliloquy: The Selected Poems of Gertrud Kolmar*. Translated by Henry A. Smith. New York: Seabury Press, 1975.

Kovner, Abba. *A Canopy in the Desert: Selected Poems by Abba Kovner*. Edited by Shirley Kaufman with Ruth Adler and Nurit Orchan. Pittsburgh: University of Pittsburgh Press, 1973.

————. *My Little Sister and Selected Poems 1965–1985*. Selected and translated by Shirley Kaufman. Field Translation Series, vol. 11. Oberlin: Oberlin College, 1986.

————. *Selected Poems of Abba Kovner and Nelly Sachs*. Translated by Shirley Kaufman and Nurit Orchan. Middlesex, England: Penguin Books, 1971.

Leftwich, Joseph, ed. and trans. "Songs of the Death Camps: A Selection with Commentary." *Commentary* 12 (1951): 269–74.

Levertov, Denise. "During the Eichmann Trial." In *Jacob's Ladder*. New York: New Directions, 1961.

Levi, Primo. *Shema: Collected Poems of Primo Levi*. Translated by Ruth Feldman and Brian Swann. London: Menard Press, 1976.

Milosz, Czeslaw. *The Collected Poems, 1931–1987*. New York: Ecco Press, 1988.

Pagis, Dan. *Points of Departure*. Translated by Stephen Mitchell. Introduction by Robert Alter. Bilingual ed. Philadelphia: The Jewish Publication Society, 1981.

Pilinsky, Janos. *Selected Poems*. Translated by Ted Hughes and Janos Csokits. New York: Persea Books, 1976.

Radnoti, Miklos. *Clouded Sky*. Translated by Steven Polgar, Stephen Berg, and S. J. Marks. New York: Harper and Row, 1972.

Reznikoff, Charles. *Holocaust*. Santa Barbara: Black Sparrow Press, 1977.

Rozewicz, Tadeusz. *"The Survivor" and Other Poems*. Translated by Magnus J. Krynski and Robert A. Maguire. Princeton: Princeton University Press, 1976.

Sachs, Nelly. *O the Chimneys!: Selected Poems, Including the Verse Play, Eli*. Translated by Michael Hamburger et al. Bilingual ed. New York: Farrar, Straus and Giroux, 1967.

————. *The Seeker and Other Poems*. Translated by Ruth Mead, Matthew Mead, and Michael Hamburger. New York: Farrar, Straus and Giroux, 1970.

Shayevitsh, Simcha Bunim. "Lekh-Lekho." In *The Literature of Destruction: Jewish Responses to Catastrophe*, edited by David G. Roskies. Philadelphia: The Jewish Publication Society, 1989.

Simpson, Louis. *Collected Poems*. New York: Paragon House, 1988.

Sklarew, Myra. *From the Backyard of the Diaspora*. Washington, D.C.: Dryad Press, 1976.

―――. *The Science of Goodbyes*. Athens: University of Georgia Press, 1982.

Snodgrass, W. D. *The Fuehrer Bunker*. Brockport: BOA Editions, 1977.

Sutzkever, Abraham. *Burnt Pearls: Ghetto Poems of Abraham Sutzkever*. Translated by Seymour Mayne. Introduction by Ruth R. Wisse. Oakville, Ontario: Mosaic Press-Valley Editions, 1981.

―――. *Green Aquarium*. Translated by Ruth R. Wisse. *Prooftexts: A Journal of Jewish Literary History* 2 (Jan. 1982): 95–121.

―――. *Selected Poetry and Prose*. Translated by Barbara Harshav and Benjamin Harshav. Berkeley: University of California Press, 1991.

Swirszczynska, Anna. *Building the Barricade*. Translated by Magnus J. Krynski and Robert A. Maguire. Krakow: Wydawnictwo Literackie, 1979.

Taube, Herman. *A Chain of Images*. New York: Shulsinger Brothers, 1979.

Volakova, Hana, ed. *I Never Saw Another Butterfly*. Translated by Jeanne Nemcova. New York: McGraw-Hill, 1964.

Whitman, Ruth. *The Testing of Hanna Senesh*. Detroit: Wayne State University Press, 1986.

Wiesel, Elie. *Ani Maamin: A Song Lost and Found Again*. Translated by Marion Wiesel. New York: Random House, 1973.

Williams, C. K. *Poems, 1963–1983*. New York: Farrar, Straus and Giroux, 1988.

Yevtushenko, Yevgeny. *Selected Poems*. Translated by Robin Milner-Gullard and Peter Levi. Baltimore: Penguin Books, 1974.

Drama

Amichai, Yehuda. *Bells and Trains*. *Midstream* 12 (Oct. 1966): 55–66.

Amir, Anda. *This Kind, Too*. Translated by Shoshana Perla. New York: World Zionist Organization, 1972.

Atlan, Liliane. *Mister Fuge, or Earth Sick*. In *Plays of the Holocaust: An International Anthology*, edited by Elinor Fuchs. New York: Theatre Communications Group, 1987.

Barnes, Peter. *Auschwitz*. In *Plays of the Holocaust: An International Anthology*, edited by Elinor Fuchs. New York: Theatre Communications Group, 1987.

Borchert, Wolfgang. *The Outsider*. In *Postwar German Theater: An Anthology of Plays*, edited and translated by Michael Benedikt and George E. Wellwarth. New York: E. P. Dutton, 1967.

Dagan, Gabriel. "The Reunion." *Midstream* 19 (April 1973): 3–32.

Delbo, Charlotte. *Who Will Carry the Word.* In *The Theatre of the Holocaust,* edited by Robert Skloot. Madison: University of Wisconsin Press, 1983.

Eliach, Yaffa, and Uri Eliach. *The Last Jew.* Translated by Yaffa Eliach. Israel: Alef-Alef Theatre Publications, 1977.

Frisch, Max. *Andorra.* Translated by Michael Bullock. New York: Hill and Wang, 1964.

Goldberg, Leah. *The Lady of the Castle.* Translated by T. Carmi. Tel Aviv: Institute for the Translation of Hebrew Literature, 1974

Goodrich, Frances, and Albert Hackett. *The Diary of Anne Frank.* New York: Random House, 1956. (Based upon *Anne Frank: The Diary of a Young Girl.*)

Hochhuth, Rolf. *The Deputy: A Christian Tragedy.* Translated by Richard Winston and Clara Winston. New York: Grove, 1964.

Lampell, Millard. *The Wall.* New York: Alfred A. Knopf, 1961. (Based upon the novel of the same title by John Hersey.)

Lieberman, Harold, and Edith Lieberman. *Throne of Straw.* In *The Theatre of the Holocaust,* edited by Robert Skloot. Madison: University of Wisconsin Press, 1983.

Megged, Aharon. *The Burning Bush.* Translated by Shoshana Perla. New York: World Zionist Organization, 1972.

Miller, Arthur. *Incident at Vichy.* New York: Viking Press, 1965.

Pilchik, Ely E. *Strength: A Play in Three Acts.* New York: Bloch, 1964.

Sachs, Nelly. *Eli: A Mystery Play of the Sufferings of Israel.* Translated by Christopher Holme. In *O The Chimneys!* New York: Farrar, Straus, and Giroux, 1967.

Sartre, Jean-Paul. *The Condemned of Altona.* Translated by Sylvia Leeson and George Leeson. New York: Knopf, 1961.

Schevill, James. *Cathedral of Ice.* In *Plays of the Holocaust: An International Anthology,* edited by Elinor Fuchs. New York: Theatre Communications Group, 1987.

Shaw, Robert. *The Man in the Glass Booth.* New York: Harcourt, Brace and World, 1967.

Sobol, Joshua. *Ghetto.* In *Plays of the Holocaust: An International Anthology,* edited by Elinor Fuchs. New York: Theatre Communications Group, 1987.

Sylvanus, Erwin. *Dr. Korczak and the Children.* In *Postwar German Theatre: An Anthology of Plays,* edited and translated by Michael Benedikt and George E. Wellwarth. New York: E. P. Dutton, 1967.

Szajna, Josef. *Replika.* In *Plays of the Holocaust: An International Anthology,* edited by Elinor Fuchs. New York: Theatre Communications Group, 1987.

Tabori, George. *The Cannibals.* In *The Theatre of the Holocaust,* edited by Robert Skloot. Madison: University of Wisconsin Press, 1983.

Tomer, Ben-Zion. *Children of the Shadows.* Translated by Hillel Halkin. New York: World Zionist Organization, n.d.

Walser, Martin. *The Rabbit Race*. Adapted by Ronald Duncan. Translated by Richard Gruneberger. London: J. Calder, 1963.

Weiss, Peter. *The Investigation*. Translated by John Swan and Ulu Grosbard. New York: Atheneum, 1966.

Wiesel, Elie. *The Trial of God*. Translated by Marion Wiesel. New York: Random House, 1979.

————. *Zalman; or, The Madness of God*. Translated by Nathan Edelman. Adapted for the stage by Marion Wiesel. New York: Random House, 1974.

Wincelberg, Shimon. *Resort 76*. In *The Theatre of the Holocaust,* edited by Robert Skloot. Madison: University of Wisconsin Press, 1983.

Zuchmayer, Carl. *The Devil's General*. In *Masters of Modern Drama,* edited by Haskell M. Bloch and Robert G. Shedd. New York: Random House, 1962.

Literary Criticism

Aaron, Frieda W. *Bearing the Unbearable; Yiddish and Polish Poetry in the Ghettos and Concentration Camps*. Albany: State University of New York Press, 1990.

Adorno, Theodore. "Engagement." In *Noten zur Literatur III*. Frankfurt am Mein: Suhrkamp Verlag, 1965.

Alexander, Edward. *The Resonance of Dust: Essays on Holocaust Literature and Jewish Fate*. Columbus: Ohio State University Press, 1979.

Alter, Robert. *Defenses of the Imagination: Jewish Writers and Modern Historical Crisis*. Philadelphia: The Jewish Publication Society, 1977.

Alvarez, A. "The Literature of the Holocaust." In *Beyond All This Fiddle*. New York: Random House, 1968.

Appelfeld, Aharon. "After the Holocaust." In *Writing and the Holocaust,* edited by Berel Lang. New York: Holmes and Meier, 1988.

Berger, Alan L. *Crisis and Covenant: The Holocaust in American-Jewish Fiction*. Albany: State University of New York Press, 1988.

Bilik, Dorothy Seidman. *Immigrant Survivors: Post Holocaust Consciousness in Recent Jewish American Literature*. Middletown: Wesleyan University Press, 1981.

Boas, Henriette. "Jewish Figures in Post-War Dutch Literature." *Jewish Journal of Sociology* 5 (June 1963): 55–83.

Bosmejiar, Hamida. *Metaphors of Evil: Contemporary German Literature and the Shadow of Nazism*. Iowa City: University of Iowa Press, 1979.

Brown, Robert McAfee. *Elie Wiesel, Messenger to All Humanity*. Rev. ed. Notre Dame: University of Notre Dame Press, 1989.

Denby, David. "The Humanist and the Holocaust." *New Republic,* July 28, 1986, 27–33.

Des Pres, Terrence. *The Survivor: An Anatomy of Life in the Death Camps*. New York: Pocket Books, 1976.

Ezrahi, Sidra DeKoven. *By Words Alone: The Holocaust in Literature*. Chicago: University of Chicago Press, 1982.

———. "Holocaust Literature in European Languages." In *Encyclopedia Judaica Yearbook 1973*. Jerusalem: Keter Publishing House, 1973.

Fine, Ellen S. *Legacy of Night: The Literary Universe of Elie Wiesel*. New York: State University of New York Press, 1982.

———. "Literature as Resistance: Survival in the Camps." *Holocaust and Genocide Studies* 1 (1986): 79–89.

Flam, Gila. *Singing for Survival: Songs of the Lodz Ghetto, 1940–45*. Urbana: University of Illinois Press, 1992.

Grynberg, Henryk. "The Holocaust in Polish Literature." *Notre Dame English Journal* 11 (April 1979): 116–38.

Haft, Cynthia. *The Theme of Nazi Concentration Camps in French Literature*. The Hague: Mouton, 1973.

Heinemann, Marlene E. *Gender and Destiny: Women Writers and the Holocaust*. Westport: Greenwood Press, 1986.

Howe, Irving. "Auschwitz and High Mandarin." In *The Critical Point: On Literature and Culture*. New York: Horizon, 1973.

———. "How to Write About the Holocaust." *New York Review of Books,* March 28, 1985, 14–17.

———. "Writing and the Holocaust." *New Republic,* Oct. 27, 1986, 27–39.

Knopp, Josephine Zadovsky. *The Trial of Judaism in Contemporary Jewish Writing*. Urbana: University of Illinois Press, 1975.

Kremer, Lillian. *Witness Through the Imagination: Jewish American Holocaust Literature*. Detroit: Wayne State University Press, 1989.

Lang, Berel, ed. *Writing and the Holocaust*. New York: Holmes and Meier, 1988.

Langer, Lawrence L. *The Age of Atrocity: Death in Modern Literature*. Boston: Beacon Press, 1978.

———. *Holocaust Testimonies: The Ruins of Memory*. New Haven: Yale University Press, 1991.

———. *The Holocaust and the Literary Imagination*. New Haven: Yale University Press, 1977.

———. *Versions of Survival: The Holocaust and the Human Spirit*. Albany: State University of New York Press, 1982.

Leftwich, Joseph. *Abraham Suzkever: Partisan Poet*. New York: Thomas Yoseloff, 1971.

Lifton, Robert Jay. *Death in Life: Survivors of Hiroshima*. New York: Vintage, 1967.

Lind, Jakov. "John Brown and His Little Indians." *Times Literary Supplement,* May 25, 1973, 589–90.

Milosz, Czeslaw. *The History of Polish Literature*. London: Macmillan Company, 1969.

————. *The Witness of Poetry.* Cambridge: Harvard University Press, 1983.

Mintz, Alan. *Hurban: Responses to Catastrophe in Hebrew Literature.* New York: Columbia University Press, 1984.

Murdoch, Brian. "Transformations of the Holocaust: Auschwitz in Modern Lyric Poetry." *Comparative Literature Studies* 2, no. 6 (1974): 123–50.

Niger, Samuel. "Yiddish Poets of the 'Third Destruction.'" *Reconstructionist,* June 27, 1947, 13–18.

Rosen, Norma. *Accidents of Influence: Writing as a Woman and a Jew in America.* Albany: State University of New York Press, 1992.

————. "Notes Toward A Holocaust Fiction." In *Testimony: Contemporary Writers Make The Holocaust Personal,* edited by David Rosenberg. New York: Random House, 1989.

Rosenbloom, Noah H. "The Threnodist and the Threnody of the Holocaust." In *Yitzhak Katzenelson: The Song of the Murdered Jewish People.* Tel Aviv: Ghetto Fighters' House, Hakibbutz Hameuchad Publishing House, 1982.

Rosenfeld, Alvin H. *A Double Dying: Reflections on Holocaust Literature.* Bloomington: Indiana University Press, 1980.

————. "Jakov Lind and the Trial of Jewishness." *Midstream* 20 (Feb. 1974): 71–75.

————. "Paul Celan." *Midstream* 17 (Nov. 1971): 75–80.

Rosenfeld, Alvin H., and Irving Greenberg, eds. *Confronting the Holocaust: The Impact of Elie Wiesel.* Bloomington: Indiana University Press, 1979.

Roskies, David G. *Against the Apocalypse: Responses to Catastrophe in Modern Jewish Culture.* Cambridge: Harvard University Press, 1984.

————. "Yiddish Writing in the Nazi Ghettos and the Art of the Incommensurate." *Modern Language Studies* 16 (Winter 1986): 29–36.

Steiner, George. *Language and Silence: Essays on Language, Literature, and the Inhuman.* New York: Atheneum, 1967.

Syrkin, Marie. "Nelly Sachs: Poet of the Holocaust." *Midstream* 13 (March 1967): 13–23.

Szeintuch, Yechiel. "The Corpus of Yiddish and Hebrew Literature from Ghettos and Concentrtation Camps and Its Relevance for Holocaust Studies." *Studies in Yiddish Literature and Folklore.* Research Project of YIVO, the Institute of Jewish Studies. Monograph 7. Jerusalem: Hebrew University of Jerusalem, 1986.

Weimar, Karl S. "Paul Celan's 'Todesfuge': Translation and Interpretation." *PMLA* 89 (Jan. 1974): 85–89.

Wisse, Ruth. "The Ghetto Poems of Abraham Sutzkever." *Jewish Book Annual.* New York: Jewish Book Council, 1979.

Young, James E. *Writing and Rewriting the Holocaust: Narrative and the Consequence of Interpretation.* Bloomington: Indiana University Press, 1986.

Historical, Philosophical, Theological, and Related Studies

Arendt, Hannah. *Eichmann in Jerusalem: A Report on the Banality of Evil.* Rev. ed. New York: Penguin Books, 1987.

Bauman, Zygnunt. *Modernity and the Holocaust.* Ithaca: Cornell University Press, 1989.

Bridenthal, Renate, Atina Grossman, and Marion Kaplan. *When Biology Became Destiny: Women in Weimar and Nazi Germany.* New York: Monthly Review Press, 1984.

Chalik, Frank Robert, and Kurt Jonassohn. *The History and Sociology of Genocide: Analysis and Case Studies.* New Haven: Yale University Press, 1990.

Dawidowicz, Lucy S. *The Holocaust and the Historians.* Cambridge: Harvard University Press, 1981.

———. *The War Against the Jews, 1933–1945.* 10th ed. New York: Bantam Books, 1986.

Fackenheim, Emil L. *To Mend the World: Foundations of Post-Holocaust Jewish Thought.* 2d ed. New York: Schocken Books, 1989.

Friedman, Philip. *Their Brothers' Keepers: The Christian Heroes and Heroines Who Helped the Oppressed Escape the Nazi Terror.* New York: Schocken, 1957. Reprint. New York: Holocaust Library, 1978.

Gilbert, Martin. *The Holocaust: A History of the Jews of Europe during the Second World War.* New York: Holt, Rinehart and Winston, 1986.

Green, Gerald. *The Artists of Terezin.* New York: Schocken Books, 1978.

Hallie, Philip Paul. *Lest Innocent Blood Be Shed: The Story of the Village of Le Chambon and How Goodness Happened There.* New York: Harper and Row, 1985.

Hilberg, Raul. *The Destruction of the European Jews.* 3 vols. Rev. ed. New York: Holmes and Meier, 1985.

Katz, Esther, and Joan Miriam Ringelheim. *Proceedings of the Conference Women Surviving the Holocaust.* New York: Institute for Research in History, 1983.

Koonz, Claudia. *Mothers in the Fatherland: Women, the Family, and Nazi Politics.* New York: St. Martin's Press, 1986.

Krakowski, Shmuel. *The War of the Doomed: Jewish Armed Resistance in Poland, 1942–1944.* Translated by Orah Blaustein. New York: Holmes and Meir, 1984.

Laska, Vera, ed. *Women in the Resistance and in the Holocaust: The Voices of Eye Witnesses.* Westport: Greenwood Press, 1983.

Levi, Primo. *The Drowned and the Saved.* Translated by Raymond Rosenthal. New York: Summit Books, 1988.

Levin, Nora. *The Holocaust: The Destruction of European Jewry, 1939–1945.* New York: Crowell, 1968; New York: Schocken Books, 1973.

Lindwer, Willy. *The Last Seven Months of Anne Frank*. Translated by Alison Meers-schaert. New York: Pantheon Books, 1991.

Littel, Franklin Hamlin. *The Crucifixion of the Jews*. Macon: Mercer University Press, 1986.

Mark, Ber. *The Uprising in the Warsaw Ghetto*. Translated by Gershon Freidlin. New York: Schocken Books, 1975.

Marrus, Michael R. *The Holocaust in History*. Hanover: University Press of New England, for the Tauber Institute for the Study of European Jewry, 1987.

Miller, Judith. *One, by One, by One: Facing the Holocaust*. New York: Simon and Schuster, 1990.

Morse, Arthur D. *While Six Million Died: A Chronicle of American Apathy*. New York: Hart Publishing, 1967; Woodstock: Overlook Press, 1983.

Poliakov, Leon. *Harvest of Hate: The Nazi Program for the Destruction of the Jews of Europe*. Rev. ed. New York: Holocaust Library, 1979.

Ringelheim, Joan. "Women and the Holocaust: A Reconsidertion of Research." *Signs: Journal of Women in Culture and Society* 10, no. 4 (1985): 741–61.

Rosenberg, Alan, and Gerald E. Myers, eds. *Echoes from the Holocaust: Philosophical Reflections on a Dark Time*. Philadelphia: Temple University Press, 1988.

Rossiter, Margaret L. *Women in the Resistance*. New York: Praeger Publishers, 1986.

Rubenstein, Richard L. *After Auschwitz: Radical Theology and Contemporary Judaism*. Indianapolis: Bobbs-Merrill, 1966.

———. *The Cunning of History: The Holocaust and the American Future*. New York: Harper and Row, 1987.

Rubenstein, Richard L., and John K. Roth. *Approaches to Auschwitz: The Holocaust and Its Legacy*. Atlanta: John Knox Press, 1987.

Suhl, Yuri, ed. *They Fought Back: The Story of Jewish Resistance in Nazi Europe*. New York: Crown Publishing, 1967; New York: Schocken Books, 1975.

Tec, Nechama. *When Light Pierced the Darkness: Christian Rescue of Jews in Nazi-Occupied Poland*. New York: Oxford University Press, 1986.

Trunk, Isaiah. *Jewish Responses to Nazi Persecution: Collective and Individual Behavior in Extremis*. Translated by Gabriel Trunk. New York: Stein and Day, 1979.

———. *Judenrat: The Jewish Councils in Eastern Europe under Nazi Occupation*. New York: Stein and Day, 1977.

Wyman, David S. *The Abandonment of the Jews: America and the Holocaust, 1941–45*. New York: Random House, 1984.

Yahil, Leni. *The Holocaust: The Fate of European Jewry, 1932–1945*. Translated by Ina Friedman and Haya Galai. New York: Oxford University Press, 1990.

Copyright Acknowledgments